OUT TOWNS

nunyi

• Tuckaseegee

ETTLEMENTS

• Kanasia

Tuckaseegee R.

SOUTH CAROLINA

ooga R.

• Estatoe

Keowee R.

• Toxaway

TOMASSEE

R.

• Fort Prince George

Oconee Keowee

WALHALLA

• Tunnissey

sway • Seneca •

CALHOUN

Seneca R.

• Noyowee

• Tugaloo

TOWNS

Tugaloo R.

Saluda R.

Savannah R.

A LAW OF BLOOD

A LAW OF BLOOD

THE PRIMITIVE LAW OF THE CHEROKEE NATION

by John Phillip Reid

New York
New York University Press
1970

For Peter Noel Reid, M.D.

CONTENTS

A LAW OF BLOOD

CHAPTER ONE

A RACE OF MOUNTAIN MEN

—THE PEOPLE

Law is the signet of a people and a people are the product of a land. The primitive law of the eighteenth-century Cherokee nation reflects the mores, the integrality, and the rapport of the Cherokee people just as the characteristic traits of the Cherokees themselves reflect the physical environment of their existence: the mountains upon which they lived, the harvest reaped from forest, field, and stream, and the enemies—both in nature and mankind—that their geographical location required them to fight.

Neighboring tribes gave them the name "Cherokee" (the cave people), for they were believed to have come from the ground. They called themselves "Tsulakees" or "Tsalakees" (the principal people)[1] and their personality as a race defies summation. A visitor to the Cherokee nation in 1766, disturbed by "their propensity for strong drink," was content to say, "They love strangers among them and are hospitable, but poor." [2] Four generations later, after the old ways and primitive law had long since vanished, a Cherokee would write of her ancestors: "Holding this place of

3

Supremacy made them self-confident and independent. In disposition they
were friendly and generous, though always reserved before strangers.
Fearless in danger, intrepid and daring when occasion required, they were
slow to take offence at fancied injuries or insults." [3] This description must
be accepted with a grain of salt, for it is largely filial *fanfaronade*. The
Cherokees were generous and independent, true enough, but by the common standards with which we judge mankind, they were either self-confident nor fearless; indeed, if anything they were indecisive and
pusillanimous. Far from slow at taking offense, the Cherokees, we are told
by an impartial observer, "are known for their quick tempers, and some
of their friends have said that they are shrewd and crafty in their
dealings." [4]

Perhaps the best summation of their national character has been furnished by a leading scholar of Cherokee ethnology, who writes:

> Most authorities concur in the opinion that both physically and tem-
> peramentally the older Cherokees made a most favorable impression.
> They delighted in athletics and excelled in endurance of intense cold.
> Well featured and of erect carriage, of moderately robust build, they
> were possessed of a superior and independent bearing. Although
> steady in manner and disposition to the point of melancholy and
> slow and reserved in speech they were withal frank, cheerful, and
> humane, as well as honest and liberal.[5]

In common with other American Indians, the Cherokees of the eighteenth century honored a symbolism that has intrigued folklorists. Color
held meaning, stirring a response when used in customary ways, as in the
black of the wampum sent by an enemy nation challenging the Cherokee
to battle, or the red of the sticks of war sent by the town which received
the black wampum, summoning other towns to its aid. White was emble-
matic of peace and happiness, red of power and success, blue of trouble
and defeat, black of death.[6] "The South wind was white and brought
peace; the North wind was blue and meant defeat; the West wind was
black and brought death. The wind from the East was red. It brought
power, and war." [7]

Physically the Cherokees have been classified as a mixture of the
Algonquin-Iroquois dolichocephalic type and the Eastern and Southern
brachycephals.[8] Their most marked feature was their height. Although
Lieutenant General Oglethorpe did not think them as tall as some of their
neighbors [9] (possibly the Creeks, who often ranged above six feet),[10] the
botanist William Bartram called the Cherokees "by far the largest race of

men I have seen." He thought them more robust than the Creeks, and admired their complexions as being "brighter and somewhat of the olive cast, especially the adults; and some of their young women are nearly as fair and blooming as European women." [11]

Despite his height and olive complexion, the average Cherokee probably did not appear notably different from the other aborigines first encountered by Europeans in the eastern half of North America. The scalp lock rising behind the bare eggshaped dome of his high forehead, the tatooed body, and the slit ear lobes which, distended by silver bangles, stretched to his shoulders, were a familiar sight from the Gulf north to Virginia. But these were superficial similarities of custom and costume, physical and visual, not psychological or inherent. From the moment of the first contact, the Europeans—British, French, and Spanish—noted at least two national characteristics marking the Cherokee as distinct from his neighbors. The first was hardly to the Cherokees' credit, at least not in the civilization of the eighteenth-century American Indian, which throve on warfare and bestowed its rewards only upon the brave. For despite their own legends of daring battles and of victories won,[12] the Cherokees were the least warlike of all the great nations in the eastern half of the continent. Indeed, the other Indians thought them cowards. Both the Shawnees and the Chickasaws called them "old women," and there was little glory for the Iroquois warrior who came home with a Cherokee scalp.[13] White contemporaries treated the nation with equal contempt [14] and so they have been recorded: first entering history as a defeated people, forced by the Delawares to flee the Ohio Valley,[15] and finally in the late eighteenth century laying aside their arms forever, crushed by small bands of American frontier irregulars.[16]

Yet there was a compensating factor. If their martial inferiority placed them at a disadvantage in the old world of Indian warfare, their native abilities were destined to serve them well in the new world being imposed by European civilization. For it is generally agreed, by whatever standard is devised, that the Cherokees were among the most talented, the most intelligent, and were one of the least barbarous of the American nations.[17]

As early as the 1560s. a Spanish Jesuit found the Cherokees superior to any other tribe he had encountered,[18] and a century later a British superintendent of Indian affairs reported that the Cherokees "are the most Ingenious Indians." [19] This attribute, plus an ability to adjust their laws and institutions to changing circumstances, enabled them, almost alone among the Indian nations, "to pass through the ordeal of more than two centuries of wars, councils, and litigation with the white man." [20] In so doing, they emerged into such a position of leadership that during the nineteenth century many of their former enemies, the Delawares, the Iroquois, the Catawbas, bewildered by American politics and harassed by American greed, would forget their contempt for the cowardly foe of another era and beg for sanctuary beneath the protective shelter of that most remarkable achievement of Indian jurisprudence—the Cherokee constitution.

All this lay in the future, however, and if we ask how a nation inept at warfare survived in that epoch of strife and bloodshed before the Americans imposed peace, we must point to the two dominant features of the eighteenth-century Cherokees—their numbers and their mountain homeland. They are generally believed to have been the largest Indian nation in the east,[21] although the more remote Choctaws may have exceeded them.[22] Surely only the Choctaws and the Creeks rivaled them, and most other tribes were dwarfed in comparison.

Because the Cherokees lived in up to 60 towns scattered over an extensive, rugged, often inaccessible territory, it was impossible for anyone to make a precise head count. One authority has estimated that there were 22,000 in 1650, when the only white men to know of their existence were a few Spaniards.[23] Neither the British nor the French were to encounter so many. The first meaningful census, drawn in 1715 by South Carolina officials from the journals of traders in the Cherokee nation, reported 60 towns with a population of 11,210.[24] This number included 2,370 fighting men, always an unreliable figure as seen by the fact that 11 years later, in 1721, when the population was roughly the same, there were said to be either 3,510 or 3,800 Cherokee warriors.[25] By 1729, based largely on the estimates of the historian James Adair who 40 years later interviewed fellow traders, scholars believe there were 6,000 warriors out of a total of 20,000 people.[26] After this there was a rapid decrease, due to the smallpox epidemic of 1738 which either killed, or drove to suicide, one half of the nation.[27] In 1741 it was calculated in Charles Town that 10,000 Cherokees, or 2,500 warriors, were left.[28] Although one authority put the population in 1758 at 7,500, an all-time low, the figure of about 10,000 men, women, and children, and of between 2,000 to 2,590 fighters is generally accepted for the period from 1745 to the Cherokee War of 1760. Then the nation was dispersed for the first time, and its era of primitive law began to draw to a close.[29]

These numbers may seem low to twentieth-century man, but their meaning can be placed in eighteenth-century perspective when we recall that the mighty Chickasaws—the people who for 40 years denied the French domination of the Mississippi Valley, drove the Shawnee from the Cumberland in 1715, crossed the "Father of Waters" to defeat the Yatasi in 1717, and won an unbroken series of wars against the Choctaws to the south and the Creeks and Cherokees to the east, sometimes against overwhelming odds—probably numbered little more than 3,000 men, women, and children at their greatest. They could not have been much more than 2,300 when they decisively vanquished the Cherokees at the battle of Chickasaw Old Fields in 1768.[30]

The size of the Cherokee population, great as it was in comparison to the nations which surrounded them, may have been a major factor in their survival and their importance, but had little appreciable effect upon their institutions and their law. More significant was the land on which they lived. The centralized government and sense of national identification that one might expect to find among a numerous people never materialized among the eighteenth-century Cherokees, partly because geography dictated a dispersal into many towns connected only by narrow, often dangerous paths. For the Cherokees were America's first known mountaineers, living in the valleys and along the streams of the southern Appalachian range, for the most part at 1200 feet in altitude. This was a rugged, often marginal area, capable of supporting human life only on isolated patches of fertile fields and sheltered caves; even after it passed into the domain of white men, the region would sprout a population of individualists, contemptuous of authority and self-reliant in law.

Today this area forms the border lands of five states, the two Carolinas, Georgia, Tennessee, and southwestern Virginia. Here explorers first discovered the western waters, sources of the great streams which one day would carry the settlers westward: the Cumberland, the Alabama, the Kentucky, and the mighty Tennessee, named by the French and known for so long as "the Cherokee River." Here, too, were the headwaters of the eastern streams that flowed into the Carolinas, or down into Georgia —the Savannah, the Catawba, the Saluda, the Keowee, and the Peedee. They all led out of the Cherokee nation, they did not link it; they were roadways of invasions, not avenues of communication.

It would be misleading to define the boundaries of the eighteenth-century Cherokee domain, perhaps even inaccurate to speak of "boundaries" and of "domain." The Cherokees did not do so; they knew only what belonged to them. The day would arrive when they borrowed European legal terminology to proclaim that their fathers had held their lands "from time immemorial." [31] Once they might have believed this boast, for they were one of the few Indian people without a legend of migration.

The traditional explanation of how they had settled their mountain homeland was that their ancestors had emerged from the ground.[32] But later,
when it became legally useful to rely upon an argument of possession from
time immemorial, they knew they were talking the rhetoric of law, not
the facts of history. Tradition, taught them by other Indians and supported
by scientific investigation, showed they were not native to the Appalachians.[33] There is no agreement as to when the Cherokees reached the
heartland of their country, the valley of the Little Tennessee, but there is
evidence that they may not have been there even in 1540, when DeSoto
passed nearby.[34] Whether they came from the west or north, and whether
during the second half of the sixteenth century or earlier, they stopped
trekking when they encountered the Muskhogean nations to the south and
the Siouan tribes to the east. This is the crucial and only realistic factor
when speaking of Indian boundaries. Like all other American nations, the
Cherokees held sway over that part of the continent their enemies did not
dare contest.

It is the Cherokee language that furnishes the best clue to their origin,
for they belonged to the Iroquoian family and thus were a southern off-
shoot of the great migration that brought the Iroquoian people from west
to east.[35] This fact would have been incomprehensible to the preliterate
Cherokees who believed their language distinct from that of other
Indians,[36] and who felt no affinity with those nations who are now classified as their kinsmen. Indeed, had an eighteenth-century Cherokee been
asked to name his most dreaded foe, he might well have selected the Six
Nations of the Iroquois League: the Senecas, the Mohawks, the Cayugas,
the Onondagas, the Oneidas, and the Tuscaroras. The last of these were
once his neighbors in North Carolina, but the Cherokees aided the British
to crush the Tuscaroras in 1713 and to send them fleeing north, where
they added a sixth lodge to the old confederacy of the Five Nations. From
their northern homeland in New York, the Iroquois ranged far and wide
in search of enemies, stalking the Cherokees' towns for days on end; small
parties of two or three would sometimes return to their nation with a
string of scalps, seldom failing in some way to show their contempt for
Cherokee manhood by devising special insults and displaying daring
bravery.[37] If any external factor gave the Cherokees a sense of national
unity, it was fear and hatred of their Iroquois cousins.

If one wishes to group the Cherokees with other nations, it would be
useful to forget their linguistic origins and to classify them with their
neighbors to the southwest—the Creeks, the Choctaws, the Chickasaws,
and the distant Seminoles—those great Muskhogean-speaking tribes with

whom the Cherokees are linked in American history as "the Five Civilized Nations." True, the Cherokees were seldom at peace with these Indians, except for the Chickasaws who were their traditional friends.[38] They were forever at odds with the Creek confederacy, waging against them a costly war which lasted, on and off, from 1715 to 1753. Yet despite lack of blood relationship, common language, or sustained periods of peaceful intercourse, the Cherokees and their Muskhogean neighbors form a cultural unit, an Indian community of common customs, common institutions, and common social and economic patterns.[39] Of course there were vast differences. Yet the points of similarity provide invaluable guideposts in the search for early Cherokee law. If used cautiously to fill gaps where Cherokee records are silent, by telling what questions to ask, not what answers to give, these similarities reveal much that might otherwise be overlooked.

While dealing with those nations to the south and west, some Cherokees are believed to have spoken Choctaw, the common trading language of the region. Surely they did not expect other Indians to know Cherokee, as it was exceedingly difficult to learn. It is reported that in later years a Cherokee child with equal opportunities to speak his own language or English was almost certain to master English first.[40] Most authorities agree that the eighteenth-century Cherokees were confronted with a serious problem; their language was divided into dialects and a Cherokee who spoke one dialect might not understand a Cherokee speaking another.[41]

While today these dialects remain incompletely identified,[42] it is now generally believed that there were once three Cherokee dialects, the Lower or Elati, the Middle or Kituhwa, and the Upper or Atali.[43] Some historians classify Elati, the dialect of the Lower towns, as extinct, Kituhwa, the dialect of the Middle Cherokee settlements, as the dialect now spoken in North Carolina, and Atali, the dialect of the Overhills and of the Valley towns during the eighteenth century, as the dialect now spoken by the Oklahoma Cherokees.[44] However, scholars of the language do not agree. The Kilpatricks, for example, tell us that the Cherokees who remained behind in North Carolina, after the remainder of the nation was driven to Oklahoma during the 1830s, "did not all speak the same dialect, just as those who came West did not, nor do their descendents today." [45]

This matter of dialects is important, especially if one dialect was incomprehensible to persons who spoke a different dialect. What could have put the unity of the nation under greater strain? The day would come when the Cherokees eliminated some problems by making English the official language of their courts and legislative assemblies, translating proceedings into English and back again even when few present understood little except their own dialect. However, during the eighteenth century there was no substitute for the native tongue, and no way to surmount the divisions nurtured by the dialects except through cultural ties and legal institutions. Much as we may in the following chapters disparage the primitive law of the Cherokee as weak and inefficient, at least when measured by European standards, we must here concede that despite all its faults Cherokee law racked up one remarkable achievement. Throughout much of the eighteenth century, law helped hold together the Cherokee nation. It gave a degree of unity and national identification to a people who might easily have been pulled asunder by the dynamics of mountain geography, by the trichotomy of their language, and by the decentralization inherent in a system of government based on towns and not on nation.

CHAPTER TWO

A SOURCE OF DISUNITY

—THE REGIONS

Perhaps the greatest challenge to Cherokee unity, and the feature of their constitution that placed more stress on their sense of national identification than even their dialects, was the regional system into which their nation was divided. It was serious enough that the Cherokee people were scattered throughout towns numbering from 50 to 64. Worse was the fact that these towns were grouped in clusters with which the people associated interests and loyalties that transcended interests and loyalties owed to the nation as a whole.

These town clusters or geographical regions resulted from four causes: first, topography, for natural barriers, especially mountains, separated one section from another; second, the linguistic divisions fostered by the three dialects; third, international politics, for each region had different foreign neighbors, white and Indian, and as a result, often had different friends and different enemies; and fourth, economic self-interest, for some sections were near trading outlets in direct competition with those nearer other regions of the nation.[1]

The British recognized these divisions as early as 1715, apparently attributing them to differences in dialect, for they realigned the nation into three parts. These were the Lower Cherokees with 11 towns, located in the foothills of western South Carolina, the Middle Cherokees with 30 towns in the heart of the mountains, and the Upper or Overhill Cherokees with 19 towns beyond the mountain ridges.[2] Later, after encountering frustration by attempts to deal with the nation as a constitutional unit, the British came to realize the Cherokee people were divided into at least four sections: the Lower towns in the valleys of the Keowee and Tugallo rivers and on the headwaters of the Savannah, the Middle settlements in the Tuckasegee river and on the headwaters of the Little Tennessee, the Valley towns west of the Middle settlements on the Hywassee river, and the Overhills below the Cumberland mountains on the Tellico river and on the lower reaches of the Little Tennessee.[3]

One visitor to the nation during the 1760s described the four regions as lying "in a kind of a cross," [4] a description which has been diagrammed as follows: [5]

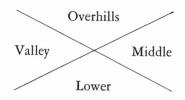

Although some historians would group the Valley towns with the Middle settlements, probably because of their location and economic unity, others suggest that the Valley towns should be associated with the Overhills,[6] perhaps because they spoke the same Atali dialect.[7] The Cherokees, however, seem to have regarded the Valley towns as a distinct entity, tied neither to the Middle settlements on one hand nor the Overhills on the other. At crucial times in Cherokee history, the headman of a Valley town might profess to speak for the region, not merely for his town. At least two, the influential Raven of the Valley, and Tacitee, King of the Valley, had titles which imply that they were recognized as war leaders of the Valley towns, and the British dealt with them as spokesmen for the region.[8] In fact, there are grounds for believing that the Cherokees divided their nation into yet a fifth section—the Out towns, located to the northeast of the Middle settlements. A vague, backwater region of the nation, the Out towns provide a curious footnote to Cherokee history. Well known to the British during the eighteenth century, they would be relatively ignored by the Americans in the nineteenth century. While the progressive and advanced part of the nation was driven westward during the 1830s, the stubborn, conservative, and backward people of the Out-town region would be allowed to remain at home. It was they who in time formed the Eastern Band of Cherokees (sometimes known as the North Carolina Cherokees), the only remnant of the nation now to occupy any part of the ancient homeland.

While keeping these regional groupings in mind, we must be careful not to misinterpret them. They were sources of disunity, not of strength. True, they provided a degree of cohesiveness for neighboring towns which might otherwise have worked at cross purposes, but they divided the nation as a whole. Europeans and Indians alike knew how to play one region off against the other. Early in the 1750s, for example, the Lower towns were reeling from Creek attacks and begging for peace. At the same time, Shawnee warriors in the pay of France were among the Overhills, receiving a friendly reception as they preached a Cherokee-Shawnee alliance against those same Creeks. To obtain their peace, the Lower towns had to send entreaties to the Overhills as well as to the Creeks. It was British pressure, not concern for their countrymen, that finally persuaded the other regions to end the war.

Thus the Cherokees furnished their enemies the means to divide and conquer. Again geography tells much of the story. From the first of the Lower towns to the last of the Overhills, as an Englishman reported in 1741, the Cherokees stretched a distance of about 500 miles.[9] He was not measuring as the crow flies but by Indian paths and ancient traces, which bypassed the innumerable escarpments, sought out the shallow fords, and, to avoid the hazard of isolated ambush, wound from town to town. Yet even at that, 500 miles was a gross exaggeration if we can believe one of the most experienced traders in the nation who, in 1729, estimated the distance from Keowee in the southeast to Great Tellico in the northwest at about 150 miles by trail.[10] Nor should the word "trail" be impressive, for as another Englishman pointed out in 1755, they were more paths than trails, and "the passage through the mountains is so narrow, that two Horses can scarce go abreast." [11]

Had an eighteenth-century traveler arrived by the trade paths from the east or south, he would have entered the nation through the Lower towns. Lying beneath the Blue Ridge barrier that marked the marchland of the old colonial "backcountry," the Lower towns were located in what are today South Carolina's most western counties—Pickens and Oconee—in the vale of the state's most beautiful stream, the Keowee, known to the

Cherokees as "the river of mulberries." [12] Here the Cherokees were first encountered by the British and here the musical names of their villages were first transliterated into English: Keowee, made famous and rich by the happy chance of being the gateway to the Carolina trade, lying about 200 to 300 miles from Charles Town, depending on the path followed; [13] Estatoe, strong and belligerent with an estimated 70 gunmen in 1756; [14] Tugaloo, near the Georgia line and called in 1725 "the most Antient Town in these parts"; [15] also Toxaway, Tomassee, Oconee, Oustestee, Cheeowie, and several others. About 2,100 strong in 1715, the Lower Cherokees possessed the gentlest land in the nation—the pleasant, fertile headwaters of the Savannah—reaped the harvest of the Carolinian trade, and formed the front line of defense against the Upper Creeks. The first to enjoy the luxury of the white man's goods, they would be the first to flee from the white man's wrath.

Should the traveler enter the nation from North Carolina, something seldom done until the Revolutionary War era, he would first encounter the Out towns on the Tuckasegee river. Unapproachable from the north, due to the Great Smokies beneath which they nestled, these towns lay off the main trade routes from the east and were remote even from the warpaths. While not numerous or important, they may have been the oldest Cherokee villages, for among them was Kittuwa, their "mother town," [16] which authorities believe was the nation's original town; a supposition supported by the fact that in some of their oldest ceremonials, the Cherokees referred to themselves as *Ani' Kitu' hwagi,* "People of Kituwha." [17]

Located near today's Bryson City, North Carolina, Kittuwa was the center of the other Out towns—Stecoe (or Steecoy, today named Whitter), Conontoroy, Tackareechee, Tuckasegee, and Oustanarle. Perhaps the majestic Great Smokies hold the answer to why these towns seldom figure in the nation's later history. They did play a role during the eighteenth century, especially Tuckasegee, which was large enough to have 70 gunmen in 1756—making it a fair-sized town—and Kittuwa, which had 50.[18] Still, the records show few instances where they produced leaders, set policy, or were consulted about events. Later, after the American Revolution, when the majority of the Cherokee nation moved southwest onto the lowlands of Georgia, Alabama, and Tennessee, adopted new ways and became the model of Indian civilization, the descendents of the Out Cherokees remained in their secluded valleys, clinging to the old customs and to the superannuated laws. In a nation of former mountaineers they became the hillbillies, the backwoodsmen in every sense of the word.

Trending on into the heart of the nation, due south from the Out towns or northwest beyond the first high ridges from the Lower Cherokees, the traveler came to the Middle settlements. Secure under the double protection of the Cowee and Balsam ranges, the Middle settlements throve and grew populous. In remote history, they had sent out the colonizers who founded the Lower towns, and later, in the 1750s, had received them back as refugees from the Creek wars.[19] Here were the towns of Watuga, Ioree, Elijoy, Cowee, Tarsalla, Coweechee, and Echoee, all of which centered around Nequasse, located near today's Franklin, North Carolina. These were among the nation's most populated villages. In 1756 Watuga was said to have 80 gunmen, Ioree had 70, and Cowee and Elijoy had 100 each, making them the second largest of all the reported Cherokee towns.[20] Yet, despite their size, they enter recorded history in the shadow of both the Overhill and Lower Cherokees. This is to be expected. The geographical advantage that gave them their prosperity and population also meant that they were seldom in the forefront of national councils. It is not possible to speak for every phase of public life, but in international affairs and Indian diplomacy the policy makers lived perforce in the border regions. It was they who bore the attacks in wartime, whose homes were burnt, and whose women were killed. It was they who moved for peace or cried for vengeance. The Middle settlements which they sheltered were carried along by events. The chance to seize national leadership occasionally came to the Middle settlements, but under the dynamics of Cherokee politics this opportunity was infrequent and was seldom expected.

If the traveler continued due west from the Middle settlements and crossed the Nantahala mountains, he came to the Valley towns located on the upper waters of the Hiwassee and in the glens of its tributary, the Valley river. Today this is Cherokee County, North Carolina, and the county seat, Murphy, contains the site of the chief town of the Valley— proud, prestigious Hywassee, the home of some of the nation's leading warriors during the struggles against the French. In this rich and beautiful land, guarded on all sides by towering mountain peaks, lay several of the leading venatic towns of the Cherokees—Enforsee, Conostee, Little Tellico, Tomattly, Nottely, Nayowee, and Cheewohee. It was especially the hunters of the Valley towns, stalking deer at the high altitudes where skins were extra fine, who made the Cherokee trade one of the mainstays of the early Carolina economy.

On October 25, 1759, at a time fraught with peril for Englishmen in the nation, Captain John Stuart prepared to leave the Valley town of Hywassee. "This day," he wrote his governor at Charles Town, "I enter the mountains." [21] He had been among mountains for several weeks, yet the governor understood his meaning. For Stuart was referring to the

Unicoi mountains, beyond which lay the Upper or Overhill Cherokees. To "go over the hills" was an expression familiar to Indian and Carolinian alike. There, northwest of Hywassee, over the Unakas, in what is today Monroe County, Tennessee, lay the most independent, remote, and energetic region of the Cherokee nation. This was the home of the Over-hills—the fertile valleys of the Little· Tennessee and the Tellico rivers, where the Warrior's Trail and the Nolochuckie war path, invasion routes from the north, entered the nation. This region was the transmontane bulwark of the Cherokees, and of Carolina, against the French and their Indians.[22]

From the base of the mountains to where the Tennessee joined the Holston, the valleys were not more than 25 to 30 miles in length. Yet here were located all the Overhill towns: [23] Great Tellico, unruly and pro-French, beneath the Unicoi mountains half a mile downstream from today's Tellico Plains; the Long Island of Holston (today called Kingsport), sacred as the place of the Cherokee's council fire; Tennessee (or Tannassie or Tunisee), which bestowed its name on a river and on a state; Chatuga, physically merged with Great Tellico yet keeping a separate council house, one of the puzzles of Cherokee government; Settico; Tallassee; Togua; and Chota, near the mouth of the Little Tennessee. Chota was the "white town" or "peace town," [24] the town of refuge, claiming to be the mother town of the Cherokees,[25] and acknowledged by many as "the Beloved Town" of the nation.[26]

Much has been made of Chota's ascendency by those who postulate a grand scheme of government under a king or "Uku" who lived in the Beloved Town.[27] But while we may doubt whether Chota enjoyed special privileges and scoff at the notion of an Uku, we cannot ignore the influence that Chota exercised. When we are able to measure that influence and discover its origin, we may begin to understand the mechanics of Cherokee government and Cherokee law.

CHAPTER THREE

A LEADERSHIP OF CRISIS

—THE ASCENDENCY OF CHOTA

The ascendency of Chota* over the other Cherokee towns is more than mystery, it is mystery compounded by myth. One cannot measure or define the meaning of that ascendency, for it was vague, fluctuating, and momentary. There is only evidence that it existed. The trouble is that much of this evidence is self-serving and hence suspect. In 1752, for example, a Cherokee named Old Hop wrote the governor of South Carolina that Chota was "the Mother Town of all." [1] But this statement may mean little, for Old Hop was a headman of Chota, and was protesting British neglect of his town. Five years later Ostenaco, better known as "Judd's Friend," wrote that Chota was "the head of all the Nation." [2] Again, there is no need to be impressed. Judd's Friend was an Overhill Cherokee closely associated in national affairs with the leaders of Chota, and he was asking Old Hop for military aid.

* Near present-day Vonore, Tennessee. Also, Chotah, Choto, Chotto, Chote, Chotte, Choate, Chateauke, and quite commonly Echota.

Admittedly there is other evidence less suspect. Some Cherokees who lived during the generation after Chota was destroyed, referred to it as "the beloved town," a term of honor that cannot be precisely defined, but that may have had political connotations.[3] Moreover, there are a few recorded incidents in which other Cherokee towns avoided unpleasant actions by placing the onus of responsibility upon Chota. Thus, in 1747 the headmen of Tennessee and Great Tellico told the British they would have put to death a French spy, "but that the Mother Town of Chotte would not give up their old right of saveing who they thought proper" and had insisted the Frenchman live.[4] Similarly in 1752 Tallassee, deferring to Chota, did not seize several French Indians who had been sent to stir up a Cherokee-Creek war. It was reported to Charles Town that the Tallassees would "have killed them had they not been afraid of Chote."[5] In both these incidents, Cherokee towns avoided British displeasure by shifting responsibility onto Chota.

Examples such as these do not prove that Tennessee, Great Tellico, or Tallassee would have obeyed Chota had they not wished, or that Chota could have made them obey. The most impressive fact is that Chota was the town used as an excuse, the beloved town to which the British thought the remainder of the Cherokee nation deferred.

There are two explanations that can be offered for Chota's ascendency. The sounder of the two is that Chota, largely by virtue of the initiative and energy of the men who lived there, was able to assume the leadership among the Overhills at a time when the Overhills was the most influential region of the nation. Before considering this theory, however, one should note the opposing argument; an argument that seeks to unravel the apparent anarchy of Cherokee government by making Chota's ascendency during recorded history a catholicon for answering all questions and resolving all doubts regarding the seat of authority in the nation; an argument that postulates a Cherokee constitution which was fixed and certain, with Chota the capital and its chief headman the ruler of the nation.

Chota, this argument tells us, ruled because it was "the grandmother town of all," [6] the home of "the one King, or Uku, the First Beloved Man;" [7] it was the capital of the Cherokees and so its headman was the headman of the nation, exercising the absolute power one would expect to be exercised by a monarch in savage society. This speculation can be supported on any one of four theories. The first theory is that because Chota was called the "beloved town" and the "mother town," it must have had a privileged function, perhaps a governmental role. The second theory is that Cherokee government was bifurcate in form, with a red hierarchy for war and a white hierarchy for peace, and Chota was the great white town. The third theory is that the Cherokee political organization was a theocracy, and Chota was the home of the high priest. The fourth theory is that because authority must rest somewhere, in a nation of town governments it probably rested in the leading town—and Chota was the leading town.

The first theory is the easiest to dismiss. It is simply too speculative. No one today can define what the terms "beloved town" or "mother town" meant in Cherokee law. The soundest evidence in Chota's case is that "beloved town" referred to the fact that Chota was the Cherokee village of refuge, a legal concept relating to the law of homicide. Chota was the town in which blood could not be spilled, the one place where a killer was free from the vengeance of his victim's kinsmen.[8] The term may also have been applied to Chota as the Cherokees' most important town, a fact which need not be disputed if it is qualified by noting that there is no evidence of Chota's being the most important town at any time except when records are clear, or of its being important because it had a governing function.

As for the term "mother town," we need only consider that Chota was not the only "mother town." A visitor to the nation in 1730 was told that there were seven mother towns, of which Chota was not then one.[9] The number is significant for there were seven clans in the nation, and it is possible that these seven towns, if they served a legal function, were the mother towns of the seven respective clans. If so, and if we dare force sophisticated legal concepts upon primitive institutions, then they properly should be classified under private, not public law.

The second theory explaining Chota's position at the head of a Cherokee government is based on the assumption that national leadership was divided between "red towns" and "white towns." The red were "war" towns, and the white were "peace" towns and places of refuge. In time of invasion, or for the duration of a martial emergency, the red group assumed command. In time of peace the white towns provided leadership. This theory postulates two sets of political officials with largely independent activities, two moieties which knew when they should exercise exclusive authority, and when they should yield to the other. It is an attractive soluion to the puzzle posed by the confusion of Cherokee government, and it has been adopted by several historians.[10] Unfortunately there is slight proof to support such a theory.

One Carolinian official, Tobias Fitch, told the Cherokees in 1726 that he understood that "making peace belongs to the head men of your white Towns," [11] and this evidence is surely impressive, for Fitch was then in the nation and was an expert on Indian affairs. But Fitch was equally if not more familiar with the government of the Creeks, and the Creeks are believed to have had a red-white division of leadership.[12] It may be that Fitch made the same assumption as later historians: that Creek governmental structures were duplicated among the Cherokees.[13] At least, more facts are needed before accepting generalities drawn from a chance remark, or from anthropological arguments assumed by comparing neighboring institutions. Comparative anthropological jurisprudence is a perilous discipline when employed to provide answers, not merely to frame questions. The existence of a red-white dichotomy among the Creeks raises the legitimate issue whether the Cherokes, who paralleled the Creeks in many respects, had a similar governmental moiety. It is a problem, however, that can be solved only by Cherokee evidence. Frederic William Maitland warned against filling in blanks that occur in the history of one nation by institutions and processes observed in another.[14] "Explorations in foreign climes," he said, "may often tell us what to look for, but never what to find." [15] There is nothing in Cherokee history to substantiate the notion that "red" towns and "white" towns performed different governmental functions. All towns seem to have operated in a similar manner; any one might wage war, any one might negotiate peace. Chota, for example, often did both at the same time. Nor can it be proven that there was even a division of peace-war duties on a personal basis. The very men who led raiding parties against an enemy often were the ones who concluded peace. On one occasion the Little Carpenter, a Chota headman, even returned from a sortie against the Shawnees by way of the Chickasaws and used his oratory, as well as scalps he had just taken, to avert a threatened Chickasaw-Cherokee war. When confronted with the facts of recorded history, it is impossible to sustain a theory of red-white leadership.

Moreover, were we to rely solely on comparative anthropological jurisprudence, we might still be skeptical. Even the Creeks do not seem to have had the compact governmental structure envisioned by the theorists. "There are two great Men that agree to Peace or who order War," a Creek headman explained in 1753, implying that the power of war and peace among the Creeks was united under two leaders, and not divided between them.[16] Even this statement offered too simple an explanation of constitutional practice, as seen by the actions of the Gun Merchant, an Upper-Creek headman during the late 1740s and early 1750s. The Gun Merchant was a successful war leader who publicly boasted of fighting several battles against the Cherokees. Far from acting as though he were limited to a red phalanx of power, he was the prime mover among his people for a Cherokee peace during the 1750s. He not only led the peace party among the Upper Creeks, but when peace was negotiated, he sought to bind the Creeks and Cherokees into a firm alliance by starting a war with the Choctaws—thus combining red and white powers to achieve one diplomatic stroke.[17]

It is not necessary to quarrel with the notion that there were "red" and "white" towns among either the Cherokees or the Creeks. We need only doubt whether they played any taxonomic, or fixed role in government. As will appear, Cherokee government was less a structural fact than a fluid, changing reality.

The third theory which has been advanced to explain Chota's ascendency in the nation as constitutional authority, and not mere accident, can be traced to ethnological conjecture about an ancient Cherokee religion. Some towns, so the story goes, possessed "a mother fire," and the towns without a mother fire looked to them for leadership.[18] Chota, with the oldest fire of all, was naturally the first among the leaders.

That we have no evidence to support the notion of political leadership among the Cherokees does not seem to trouble the supporters of this theory. From scattered tidbits of unsubstantiated tradition, a grand scheme of priests and holy men has evolved to fill places of power and authority conventional to the experience of western man. The Cherokees, it is further asserted, created a state in which the major offices were held by priests [19] who formed a separate class in society; a hierarchy of privilege that may have been possessed by one family by hereditary right, reminding at least one writer of the priestly rulers of the Aztec and Mayan—"of the historic Hopi priests of fire, heat, and fertility, whose voices on occasion the laity heard in the night expressing the will of heaven as they moved in the dark toward such women as they choose." [20] The time came when the Cherokee priests abused their power by choosing the wrong woman, the wife of a young hunter who, with his brother, led a rebellion that toppled the holy men from power, leaving their priestly functions to doctors and conjurers.[21] A second version of the same myth leaves the priests weakened but not broken, forced to share leadership with the nation's warriors.[22] All these events lie beyond the pale of history; as tradition they may possibly have some foundation in truth, though it cannot be proved one way or the other.

Legends such as these would lead no one to claim that the Cherokee government was a priest-state, were it not for the fact that when Chota begins to appear on the records, Chota's headman is Old Hop, whom James Adair called a priest.[23] Adair lived among the Cherokees and knew them well, but his statement cannot be cited as proof that the Cherokees were a theocracy. For one thing, Adair did not like Old Hop and by calling him the "Archi-magus," a chiefship with ultimate power which we know Old Hop never possessed, Adair blamed him for the disastrous Cherokee War of 1760. Moreover, Adair was trying to prove that American Indians were descendants of the ancient Jews, and he was all too anxious to make ordinary Cherokee headmen resemble leaders of biblical times. He does not define what he means by "priest," nor does he furnish examples of priestly functions. Other authorities who believe there were priests in the nation say that they could not spill blood, which would exclude Old Hop who had been a warrior in his younger days.[24]

The problem, to be sure, is not whether Old Hop was a priest but whether he occupied a political office in Cherokee government by virtue of a religious function. We may discount a nation's religion as a factor in its law only if that nation's clerics exercised no constitutional power *ex officio,* and if religious doctrine did not determine individual rights, or play a role in the settlement of judicial disputes. It is possible that if all the necessary evidence were available, we would find that Cherokee religion met this test. However, at the present state of knowledge this seems improbable, for at best, it appears to have been a religion with slight pretensions at dogma and without any discernible organizational structure. It is known that during recorded times, the Cherokees had conjurers who prepared physics to purge their clients of sickness, and who offered prophesies that were used as excuses for avoiding warfare or other unpleasant duties. Perhaps, as one writer has suggested, the conjurers were the remains of the ancient priestly class of legend.[25] However, if we took the sounder approach and reversed the supposition by arguing from the known of recorded history to the unknown of pre-history, we could contend that there never was any Cherokee religion more sophisticated or more organized than professional conjuring, a form of free enterprise more related to superstition than to theology.

A few writers, apparently on their own authority, have asserted that the Cherokees believed in a Great Spirit, in an evil spirit who on the last day would be the accuser of all nations, and in a future life where the good are rewarded and the bad are condemned to menial tasks.[26] Although extant records do quote some Cherokees as speaking of "The Great Man above," [27] references to God almost invariably turn up when they are excusing their conduct to the British, and seem to have been a shrewd form of special pleading. At the very most, they may have honored a celestial diety,[28] but even this possibility is doubtful. The best available evidence points to the conclusion that the Cherokees had no theology based on belief in a supreme being, or in an universal evil spirit.[29] What religion they had was zootheism in nature.[30]

> The Cherokee religion is a polytheistic form of zoolatry, or animal-worship, which may possibly have had a totemic origin. No great central figure, no creative cause, is evident in this system. To the Cherokee the Land of Spirits is merely a shadowy extension of the world in which he dwells. He recognizes neither a Paradise nor a place of punishment, neither a Supreme Being nor a Spirit of Evil.[31]

Too much importance should not be attached to the notion of animal worship. That was at most a personal factor, not an institutionalized ritual of theology or ceremony. A Cherokee might beg the pardon of an animal he had slain to appease the anger of its spirit, or he might consider it unlucky to kill a wolf because the soul of a dead wolf could spoil his gun.[32] But if, on occasion, he hired a conjurer to recite a prayer for forgiveness over the body of a dead animal, he seems never to have left offerings at the numerous places where he believed supernatural beings lived.[33] He merely avoided such places. The first white clergyman to investigate the Cherokee religion was disappointed by the evidence he uncovered. A Presbyterian missionary, he was in Chota during January, 1759, where he witnessed a dance "which I took for some religious Ceremony paid to the Fire, as they frequently bowed to it, but was afterwards informed by them it was only a custom they have & they dont seem to worship any Thing." [34]

The conclusion is inescapable. The Cherokees may have been superstitious. They may even have been religious. But they had no organized theology. They hired conjurers to intercede on their behalf with animal spirits, especially when they were sick. But individuals were on their own as far as religious philosophy was concerned, and conjuring seems to have been a private business, not a function of state.] We must not deny that superstition was important in their lives, or that ritual, especially the ceremonies attendant upon purification following birth or preceding battle, was a vital element in their social behavior. We need only recognize that their religion was not well enough organized to guarantee priests the leadership of government. The conjurers who rose to position of influence

—and there were several—were no different from other headmen. What power they had came from the civil, not the religious, side of Cherokee life. Their leadership was derived from a mastery of Cherokee politics, not from inherited priestcraft or theocratic privilege.」

The fourth theory explaining Chota's ascendency rests on the assumption that national authority must be vested somewhere; and because Chota was the most active Cherokee town, it follows that authority was vested in Chota. But this notion of "authority" is European authority, not Cherokee authority. It is premised on the concept of the coercive state, a level of government the Cherokee would not adopt until the first decade of the nineteenth century, when their political and legal institutions were drastically revised. During the era of their primitive law, the Cherokee nation was an aggregate of independent towns. There was no governmental machinery to formulate a coordinate domestic program, or to frame a uniform international policy. And even when a course of action was supported by a consensus of the nation, there was no constitutional means to enforce its acceptance upon individual towns or upon individual Cherokees. The Cherokees may not have felt completely free; they may have recognized the duty to obey, resulting from a coercion that we might label public opinion or social ostracism. But a Cherokee did not fear the police power of Chota, for Chota had none to exercise.

The problem was not merely that fractional and regional rivalries made it impossible for the national government to bind all the Cherokees into a political unit.[35] The problem was that there was no national government at all. It cannot be said that the Cherokees recognized this as a problem. They probably would not have understood it anyway. The British tried several times to persuade them that responsible authority was better than anarchy, but the Cherokees could not be moved to think of change. They knew any solution was so radical that it would be almost impossible to effect. We may suspect that the Cherokees were able to understand the advantage of having each region fight on behalf of the whole nation, to acknowledge that the invaders of one were invaders of all. But we may doubt if an eighteenth-century Cherokee could have contemplated any scheme to force his countrymen to wage the same war and negotiate the same peace. The Overhill Cherokees spent a good part of recorded history fighting the French Indians, while the Lower towns were at war with the Creeks.[36] There was no unit of the national government to tell the Overhills to attack the Creeks, or even to be unfriendly toward them. When two white men were killed in 1758 and South Carolina threatened vengeance, the Lower towns told the British the killers were Overhills, while the Overhills said they were Lower Cherokees.[37] Neither region showed any compulsion to shield the other, even though a British war against one would almost certainly have involved all. Under the same circumstances one Overhill town was as likely to blame another Overhill town as to blame a Lower or a Valley town.

In a nation without political unity and lacking the machinery to coerce unity, it follows that governmental leadership was not a matter of constitutional authority but the filling of a constitutional vacuum. This explains Chota's ascendency. Back during the 1720s and 1730s, when the British first encountered the Cherokees, the records hardly ever mentioned Chota. The Overhills, of which Chota was a part, were harassed by enemy attacks and in 1724 even fled to the Lower Cherokee country.[38] The Lower towns were relatively secure, and proximity to the Charles Town trade gave them a wealth which enhanced their influence in national affairs.[39] For a while Tugalo was the most energetic of the towns and seems to have been the most important. "I take the people thereabout to be the most turbulent in the Nation," a British agent wrote of Tugalo in 1725, "& also the most taken notice of by the other towns." [40] Fifty-two years later, at the very time Old Hop emerges as a Chota headman, the fortunes of war were reversed and the Lower Cherokees fled their country to take refuge among the Overhills.[41] Moreover, the French wars of attrition had begun to wear down the Chickasaws, and the British were forced to deal with the strategically-located Overhills as their first line of defense.[42] Whereas in 1725 the Lower headmen had negotiated with Charles Town on behalf of the nation, in 1753 the Governor of South Carolina observed that the Overhill headmen had "now the great Sway in every Part of the Nation." [43]

To gain an idea of the primitive theory of government in the Cherokees, we can do no better than consider Chota's record during the early 1750s, when the nation was harassed on all sides. Creeks were destroying the Lower Towns, French Indians were attacking the Overhills, and Catawbas, fierce neighbors to the east, were threatening war unless the Cherokees ceased providing sanctuary for their enemies. Even more critical, the Cherokee-British alliance, the prop of the nation's foreign policy for over a half century, was coming unstuck. Disgruntled hunters in several towns had sought to escape the vise of rising debts and falling prices in the only way they knew how—by robbing and in some cases killing the traders, a crime South Carolina could not let pass without demanding satisfaction. Many Cherokees, especially some of the most influential headmen in the nation, were so annoyed by the tactics of British agents (who were recruiting, for service in General Braddock's offense against Fort Duquesne, Cherokee warriors needed to defend their towns), that they were ready to make peace with the French. To these crises the headmen of Chota applied themselves. We might not call the action they took "leadership." They did not furnish our kind of political leadership, but they did furnish Cherokee leadership. Indeed, they did more. They furnished Cherokee "government." Seizing the initiative, the Chotas attempted to formulate a new national policy. They did not order, decree, direct, or legislate. They conferred, discussed, proposed, and conciliated, with more energy and greater conviction than did their rivals in other towns. They scored a small point, for example, when a talk they sent the Catawbas pleased that nation's headmen so much, they said they would henceforth deal only with Chota.[44] Neither the Catawbas nor the Cherokees were bound by this statement, and likely as not the Catawbas would soon forget they had ever made it. However, for the moment, Chota enjoyed the national leadership in Catawba affairs—and for that moment Chota was, in Catawba affairs, the closest thing the Cherokees had to an effectual government.

In more important matters, the Chota headmen assumed national leadership by concluding a long-desired peace with the French Indians,[45] by formulating a new British alliance brilliantly designed to end the Carolinian monopoly with a rival Virginia trade negotiated by Chota,[46] and by shielding the murderers of the traders behind protracted diplomatic maneuvers frustrating British demands for satisfaction. They also persuaded the British to build a fort in the Overhills to protect Cherokee women and children, before any more warriors were recruited for Braddock's army. None of these efforts except the last was totally successful, but the result was not important because appearance was as significant as reality in Cherokee politics. When both South Carolina and Virginia constructed forts near Chota, that town was acknowledged by British and Cherokee alike to have seized political leadership in the nation.

Political activity centered around Chota because the headmen of Chota were politically active, and the actions they took politically successful. During the 1750s they, more than the headmen of other towns, seemed to offer leadership and thus filled the vacuum of leadership inherent in Cherokee government. It was they and the programs they offered, plus the fact that the British, French, foreign Indians, and the other towns all paid them heed by either dealing with or following them, which gave Chota its ascendency in national affairs, and led the Cherokees to call it "the beloved town" or "the mother town."

Chota's political leadership was based on political crises: (1) the crisis of the Lower towns almost annihilated by the Creeks; (2) the crisis of the British need for allies giving the Overhills, as guardians of tramontane Carolina, a new importance in military affairs; and (3) the crisis of the violence committed against Carolinian traders that turned the nation toward Chota, the gateway to the Virginia trade. Cherokee national government was in fact a government of crisis. National leadership functioned best in response to crisis, because the nation responded to leadership only when in peril. If Chota's ascendency demonstrates this, so does its downfall. It lost its leadership when unable to cope with the crises of wars against the British in 1760, and the Americans in 1776.

CHAPTER FOUR

A RULE BY CONSENSUS

—THE TOWNS

To say the Cherokees had no national government, just crisis leadership, is not to say they had no government at all. At the local level there were the towns, and to the average Cherokee the town was the only governmental unit he acknowledged. There were at least 50 towns in the nation, with some authorities counting up to 64.[1] The best guess is that they averaged between 350 to 600 people each, seldom getting larger, probably because they divided once the population grew too numerous.[2] The reason was topography. It was rare to find a level tract of 400 acres in the mountain country, and the Cherokees were a sedentary people who tilled the soil, depending largely upon agriculture and fishing for subsistence. Moreover they were not in the habit of traveling to their fishing beds, and so their towns had to be located along the banks of rivers and streams; not the great rivers such as the Tennessee and the Savannah, which would have exposed them to attack, but along the small affluents hidden between the mountain ridges.[3]

In appearance, Cherokee towns physically resembled the open-field villages of medieval England. They were nucleated settlements with houses clustered together at some central point, and the planting stretched out in several directions. No Cherokee family maintained a unit farm, with house, field, and pasture joined in one piece away from neighbors. It was not a primitive distaste for isolation that made the Cherokee a village dweller,[4] but the security of mutual protection. It is doubtful if his wife worked in the field alone. With enemies lurking in the woods beyond, she was not safe unless fellow townswomen labored at the same hour. The regulation of these hours was surely a prime function of town government, although one must be cautious at this point as there is little direct evidence one way or the other. The town government may also have assigned the fields and house lots, and there is some support for the thesis that the town maintained a common grainary and even directed work. But both these matters must be deferred, as they more properly belong in a discussion of the Cherokee law of property.

The governing body of each town was the council, an assembly of all the men and women, who met every night except during the hunting season. The council house was the largest structure in the village, a seven-sided amphitheatre around which the people sat, with the headmen near the center and the others on benches along the sides, each person sitting with his clan. A British army officer reported that Chota's council house resembled "a small mountain at a little distance,"[5] and it may not have been the only one capable of holding up to 500 people.[6]

We must not attribute too much to these councils, except to acknowledge that they were completely democratic. They undoubtedly followed some rules of procedure. No one, for example, was allowed to bring weapons into the council house.[7] Yet, everyone was permitted to speak, and custom required that everyone be heard. This, in fact, was the essence of their function. For they were deliberative bodies; they did not legislate or adjudicate. The town council met to seek a consensus on policy, to compromise between viewpoints, not to pass laws or to regulate conduct. If any man could not agree with the emerging consensus, Cherokee habit and Cherokee custom called for him to withdraw, to disassociate himself. He was not expelled. To have ousted him would have caused friction, and the town council existed to promote harmony. Dissenters were ignored, never chastised.

During the 1750s, a headman known as the Mankiller of Great Tellico persuaded the people of his town to seek an alliance with the French. They followed his lead, even abandoning their village and moving closer to the French. But when the promised presents of the French failed to materialize, and they found themselves cut off from British presents and scorned by other towns, the people of Great Tellico drifted back to their old town site and sought to regain the good will of the British and their fellow Cherokees. The presence of the Mankiller in their midst made it impossible to convince the British of their sincerity, yet there was nothing they could do but treat him and his lieutenants as social but not legal outcasts. Finally, when the Mankiller announced a change of heart, a festival was held to celebrate restored harmony.[8] The council—the consensus of the people—had performed its task. It does not matter that an English lawyer might conclude nothing had been resolved. The town councils must be judged on their own terms. In a sense they typified the legal theory guiding Cherokee governmental institutions. They were designed not to resolve difficulties, but to avoid them; not to command, but to conciliate.

We cannot leave our discussion of the Cherokee town on such an indecisive note. Town government may seem ineffective by our standards, but nonetheless the town was remarkable in at least one respect. Legal fictions and legal abstractions may be common in primitive law, but were rare among the Cherokees. Yet the "town" may have been a legal abstraction that every Cherokee understood. It was more than a collection of houses within a geographical area, bound together by a common council. We know that for at least 40 years and undoubtedly much longer, the houses of two towns, Great Tellico and Chatuga, were physically intermixed, yet they maintained separate councils. Their location on the nation's northwestern frontier left them exposed to enemy attack and therefore, as one colonial officer put it in 1725, they were "very Compact and thick Settled." [9] He seemed a bit puzzled that they were two towns. So, too, was a French soldier who reported 16 years later that there were "two different councils, though the cabins are mingled together indistinguishable." [10] We may be certain the Cherokees knew they were two towns. In December, 1756, when Great Tellico voted to move nearer the French, it was hoped Chatuga would go along. But to a man, that town rejected the leadership of the Mankiller. The Chatugas thrashed out the issue in their own council and adhered to the pro-British sentiments of their headmen. It is possible to imagine two Cherokees, one a Chatuga, the other a Great Tellico, living in adjoining houses and perhaps even belonging to the same clan: one aiding the British to kill French Indians, the other plotting with French Indians to kill Englishmen. Something of this sort occurred in June, 1757, when the Black Dog Warrior of Chatuga assisted a party of South Carolina soldiers to ambush 8 Shawnees negotiating with the Mankiller. He kept the Great Tellico escort a few yards back by engaging them in conversation while the white men killed the Shawnees, thus keeping the Cherokees out of the line of fire. For had a Great Tellico been shot, all the Cherokees of his clan, even those living in Chatuga, could have demanded vengeance and the British-Cherokee alliance might have been broken.

Accepting the town as the basic unit of government, it cannot be said that either the Black Dog Warrior of Chatuga, or the Mankiller of Great Tellico, was an insurgent or even acting outside the law. We might be reluctant to think both were acting legally when we realize that the things they did were at such cross purposes as to endanger the peace and safety of the nation. However, it would be error to say that one man or the other acted illegally. What we can say is that they and other eighteenth-century Cherokees regarded their towns as corporate entities, a legal abstraction they apparently found too sophisticated to apply to the nation as a whole.

We may go a step further and note a final point regarding Cherokee towns. In addition to being treated as a corporate entity, as the basic unit of government, the town was one the two legal institutions to which Cherokees applied the doctrine of collective responsibility. The second was the clan. We shall see many instances of the doctrine of collective responsibility, especially when we examine Cherokee homicide law and international law. Let one illustration suffice here. During the spring of 1751, a number of disturbances occurred in the nation. It had been a poor winter for hunting, and with many Cherokees heavily in their debt the British traders refused to extend further credit, thus leaving a large segment of the population with no means to obtain supplies. Dissatisfaction became widespread, and in several towns the people looted the stores of the traders. Most headmen were able to adjust matters on behalf of their own towns. In Chota, for example, Old Hop took the local trader into his house and persuaded the thieves to return much of the stolen property. But in two towns, Ustanali and Stecoe, the goods disappeared. When the other towns disowned them, and they realized they were open to British retaliation, the people of Ustanali and Stecoe gave way to panic. The Ustanalis were so alarmed they broke up their town and fled a hundred miles westward beyond several mountains, where they permanently settled.[11]

The Stecoes also fled. It is possible to argue that perhaps every person in Ustanali and Stecoe may have taken part in the depredations, and that their flight resulted as much from individual guilt as from a sense of collective responsibility. What is legally significant is the action of the Raven of Hywassee. In order to protect the Valley towns and perhaps even the whole nation, he sent his son to Stecoe, an Out town, to demand that Stecoe pay for the stolen property.[12] The entire town was held collectively responsible by the Raven, and the matter was settled when the town itself pledged that it would reimburse its trader for his losses.

Incidents such as this were frequent in the nation's history. Sometimes only one individual was guilty in the sense that the common law defines the word "guilt," yet the whole town was held collectively responsible. One of the great dilemmas of Cherokee law was that the Cherokee understood the doctrine of collective responsibility as applied to a town, a clan, or another Indian nation, but they were unable to apply it in a meaningful manner to their own nation.

It might be asked whether we can even speak of "Cherokee government." There was a Chota government, a Keowee government, a Hywassee government, and up to 60 other governments. But was there a "Cherokee government"? Certainly there was no authority, no head of state, no lawmaking body with which other nations could deal. It is too strong a term to call the Cherokee nation a confederacy of towns. At best, it was a collection of towns populated by a common people. At worst—in times of strife—it was anarchy. Yet we cannot conclude that there was no national government. When the headmen of certain towns furnished a leadership that others would follow, the nation became a functioning reality, and this occurred as often as not.

Should we, therefore, define the Cherokee nation as a government of independent towns joined together by a shifting, changing leadership, which arose to meet individual crises, and which arranged and rearranged itself to meet the problems at hand? This definition leaves two remaining questions. What was it that united the nation, if not a coercive government? And how did the headmen rise to influence? The answer to the first question is the clans, and to the second, the will of the people.

CHAPTER FIVE

A FAMILY WRIT LARGE

—THE CLANS

It could be argued that if the Cherokees had no national government, they should not be called a "nation." A few historians have in fact refused to use the word, and one even insists that a colonial governor was guilty of error when he spoke of Indian nations rather than Indian tribes.[1] But in truth "tribe" was a nineteenth-century term, and if an eighteenth-century governor had used it, he might have confused his correspondents because "tribe" usually referred to "clan" or some other national sub-division. "Nation," on the other hand, described both an ethnic group and a piece of geography. Colonial officials spoke of going into "the Cherokee nation," or into "the nation," or into "the Cherokees," or they might speak of sending a message or "talk" into "the nation"; only after independence would men speak of entering the "Indian country." Not until Americans were brought into contact with the nomadic Indians of the Western Plains did it become common to use the word "tribe." True, the constitution of the United States speaks of "Indian tribes," but this occurs in the commerce clause where Indians are contrasted with foreign nations and states.[2] For several decades, the federal government called the larger tribes "nations"; in official documents, legislation, treaties, and law suits, the Cherokees, the Choctaws, the Creeks, and the Chickasaws were always referred to as "nations." The Cherokees themselves took the question of whether they were a "nation" to the Supreme Court of the United States, and the court was so confused that it divided.[3]

The issues which divided the justices were legal issues of constitutional interpretation and sovereignty, not issues which help to resolve the problem of whether the eighteenth-century Cherokees formed a "nation." To find an answer, it is better to reply on Cherokee law than American law, and from the perspective of the Cherokees' own domestic situation, from their social and legal institutions, it is possible to argue that they constituted a nation but not a state. The disinction between "nation" and "state" may seem mere semantics, yet it reveals much regarding the substance of Cherokee government; that is, if we are willing to define a "state" as a people politically organized under a sovereign government which possesses coercive power to maintain order within the community. Coercion is the diacritical factor. It is not necessary that a state's government make law, only that it enforce law.[4] The national government of the Cherokees lacked authority either to make or enforce law. When it acquired the authority to do both during the first decade of the nineteenth century, the primitive era of Cherokee law came to an end. For the first use of coercion by the Cherokee national government was directed against the operation of customary law, and the first statutes which the Cherokee adopted abolished traditional legal institutions.[5]

Whatever hesitancy we might have about speaking of a Cherokee state using this definition, "Cherokee nation" remains a fair description. The Cherokees may not have been a political entity held together by coercive force, but they were an ethnic entity bound by ties of consanguinity. They were a nation, in the sense that they regulated their lives in conformity to a common social culture; a culture not so much the expression of esoteric ideas drawn from a social philosophy explaining the genesis, or from social patterns based on wealth, birth, or economic competition, but a social culture that stressed mutual defense, discouraged intratribal strife, and was underscored by a common tradition of unwritten laws. We may run the risk of stressing the legal, yet in a society such as the Cherokees'— a society seemingly without organized religion—the common denominator may well be law.

If we agree that the primitive Cherokees constituted a "nation—one without a coercive national government, a true, functioning "nation" without any institutionalized authority to make and enforce law—we may still ask whether they had some constitutional body, some national structure which substituted for the European system of governmental cohesiveness and provided the body politic with legal unity. For the Cherokees, as for most American Indians, this substitute was the clan. The social compages of the Cherokee nation, as well as its constitutional fabric, was woven together through a viable interrelationship of consanguinity which created legal rights and duties, both individual and collective. The towns of the nation may have been politically independent, and the people themselves may have spoken three sectional dialects, yet the legal and social structure of clanship, while providing less than perfect governmental unity, conjoined the Cherokees into one nation and one people.

There is no trace of either moieties or phratries among the Cherokees.[6] They were divided into seven matrilineal clans, that was all. These clans were the Ani'-Wa' ya, the Ani'-Kawi, the Ani'-Tsi' skwa, the Ani'-Wa' dĭ, the Ani'-Sahâ nĭ, the Ani'-Ga' tage' wĭ, and the Ani-Gilâ hĭ. Only the first four have been translated with certainty—the Wolf clan, the Deer clan, the Bird clan, and the Paint clan.[7] The remaining three have been rendered Long Hair, Blind Savannah, and Holly,[8] or Blue, Wild Potato, and Twisters.[9] The most controversy surrounds the Ani'-Ga' tage' wi clan. Early nineteenth-century researchers called them "Blind Savannahs," [10] but many authorities feel this is incorrect.[11]

It would be impossible to classify the clan in contemporary legal terms, except to say that it was the most important unit in Cherokee constitutional law. As the exogamous institution of the nation, as well as the agency responsible for the maintenance of order and the redress of wrongs, the clan seems to belong in the category of public law. But most of its functions, such as the education of children and the imposition of sanctions, were performed in a manner which we associate with private law. The Cherokees themselves described the clan as "the grand work by which marriages were regulated, and murder punished." [12]

In actuality, the clan was too basic to Cherokee society to be discussed merely by legal concepts. It was "the family writ large." [13] More than a family, the clan was a corporate entity based on kinship. More than a private corporation, it was an arm of government to which all police power was entrusted. Membership in a clan was more important than citizenship in the nation. Constitutionally speaking, there were no Cherokee citizens, only clan members. An alien had no legal security, no rights, privileges, or duties until adopted by a clan. Once adopted, he was equal to any native-born Cherokee. The members of his clan became his advocates and his sureties. They defended him in life, and should he be slain, they defended him in death by exacting from his slayer a talionic justice, the certainty of which had been the chief guarantee of his welfare. If we should say that clan membership was the single most important aspect of a Cherokee's life, we would not exaggerate.

Clanship was the most fundamental of all Cherokee legal rights. Membership was too exact to be legally challenged. The clans were enatic and descent was matrilinear. There were no agnatic factors, no patrilineage considerations. Identify the propositus' mother and you identify his clan. A Cherokee belonged to his mother's clan. If the mother was a Bird clan member her children were Birds. When her daughter married, neither the daughter nor the daughter's husband changed clans. The daughter's children all belonged to the Bird clan. When her son married, he remained a Bird. If his wife was a member of the Deer clan, she remained a Deer and all their children were Deers. They were not Birds.[14] The basic structure was as simple as the idea behind the Cherokee word for "brother." It was *ditlu-nu-tsi* which some authorities translate as "same mother." [15]

For ethnographers, clan membership answers a great many questions regarding the structure of Cherokee society. To say it was matrilineal is to say much. To describe it as "Crow" is to permit it to be compared to all the other clan systems known to anthropology. But for the lawyer, little has been revealed. To discover that clan membership was determined through the mother, and that a man belonged to only one clan, tells us how a Cherokee knew where to look for the protection of his rights, but it tells us nothing about those rights. Nor does it tell us where he looked to determine his duties. For while rights were guaranteed by clan membership, duties were imposed by relationships within the clan and not necessarily by the clan as a whole. If we knew as much about rules governing relationships within clans as we know of rules for clan membership, we would know a great deal regarding Cherokee law. Few contemporary sources enlighten us, partly because clanship did not interest whites, and partly because even those who had lived for extended periods among the Cherokees were confused. "Their method of calculating clan-kin I do not understand," one nineteenth-century missionary admitted. "I have had it imperfectly explained to me; but it appeared so incongruous that I took but little pains to learn it." The Cherokees themselves had no difficulty. "An Indian," the missionary went on, "can tell you without hesitation what degree of relationship exists between himself and any other individual of the same clan you may see proper to point out." [16]

The most obvious relationship within the clan was that between mother and child. Here the emphasis is on rights, rather than duties. The duties were the familiar duties we associate with a mother in any society. The rights flowed from peculiarities of Cherokee clan law. The children were her relatives, not her husband's. After all, they belonged to her clan, not to his. Following divorce the children stayed with her, and this was true, at least in legal theory, if her husband was a non-Cherokee or even a white man.[17] Were the mother to die, her relatives, especially her eldest brother, claimed the children.[18] Should this fact surprise us, we need only reflect that as they belonged to different clans, the father not only lacked social incentive for claiming the children but had no legal grounds for doing so. The legal theory is dramatized more graphically by the law of infanticide. The Cherokee mother could destroy any surplus or unwanted baby at, or soon after, birth.[19] If the father killed his child, even accidentally, he was liable for the consequences of homicide. One familiar with the standards of European Christianity may marvel at these doctrines, but should not wonder how they came about. They are consistent with the rules of clan membership and follow with brutal logic from the legal concepts of clan law.

A more basic clan relationship than that between mother and child was the relationship between brother and sister—that is, if they had the same mother. The consanguine kinship existing between uterine brothers and sisters is said to have been the warmest, strongest, yet most respectful in North American Indian culture. Echoing the lament of Antigone, the Kiowas summed up the sentiment in the saying, "A woman can always get another husband, but she has only one brother." [20] Unfortunately, we do not have sufficient data to translate this relationship into legal doctrine. We suspect that the duties lay on the brother, that the sister enjoyed most of the rights. There is no evidence that he had to support her, at least while she was married, but he was the head of her family, her guardian, and the guardian of her children. Should we object that there were no legal sanctions binding him to the task, we would be asking too much of primitive institutions and ignoring the force of Cherokee social custom. We must think in terms of the blood family, not of the connubial family. A Cherokee performed his duty not because of conjugal ties but because of clan structure. It will not do to say that he neglected "his" children, for they were his wife's children and the responsibility of her brother. His sister's children were his responsibility.

The fundamental clan relationship, therefore, was between uterine uncles and nephews. Avuncular responsibility was the keystone of Cherokee education. So too was avuncular authority. The Cherokee youth was instructed and disciplined by his mother's brother. Matrilocal residence was one reason, clan law another. As the Cherokee father did not belong to the clan of his son, he was a legal stranger to him, and to have inflicted a parental punishment could have been legally risky. Should the father harm his son, he might be held to account by the son's clan. Should the father kill his son, the dead boy's clan might kill him in return.

The uterine uncle was, by necessity of law as well as social custom, the disciplinary and tutorial authority in the family.[21] It would be error to think of his position as based on the maternal relationship, rather than on clan law. "At first sight," one historical jurisprudent has written, "it may seem odd that the mother's brother and not the mother's father is the male protector, but the brother is the contemporary and remains when the older generation, in the person of the father, has passed away." [22] This explanation is not correct. The mother's father is not the male protector because he does not belong to the clan of his daughter and daughter's children, any more than does the father of those children. Should the child lack a uterine uncle to guide and protect him, his mother's father and his own father were still not the responsible authority. Rather, the extension of kinship through the clan meant that a "classificatory uncle" was available to assume the responsibility of the mother's brother.[23]

A notable aspect of the avuncular relationship was its strength. It was destined to last longer than most other Cherokee social institutions, surviving with remarkable resilience even the shift from the consanguine to the conjugal family organization, after most of the legal duties once performed by the uncle were taken over by the Cherokee state.[24] Among American Indians with a Cherokee-type clan structure, it was the uncle who during the acculturation period enrolled the nephew in school,[25] and to whom the boy continued to look for guidance.[26] A story is told of a young Cherokee, probably during the early years of the nineteenth century, selected by his uncle for the native priesthood. Later the nephew became a Christian and his uncle, stricken with grief and mortification, left home, and retired into the mountains to mourn his loss.[27] The story makes no mention of the father's reaction. There is no need. We cannot say he did not care. He may have cared as deeply as did the uncle. But the disgrace was not on him.

Fundamental as was the clan relationship between maternal uncle and sororal nephew, even closer was that of brother and brother. In many American Indian nations this was the strongest of all kinship bonds,[28] and the Cherokees were no exception. In their terminology they even distinguished an older brother from a younger brother, though they did not do the same with sisters.[29] Again we must stress duties and not rights, for the honored position of the elder brother was not one of privilege, as in the English law of primogeniture or of sex as in the salic law, but of responsibility. He possessed no rights over his sisters or his younger brothers, rather he had the duty of primary protector. This topic is one we must defer, as it belongs more properly to a discussion of the law of homicide. Enough is said by noting that an older brother's function was to protect and avenge his sisters and his younger brothers, and when old enough to do so, to assume toward them the role of a European father and a Cherokee uncle.[30]

We cannot overemphasize the importance of the clan in Cherokee law, if for no other reason than that clan relationships determined how much of that law should operate. Thus it is well to summarize by noting that the close ties of clan kinship, in terms of a Cherokee's legal responsibilities, were between brother and sister, and between mother's brother and sister's child. In terms of mutual rights and of clan dependency, the average Cherokee when he sought legal redress or felt obliged to avenge wrongs done by others, looked to his own brothers, to his mother's brothers, to his sisters' sons, to his mother's maternal uncles, and to his sisters' daughters' sons. In legal doctrine these were his close "brothers"— closer than the other members of the clan, who in Cherokee terminology as well as law were his clan brothers.[31]

It may seem incongruous that the Cherokee language had terms for distinguishing maternal uncles and elder brothers, but no way of reckoning kinship on the father's side. There is logic here, however. No matter what social intercourse a Cherokee may have had with his father's close clan kin, no matter if he regarded them as special friends or even as relatives, there was only one legal rule governing his conduct toward them. He was forbidden to marry them, or any other member of his father's clan. The clan was the exogamous unit of Cherokee society, and marriage within one's own clan or one's father's clan violated exogamy.[32] This principle contains the Cherokee law of incest, for it seems reasonable to suppose that it was broad enough to cover sexual intercourse as well as marriage.

"It is an axiom of Anthopology," the greatest of all legal anthropologists, Bronislaw Malinowski, has observed, "that nothing arouses greater horror than the breach of this prohibition," [33] and scholars of Cherokee customs, as if to underscore this argument, have insisted that the Cherokees punish incest with death.[34] It has been suggested that the clans themselves executed the violators,[35] or that the clan women somehow formed a group to administer the penalty.[36] If there was capital punishment for incest, surely it could have been imposed by no other authority than clan authority —and since every writer on the subject tells us there was a death penalty, we have grounds for believing there was. Yet no one can cite a specific case where intraclan marriage led to an execution, nor is the concept of punishment imposed by the clan upon its own members consistent with the general principles of Cherokee law, which was traditionally without physical sanctions except in regard to vengeance for homicide. Were we permitted to guess from analogies, we might conclude that a Cherokee writing in 1829 was correct when he suggested that his ancestors probably never violated the law against incest.[37] As an eighteenth-century visitor to the nation put it, they did not "dare" marry within their own clan or the clan of their father,[38] but the sanctions were more likely social than capital.

It should be noted that in some ways the Cherokee law prohibiting incestuous marriages was much broader than that laid down by Christian nations. A Cherokee could not marry anyone in his own clan or his father's clan, even members whose relationship to him was by our standards so remote that we would not think them kin. On the other hand, Cherokee law was narrower than Christian law. It is conceivable that a Cherokee man might have two wives belonging to different clans. The daughter of one wife would, in English law, be the half-sister of the son of the second wife, yet by Cherokee law they would belong to separate clans and would be free to marry. Cousinage was not a Cherokee legal concept; at least not outside of one's own clan. The son of a Cherokee was not related to the daughter of his father's brother. The daughter was forbidden to marry the brother of her father because he belonged to the same clan as her father. But there was no restriction against marrying her father's brother's son.

To make this point is to make a point about law, about the legal customs of the Cherokees, by carrying their exogamous clan rules to a logical conclusion. But logic is an uncertain tool in primitive law, just as it is in civilized law, for social customs and legal customs sometimes blend one into the other, with social customs often commanding an obedience equal to that paid legal customs. We are treading on uncertain grounds when we try to separate the two in terms of legal doctrine, and we may be certain no Cherokee would have tried. Yet it is possible to apply the word "law" to the rule that no one could marry into his father's clan or his own clan, because this was a prohibition clearly understood and enforced by tribal disapproval if not by outright sanctions. There was no comparable rule requiring that a Cherokee marry within certain clans, and thus we are tempted to conclude that Cherokee law did not enforce endogamy. Social custom however makes us cautious, for there may have been a social endogamous custom so widely respected that it had the same force as a rule of law. Most of our evidence comes from anthropological studies of the Eastern Band of Cherokees, conducted during the 1930s, which show a pattern of marriage within preferred clans—the father's father's clan and the mother's father's clan.[39] Several students have transposed this evidence onto the primitive Cherokees, thus using the known of today to answer questions about the unknown of yesterday.[40] They would be on surer grounds, had not the Cherokee institution of marriage undergone such changes between the primitive era when it was polygamous and informal, and the 1930s when it more closely resembled the Christian standard of American life. Still there is good reason to believe that the social custom of preferential marriage within two clans existed among the primitive Cherokees, for the reasons supporting it among the Eastern Cherokees duing the 1930s would have operated with even greater force in primitive times.

The argument is that Cherokees tended to marry within two preferred clans, the clan of the father's father or the clan of the mother's father. This is not the same as saying that they married into what we would call their grandparents' clans, for the clan of the father's mother was the same as their father's clan and the clan of their mother's mother was their mother's clan and their own clan, into both of which they were forbidden to marry. But the two clans of their male grandparents were not barred by the exogamous rules.

The endogamous custom can best be illustrated by considering the relationships of a typical Cherokee, the Catawba Killer, living let us say in 1740. The Catawba Killer is a youth, but not a boy, for as his name implies he has been on the warpath, apparently with some success. His mother is a member of the Paint clan, as are he, his brothers and sisters, his maternal uncles, and his mother's mother. His father is a member of the Deer clan, as is his father's mother. His father's father must belong to yet a third clan—for had he been a member of the Paint clan, father would not have been permitted to marry mother, and had he been a member of the Deer clan, he (father's father) would have never married father's mother. So father's father belonged to, let us say, the Wolf clan. This leaves mother's father. For the same reasons as father's father, he could not belong to either the Deer clan or the Paint clan. Had he been a Paint, he could not have married mother's mother and had he been a

Deer, mother could not have married father. It is possible that he was a Wolf like father's father. First of all, mother's father and father's father could have been the same person. If the Catawba Killer's grandfather was married twice, first to a member of the Deer clan (that is to father's mother), and later to a member of the Paint clan (to mother's mother), father and mother would not have been brother and sister, they would have been free to marry, and the Catawba Killer would have had one grandfather and the clan of father's father and mother's father would have been the same—the Wolf clan. If, on the other hand, father's father and mother's father were different individuals, and father's father was a Wolf, there was no reason why mother's father could not also have been a Wolf. Mother, who was a Paint, was prevented from marrying only a Paint and a Wolf, but father was a Deer. He, like mother, could not marry a Wolf but this fact would not interfere with his marrying mother. Both father and mother were forbidden to marry Wolfs, but they could still marry each other. Thus in these two instances the Catawba Killer would have been "related" to three clans—his own Paint clan, his father's Deer clan, and the Wolf clan of mother's father and father's father.

We may safely suppose, however, that if the Catawba Killer were our average Cherokee of 1740, that he was "related" to four clans; that mother's father would have belonged to a different clan than father's father. This supposition follows both from the law of averages (after all, there were seven clans) and also from the endogamous social custom of marrying into preferred clans. This means that for the Catawba Killer we should postulate a fourth clan, which we can call the Bird clan, the clan of mother's father. Thus in the life of the Catawba Killer, as in the lives of most Cherokees, there were four clans to which we would say he was "related," the Paint clan to which he belonged, the Deer clan to which his father belonged, the Wolf clan of father's father, and the Bird clan of mother's father.

The first two clans were the most important: the Paint clan, which furnished him his rights and imposed upon him his duties as a Cherokee; and the Deer clan, to which he owed no obligations and from which he could claim no protection, and into which he could not marry. The Catawba Killer looked upon all members of the Paint clan as his brothers and sisters, no matter how remotely connected, though he had special terms of endearment for his close clan kin: his blood brothers and sisters, his eldest brother, his mother, and his mother's brothers. With the members of the Deer clan, he had no connection we would term "legal" except for the ban against marriage. Yet the Catawba Killer treated them all with respect and, making no distinction between his mother's husband and a total stranger, or between generations, called the males "father" and the females "father's sister." [41] Thus his father's brothers, his father's sister's sons, and his father's sister's daughter's sons were all called "father" by the Catawba Killer, as were the other men and boys in his father's clan. The only suggestion we have that the Catawba Killer may have distinguished father's clan kin from the other members of father's clan was that he had a special name for father's sister's husband.[42] This man (who of course did not belong to father's clan) not only was father's brother-in-law, but (if he had children) was also the father of the "fathers" and "father's sisters" over whom the Catawba Killer's father exercised avuncular authority.

The two remaining related clans—the Wolf clan of father's father and the Bird clan of mother's father—demanded very little of the Catawba Killer. Neither gave him legal rights, neither imposed legal duties. They were not exogamous; he could marry into either. Whether they were endogamous is a fine question that cannot be answered with complete satisfaction. A possible solution is to say they were not legally endogamous, but were socially endogamous. The evidence from the 1930s tends to show that the Catawba Killer was expected to marry into one or the other, that he was to treat them as preferential clans when seeking a wife, but was not bound to find a wife in either.[43] From the time the Catawba Killer was a young boy, his father may have told him, "You will marry my father's sister," meaning that he would marry someone from his father's father's clan. Of course he would not have meant the women we would call "aunt"; he was referring to any female of the Catawba Killer's generation in his father's clan. At the same time, we suspect, the Catawba Killer's maternal uncle was telling him he would grow up and marry his mother's aunt, that is, some member of his mother's father's clan, a girl whom his mother and his uncle called "father's sister." In this way preference was created for two of the five clans into which the Catawba Killer could marry.

The force of this preference is measured by the fact that statistics gathered in the 1930s show that more than half the Eastern Cherokees married into the clans of their father's father or their mother's father. The reason why the preference existed is elusive and may never be established. One explanation is reciprocity. The thought is that the father's father's clan and the mother's father's clan both lost members when father's father married father's mother and mother's father married mother's mother— and both men went to live, hunt, and fight with the clan of his wife. The

Catawba Killer, as a grandchild, belongs to the first generation of the clans which received benefit from the marriage of father's father or mother's father, and who can redress the loss to either father's father's clan or mother's father's clan by marrying back into them.[44] This explanation is plausible and makes sense from the perspective of social pressures, if males did in fact leave their clans when they married. Perhaps they did but we cannot be sure. They did not leave them legally as we shall see, and it is doubtful if they left them socially, for they were still the guardians of their sister's children and the heads of their sisters' families. That they left them economically, by providing for their wives rather than their sisters, is likely. However, the reciprocity redressing this loss would come not from having their daughters' sons or their sons' sons marry back into their clans, but from the fact that their own sisters were provided for by husbands coming from different clans.

A better explanation of why a Cherokee such as the Catawba Killer was likely to marry into his father's father's clan, or his mother's father's clan, is that he placed the members of these two clans into a special category. He called the males "grandfather" and the females "grandmother," just as he called the men in his father's clan "father" and the women "father's sister." [45] The reasons he did so seem to be part of the Cherokee social structure which depended upon the clan system to maintain order, and are better left to our discussion of the law of homicide. For the purpose of unraveling the mystery of marriage within preferential clans, it can be said that these terms of familiarity gave the Catawba Killer an opportunity to know the women of his father's father's clan and his mother's father's clan, better than he knew the women of the remaining three clans into which he was permitted to marry. Social restraint and formality of manner are hallmarks of primitive culture. A Cherokee was on his guard when he spoke with strangers and could joke only with certain people. Among these were his "grandmothers," and we must not forget that a Cherokee such as the Catawba Killer called even girls of his own age "grandmother" if they belonged to the preferential clans. With them he could be on more familiar terms than he could be with the girls of the remaining three clans, social intercourse was less strained, there were fewer taboos, and hence opportunities for intimacy were greater. Even without the force of law, it is not surprising that he should find a wife among them. "I have," the anthropologist A. R. Radcliffe-Brown wrote in 1952, "observed in certain classes in English-speaking countries the occurrence of horse-play between young men and women as a preliminary to courtship, very similar to the way in which a Cherokee Indian jokes with his 'grandmothers.' " [46]

We must not draw too many analogies between primitive and civilized institutions, yet if it is fair to think in terms of a Cherokee government, it is fair to ask how the Cherokees accomplished certain tasks which we associate with government or law. The clan system holds many of the answers. By embodying in their very structure the customs of the people, and by furnishing the procedural framework through which rights were enforced and duties performed, the clans gave the Cherokees a substitute for many of the statutes and most of the courts which characterized European governments. By shaping the contours of society, they determined the contours of law. Stressing as they did ties of kinship, the clans grouped the Cherokees into seven corporate bodies, which on one hand slightly resembled the patripotestal family organizations of Roman law, while on the other hand they compensated in part for the lack of a national government by being the agency through which law was enforced.

The clan system permitted the Cherokees to divide society into easily definable legal groups, first into the seven clans themselves, and second into groups of "brothers," "sisters," "uncles," "fathers," "father's sisters," "grandfathers," and "grandmothers." The emphasis was on the relationship of the classifying person to the group and not on degrees of consanguinity, thus stressing lineage, not generation. A Cherokee looked upon the members of his father's clan as persons he must respect but could not marry, calling the males "father" and the females "father's sister," speaking of them as though they belonged to the generation of his parents.[47] With "grandfathers" and "grandmothers," he knew he could joke and he could marry. These terms of kinship therefore impressed upon each Cherokee the rules of legal relationship, and in addition to mitigating friction, helped to define the rights and duties of each individual.

It is in the area of public law, however, that the clans had their most unexpected impact. This fact may seem ironic, but the clans, which at first glance might be thought to divide the nation into seven antagonistic groups, gave to the Cherokees their structural unity. There was apparently no national clan government, nor clan chiefs who spoke for the clans in the councils of the nation. When the clan members sat together in council, it was usually in the town councils. Yet in each town there were members of the Wolf clan, the Deer clan, the Paint clan, and so on. If a Cherokee left his town to visit another, he knew there were clan brothers to welcome him, to defend his rights, and to perform the duties owed a fellow

member. It was this knowledge which permitted a feeling of blood relationship and solidarity to extend beyond the precincts of each town, and
which bound each individual to the nation as a whole.[48] We should stress
not the familial divisions of clanship, but the legal cohesiveness provided
by the mutual rights and duties existing between clan members—for it
was this which united the Cherokees into a "nation" in the fullest sense
of the term.

CHAPTER SIX

A NATIVE POLITENESS

—THE HEADMEN

Some of those scholars of early Cherokee institutions who believe Chota was the capital of the nation have constructed a scheme of government centered around the hereditary king of that town. "The whole," we are told, "was a rude copy of the Jewish monarchy." [1] At the head of the nation was the *Uku* or *Ookah* or *Ugutuyi,* the "Fire King," whose word was law and whose commands, at least in peacetime, had to be obeyed. He was assisted by a white national council of beloved men, somewhat vague in composition but perhaps representative of the towns, and by a permanent right-hand man, a group of seven counselors (one from each clan), a chief speaker, and several messengers. In the red hierarchy, complementing the *Uku* and commanding the nation in wartime, was the high priest of war (or the Great Warrior), usually elected to office by the warriors with the approval of the white leaders. He was assisted by seven war counselors empowered to order war, who also directed the activities of the scouts, the surgeons, and other war officials such as the "Ravens" and the "Mankillers." [2]

Perhaps we should not ask for documented evidence supporting this detailed scheme of government, for to do so raises issues concerning conflicting methods of proof. The ethnologist can be satisfied with evidence based on tradition, analogy, and supposition, and can rightly claim that the lawyer is narrow and unimaginative when he asks for proof that each office had a function, and that this function was supported by authority. The test of law may in fact be too confining for the cultural anthropologist, and he is correct in thinking the lawyer asks more of anthropological evidence than anthropological evidence can provide. But if we insist that schemes of government are essentially schemes of law, we still need not quarrel with those who say the primitive Cherokees had *Ukus,* Great Warriors, counsellors, and other national officials. We need ask only how these officials "governed," and when function is tested against theory by legal facts drawn from historical records, the whole scheme crumbles as an operating system of government.

Searching for the source of Cherokee governmental leadership, it is best to return to the basic unit of Cherokee government, the town council. We are told by the theorists that even on the town level, the Cherokees were ruled by a white chief, a right-hand man, and seven clan counselors who constituted the decision-making area of town government or the town court.[3] In other words, town government was a mirror of the national government on a small scale. But at the very most, any decision-making function of the town government must be associated with administration, not with legislation. No group of officials have been shown who set policy; only the town council could do this, and even it did not pass laws or issue mandates. The procedural function of the council was to crystallize opinion. It was a forum in which the conflicting interests within the town discussed their points of view, often for days on end, over and over again, with every man permitted to speak and every voice having equal weight, until finally a consensus emerged. But consensus came not by vote. It came with the disappearance of opposition, through compromise or withdrawal, not by the minority acknowledging that it was constitutionally bound to yield its views to majority rule.[4]

In an age when volumes have been written on parliamentary procedure, it may seem unrealistic to suppose that even a primitive people could have managed affairs in villages the size of Cherokee towns with such informality. But what is anarchy to us may have been order to them. It must be remembered that one of their most honored social customs—a custom shared with other American Indians—required that a speaker be heard with attention and respect, no matter who he was, how long he spoke, or how distasteful his views. It would have been unpardonable to interrupt him, had anyone thought of doing so, which was unlikely as Cherokees were taught from birth never to give offense, just as they were taught to avoid controversy. James Adair who lived among the Cherokees and the Chickasaws, and who knew well the Creeks and Choctaws, summed up these social traits when he described how headmen of those four nations conducted foreign affairs:

> They are very deliberate in their councils, and never give an im-
> mediate answer to any message sent them by strangers, but suffer
> some nights first to elapse. They reason in a very orderly manner,
> with much coolness and good-natured language, though they may
> differ widely in their opinions. Through respect to the silent audi-
> ence, the speaker always addresses them in a standing posture. In
> this manner they proceed, till each of the head men hath given his
> opinion on the point in debate. Then they sit down together, and
> determine upon the affair. Not the least passionate expression is to
> be heard among them, and they behave with the greatest civility to
> each other. In all their stated orations, they have a beautiful modest
> way of expressing their dislike of ill things. They only say, "it is not
> good, goodly, or commendable." And their whole behaviour, on
> public occasions, is highly worthy of imitation by some of our
> British senators and lawyers.[5]

There was a second social custom, equally important in maintaining order in town councils: the custom that the young men were expected to defer to the judgment of their elders and obey their wishes.[6] This custom has been noted by most commentators on Cherokee life, and of course was not always an effective tool for political restraint on the national level when the young men, aroused by depredations of an enemy, opted for war and the older men cautioned peace. But there is every reason for be- lieving it controlled passions on the town level, when less explosive issues were debated. Moreover, we should remember that the seven clans in each town sat as units around the sides of the council house, and this may have aided harmony by discouraging stubborn opposition on the part of small groups or individuals. For the clans could have acted as seven separate caucuses which reached corporate opinions among their members, thus narrowing the number of debaters, eliminating extreme positions, and making compromise or withdrawal easier to obtain.[7] Finally we should remember that the town councils were not asked to resolve some of the more difficult problems of primitive life, such as homicide or family strife. These matters were left to the clans to be settled according to the rules of customary law.

With such a system of "legislative" powers, it is difficult to imagine a town "executive" with decision-making powers. In fact, it is difficult to think of any governmental institution on the town level existing separately from the council. The best contemporary evidence, as well as the consistency of legal principles, point to the conclusion that the leader of a Cherokee town was either the person who presided over the council, or the politician who most frequently expressed or created the consensus resolving major issues. It is very likely that the people elected a speaker for the council who also may be called a headman, or even the headman of the village. As speaker of the council, he was elected by the council, that is by the town, and as speaker of the town was sometimes more than the magistrate presiding over the council at its daily sessions. He was on occasion the spokesman for the town, when dealing with other towns or with foreign governments. Available evidence, however, makes it difficult to support the theory that his authority extended beyond specific instructions issued by the council on each occasion.

We have no other term for this official except "headman," the word the Cherokees used. In the nineteenth century, they would adopt the American title "chief," which they thought was equivalent to eighteenth-century "warrior," [8] an appellation with few political connotations. They also had the term of "beloved man" which may have referred only to age statuses —the three ages of Cherokee men being "boy," "young man," and "beloved man," [9] although the British sometimes used "beloved man" synonymously with "headman." South Carolina, for example, would speak of "sending a beloved Man to the Cherokees" as ambassador.[10] The Cherokees once asked the Creeks to send them as ambassadors "two head warriors (not beloved men)." [11] They were seeking a military alliance with the Creeks against the British, and apparently did not want cooler heads to prevail.

Village headmen might be beloved men chosen for superior wisdom or warriors selected for military prowess, although martial fame was by no means a decisive factor;[12] the ability to obtain gifts for the town,[13] or to negotiate peace, or merely to avoid controversy were all well-travelled avenues to influence. As a British officer who was a hostage in the Cherokee nation during 1761 put it, "policy and art are the greatest steps to power." [14] But that same year, a Carolinian argued that "power" was not the correct word, for headmen among the Cherokees "are rather as Fathers than Magistrates." [15] They could persuade, they could not command, they led by virtue of their personal credit, not their constitutional power. Thus their influence over political affairs was the only material determinant, and by its very nature, political influence could be neither permanent nor definable. One town might follow a headman during a lifetime of wise leadership, a second might have no discernible headman except as each crisis presented opportunities for individuals to formulate temporary policy, and a third might have several headmen, all equally influential.

A colonial militia captain, Raymond Demere, summed up the elusive nature of the headman's office when he explained to his superiors in 1757 why it was difficult to deal with the Cherokees, even while living in their midst.

> The Savages are an odd Kind of People; as there is no Law nor Sub-jection amongst them, they can't be compelled to do any Thing nor oblige them to embrace any Party except they please. The very lowest of them thinks himself as great and as high as any of the Rest, every one of them must be courted for their Friendship, with some Kind of a Feeling, and made much of. So what is called great and leading Men amongst them, are commonly old and middle-aged People, who know how to give a Talk in Favour of whom they have a Fancy for, and that same may influence the Minds of the young Fellows for a Time, but every one is his own Master.[16]

James Adair sought to clarify just how a southern-Indian headman influenced the minds of men whom he hoped to lead, yet who were his constitutional equals. "The power of their chiefs, is an empty sound," he explained. "They can only persuade or dissuade the people, either by the force of good-nature and clear reasoning, or colouring things, so as to suit their prevailing passions. It is reputed merit alone, that gives them any titles of distinction above the meanest of the people." [17] A Cherokee de-scribed this merit as "native politeness," [18] we might call it political sagacity; by any name it was the means to leadership in the nation and made oratory the most valuable attribute an aspiring leader could possess.

We must not overestimate the significance of oratory, for we know of at least two important national headmen who were not orators—Old Hop, whose nephew the Little Carpenter spoke for him when negotiating with the British,[19] and Oconostota, the Great Warrior of Chota, who had his nephew Savanooha, the Raven of Chota, speak for him in national councils.[20] But in almost every other instance, the headmen depended upon oratory to drive their people, in Thomas Jefferson's words, "to duty and to enterprise." [21] Jefferson knew the famous Overhill headman, Judd's Friend, a frequent guest at Jefferson's house, and once described to John Adams a talk he heard given by Judd's Friend, as he took leave of his followers on the eve of a journey to London: "His sounding voice, distinct articulation, animated action, and the solemn silence of his people at their several fires, filled me with awe and veneration, altho' I did not understand a word he uttered." [22]

The question of just what a Cherokee could accomplish, once he persuaded people to follow his leadership (thus becoming a headman), is best left to the chapters dealing with the Cherokee war machine, and the Cherokee law of coercion. In this chapter we are considering the office of headman, its attainment and its functions, facets of Cherokee government lost in time and only partly uncovered by drawing analogies to similar institutions among other American Indians. In terms of constitutional function, the Cherokee headman stood somewhere between the sachem of New England's Algonquian tribes and the Comanche headman. Sachemship was by no means as secure or as well defined as European kingship, yet it was certainly more institutionalized than Cherokee headmanship. The New England sachem exercised property rights over the possessions of his people, could exact tribute from subtribes, and was expected "to pronounce rules, administer punishments, and make major decisions for all his subjects." [23] The Cherokee headman enjoyed none of these functions except the last, and then with a difference. He made decisions only because someone had to make them, not because he was empowered to do so, and their validity, force, and effectiveness depended upon public opinion. If public opinion supported his decisions, they were the decisions of a headman; that some individuals resisted did not matter. Acquiescence by most, not lack of opposition by a few, was the fulcrum lifting the decisions of a Cherokee headman above the mere proposals of a nonheadman. The opponents were neither rebels nor outlaws, they were merely potential headmen waiting to replace him if he should fail.

The Comanche headman, on the other hand, may not have had a decision-making function. The American anthropologist, E. Adamson Hoebel, found that the influence of the Comanche headman was so subtle that it almost defies explicit description. "He worked through precept, advice, and good humor, expressing his wisdom through well-chosen words and persuasive common sense." [24] Of course he made decisions, but in a different manner than did the Algonquian sachem or the Cherokee headman.

The distinction between the sachem and the Cherokee or Comanche headman can be explained in terms of governmental power—the sachem had power to make decisions as long as he was sachem. The distinction between the Cherokee and Comanche headmen, however, was one of governmental structure, rather than power. The Comanches were a tribe of roving bands, and their headmen were magnets at the core of the band [25]—while the Cherokees were a sedentary people, and their town councils gave their headmen institutions through which to operate. Like the Comanche headman, the Cherokee headman ruled "only by calm reason and friendly exhortation," [26] yet if he gained the backing of his council, his prestige and influence surpassed that of any Comanche headman.

The constitutional underpinning lending substance to the office of headman among the Cherokees came from the town council, and if we define the Cherokee headman as a person who led but did not rule, who had to justify every decision, and seldom acted on impulse but only after long deliberation, we are recognizing him as an extension of the council, both in theory and in function.

CHAPTER SEVEN

A NATION'S MOUTH

—THE NATIONAL COUNCIL AND SPEAKER

Whatever our difficulty defining the office of town headman, the problem is compounded when we try to define the office of national headman. It will not do to project the town headman onto the national scene, and to assume that the national headman is a town headman acting on a national level. We have seen that there was no national government structure, only a collection of independent towns, and thus there was no institution to give substance and purpose to the office of national headman in the way that the office of town headman was patterned by the town council. Should we try to equate the national headman to the town headman, it would be necessary to equate the national council with the town council, and this we must not do. They simply were not the same.

The town council met every evening and was primarily a social gathering. The national council met infrequently and only in an emergency, generally to settle problems which could no longer be shunted. The town council was an indigenous institution which the Cherokees shared with the other southern nations whose economic and social life were similar to their own. The national council, on the other hand, may have been imposed from without; it was the Cherokee agency for foreign negotiation, seldom concerned with domestic affairs, always convened to resolve an international rather than an internal crisis.

At the danger of stressing the obvious, it is important to clarify what the national council was not, as well as what it was. It was not a meeting of town headmen, not a legislative tribunal with definitive powers convening twice a year in Chota to advise a king or *Uku* and to vote approval on questions that concerned the whole tribe. It was rather the simplest, yet the most awkward, and at the same time the most compossible of all Cherokee governmental agencies—a general convention of the entire nation, with every Cherokee a member and every member possessing a theoretical right to be heard.

Should we object that so unwieldy a body hampered the formulation of effective policy and diminished the efficiency of national government, we would be guilty of imposing modern needs upon primitive man and of ignoring the basic precept of Cherokee public law—that every individual was free from restraint and bound only by personal contract. Fundamental constitutional doctrine made the national council an institutional necessity. Edmond Atkin, the first superintendent for Indian affairs in the southern colonies, explained the legal function of the national council to his British superiors when he warned in 1757 that many agreements negotiated with headmen alone had no validity, that the direct consent of the entire nation was required for important decisions.[1] This rule was to remain operative until the adoption of the Cherokee constitution in 1827. As late as 1823, American commissioners sent to the nation to negotiate the purchase of land asked that "at least a majority of the Cherokee Nation" attend the council and vote on their offer.[2] There were at that time over 16,000 Cherokees and convening a majority was both expensive and inconvenient, yet to have dealt with less would have left the legality of any sale open to challenge.

The British had difficulty adjusting to the principle that binding international business with Indians had to be conducted through the national council. They preferred to deal with an institution less cumbersome in structure, but try as they might they never succeeded in imposing on the Cherokees the concept of delegated authority vested in a few headmen. The desire to negotiate with more manageable numbers sometimes led colonial officials to stumble into diplomatic blunders. For example, when James Glen was the newly-arrived governor of South Carolina, he was told that 300 to 500 Cherokees were converging on Charles Town.

Alarmed at the prospect of so many savages in his capital city and fearful
that the expense of their entertainment might be too great for the colony's
finances, he ordered that none but "the King or the Chief of the Nation
with Six of His assistants be allowed to come and one man from Each
town." [3] The Cherokees were spared a diplomatic insult when men more
experienced in Indian affairs persuaded Glen not only that he had to
receive each Cherokee who wished to attend the council, but that he had
to treat all with equal respect.[4] Glen learned his lesson and in time became the most knowledgeable of Indian experts. He was the first colonial
governor to travel to the nation when negotiating with the Cherokees,
always bringing sufficient presents to attract the widest possible representa-
tion. By 1755 when he sought to purchase land for a fort, Glen knew
better than to think he could deal with a few chiefs. Instead he asked the
Cherokees to convene a national council and drafted the instrument of sale
in words implying that the entire population was party to the transaction.
"I had," he wrote, "the deeds of conveyance formally executed in their
own Country, by their head men, in the name of the whole people, and
with their universal approbation and good will." [5]

The pungent aspect of the national council is not that the British were
forced to acquiesce in its existence but that it produced the first national
office cognizable under the primitive Cherokee constitution—the speaker
of the national council.

We might unravel more of the mysteries of Cherokee town government
if we knew as much about the origin of the national speaker's office as we
know about its functions. In the last chapter, the possibility was suggested
that each town had a speaker—that the headman or a headman of the
town was chosen to preside over the town council, to express the consensus once discussion ended, or to speak for the council when repre-
sentatives of other Cherokee towns or foreign powers were in attendance.
Of course, the same headman might not perform all three functions or
even perform one of them at all times, but when he did we may think of
him as the speaker of the town in the same sense that the national speaker
was speaker of the nation. There is one reservation however. The national
speakership is a readily identifiable institution, while the town speakership
is at best a deductable conjecture, for the national speakership appears
clearly in extant records but the town speakership must be implied largely
from the existence of the national speaker.

The complexity and sophistication of Cherokee jurisprudence assume
new dimensions when we consider the office of the national speaker, for
his duties were well defined and his power circumscribed by clear legal

concepts. Consider the first speaker of whom we know, the Head Warrior of Tennessee. In 1725 Colonel George Chicken was at Ellijay, to deliver a talk to the Cherokees on behalf of the government of South Carolina and to receive their answer. According to custom, the Cherokees heard him out and then, after conferring together, elected as speaker to deliver their reply the Head Warrior of Tennessee.[6] He was free to use his own phraseology, indeed he may have been chosen partly for his fame as an orator, but in law he was not free to say what he pleased. He was bound by his instructions and should he depart from them, his words were not the words of the nation.

It may be objected that this definition of the speaker's function relates his office too closely to that of a medieval European attorney, yet such is the inescapable conclusion from all available evidence. On the evening before the start of an important national council held at Saluda during the summer of 1755, the Little Carpenter went to Governor Glen to announce his election as speaker of the nation. He told Glen that he was limited to act within his instructions which he could not properly reveal, except to say he was charged not to be disagreeable toward the British.[7] This statement did not mean that had the British introduced a topic not covered by the instructions and asked for an answer, the Little Carpenter had discretion to formulate his own reply. Four years earlier, Governor Glen had held a council with the Lower Cherokees at which Skiagunsta, the Warrior of Keowee, was the elected speaker. Glen had surprised the Cherokees by saying he might raise the prices of certain goods and Skiagunsta had wanted to protest but did not, as he later explained, because "I had no Directions from my People to talk about it."[8]

The examples could be multiplied, but these illustrations tell the story. There is no public office about which we have more direct evidence and what we know covers a century of time, yet over the years the basic principles remained unchanged—the speaker was instructed, and the speaker was not to stray beyond his instructions. The marvel is not that a potentially complex procedure had been reduced to two simple rules. The marvel is that every Cherokee understood the law and controversy was avoided. To ask whether they regarded the speaker as an agent who bound them if he conceded more than he was instructed to concede, or if he spoke of matters he was supposed to ignore,* would be to ask a question the Cherokees did not contemplate. They expected their speaker to guard

---

* The Cherokees avoided controversy and unpleasantness by ignoring questions, rather than by giving negative answers.

his words, and he expected them to honor his commission. Once, after
Skiagunsta had spoken at a council and Governor Glen had acknowledged
him "the Speaker and the Mouth of his Nation," Glen asked if there were
any other Cherokees who had anything to say. "I have spoken for them
all," Skiagunsta quickly replied.[9] We may suppose that Skiagunsta expected them to remain silent, surely a test of Indian restraint when we
recall that the British, apparently assuming that speaking indicated importance, gave more presents to those who spoke than to those who said
nothing. A distinction was made between speaking for all those present,
speaking for one town on a local problem, or speaking as a private individual, as Skiagunsta implied when he told Glen that he wished to be
heard again. "I have spoken all ready for the Nation," he explained. "I shall
now speak Something concerning myself." [10] A white man had recently
stolen his horse and he wanted compensation. Personal business might be
intermingled with national business but the credentials of the speaker
were not confused.

While the speakership of the national council was the first recognizable
office of Cherokee national government, it was never the highest office.
This is a bold statement and must be made with reservations, yet if the
retrogressive method of writing legal history has validity, the statement
is both reasonable and useful. As time goes on, a second office will begin
to emerge, separate from that of the speaker, an office which was almost
indiscernible during the eighteenth century and can be located with safety
only by looking back from the perspective of post-primitive institutions.
This is the office of principal chief, a title we would not dare confer on
any Cherokee, at least until Old Tassell is chosen to lead the Upper Cherokees, more than a half century after the Head Warrior of Tennessee
spoke for the nation at that early council held at Ellijay.

While admitting that there was no principal chief during the period of
Cherokee primitive law, it is useful to keep the office in mind because
many headmen, by offering to fill a vacuum of national leadership which
the speaker did not fill, were aspiring to that office though they may not
have realized they were doing so. When the Cherokees, during the first
decade of the nineteenth century, began to structure their government
upon the American pattern, the speaker emerged as the head of the
legislature, certifying laws for the approval of the principal chief, who
was the head of the executive branch.[11] This division of powers can be
projected back into the eighteenth century without raising havoc with
primitive institutions because the national council was fundamentally a
legislative organ. The purpose of convening the entire nation was not to

reach agreements on international questions with foreign commissioners, for it was the headmen who did the negotiating and they could have done as much without calling together hundreds of spectators. The purpose of the national council was to make these agreements binding upon everyone, to give them the force of law, that is to legislate. When, in 1827, the Cherokees adopted their first written constitution, treaty making remained a legislative function, treaties were acknowledged to be "the Supreme law of the land," and the legislature was given "the sole power of deciding on the construction of all Treaty stipulations." [12]

Perhaps it is pressing contemporary political analogies too far to say that the national council was solely concerned with diplomacy, while insisting that it was fundamentally a legislative body. Yet such was the nature of Cherokee government that legislation in the sense of binding enactment was first performed in the sphere of international rather than domestic law. In time the national council would not only elect the principal chief, but the appellate and trial courts, as well as both houses of the Cherokee legislature, would trace their constitutional powers back to the national council. Indeed, during the crisis of the 1830s when the constituted branches of the government were suppressed by Georgia, the continuity of legitimate authority in the nation was preserved by reconvening the national council. To tell the story of the national council's contribution to Cherokee institutions would be to tell the story of the growth of organized Cherokee government, but as that is a story which would take us beyond the era of primitive law, it provides a temptation we must avoid.

CHAPTER EIGHT

A DARLING PASSION

—THE LAW OF COERCION AND OF EQUITY

If a good deal of primitive Cherokee law must remain a mystery, the constitutional principle underlying the national council does not. We may speak of it with some confidence, and it is as simple as the Cherokee constitution itself: every Cherokee was equal and every Cherokee had an equal right of participation. While this principle reveals much about Cherokee government—that it had not yet advanced to the stage of delegated authority—it reveals but one facet of Cherokee equality, the right to be bound only by personal consent. In fact, equality was a constitutional concept of unlimited consequence, permeating every aspect of Cherokee life, a source of anarchy in leadership, and one reason why the primitive era of Cherokee government knew neither a Cherokee state nor a law of coercion.

When an eighteenth-century colonial official told the Cherokees they would "never be a people" until they obeyed a king, he was doing more than urging them to establish responsible government; he was warning them that absolute equality was a constitutional luxury they could no longer afford. When a British trader took note of the fact that the Cherokees had no sanctions with which to punish wrongdoers, he was not only saying that they lacked a concept of police power or a method of enacting criminal legislation, he was stating in positive-law terms the consequences of absolute equality. The salient characteristic of Cherokee equality was not its universality—that it extended over the average as well as the great, over women as well as men—but the lengths to which it was carried.

Eighteenth-century records are replete with instances where the headmen knew they must act for the good of the nation but lacked power to act. White men stood by in angered frustration and Cherokees wrung their hands in despair, yet time and again the security of the nation was jeopardized because absolute equality made coercion constitutionally unthinkable. "Subjection is what they are unacquainted with in their own state, there being no such Thing as coercive Power among them," an eighteenth-century Carolinian wrote: "their Chiefs are such only in Virtue of their Credit and not their Power; there being, in all other Circumstances, a perfect Equality among them." [1] If life in the Appalachian forests made incarceration physically impossible, equality made all other sanctions constitutionally impossible. Fines, for example, were out of the question, "for they had no way of exacting them from free men." [2]

Perhaps the most striking description of equality among the Southern Indians has been furnished by James Adair. "Their darling passion is liberty," he wrote. "To it they sacrifice everything and in the most unbounded liberty they indulge themselves through life." [3]

The unbounded liberty in which the Cherokees indulged themselves marked at least three areas of their public law. First of all, equality explains the Cherokees' abhorrence of any form of coercion; an abhorrence which inhibited the use of official aggression, even to force conformity to policies arrived at by popular consensus and designed to promote the common good. This tradition was responsible for a second legal consequence of unbounded liberty: the lack of coercive powers vested in the one effective instrument of Cherokee politics, the town councils; a lack which naturally was carried over into the more weakly structured national apparatus of government. The third public-law manifestation of "unbounded liberty" was of course the constitutional principle of equality itself, extending to women and children as well as to men, giving hunters and farmers the same legal status as warriors, and making headmen dependent upon public opinion for influence.

While many other American Indian nations possessed similar attitudes regarding official coercion, we need not rely upon comparative studies for explanations. Due to the investigations of Frederick O. Gearing, the only anthropologist who has attempted to decipher the Cherokee legal psyche, there is more direct evidence to which we may turn. The Cherokees, he argues, believed that "the exercise of coercion, in personal relations within the village, was wrongful." [4]

> The shared Cherokee idea about aggression forbade as wrongful virtually any public act which was coercive; ideally, decisions by villages were reached through unanimity and, ideally, village actions were co-ordinated through the voluntary effort of individuals.[5]

"Personal aggression, according to that shared idea, was any act which made it impossible for one villager voluntarily to defer to the wishes of another." [6] As officially sanctioned force would have been "aggression," its use was psychologically and therefore legally impossible, even if the Cherokees had possessed the governmental machinery to implement it. "Where village opinion had crystallized, a few who opposed were expected soon to defer to the wishes of others," Gearing concludes. "However, if the few should fail to defer, the many could not properly coerce them. That, too, would be aggression." [7] As a result, the basic Cherokee sanction was withdrawal;[8] a sanction which operated effectively upon individuals only on the town level, that is, in "the face-to-face community." [9]

Typical of the legal consequences resulting from Cherokee abhorrence of aggressive force was the inability of the nation to police the activities of resident or transitory aliens. A trader might be told he could not trade in a town, or a preacher that he could not preach,[10] but the trader and preacher were white men without the security of clan membership who, when requesting permission of certain headmen to trade or preach, may have believed they were seeking official authorization yet in fact were asking those headmen for personal protection. The headmen who told white men in the nation that they could not do such-and-such, were refusing to cooperate or to persuade their fellow townsmen to cooperate, but they were not necessarily threatening coercive restraint. Indians of other nations—for example, Shawnees—moved in and out of Cherokee towns at will, and the headmen confessed they were helpless to control them. Should the Shawnees kidnap a settler from the Carolina back country and bring him in to the Cherokees, he could be rescued only by private enterprise, by hiring a party of warriors to attack the Shawnees—for even British threats that the nation would be held collectively responsible for the behavior of the Shawnees did not embolden or empower the headmen to order the Shawnees arrested.[11] Should Shawnees in the pay of France spread bad talks throughout the towns, the separate councils might announce that they would not listen, but they could not silence the talks. The British, with tacit consent of some headmen, might act, or an individual Cherokee might act, but there was no Cherokee governmental unit with authority to act.[12] Should a Cherokee kill a British subject or a foreign Indian, and should South Carolina or the victim's nation demand satisfaction, there was no coercive machinery by which the nation could extricate itself from the threat of war. A headman might promise to have the manslayer killed,[13] and sometimes the headmen might convince the British that through guile and trickery they had managed to have him killed,[14] yet the task was virtually impossible whenever the clan of a manslayer refused to cooperate.

During January, 1760, the nation faced its hour of greatest peril. A party of Cherokees had killed white settlers in Virginia and the Carolinas, and the British, demanding satisfaction, seized as hostages 24 Cherokee headmen and threatened to kill them and invade the nation unless the "murderers" were handed over. The most influential leaders from every section of the nation, warriors as well as beloved men, dreaded the prospect of a war, yet they could not arrange satisfaction. With a British army under Governor Lyttelton of South Carolina marching up to Keowee from Charles Town; with the trade cut off and ammunition low; with the colonial garrisons preparing for war and the dream of a French alliance shattered by Wolfe's victory at Quebec; with the Catawbas menacing their eastern flank and the Governor of Georgia arming the Creeks to attack from the south—the two most influential men in the nation, the Great Warrior of Chota and the Little Carpenter, confessed that they were helpless. Try as they might, they explained, they could not seize the wanted men "owing to the Obstinacy of their Relatives who only have power to punish them by the Custome of the Country and who would not be prevailed upon to Deliver them." [15] And so war came and the nation was bloodied.

Even during that war, even when the very life of their nation was in jeopardy, the Cherokees clung to "unbounded liberty" and maintained without dilution their constitutional bar to personal aggression. As a result, they had neither a concept of treason nor a means of coercing loyalty. Their treaties might speak of asking extradition from British colonies of Cherokee "Rebels," "Traitors," "disobedient Subjects," or "Fugitives," [16] but these were English words and defined offenses which their legal premises did not permit them to contemplate. Thus, during the highpoint of organized hostilities, when the energies of the nation were focused on the capture of Fort Loudoun, the Little Carpenter—who opposed the war —twice warned the garrison of Cherokee strategy, thus frustrating the attackers led by his own close-clan kin, Willenawah.[17] When Willenawah tried to starve the British into submission, South Carolina smuggled in ribbon and paint with which to buy provisions from women living in nearby towns. A yard of ribbon could purchase food to support one man for a month, and the commandant bought enough to sustain the fort for two weeks. Willenawah tried to stop the trade by threatening the women with death, but they laughed at him, saying that if he killed them their clans would kill him. "Willinawaw," a British army officer noted, "was too sensible of this to put his threats into execution, so that the garrison subsisted a long time on the provisions brought to them in this manner." [18] The only solution the warriors found to their legal dilemma was to hide the corn from the women.[19]

Willenawah's dilemma, a compound of public and private law, was well nigh irresolvable. Had he offended Cherokee constitutional sensibilities by using force to coerce the women—even force sanctioned by the vast majority of the people and by all the warriors—he would have run the risk of killing them. Had he killed them, their clan members had the right to kill him in return, and even had they resolved not to do so, he would never again have felt safe, for there always loomed the possibility that one of them might change his mind. So, too, by the same law of revenge would the lives of those who might have helped him kill the women been put in jeopardy, making it improbable that he could have persuaded many of his followers to assist the executions. Indeed, even by suggesting action he might have lost his influence over them all. We may even think of a Cherokee warrior risking his life to capture the fort, while watching his own sister supply his enemies with food. He might condemn his sister and feel shame, yet had anyone harmed her, his attitudes and loyalties would have been altered, the national war effort would have assumed a secondary importance, and his duty to avenge blood would have been given precedence. The women laughed at Willenawah because they knew he was legally impotent. So did he, and the remarkable aspect is not that the women were left unmolested but that he had threatened them—an indication of his frustration and his desperation.

There was a second legal consideration underlying Willanwah's dilemma—the equality of women. That the rights possessed by Cherokee women were equal to those enjoyed by Cherokee men need not surprise us, if we keep in mind the fact that legal status and social standing need not depend on physical labor. While there are few extant comments regarding eighteenth-century Cherokee women, visitors to the Indian nations in general thought the native American female a creature to be pitied. Seeing her labor in the corn fields and about the house, leading a life of unending drudgery, some observers concluded that her status was servile and depressed. English women were not politically or legally equal to English men, yet lived better lives socially and physically than did Indian women, and hence it followed that Indian women were that much worse off politically and legally. But politics and law are not always reflected in social and physical conditions, and this conclusion may be challenged by the facts. "First of all," as Robert H. Lowie has pointed out, "it should be noted that the treatment of woman is one thing, her legal status another, her opportunities for public activity still another, while the character and extent of her labors belong again to a distinct category." [20] That Cherokee women did the farm work may show that in society their role was one of manual labor; in law it may reveal only that they owned the farms.[21] And even from a social point of view, female servitude does not necessarily connote inferior status, rather it left the men free to meet sudden attack and to endure the hardships of the hunt,[22] "which in savagery are always toilsome, frequently dangerous, and not rarely fatal, especially in winter." [23] The division of labor was dictated by the Cherokee mode of life and should not be compared to contemporary European norms. Indeed, the decline of hunting and the adoption of American ways during the nineteenth century, with the substitution of factory-made for home-made goods, may have freed the Cherokee woman from outdoor labor, placing her in the kitchen and her husband in the fields, but it also deprived her of economic independence, making her politically and legally more like her white sisters.

Although Cherokee women during the nineteenth century, at least when compared to American women, would remain legally emancipated, fully competent to own separate property and to transact business, they would be politically disenfranchised, barred from holding public office, and prohibited from voting in elections [24]—a drastic and fundamental departure from eighteenth-century constitutional practice. Although it has been suggested that Cherokee women during the primitive-law era could speak in town councils only under "certain circumstances, unclear in the record," [25] the better view seems to be that they could participate as freely as men.[26] Of course a woman was less likely to play a leading part than was a man, just as an insignificant male was less likely to exert influence than was a leading warrior. Yet on some occasions, Cherokee females won by personal merit positions of influence, most notably Nancy Ward who made a remarkable reputation in warfare, rose to the honorific of "the Beloved Woman," spoke in national councils and was commissioned in 1781 by the more timid headmen to negotiate a peace with an invading American army.[27] A generation earlier, her uncle, the Little Carpenter, while attending a council in Charles Town, had underscored the political equality of Cherokee women when he asked the startled Carolinians why they were all males. It was the custom among Indians to admit women to their councils, he told Governor Lyttelton. "White Men as well as the Red were born of Women," he pointed out and "desired to know if that was not the Custom of the White People also." [28] It took Lyttelton two or three days to come up with the rather lame answer that "The White Men do place a Confidence in their Women and share their Counsels with them when they know their Hearts to be good." [29]

We can be less confident about the social equality of Cherokee women than we can about their economic and political equality, but we may speak with certainty of their legal equality, a topic best illustrated by the law of adultery. Discussion of adultery more properly belongs in the chapter dealing with marriage; at this point we need only note that in Cherokee law adultery was not an offense. It was a crime, however, in neighboring nations, the Creeks punishing the adulteress much more severely than the adulterer, and the Chickasaws punishing only the adulteress. When James Adair asked the Chickasaws "the reason of the inequality of their marriage-law, in punishing the weaker passive party, and exempting the stronger," he was told that "if they put such old cross laws of marriage in force, all their beloved brisk warriors would soon be spoiled,* and their habitations turned to a wild waste." [31] It is difficult to imagine an eighteenth-century Cherokee reasoning in this manner, and the law, or lack of law, governing adultery is a striking indication of the extent to which the Cherokees carried the concept of personal liberty and female equality. All of the southern Indian nations were committed to the constitutional principle of individual freedom, but only Cherokee men permitted it to take precedence over pride in their manhood and insults to their vanity. Like Cherokee women, Creek women and Chickasaw women seem to have been the political and social equals of their menfolk; yet it was the Cherokees, almost alone, who insisted that legal equality included the right of women to sin, as well as to be sinned against.

The refusal of the Cherokee legal mind to contemplate a law of

---

* The Chickasaws cut off the upper lip of an adulteress.[30]

physical coercion or to modify the doctrine of legal equality, might lead us to imagine that the Cherokees lived in a chaotic state of political anarchy. Nothing could be further from the fact. The Cherokee distaste for official aggression meant only that there could be no sanctions applied against wrongdoers in the name of the nation. There were substitute or private sanctions—indeed, the prospect of withdrawal, ostracism, public reprobation, and mockery were to the primitive Cherokee forms of coercion at least as terrible as is the prospect of punishment by a court of law for civilized man.[32] And the principle of absolute equality must not be thought of as a doctrine guaranteeing social disintegration. Rather, equality should be seen primarily as the constitutional norm underlying customs and explaining rules that every Cherokee understood and almost every Cherokee obeyed. "It cannot be too often explained," Lowie observed, "that the extreme individualism often found in primitive communities is very far from favoring universal anarchy or anything approaching it. Generally speaking, the unwritten laws of customary usage are obeyed far more willingly than our written codes, or rather they are obeyed spontaneously."[33] E. Sidney Hartland agreed. Speaking of sanction in primitive law, he wrote:

> The savage is far from being the free and unfettered creature of Rousseau's imagination. On the contrary, he is hemmed in on every side by the customs of his people, he is bound in the chains of immemorial tradition, not merely in his social relations, but in his religion, his medicine, his industry, his art: in short, every aspect of his life. These fetters are accepted by him as a matter of course; he never seeks to break forth.[34]

True, the Cherokees by being free of government restraints and living in complete legal and near social equality, seem to have enjoyed a liberty to do as they pleased; their options were many, their choices great, yet on all sides and in every aspect of life they were hemmed in by law. There were boundaries beyond which they could not step, responsibilities which they should not shun. An eighteenth-century Cherokee male might be free to commit adultery, but he knew he was not free to kill his erring wife. He might recognize no obligation to the common weal, but he never forgot his duty to his clan. The range of confining customs may have been limited, but it was exact, it was demanding, and it was certain. When beckoned by law, the Cherokee did not weigh alternatives or make distinctions, he responded automatically and without choice. He may have enjoyed much freedom from rules of law, but rules of law did not leave him free. He was the law's captive and he had to obey. That the legal institutes which he obeyed were norms of private law, not sanctions imposed by official coercion, made his obedience no less the obedience of a law-controlled man.

CHAPTER NINE

A RIGHT TO VENGEANCE

—THE LAW OF HOMICIDE

A law which the average Cherokee understood and obeyed, a law which confined his options and limited his choices, molded his conduct and heralded his responses, was the law of homicide. He knew it well, it was ingrained in his legal consciousness, the bone and marrow of his social existence. Had Europeans asked him about the law of homicide, he might not have been able to answer all their questions for these would have been European questions, not Cherokee questions, but confronted with a fact situation he knew his duties and his rights, when to be fearful and when to feel safe.

The law of homicide is the foundation of most primitive legal systems, the customary solder which holds together the social structure. The blood feud, the *lex talionis,* the law of vengeance or retaliation, which treats homicide as a personal wrong creating a personal right, has long been used by anthropologists as a cultural litmus to gauge the comparative status of developing legal institutions. Emphasis is not upon how the law served a particular people or how it operated. Rather, stress is placed on the theory that progress from primitive law to civilized law can be measured by progress from procedural remedies based on self help to the folk peace or king's peace; from legal sanctions prosecuted by the victim or his kin to sanctions imposed by a neutral court in the name of society. A related concept is that savage law seeks to secure peace while civilized law endeavors to establish justice,[1] and developments from primitive peace to civilized justice can also be measured in terms of "progress." Either approach is useful in comparative jurisprudence, but when employed to illustrate legal history both hold the danger of imposing alien standards upon working values. To understand Cherokee law we need not relate it to other primitive codes. Better to be satisfied simply to note that among the North American Indians, the law of homicide ranged in variety from the Pawnees, who may have had no blood feud at all,[2] to the Powhatan Confederacy of Virginia, which treated murder as an offense against society and executed the slayer in the name of the leader.[3] The Cherokees were somewhere in between. For them a killing was not the concern of the nation, nor was it left to blind, personal vengeance. Rather, they channelled vengeance into a set of customary rules which imposed duties, defined rights, and while privately executed were publicly obeyed.

A later generation of Cherokees were to summarize their ancestors' law of homicide by saying it rested on the fundamental "principle of retaliation." [4] When one Cherokee caused the death of a second Cherokee, the relatives of the dead man had the duty and the right to kill the manslayer or one of his relatives. It was a justice based on the talion, a universal mosaic law which may not have required an eye for an eye, or a tooth for a tooth, but demanded without fear or favor a life for a life. Some writers of popular history, seeking to explain this harsh, unyielding law of vengeance, have assumed it either to have been inherited by the Cherokees from Jewish ancestors or to have been part of the Cherokee native religion. Retaliation, we are told, was "a religious duty." [5] There is little evidence to support the second belief, none whatever to support the first. The law of the blood feud—"a life for a life"—was not only common to most primitive men, but fitted the Cherokee concept of the logical arrangement of nature, a logic that they applied to animals as well as to men. To explain why the Cherokees begged pardon of animals they had slain, an ethnologist, William Harlen Gilbert, compared that custom to "the law of blood vengeance."

> The ghosts of those animals who have been slain by the human hunter warn their friends of their own species that they must avenge

their deaths on mankind. When a deer is killed the hunter must take special precautions to prevent the deer ghost from following him into camp for if he does rheumatism will strike him down. Therefore, a special avoidance prayer is pronounced and a fire is built by the hunter on the trail in back of him to stop the deer ghost.[6]

If religion entered into the matter at all, it was to avoid vengeance, not to explain it. Legal duty, not religion, explained why vengeance had to be taken and why it was a right.]

There were two basic rules: that the commission of homicide was a clan responsibility, and that the punishment of homicide was a clan function. When one Cherokee killed another, all the members of both the manslayer's clan and the victim's clan were involved in the deed. It has been suggested that for purposes of avenging blood each clan became "a corporate individual." [7] While this concept is useful, it is not legally accurate. Let us suppose that Inali of the Bird clan was killed by Wahuhu of the Paint clan. Like any killing, this event would reorder Cherokee society, if not physically at least in legal relationships. The members of the remaining five clans would not be involved; not even the members of Inali's father's clan, for Inali's father has no recognized interests or rights at stake. The members of the Bird clan and the Paint clan will pair off against each other; in some cases where Birds are married to Paints, fathers will be opposed to their sons, and husbands to their women's brothers. But the members of each clan do not form corporate entities because their rights or duties are not the same. The members of the Bird clan, the victim's clan, have a collective responsibility which varies somewhat according to their blood relationship to Inali. Inali's mother's brother and his own brother apparently have greater responsibilities and, although we cannot be certain, greater rights. The members of the Paint clan, on the other hand, do not have a collective or corporate liability. The liability is individual, the killing of Inali by their fellow clansman Wahuhu has made each Paint liable to Inali's clan, and any one of them can be made to pay the blood price; that is, the slaying of any Paint will satisfy the responsibility which Inali's death imposed on the Birds. However, it is doubtful if every member of the Paint clan felt equally liable. Wahuhu's liability was the greatest and after him, it is likely that his near kin were more liable than other Paints. Yet to say this is not to deny that all were equally liable.

We must not use terms loosely or we will be in danger of misunderstanding Cherokee law. The killing of Inali should not be called a "crime" for it was a private, not a public wrong. Nor should we speak of "murder," for the Cherokees did not distinguish between types, degrees, or manners of homicide. In Cherokee law, the probative fact, the sole point to be considered, was the infliction of death, and neither intent, malice, negligence, accident, omission, nor excuse was a plea to be entered or an element to be weighed. Causation was the only factor to be proved, lack of causation the only defense to be entered. Death had to be caused by the act of another, but the nature of the act, its rectitude or turpitude, was no issue. Thus liability, not culpability, was the operative legal concept, and a third word to be avoided is "guilt"—at least as used in the sense that a manslayer was "guilty," or that his clan shared a collective "guilt." They shared an equal liability, and the law was not concerned with guilt. The relatives of the victim may have thought of "guilt" by considering personal responsibility, for it is likely they preferred to take vengeance on the manslayer rather than a stranger (a supposition we may reasonably draw from the fact that in mythology animal spirits always plagued the hunter rather than just any human), but they were not bound to do so.

If a horse tied to a tree became unruly and killed a passing Cherokee, the owner of the horse or the person who had tied it was responsible, and the clan of the victim could slay either.[8] If a Cherokee borrowed the horse of a friend and the horse threw and killed him, the clan of the deceased could slay the friend.[9] Self-defense was no excuse.[10] In fact the only excuse for a killing was the blood feud itself, and this was more a right than an excuse; a set-off of killings, one wiping clean the debt owed by the other.

Abstract principles are not the best tool for discussing Cherokee law, for the Cherokees themselves did not use them. The Cherokees acted on instinct and when confronted with a fact situation, knew immediately how to act. We may imagine that had they been asked to explain the law of homicide, they would have cited examples and few examples could have been more revealing than the case of James Vann. He belonged to the Blind Savannah clan as well as to the last Cherokee generation governed by the *lex talionis,* and lived at a time when there was a liberal sprinkling of white blood in the nation and many Cherokees had adopted English surnames. Another member of the Blind Savannah clan was Sour Mush, an aged warrior of some prominence. One day, while at a drinking party, Sour Mush was beaten up by a member of the Paint clan. Displaying the proud dignity of an elderly Indian, Sour Mush seems to have been less disturbed by the beating than by the fact that no one planned to avenge him, not even the other Blind Savannahs present. He scolded the younger Blind Savannahs, complained that during his youth no member of the Blind Savannah clan would have seen an old clansman mistreated, and apparently suggested they had a duty to avenge him. While we suspect Sour Mush was appealing more to clan pride than any rule of law requiring retaliation, the distinction is thin, and he himself may have been counting on the customary respect in which Indian youths held their elders, and the shame which his upbraiding caused the Blind Savannahs. In any event he got his revenge. Following a second whiskey bout, some Blind Savannahs, led by Charles Hughes, set on the Paint clan member who had beaten Sour Mush and gave him such a thrashing that he died.

The Blind Savannah clan now was liable to the Paint clan for one life. Were it a question of guilt rather than liability, Charles Hughes probably would have been selected to die. We cannot doubt that he was the prime candidate for vengeance and in most cases would surely have been put to death. When the Paint clan members interested in the affair consulted about what action to take, Hughes intervened (through intermediaries, perhaps, although it is possible he approached the Paints in person) and persuaded them to leave him alone. In his place Hughes suggested that the Paints kill James Vann. We do not know whether Vann had been a party to the death being avenged, but in legal theory it would not matter. He was a Blind Savannah, and equally liable whether he had committed the killing himself or had risked his life to prevent it. The rationale of the law was summed up by Hughes's argument why Vann should be sacrificed, and he spared. Vann, Hughes pointed out, was an ungovernable and unpromising boy, who had done nothing for his people and who could be killed without regret. We may assume Hughes was comparing Vann to himself and that the Paint clan agreed the nation would be better served with Hughes alive and Vann dead.

James Vann was told of the decision and apparently reconciled himself to his fate, even deliberately riding into one ambush from which he luckily escaped. We may suppose that as time went on, life became more precious and he sought ways to avoid the inevitable. It is possible, although we cannot be certain, that he ventured forth in public only in company with his uterine uncle. In any event he was attending a gathering with his uncle when some of the Paint clan appeared and he realized that the moment of decision was at hand. Taking a rifle or a pistol, he walked over to his uncle and shot him through the head. This action, to use the Cherokee phrase, "quieted the claim." [11] The Blind Savannahs had paid the blood price, and the Paint clan was satisfied.

James Vann went on to lead the troublesome life Hughes had predicted. He became a successful businessman and a large property owner, but he was a scandal to the authorities of the nation, quarrelling with his neighbors and maintaining a tavern in violation of the prohibition laws. In 1807 Vann accused his brother-in-law, John Falling, of instigating his negro slaves to insubordination. The two men fought a duel, and Falling was killed. As brothers-in-law they belonged to different clans and Falling's clan had a right to vengeance. Two years later, while Vann was helping to drive a gang of thieves out of the Cherokee nation, he was killed by Falling's relatives.[12]

The first rule of the Cherokee law of homicide illustrated by the Vann case is that the clan of the victim has a right to retaliation. This right imposed on the clan of the slayer a duty to be "indifferent"; [13] a duty, as one Cherokee expressed it, "to remain neuter by the law of the Nation." [14] A killing did not produce a cycle of retaliatory killings, there was one retaliation and this was the end of the affair.

We may be surprised that the relatives of a slayer would acknowledge the duty to stand aside, but if they had not, there would have been anarchy. When Vann was killed in 1809, no attempt was made by his clan to discover who shot him, [15] and in every other known case the avengers of blood seem to have acted without fear of retaliation. There is no record of Cherokee thoughts regarding the binding force of this duty to tell us whether they rationalized it, or merely acquiesced in it as a custom, but we do have the myth of "The Rattlesnake's Vengeance," which illustrates how readily they obeyed it. This is a typical Cherokee myth, perhaps told as much to teach children their legal duties as to entertain, and describes a Cherokee hunter who heard a strange wailing sound while returning home.

> Looking about he found that he had come into the midst of a whole company of rattlesnakes, which all had their mouths open and seemed to be crying. He asked them the reason of their trouble, and they told him that his own wife had that day killed their chief, the Yellow Rattlesnake, and they were just now about to send the Black Rattlesnake to take revenge.
>
> The hunter said he was very sorry, but they told him that if he spoke the truth he must be ready to make satisfaction and give his wife as a sacrifice for the life of their chief. Not knowing what might happen otherwise, he consented. They then told him that the Black Rattlesnake would go home with him and coil up just outside the door in the dark. He must go inside, where he would find

his wife awaiting him, and ask her to get him a drink of fresh water from the spring. That was all.

He went home and knew that the Black Rattlesnake was following. It was night when he arrived and very dark, but he found his wife waiting with his supper ready. He sat down and asked for a drink of water. She handed him a gourd full from the jar, but he said he wanted it fresh from the spring, so she took a bowl and went out of the door. The next moment he heard a cry, and going out he found that the Black Rattlesnake had bitten her and that she was already dying. He stayed with her until she was dead, when the Black Ratlesnake came out from the grass again and said his tribe was now satisfied.[16]

The hunter did more than stand "neuter" while his wife was killed. He actively arranged her death, a point stressed in the story when he demands water fresh from the spring. We cannot say the average Cherokee understood there was a postive duty to sacrifice his kinsman to lawful vengeance, yet this is the lesson the myth teller seems to teach. What we can say is that the average Cherokee had every reason to aid the avengers of blood—for if they did not kill his relative, they might kill him.

The British and French never understood the Cherokee law of homicide, they never tried to discover how it operated or if it served the needs of Cherokee society. They simply noticed that the "innocent" were sometimes executed in place of the "guilty," and so urged the Cherokees to be more civilized. Time and again, the governor of South Carolina preached the humane lesson that "no man ought to be punished for what another does"; [17] time and again, the Cherokees listened in apparent bewilderment, not comprehending the point the white men tried to get across. The day would arrive when they understood, but during the primitive-law era, they were more impressed by the pragmatic logic of holding one man answerable for the acts of another, a logic unrelated to any theory of vicarious liability based on clan relationship. By making each member of a clan liable for deaths caused by fellow clansmen, the law of homicide utilized the clan (the one viable constitutional unit of Cherokee society) as a sort of tithing, enforcing on an informal basis a system of frankpledge. Knowing they might serve as his substitute, the relatives of the manslayer were hardly anxious to help him escape, but on the contrary had good reasons for not obstructing the course of retaliation. Although we may doubt the assertion made in later years that the clansmen of a manslayer "were generally the first to apprehend" him, [18] we may believe it possible that the brothers of a manslayer would sometimes execute him in order to save one of themselves.[19]

It must be understood that the Vann case was not typical. In the average situation, the clan of the victim wanted to take revenge on the manslayer, and Charles Hughes could not have shifted liability to James Vann. Moreover, it is unlikely that even had Charles Hughes fled the nation, the Paint clan would have selected just any Blind Savannah to pay the blood price. Surely custom favored killing the manslayer's brother or his nearest clan kin.[20] Like the Creeks, the Cherokees must have realized that by placing in jeopardy the life of the manslayer's brother or uncle—the person most likely to aid his escape—they increased the certainty the manslayer himself would be produced.[21]

There is a counterconsideration not to be overlooked. The fact that a brother might be killed in his stead could lead the manslayer to surrender and accept his fate. We must not scoff at this possibility, as there are too many documented examples for us to doubt the moral persuasion of customary law among the southern Indians. True, there are few (if any) records of Cherokee manslayers rushing to save their brothers from being killed in their place, but there are also no records of Cherokees leaving their brothers to die for them. Scarcity of records is a handicap when making generalizations, yet on this point we may safely draw from what is known of neighboring Indian nations. The Choctaws, for example, had a law of homicide similar to the Cherokees, and no Choctaw was known to miss his own execution.[22] The avenging clan told him they would exact the blood price, gave him the date and location, and knew he would appear.[23] Indeed, among many Indian nations, there are instances of men substituting for their condemned brothers or uncles. Once a Choctaw arrived at his execution so fearful that his brother, seeing he was afraid to die, stepped forward and took his place. "My brother, you are no [sic] brave," he said, "stay here and take care of my family—I will die in your place." And he did.[24]

Cherokees were not always this courageous or self-sacrificing, yet we may be certain that they too acknowledged a right of substitution; a right upon which James Vann acted; confident that the avengers of blood would accept his uncle's death in substitution of his own. It was a rule so generally honored among southern Indians that it may have been universal. During the early 1750s a Chickasaw living in the Upper Creek nation killed a white man, and the British demanded his life in retaliation. The Creeks, who had much to lose from British displeasure and no reason to protect the Chickasaw, answered that it was "just and reasonable that

Blood for Blood should be given." [25] Unhappily the manslayer did not agree and refused to be a sacrifice. There was no Creek or Chickasaw who could kill him as, of course, none belonged to the clan of the victim, a white man. The Indians would have permitted the British to execute him but the British, insisting on following their own norms, demanded that the Indians themselves kill him, which was legally risky. If any Indian had done so, he would have been liable to retaliation. The matter might have reached an impasse, had not the Upper Creeks intervened. There were a large number of Chickasaws in their nation, refugees from the French wars, whom they threatened to expel if the British did not receive satisfaction. The manslayer's uncle tried to show him his duty. "I have heard all your Talks and find you are mad," he told his nephew. "The Blood of a white man is spilt and by your own Laws Blood ought to be in Satisfaction. In Case you throw away the English, you, your Women, and Children must become miserable or be made Slaves to the French." [26]

The uncle then sent word to Thomas Bosomworth, the British agent, that if his nephew was unwilling to die, he would take his place. The Creeks and Chickasaws thought this a reasonable solution and appeared surprised by British objections. The manslayer must die and no one else, the agent told them, because he alone was "guilty." The Chickasaw headman did not understand and assured Bosomworth satisfaction would be given, for either the manslayer or his uncle "would be the Attonement." But Bosomworth, an Englishman dealing with natives, had the advantage of knowing his institutions were superior to native institutions. "I then informed him that it was not our Laws that the Innocent should suffer for the Guilty, to which he replyed that by the Laws of their Nation one of the same Blood was equally satisfactory, but in Case neither of them was killed before he returned to the [Chickasaw] Camp the guilty Person should suffer." [27]

Perhaps the Chickasaw headman understood what was expected of him, more likely he did not. It hardly mattered for the issue had already been resolved. While the headman was conferring with Bosomworth, the manslayer's uncle ended the crisis.

> The Uncle retired to a Conferrence with his Nephew and told him that the Day was come, that one or other of them must dye. He asked him the Question if he was willing to suffer Death, to which the Nephew made no Answer. Without further Hesitation the Uncle replyed, I see you are affraid to dye, therefore I must dye for you. Upon which he immediately repaired to his own House

to seek for his Gun which his Wife had hid from him, but finding a long French Knife, with that in one Hand and Paint in the other with which he besmearhed himself, came out into the open Street and made a publick Declaration that as one of his Family had spilt the Blood of a white man and was affrayd to dye for it, he was now going to pay the Debt for him for the Good of his People and for Satisfaction to the English, and with the greatest Undauntedness struck the Knife into the Gullet and immediately dyed with the Wound.[28]

The British were angry but helpless. "We must be satisfied with what has been done since that is your Way," Governor James Glen told the Upper Creeks, but in the future he wanted no more nonsense.[29] What interests us is the uncle's public declaration which, while admittedly reported secondhand as Bosomworth was not present, implies that he was asserting a right to act as his nephew's substitute, and that he had no doubt this action was legal. "I am now going to purchase your Life with mine," he had told his nephew. "Take care you do no more Mischief to the white People, or you will have no Body to pay the Debt for you when I am gone." [30]

We must stress legal principles, not events. James Vann killed his uncle to save himself, while the Chickasaw uncle killed himself to save his nephew and his people. Thus two nephews, one by his own action, the other by being impassive, escaped paying the blood price; yet the price was paid and the debt satisfied. Both men stood free in the eyes of the law, no liability attached to either, though we cannot say how public opinion looked upon them. It seems likely that public opinion condemned their physical cowardliness while tolerating their legal subterfuge. The Cherokees were sophisticated enough jurisprudents to distinguish between law and public opinion, not always an easy distinction, as they depended largely upon public opinion to enforce law. One way to define Cherokee law, after all, is to say law is social custom supported by public opinion. It is, of course, not so simple, yet it must be acknowledged that the same respect for public opinion that made an American Indian oblivious to physical discomfort, disdainful of his enemies, and stoical in the face of torture, also motivated him to perform his legal duty even when it meant his certain death.

Fear of social stigma may not have been a strong enough motive to bend the Chickasaw nephew to his legal duty, but there are instances of Indians who killed white men voluntarily surrendering to British retaliation, in order to save their nation from threatened reprisals. The point may be better illustrated by considering another aspect of the law of homicide. We have seen that the clan of a manslayer was expected to "stand neuter" when the victim's clan retaliated, and that duty toward a brother who might be killed in his place deterred the average slayer from fleeing to safety. It does not follow, however, that he submitted meekly to his fate. We know of instances where the avenging clan exacted the blood price from ambush, implying that they, at least, feared he might defend himself. Yet we cannot doubt that the ideal standard of conduct was for the slayer to succumb with longanimous indifference. Again, the Choctaws provide the best examples, as they made submission at least a virtue, if not a duty. A revealing case was reported in 1823, an especially significant date since by then a large number of whites and blacks lived in the Choctaw nation, and the presence of both these races tended to break down traditional Indian institutions, especially the duty of voluntary submission and the custom of personal courage.

A Choctaw Indain, calling himself doctor Sibley, and belonging to a wandering tribe of that nation, who have resided in the neighborhood of Red river for some years past, while in a state of intoxication, stabbed another Indian to the heart, who immediately expired. After the murder, a brother of the deceased Indian came to Sibley, and told him that he must have revenge for the death of his brother, by taking his (Sibley's) life. To this proposal Sibley readily assented, and proposed that his execution take place on the following morning which was also assented to by the other party. In the meanwhile, Sibley was kept under no restraint whatever, but was permitted his freedom as usual, without showing the least disposition to make his escape. When the morning arrived on which he was to suffer death, Sibley went out with the rest of the party, and aided in digging a grave for the deceased Indian. After it was finished, he observed to the party, that he thought it large enough for both of them to lie in, and signified a wish to be buried in the same grave. This not being objected to, he placed himself in a standing position over the grave, with his arms stretched out and gave the signal to fire, when the brother of the deceased Indian placed a rifle to his breast and discharged its contents through his heart. He dropped into the grave, and instantly expired.[31]

There is one final rule relating to the law of homicide which should be noted. The Cherokees, like some other Indian nations, practiced a form of outlawry, permitting a clan to formally announce that it would no longer protect a member who frequently involved the clan in controversy.[32] It is doubtful if this freed the members of a Cherokee's clan from liability for his past acts, and we cannot be sure it excused them from liability for future homicides, although it is possible. But it did mean that if the "outlaw" were killed, there would be no effort to avenge his blood. We know little about the mechanics of the decision although surely it had to be made by a close-clan kin, otherwise it would have little force, the remainder of the clan having less interest in the matter than he and so likely to follow his wishes. Also it is probable that a man was not declared a general "outlaw" in the sense of old Germanic and English law, but was told he would not be avenged if he persisted in conduct, or took certain actions, of which his brother and his clan disapproved. Thus, in 1792 Unacata said he would not retaliate against the Americans if they should kill his brother, John Watts, in battle. Watts had joined the rebellious Chickamagua Cherokees to avenge the killing of his uncle, Old Tassel,[33] and Unacata had gone with him. But by the early 1790s, it was apparent that the cycle of retaliatory killings had to stop or the Cherokee nation would be wiped out. "If Watts goes to war and falls, he may lie there," Unacata declared. "I will not pick him up." [34]

CHAPTER TEN

A WAY OF PEACE

—THE MECHANICS OF VENGEANCE

Although we may be certain of the general rules governing the law of homicide—that any killing, accidental or deliberate, vested a right of vengeance in the victim's clan and imposed a liability upon the members of the manslayer's clan—there are many questions that we cannot answer, and a few that probably even the Cherokees could not have answered. Customary law was, after all, general—not specific; it provided rules in broad outline, not in precise detail.

What, for example, happened when a Cherokee killed two men? Was the manslayer's clan liable for two lives, or would his death alone quiet the claim? Since in legal theory it was two deaths that were being revenged, and not a murderer that was being punished, one may suspect that the avenging clan had the right to two lives, but we cannot be certain. What if the two men killed belonged to different clans? Were the clans of both victims to be satisfied by the manslayer's death? We know that if two Cherokees of the same clan killed a member of a second clan, the avenging clan would be satisfied with one death; it did not have the right to kill both manslayers. But how was it determined which was sacrificed? And what if the two killers belonged to different clans? The avenging clan still had the right to only one blood price, but which clan was liable, and how did the avenging clan choose? These are questions we cannot answer, and which we suspect would not have troubled the Cherokees. Had the fact situations occurred, they would have solved each in some manner, and if the acts were repeated often enough, would have recognized a custom, a rule of conduct, a law. But until the solution evolved, the problem did not exist.

A more pressing series of questions, which surely the Cherokees had to face, relate to homicide within clans. The law of retaliation was based on a theory of clan vengeance and made no provision, indeed seemed to ignore the possibility that a Cherokee might kill a member of his own clan. Of course such killings took place and of course the Cherokees had a solution, though we can only guess what that solution was.

Charles Hicks, one of the highest ranking officials under the first of the Cherokees' written constitutions, has given us a hint how intraclan killings may have been resolved in primitive-law times. Writing in 1818, after the blood feud had been abolished and a law of murder adopted, Hicks said that a convicted murderer who had killed a member of another clan was always punished with death. But if the slayer and the victim belonged to the same clan and the slayer was found guilty of murder, "it frequently happens that the clan intercedes with the chief head of the nation, and obtains a pardon, which pardon is published in the national council when convened." [1] Now if this attitude of forgiveness prevailed after the clan responsibility for homicide had been abolished, and murder was limited to killings with "malice intended," [2] it is reasonable to conclude that there was a strong reluctance among clan members to see a fellow clansman die, even for an intraclan killing. Projecting this reluctance back to the era of the blood feud, when clan ties were legally stronger than in 1818, it seems just as reasonable to believe that intraclan homicides were adjusted either by accommodation or by forgiveness. We cannot rule out the possibility that a brother might retaliate against a fellow clansman who killed his brother, or that he had a right to retaliate. We can only assume that in these cases the pressures operating to mitigate absolute liability* were particularly strong.

Of only two types of intraclan slaying can we speak with certainty. A brother who killed a brother was amenable to no one, not even to a third

* Discussed in the next chapter.

brother,[3] and as previously noted, a mother could kill a newly-born babe and apparently not even the child's older brother could object.[4] Thus we may state as a general rule that fratricide and infanticide were exceptions to the law of homicide. How far the privilege extended, however, we cannot say. Could a mother, for example, kill a six-month-old child? If a nephew killed his uncle, was he immune from retaliation or could a second uncle kill him? There may have been no answer to these questions, and even the case of James Vann tells us nothing. He killed his uncle, true enough, and was not killed in return, not because uncle-slaying was privileged but because his uncle's death satisfied the blood debt which was owed the Paint clan.

The uncertainty of the law governing intraclan homicide may be illustrated by an event that occurred in the Creek nation during 1752. The British were demanding that the Lower Creeks execute a headman called the Acorn Whistler, who had killed Cherokees, and the Lower Creeks had agreed, but no one was willing to be the executioner. A headman named Chiggilli told two other headmen, Estepaichi and the Ollassee King, that they could act without fear of retaliation. "You are his own Flesh and Blood," Chiggilli argued. "Either of you or any of his own Relations may kill him and who has any Thing to say to it?"[5] That both Estepaichi and the Ollassee King insisted Chiggilli was wrong, and that their own lives would be jeopardized if they killed the Acorn Whistler, is evidence the Creek law of intraclan homicide was ill-defined. That they feared vengeance meant they feared it from members of their own clan, undoubtedly from the Acorn Whistler's close-clan kin. The matter was resolved by having the Acorn Whistler's nephew do the killing, but even he would not act without a pledge of secrecy.

It must not be assumed that a brother was free to kill a brother merely because the feud did not extend to fratricide. Nor should we think this oversight a flaw inherent in a legal theory too closely tied to the logic of clan vengeance. True, a system of justice based on personal retaliation is bound to arrive at a manslayer so closely related to his victim that there is no nearer kin to exact the blood price. However, the same social patterns which generate personal-retaliation law also generate an atmosphere of mutual dependence and selfless identity, making deliberate fratricide unthinkable. Among the Kiowas, we are told, killing a brother was "the most terrible thing" a man could do,[6] and there is every reason to believe the same was true among the Cherokees—indeed, among most American Indians. Yet the possibility of fratricide, especially accidental fratricide, did exist and it may have occurred; at least, this is one inference which can be drawn from the fact that when the Cherokees in 1810 abolished the feud, they took the trouble to make clear that fratricide committed with malice came within the definition of murder. The statute provided "That should it happen that a brother, forgetting his natural affection, should raise his hand in anger and kill his brother, he shall be accounted guilty of murder and suffer accordingly." [7]

But what if a son should kill his father? Again we cannot be sure of the answer. In stark, uncompromising law there is no doubt that patricide and filicide invoked the blood debt, for a father belonged to a different clan than his child, and for one to kill the other created a liability under the law of homicide. A parricide who killed with malice might expect to pay the blood price; yet it is difficult to believe that a son slayer would be held to absolute liability, for he (after all) is father, husband, and brother-in-law to the close clan kin of the victim. So, especially if the killing was unintentional, it is likely that the rules of mitigation*—if not outright forgiveness—would determine his fate. Still we cannot be certain, as some authorities tell us Cherokee fathers did not discipline their children for fear of blood revenge if they should be harmed.[8] This rationale seems doubtful, for a sounder explanation is that discipline was not the father's task.

There was also, of course, the problem of a son killing a member of his father's clan. Did the father join the avengers of blood, or did he in the councils of his own clan plead the case of his son? Here we are asking questions about conduct and not law, for the law is clear—the father's clan is owed a life and the father's first duty is to his clan. We may imagine the average Cherokee father taking every conceivable course that interest or affection dictated, except one: he would never have physically defended his son against his fellow clansmen. It must have been a difficult hour for a man who took seriously his parental ties, and we may assume that homicides between clans of a father and son created one of the situations where liability was mitigated along lines to be discussed in the next chapter.

Our questions can become as complicated as they are insolvable. What if the father of the victim is a member of the manslayer's clan? Can his son's clan kill him, in satisfaction of the blood price? There must have been limits but they were limits set by social attitudes, not by legal doctrine.

Again it must be emphasized that homicide created absolute liability,

* Discussed in the next chapter.

and that the hard cases we have been postulating might not to a Cherokee have raised issues of liability, but issues governing the mitigation of lia- bility. To say as much may be the same as saying that post-homicide miti- gation was the determinative factor in the resolution of the feud between related Cherokees. This point may be accepted, if we also note that there was a pre-homicide preventative built into the Cherokee social system, an institution or custom which decreased the likelihood of killings between certain clans. We have previously considered this custom: the use of kin- ship terms, rather than proper names. It was more than a method for arranging marriages within preferred clans; it was a device by which controversy was prevented.[9] A Cherokee called all the male members of his father's clan "father" and all the female members "father's sister," according to each some of the respect and deference he showed his blood father and paternal aunt, thus decreasing the possibility of animosity and petty quarrels that might develop into acts of homicide. Moreover, he had kinship terms for the members of the clans to which belong most of the persons in an extended European family; in addition to his father's clan, he called the males of his father's father's clan and his mother's father's clan "grandfather," and the females "grandmother." These kinship terms allowed him to joke with members of those clans without giving offense, to treat them with a familiarity that must have bred both a sense of rela- tionship and a feeling of respect, thus eliminating some of the friction inherent in the formal conduct of primitive peoples. Of course there was the counterdanger that close association encouraged by kinship terms might increase the chances of accidental homicide, by bringing a Cherokee into frequent contact with the members of the three clans to which he was "related." But this danger may not have contributed to the blood feud for, as we shall see, accidental killing was probably the chief occasion for mitigating liability. It is no exaggeration, therefore, to regard kinship terms as social customs more relevant to the law of homicide than to the law of marriage, and in accepting this conclusion, we may understand why J. W. Powell called the use of proper names by certain relatives "illegal." [10]

Most of the questions we have been unable to answer are of a type which would have been asked by an English lawyer, not by a Cherokee. Lawyers grasp the implications of rules only after postulating hypotheticals from a wide range of the possible. The primitive legal mind, on the other hand, formulates patterns of conduct upon past experience, and what has not occurred holds no law for him. We might regret some questions that remain unanswered, the Cherokee would not. Even more regrettable for us are the questions we cannot answer but which the Cherokee could, questions relating to the mechanics of vengeance: who was permitted to exact the blood price, how were the avengers of blood designated, and did the right of vengeance impose upon any persons the duty to enforce that right?

We may be sure a Cherokee could answer these questions, they were too fundamental to have been left for solution as the occasion arose. The right of vengeance may have belonged to the clan, but surely not any member of the clan was supposed to exercise it as a right, for it belonged to some more than to others. Unfortunately we do not know how priority was assigned, or whether there was any clan machinery for designating an avenger of blood. There is little direct evidence and even that is contradictory. A contemporary writing in 1761 says the decision was left to "the Heads of the nation," which seems clearly wrong;[11] an authority more knowledgeable in Cherokee affairs, writing in 1842, says that the clan made the decision, a statement which is hardly helpful;[12] the only Cherokee myth hinting at a method of organized retaliation makes the retaliatory force a town, not a clan, which may be an incorrect statement of law.[13] Also, the one reference in a legal document, a deposition filed with the Cherokee Supreme Court during 1833, implies that the town council was sometimes convened, but the case described in the deposition involved a white manslayer with consequential dangers of international conflict, should the avengers of blood act before colonial officials were notified.[14] Where a Cherokee was the manslayer of another Cherokee, the town council, in which the manslayer's clan took part, was probably an inappropriate agency for ordering the method of retaliation.

Perhaps the most reliable statement that we have is from the instructions given to a jury by the presiding judge in a murder trial held in 1840, shortly after the main part of the Cherokee nation was reunited with the Cherokee West in what is today northeastern Oklahoma. The Cherokee West were a conservative minority who had migrated to Arkansas over two decades earlier, partly in order to retain their old customs, including the blood feud. It may be for this reason that Chief Justice Bushyhead, in his charge, felt it necessary to explain why the new law of murder was more just than the primitive law of homicide. "Before the introduction of written laws among our people, we had a custom which often made the innocent suffer for the guilty," Bushyhead argued. "There was no specific injunction with regard to the manner of execution, nor was there any rule prescribed even as to the person to be selected for death, in the event of difficulty in finding the slayer himself;—the nearest relative of the slain was to take the life of any one he chose in the slayer's clan." [15]

Again, we are not certain as to the accuracy of Bushyhead's facts, but he was a student of his nation's customs and what he says jibes with our general sources, anthropologists and traders, who tell us that the male next of blood to the victim had the right, if not the legal duty to inflict clan revenge.[16] Among the Creeks an uncle may have had priority,[17] but among the Cherokees all authorities agree that retaliation was the function first of the oldest brother, and then of the nearest male clan kin.[18] As late as 1895, the Choctaws permitted the closest male relative of a murder victim to take the sheriff's place at an execution and shoot the killer [19]— a civilized adaptation of a primitive right indicating that the avenger of blood may have been determined by rules of consanguinity.

To conclude that the older brother of the victim was the avenger of blood does not tell us how he performed his mission. It may not be important whether he consulted with members of his own clan or asked any of them for help, but we would better understand the Cherokee law of homicide if we knew whether he had the right to tell his clan kin not to act without his consent, if he decided which member of the manslayer's clan should be killed, and if he could invite relatives from other clans to participate. This last question becomes important when we note that contemporary records speak of fathers setting forth to avenge the deaths of sons. We cannot be confident that interpreters, when they quoted an Indian as saying, ". . . as they killed my Son we must have Blood for Blood," [20] translated the word "Son" correctly. They may have rendered into English a clan term without much heed to precise definition. Still, the word "son" appears frequently enough to imply that fathers were moved by the killing of sons and sometimes joined the cry for blood. But could they be parties to the vengeance? Suppose the father killed the manslayer, would he be immune from retaliation by the manslayer's clan, or would he be a stranger whose actions under the law of homicide would have to be avenged? Again there may have been no certain answer, although we suspect that if invited by the avenging clan to join the feud, his conduct was privileged or he would not dare participate.

Perhaps it does not matter that there are many questions which we cannot answer regarding the mechanics of the Cherokee law of homicide. Civilized man may be too far removed from savage man for us fully to comprehend the legal theory of the blood feud as a primitive Cherokee comprehended it, even if we knew every rule and could explain what would have happened in any hypothetical case. We cannot think as a Cherokee would have thought, and this is our undoing. The inbred concept of lawyer-entrusted justice, contained in certain rules of procedural due process geared to an adjudicatory system of advocacy defense and impartial judgment, keeps getting in our way. It is not enough to say that the legal mind of the Cherokee was too primitive to value the rule-of-law institutions of civilization, for this might be the same as saying that his sense of injustice was inherent rather than taught. Rather, we must try to understand that the Cherokee did not view his version of the universal talionic feud as a method for channelling legal violence in accordance with rules of blood retaliation and sanctions based on personal vengeance. On the contrary, he saw it as a self-evident necessity derived from the clearest tenets of natural law, which followed with perfect logic the clan-oriented arrangement of his social world and sensibly entrusted his security to men who loved him, not men who ruled him.

"In civilization," J. W. Powell has written, "law is theoretically founded on justice; but in savagery, principles of justice have little consideration. There are two fundamental principles at the basis of primitive law: viz. first, controversy should be prevented; second, controversy should be terminated." [21] This distinction provides a usable test with which to judge the Cherokee law of homicide, though it is a test of civilized man, not primitive man. From the Cherokee perspective, the law of blood may be thought of as a law of prevention and a law of termination, but not as a law of violence. It was rather, like all law, a law of peace: a law which imposed upon society a degree of peace by the very fact men knew that if controversy were carried too far, organized and certain violence would follow in its wake. Should civilized man object that accident was punished equally with malice, he would be objecting that the Cherokees, without police, courts, or legal sanctions, found that the surest method to maintain social order was to blame the act and not the actor. Order, not justice, was their ideal, and order—not justice—is the standard by which their law of homicide must be judged.

CHAPTER ELEVEN

A TOUCH OF JUSTICE

—THE MITIGATION OF LIABILITY

There is danger to defending the Cherokee law of homicide in terms of a dichotomy between order and justice—danger not so much that we may be imposing our values upon Cherokee institutions, but that we may misrepresent Cherokee legal thought by implying that the primitive Cherokees were not concerned with formulating a system of justice, only with administering rules of law which were predictable in their result, certain in their execution, and equal for all men. The danger, in other words, is that emphasis upon order, as distinguished from justice, assumes that elements such as responsibility or guilt were alien to Cherokee jurisprudence. Just as we would never understand American criminal law, were we to dwell upon statutory definitions of crime without mentioning the prosecutor's discretion in permitting an accused to plea guilty to a charge less serious than the letter of the law, or of a judge to impose a flexible sentence tempered by considerations of clemency, so we would not understand the Cherokee law of homicide if we were to defend it as a system for maintaining order, while ignoring the fact that it contained several avenues by which the rule of absolute liability was mitigated in practice. Justice, even as we define it, was not always absent from primitive law. The Cherokee law of homicide may seem harsh when we consider only the rules demanding vengeance, regardless of circumstance or excuse, but the enforcement of the law was more lenient than its rules imply.

One mitigating force working against the imposition of strict liability in every case of homicide was the human fact that there usually were blood relatives on each side of a feud. After all, just seven clans existed in the Cherokee nation, and it is virtually certain that even in a small town, each clan contained at least one member married into one of the other six. Considering only the attitude of a father, we may expect that every avenging clan contained one member likely to urge his fellow clansmen to proceed cautiously. "It is difficult to imagine," Fred Gearing has observed, "that he could be unmindful of his own sons who in principle shared the corporate guilt and were subject to be killed, and that that compelling sentiment was not publicly recognized and publicly handled through structural arrangement." [1]

A second mitigating factor was accidental homicide. True the law took no notice of accident, treating all homicides as equally culpable no matter what their circumstances. But this does not mean that the Indians themselves did not consider the circumstances of a killing when deciding whether to enforce the rule of absolute liability. During the 1790s, Benjamin Hawkins, the famous United States agent to the Cherokees and Creeks, asked Efau Haujo, the speaker of the Creek national council, his opinion on the custom of punishing accidental death with the same severity as malicious homicide. Efau Haujo replied,

> The custom of ours is a bad one, blood for blood; but I do not believe it came from E-sau-ge-tuh E-mis-see * but proceeded from ourselves. Of a case of this sort, I will give you my opinion, by my conduct. Lately, in Tookaubatche, two promising boys were playing and slinging stones. One of them let slip his sling, the stone flew back and killed his companion. The family of the deceased took the two boys and were preparing to bury them in the same grave. The uncles, who have the right to decide in such cases, were sent for, and I was sent for. We arrived at the same time. I ordered the people to leave the house, and the two boys to remain together. I took the uncles to my house, raised their spirits with a little rum, and told them, the boy was a fine boy, and would be useful to us in our town, when

* "The Master of Breath"—God.

he became a man; that he had no ill will against the dead one; the act was purely accidental; that it had been the will of E-sau-ge-tuh E-mis-se[e] to end his days and I thought that the living one should remain, as taking away his life would not give it to the other. The two uncles, after some reflection, told me, as you have advised us, so we will act; he shall not die, it was an accident.[2]

The Cherokees were also prepared to plead accident in extenuation of homicide, and to consider the absence of intent or malice, the reputation of good character, and the necessity of self defense as factors which might be argued in mitigation of liability. We know of one case in which a Cherokee made several of these defenses, the case of Andrew White, which is particularly significant as it occurred at the comparatively early date of 1752. White, a Cherokee warrior, was in search of Creek scalps to avenge Creek killing of fellow clansmen, when his party surrounded a house in South Carolina and inadvertently killed a British subject.[3] The governor of South Carolina demanded that he come to Charles Town to be punished, and White was apparently willing if there was no other way to prevent trouble between Carolina and the Cherokee nation. Before surrendering, however, White sent the governor a "talk" which is the nearest analogy we have to a Cherokee defense brief. Even allowing for the fact that a British trader probably aided its composition (typically the translator alternates between the third and first person), it is a revealing summary of the Cherokee legal mind: arguing not only accident and good intent, but that no causation could be imputed to White, and that the Creeks were at least constructively liable. In his talk, White pleaded,

That he never had any Harm against any white man, and never intended any, but this Accident happened when he was out at War. He saw a Horse that the Creeks took away when they killed one of his Relations, and thought then he should have Satisfaction, not knowing there was any white Man in the House, and a young Fellow, one of his Relations put him in a Passion, and seeing a white Man come out he run up, and gave him one stroke with a Stick of Wood, though it was not that that killed him for he was shott before in the House, and after he says he came to consider what he had done to think that he had killed his Father as he calls white People he was troubled to his Heart to think he should strike a white Man through the Creeks' doings. He looked on it then that the Creeks was Accessary to the Death of the white Man, and he has been constantly at War with them to take Satisfaction for it [is]

> true I have been guilty of what the white People calls me a Rogue,
> for but it was not my Intent ever to have given them Occasion to
> have called me [that].

Having pleaded accident and lack of intent, White went on to argue good
character, and urged the governor to ask the Cherokee traders

> if ever he behaved any Ways disrespectfull to them in any Ways,
> and he says he believes they will say they never knew any Harm of
> him only this, that that call him Harm, striking this white Man
> through Mistake, which was not the Cause of his Death, and says
> that he was not satisfied since that happened, and has been constantly
> at War since, and just came in with three Slaves and two Scalps
> from the Creeks for Revenge for the white Man that was killed
> through their Doings.[4]

We must appreciate Andrew White's legal dilemma. He was charged
by South Carolina with a crime resembling common-law murder, yet he
was to be judged not by the law of Westminster Hall, but by a law of
summary retaliation which the British had borrowed from the American
Indians. A lawyer could not have drafted a better defense brief than this
talk which White sent the governor from the forests of the Appalachian
highlands. Like the charge against him, White's talk was a composite of
conflicting legal principles, setting up six defenses. Two of these were
known to English common law, two peculiar to Cherokee law. One defense
—the plea that he was not the cause of the white man's death—was
common to both British and Cherokee law, and another—the argument
that the Creeks were constructively liable—may have been recognized in
Cherokee law, or may have been *sui generis*. We may suppose that the
governor understood and weighed the common-law defenses of accident
and absence of malice. It is doubtful, however, if he realized that White's
request for forgiveness and his argument that the blood debt had been
satisfied (by enemy scalps taken subsequent to the crime) were defenses
with a meaning in Cherokee law; that they were more than mere pleas in
abatement of punishment, which more properly belonged in a petition
for clemency than in a defense brief; that they were, in fact, well-
established doctrines mitigating liability in the Cherokee law of homicide.

Forgiveness of liability was surely a tenuous legal doctrine. After all, a
clan or brother who failed to avenge a homicide was disgraced [5] and the
Cherokees even had a word of reproach, *Hv tsa,* for the man who feared
to exact the blood price.[6] Yet we are told that "under very peculiar cir-

cumstances & very, very seldom" [7] a clan might forgive a homicide, and there were at least two minor cases in which this is said to have happened. In one case, "two individuals, supposed to be guilty, who had escaped with their lives, all snares laid for them and were at last let alone, and suffered to live." [8] In the second instance, admittedly a "tradition" even though related by a North Carolina historian who claimed to know the principals, the avenger of blood, moved by the tears of the manslayer's white sweetheart, forgave the killing.[9]

Before considering documented Cherokee evidence, it should be noted that forgiveness as a method for mitigating liability seems to have been recognized among some of the other southeastern nations, for example, the Creeks as shown by the case narrated by Efau Haujo, where the uncles forgave the young boy who accidently slew his friend with a rock. In an earlier Creek case, self defense was accepted by a victim's relative as sufficient reason for forgiveness. During 1756 the killing of three Creek warriors by a party of Carolinians led to Creek demands for satisfaction, and a national council of the Upper Creeks was called at which a headman named the Wolf Warrior of the Mucklasses argued that the three victims had been "straggling of their own Accord," and had been killed in self defense. "He added that if any Person there had any Thing to say in the Affair to speak then or for ever hold their Peace and Let the Affair be buried in Oblivion." Someone whispered that none of the relatives of the dead men was present, implying the homicide could not be forgiven unless they were. "He, the Wolf, told him it was false for he him self was Relation to one, and thought the White People were not to be blamed." [10]

A somewhat similar case occurred in the Cherokees one year later, in December, 1757. Samuel Benn, a trader who had been in the nation for 19 years, his 11 year-old son, and his black slave were on their way to Benn's store at "Tannissee [Tennessee] Town" with a cargo of goods from Ninety Six, South Carolina, when four Cherokees attempted to rob them near Natalee. Benn shot and killed one of the thieves and, leaving the Negro to guard the property, fled to the safety of Fort Loudoun, a British garrison located among the Overhills. The commander of the fort sent word of the incident to Old Hop, who replied that Benn need not fear vengeance, that as he had acted in self defense the towns of Chota and Tennessee would protect him.[11] Old Hop then sent a Chota headman to the headmen of Natalee "with a String of white Beads and to tell them, that as the Indian was seeking his Death, he desired them to think no more about it, but to leave the Path clear for all the white People." [12]

The Cock Eye Warrior of Natalee, a "cousin" of the victim, had been hunting at the time of the killing, and so decision apparently was delayed awaiting his return—a significant fact (if "cousin" means he was not the victim's closest clan kin), for it implies that the avengers of blood may have consulted with those clan members who were influential in town or national councils.

When the Cock Eye Warrior got back to Natalee, he was persuaded by the Warrior of the Long Savannah, another intermediary, to forgive Benn. "He says you may think that he may take Revenge of sum other white Man," the Warrior of the Long Savannah wrote the British, "but he was a better Thought then that." [13] The Cock Eye Warrior himself let Benn know what that better thought was: "That he himself was the Head Man of the family of the young Man that was killed, the most numerous in all the Cherokees, and that he had quite forgotten [the event], as he knew very well, that it was his own Seeking." [14]

That forgiveness was an institutionalized method of mitigating liability for homicide is supported by evidence from three sources other than recorded domestic Cherokee and Creek law. The first is the extreme reluctance of the Cherokees, as a people, to tolerate punishment of wrongdoers, a psychological factor better considered in the chapter dealing with the Cherokee legal mind. The other two sources are Cherokee mythology, and the international law of American Indians.

We have already noted that after killing an animal, Cherokees wishing to escape the vengeance of the animal's spirit asked its pardon. A hunter shooting a deer approached the carcass and begged forgiveness, otherwise the chief of the deers, the Little Deer, might strike him with rheumatism. [15] All human diseases were imposed by animals in revenge for killing and each species had invented a disease with which to plague man. The fishes and reptiles, for example, retaliated by sending bad dreams that caused the hunter to lose his appetite, sicken, and die. The one exception was the bear, who instead of inventing a disease tried to use man's own weapon, the bow and arrow, against man, but finding he could not shoot without cutting his claws, gave up in disgust and forgot the need for vengeance. As a result the Cherokees never asked pardon of a slain bear, [16] leaving the unmistakeable impression that they asked pardon of other animals not because they were sorry or had done wrong, but to avoid retaliation through forgiveness. The animal tribes had the same right of vengeance as the clan of a slain Cherokee, yet the hunter acted on the premise that a killing could be forgiven and forgotten.

Other evidence that forgiveness was an institutionalized method for terminating homicide liability comes from the international law of American Indians. Many of the domestic laws of the Cherokees are paralleled in their international law—the several Indian nations dealing one with the other by much the same rules as followed in interclan domestic law—and an established method by which Indian nations avoided conflict was to announce that they would forgive offenses. The common expression, occurring so often in the records that we may view it as legal terminology, was to say the wrong would be overlooked "as a thing done in the dark." [17] Sometimes the offending nation requested forgiveness, as Skiagunsta, the Warrior of Keowee, did in the case of Andrew White by advising the governor of South Carolina that because White had risked his life against the Creeks after killing the white man he should be forgiven.[18]

Skiagunsta, to be sure, was stressing the point that Cherokee-Carolina relationships would improve if a valuable warrior was forgiven by the British, yet his argument reflected a defense which White himself had raised. It will be recalled that White told the governor he had "just came in with three Slaves and two Scalps from the Creeks for Revenge for the white Man that was killed through their Doings." He was neither boasting of war feats nor begging for clemency, but making a plea in abatement of liability that any Cherokee could have made without losing face. A manslayer who brought in an enemy's scalp, or who captured a prisoner in battle, would offer them to the avenging clan in satisfaction of the blood debt. We are told by nineteenth-century Cherokees that a scalp or slave was received "as full atonement," and the manslayer was henceforth a free man.[19] However, it is difficult to believe the avenging clan had no discretion. A positive rule requiring them to accept the scalp or prisoner in place of their slain clansman is not characteristic of Cherokee law. We only know that the avengers of blood could do so with honor, and we may conclude that public opinion expected them to do so, and that in most cases they probably did.

In what terms the American Indians viewed the substitution of a scalp or a prisoner for a slain relative we cannot say but apparently substitution was interpreted as evidence of sincerity and good faith; the party receiving the scalps in satisfaction of the blood debt was accepting not a symbol of barbaric savagery but a token of peace, a peace to which he magnanimously assented. Once more we may turn to international law to illustrate this concept, as substitution was commonly employed in Indian diplomacy. During 1757, a party of Cherokee warriors, scouting along the Ohio, killed five Chickasaws whom they mistook for Shawnees. A Chickasaw-

Cherokee war might have resulted, had not the Little Carpenter gone to the Chickasaws and appeased that nation with his usual eloquence, aided by a gift of two French scalps he had recently taken near Fort Toulouse, a string of beads, and a war hatchet. The offending Cherokees, he pleaded, "were young fellows" who acted rashly because they did not dare return home "without something to show." [20] The Chickasaws accepted the scalps and the nations remained at peace.

These two defenses—forgiveness and substitution—which Andrew White raised in mitigation of his liability for killing the Carolinian, in turn raise the most difficult question posed by Cherokee law. Did the Cherokees have a law of compensation in mitigation of liability for homicide? Was Andrew White offering the scalps of the Creeks as payment to satisfy the blood debt, rather than as a token of good will? The Chickasaws may have so understood the Little Carpenter's gifts, for presents given in Indian diplomacy have been compared to presents given in compensation for private killings.[21] James Mooney, the leading Cherokee mythicist, believed that the prayer of a hunter begging pardon from the spirit of a slain animal was offered to satisfy the animal's tribe, "very much as a murder is compounded for, according to the Indian system, by 'covering the bones of the dead' with presents for the bereaved relatives." [22] Mooney's supposition is that the animal's tribe accepted the prayer as compensation, that the blood debt could be paid, a principle surely carried over from Cherokee private law.

Whether the Cherokees had a law of commutation for the blood price, a system of recompense which allayed the avenging clan's duty of retaliation and released the manslayer from liability, is a question of much importance, as there is no better test for measuring the sophistication of a primitive legal system than rules governing compensation for homicide. Talionic justice was by no means an institution of uniform application. Some societies never advanced beyond simple retaliation, a life for a life, which the avenging clan had to exact if it wished to perform its duty. Others reached the stage of organized machinery, sometimes voluntary, sometimes compulsory, which brought together the manslayer and his victim's kin to discuss whether an accommodation could be reached. Procedure varied: it might be the intercession of a priest, the smoking of a peace pipe, or merely a meeting on some neutral ground, which permitted time for reflection and for adjustment. It might be limited to accidental homicide, or it might be mandatory even for deliberate killing. Still other societies—those which we might think of as "advancing" toward civilized law, such as the late Anglo-Saxons—had a predetermined schedule of value: so much for life of an earl, so much for the life of a ceorl, so much for the right arm of a thegn, so much for the right arm of a slave, and so on. If the sum were offered, it had to be accepted, and the blood feud ended. Retaliation could occur only after the folk peace had failed to produce compensation.

Among the American Indians, apparently no nation had progressed as far as had the Anglo-Saxons. The Iroquois League, which faced a particularly difficult problem since it was composed of five nations as well as clans within those nations,* convened a council immediately after any homicide in order to forestall retaliatory killing, and had a prefixed value of ten strings of wampum on a human life, which may or may not have been mandatory upon the victim's relatives.[23]

> It was decreed that the murderer or his kin or family must offer to pay the bereaved family not only for the dead person, but also for the life of the murderer who by his sinister act had forfeited his life to them, and that therefore 20 strings of wampum should be the legal tender to the bereaved family for the settlement of the homicide of a co-tribesman.[24]

The Hurons, another important branch of the Iroquoian linguistic family along with the Cherokees and the Five Nations, may have had a system of compulsory compensation as early as the seventeenth century, although the evidence is not clear. They set a definite price on a man's life—perhaps the value of a new beaver robe measured in terms of the number of presents offered, 30 or 60—and interestingly, they required

---

* To illustrate the need for mediation among the Five Nations let us suppose a case in which Odiserundy, a Mohawk of the Turtle clan kills both Onasakenrat, a non-Turtle Mohawk, and Ochionaugueras, an Onondaga. The members of Onasakenrat's clan, acting under Mohawk law, have the right to retaliate against Odiserundy, or in lieu of Odiserundy presumably against any Turtle clansman. The members of Ochionagueras' clan, on the other hand, have the duty by Onondaga law to avenge his death but their vengeance would not be privileged under Mohawk law. Moreover, if Odiserundy were not available for vengeance, Ochionagueras' relatives would hold any Mohawk liable for the blood debt, not just a member of the Turtle clan. Perhaps it would not matter whether they killed Odiserundy himself, another Turtle, or a non-Turtle Mohawk. The Mohawks would retaliate and war could result, disrupting the League. The law of compulsory compensation, therefore, was one of the most important factors unifying the Iroquois and contributed greatly to the success of their alliance.

more presents when the victims were either women (on the theory that their physical weakness deserved greater protection from the law), or aliens because, as the Hurons explained, if strangers in their nation were not secure, killings "would be continuous, trade would be ruined, and war would easily occur with foreign nations." [25]

Perhaps it is misleading to speak of compulsory compensation as a necessary step in a nation's "progress" from a primitive legal system, in which a personal blood debt is regulated by permissive violence, to a civilized law of the king's peace, or folk peace, which defines intentional homicide as murder and punishes it as a crime against the state. To the historian, the substitution of mandatory commutation for blind retaliation is not progress but change. From the viewpoint of a lawyer, however, it is possible to speak of progress. And from the lawyer's viewpoint it is reasonable to ask how far the Cherokees had progressed, in comparison to other civilizations. The supposition might be that they had advanced quite far. After all, they were destined to be the first Indian nation to adopt a law of murder enforced by state-imposed sanctions, and they apparently made the shift from the old to the new with the least difficulty and with little organized resistence. But appearances may be deceptive. Logic tells us the Cherokees should have been well along, or so drastic a step as the abolition of the blood feud decreed in 1810 would have been accompanied by confusion and dissension. Yet all our evidence tends to show that the Cherokees had not "progressed" from the most rudimentary law of blood, the automatic right of retaliation, even by the end of the eighteenth century. We may be certain they had not progressed as far as the Anglo-Saxons. The "state" did not impose a mandatory compensation upon the avenging clan. Nor had they progressed as far as the Iroquois or the Hurons. A fixed price had not been set on a man's life, nor have we any reason for believing that before taking retaliation, the avenging clan had to permit the manslayer's clan time to make an offer of settlement. Indeed, we have only the slightest evidence for saying the Cherokees allowed compensation in mitigation of liability at all.

Slight as the evidence is, it leads to but one conclusion. Some systems of compensation did exist. It was not mandatory and it was not fixed. It was at most a legal possibility, an option which the avenging clan could select in lieu of the blood debt. This fact is the very least we might expect, for in small societies surrounded by enemies and dependent on every man for survival, indemnities in goods or services would naturally be preferred by the people as a whole to taking the life of the manslayer.[26] From the reasonableness of this supposition, mighty theories could be spun—yet even ethnologists, generalizers by profession, have been cautious when converting theory into law. James Mooney tells us flatly that in cases of homicide, "the tears of the bereaved relatives" could be wiped away with presents.[27] He cites no proof, however, and may be drawing analogies from the prayers offered by hunters to the spirits of slain animals, or from the laws of other Indian nations. William Harlen Gilbert is just as positive, although he hedges his assertion by limiting compensation to cases of accidental death where "there was some doubt as to the purposeful intent of the injury." [28] Again we are furnished no evidence, yet there is reason to believe Gilbert is correct. It would be bold to claim that commutation payments were used to mitigate liability for intentional killing, bolder still to claim that they could not have been used. Admitting we cannot answer whether compensation was restricted to homicide without malice or was possible even in premeditated murder, we are still left with the lawyer's questions. Under what circumstances was commutation legally acceptable? How much payment was expected? To whom was it offered? By whom was it paid?

We cannot answer these questions with certainty, but we can make some conjectures based on what little direct evidence we have available. Most of what we know comes from international law, more particularly from that special area of international law governing the settlement of homicides committed by British subjects. Under Cherokee law, if a white man killed a Cherokee, the victim's clan retaliated by killing the manslayer or, if the manslayer had fled, by killing some other white man of the same nationality as the manslayer. In cases involving British killers, this law was in theory suspended by various treaties providing for punishment of the manslayer by South Carolina justice. In practice colonial officials seldom punished a white man for killing a Cherokee, either because the manslayer fled, or the killing was excusable under common law, or as a matter of policy (usually that public opinion would not support prosecution). Whatever the reason, the British almost always insisted that the Cherokees accept payment in lieu of blood; payment, as one Carolina official said, "Sufficient to hide the bones of the dead Men and wipe away the Tears from the eyes of their friends." [29]

We cannot say whether the British believed compensation in satisfaction for homicide was an indigenous Cherokee institution, whether they thought it a law common to all American Indians, or whether they were forcing the Cherokees to accept a method of satisfaction that they had adopted from other nations, such as the Iroquois. The best guess is that the British made mandatory a system of blood money which was voluntary under

Cherokee law, and that they extended it to intentional as well as to accidental homicide.

The important lesson revealed by recorded negotiations between the British and the Cherokees for compensation is that both parties understood that payment was to be made not to the nation or to the town in which the victim had lived, but to his "relations." [30] When the Cock Eye Warrior forgave Samuel Benn for killing his "cousin," he asked for presents to wipe away the tears of the dead man's relations.

> He says Samuel Ben is living, he may for any Hurt that shall happen to him though his Relation is dead, but he expects that he will make Retalliation to him and the others of his Relations which he says to send sum of saverell Sorts of Goods over to them will make Satisfaction for the Loss of the Dead.[31]

We may suppose that "relations" meant the victim's clan, more likely his close clan kin, and did not include his father, son, or widow. The widow's loss may not have been forgotten, but in strict legal theory it is difficult to believe she had an enforceable claim on any part of the compensation. If so, settlement may have been more easily obtained. Bronislaw Malinowski, writing of natives in the Trobriand Archipelago—a people who admittedly had a patrilocal system of marriage—made the interesting discovery that "the father or the widow is often far more keen on avenging the murdered one's death than his kinsmen are." The clan kin were more often willing to accept compensation.[32]

Granting the argument that compensation was paid to the victim's clan (more likely to his clan kin), we are faced with the further question of how much was paid. Even assuming a set price, which is highly improbable, we cannot believe that it remained constant, but fluctuated according to victim, manslayer, and circumstance. In 1768 the British agreed to pay the relatives of nine Cherokees slain by frontiersmen the value in goods of 500 dressed deer skins for each victim.[33] Since it has been reliably estimated that the average Cherokee hunter killed about 60 pounds of dressed deer skins a year,[34] and that a good skin weighed around three pounds when fully trimmed of hoofs, tail, and snout, this would mean that the British offered, and the Cherokees accepted the value of 25 years of labor by one Cherokee hunter as the price for a human life. Even if the British meant each skin to be weighed at one pound the compensation would have equaled the product of about eight and one-third years' work per Cherokee, surely higher than any Cherokee, without the help of his close-clan kin, could have paid.

The next question is, who decided to accept blood money in lieu of retaliation? We may assume that it was the clan of the victim, but was it the clan as a group or one member of the clan? James Adair, the trader-historian who probably witnessed several settlements of homicide during his years in the Cherokee nation, tells us that it was the "eldest" who permitted a killing to be redeemed by accepting "the price of blood to wipe away its stains and dry up the tears of the rest of the nearest kindred of the deceased." [35] We can only suppose that Adair meant the person we have previously identified as the avenger of blood, that is, the eldest maternal avuncular relative or the eldest brother, and not a headman of the victim's clan. Even so, the decision does not seem to have been binding upon the remainder of the clan kin, for Adair adds that compensation was "generally productive of future ills; either when they are drinking spirituous liquors, or dancing their enthusiastic war dances, a tomohawk is likely to be sunk into the head of some of his [the manslayer's] relasions." [36] If the assertion is correct—and it is no means certain that Adair was speaking of the Cherokees alone, rather than the southern Indians in general—we must conclude that the payment of compensation in mitigation of liability for homicide was a ticklish institution among the Cherokees, not yet accorded the stability of an accepted legal custom.

There is only one reported case which gives us a hint that the clan may have acted as a unit when deciding whether to accept compensation in satisfaction of the blood debt. Sometime prior to the Revolutionary War, Sam Dent, a British trader living in Chota, so severely beat and mistreated his pregnant Cherokee wife that she died. Hearing that the woman's clan was about to retaliate, Dent fled to Augusta, Georgia, where he purchased a female black slave named Molly. A petition filed at the October 1833 term of the Cherokee Supreme Court states that Dent later returned to the nation with Molly

> and did offer her to the Clans Remuneration for the wrongs he had done, a Town Council & Talk was then had at chota old Town on Tennessee River and the said Female was Then and and [sic] there Received by [the] Clan and by the authorities agreeable to the indian Law and usage in the place of the murdered wife of the Said Sam Dent.[37]

The gist of the petition is clear—Molly was received as a free member of the clan in place of Dent's wife, not as a slave—but the reference to the town council and the "authorties" is vague. As retaliation against Dent, a white man, might have involved the nation in a war with the British colonies, it is possible that public opinion was employed to persuade the dead woman's clan to accept Molly in satisfaction of the blood debt, and therefore this case would not be typical of Cherokee law. Moreover, the petition was written about half a century after the event, at a time when the Cherokee had replaced the code of vengeance with institutions copied from American criminal law, and the petitioners may not have fully understood the procedure they described. Yet the case does present the possibility that the clan, or a section of the clan, functioned as a legal unit when confronted by a manslayer's offer of compensation, and that the decision to accept commutation or to exact retaliation was arrived at by a corporate consensus. Surely this procedure seems logical when we recall James Adair's assertion that close-clan kin sometimes took vengeance on the manslayer of his relatives even after the "eldest" had agreed to commutation. If a manslayer wished to insure his own safety and to make the contract of satisfaction binding on all members of the avenging clan, what would he do but approach them through the medium of a town council at which all the close-clan kin of his victim were present?

The case of Sam Dent would seem to answer our final question—who paid the compensation to the avenging clan? Dent himself purchased Molly, brought her to Chota, and offered her to his wife's clan. But Dent was not a Cherokee and his case was not typical. Where the commutation price was either a scalp or an enemy prisoner, it is likely that the Cherokee manslayer paid it himself. During 1758, for example, a crisis arose when South Carolina demanded that the nation deliver for punishment several Cherokees accused of killing white men. Since the suspected manslayers were unwilling to go voluntarily to Charles Town, and there was no way to force them to surrender, the Cherokee negotiators proposed to the British "That every murderer should be sent out in quest of a French scalp or prisoner for every white man they had killed." [38] It is significant that the Cherokees did not suggest the British be satisfied with French scalps or prisoners taken by any Cherokee warrior. The idea seems to have been that each manslayer redeem his own blood debt. We might hesitate to make much of this example were it not supported by a tradition associated with the "city of refuge," an institution mitigating liability for homicide and discussed below. According to this tradition, a manslayer who fled to Chota was immune from the avenger of blood on the condition "that he should go out to battle in the next war that might occur; in which if he killed or took prisoner an enemy, he was free." [39]

We cannot suppose the Cherokees overlooked the fact that, in legal theory, all members of the manslayer's clan were equally liable for the blood debt. Thus it is reasonable to believe that each had an interest in seeing that compensation was paid, although it would be too great a conjecture to suggest that the Cherokees thought this placed a legal responsibility on the members of the manslayer's clan to contribute a share of the compensation. Undoubtedly matters were often adjusted this way, if adjusted at all, when goods rather than scalps and prisoners were paid. Brothers and uncles quite naturally came to the aid of their kinsman. Surely they were expected to, although we cannot say that there was a formula of contribution, or even that social disgrace visited a man who reneged on his duty.

There is a hint, a dubious hint, but still a hint that the relatives of a manslayer were not only expected to subscribe a share of the commutation, but also to initiate the bargaining. It is contained in a unique letter describing Cherokee customs, written in 1761 by a South Carolina physician named William Fyffe to his brother back in Scotland. Fyffe apparently had no association with the Cherokees, and many of his observations about Cherokee law are pure fabrication, yet he does state enough correct legal principles to give the impression that he gathered some facts from men experienced in Cherokee affairs. One of the rules which he lays down as positive (though with what accuracy we cannot guess) relates to compensation. Following a killing, Fyffe writes, the manslayer usually flees leaving his relatives (whom Fyffe calls "friends") the duty of dealing with the avenging clan.

> [H]is Friends goes to the Friends of the Deceased & makes them Presents if the Presents are accepted the Difference is made up. The Person delivering the Presents says with this string of wampum I remove the Hatchet from the Wound with this Belt I stop the Blood & as if He were curing the dead Person, but if the Presents are rejected the offender must be very cautious or He'll be murder'd.[40]

The question may not be whether Fyffe was stating a correct legal principle. Indeed, the whole matter of compensation in mitigation of liability for homicide may be one area where law, custom, and social convention are intermingled. The practice of paying blood money does not seem to have been institutionalized among the Cherokees to the extent that we can speak of rules, duties, or definite procedure. There are only two doctrines which we can state with confidence: that the Cherokees permitted compensation, and that compensation was voluntary. Should we attempt to go further, we would run the risk of borrowing alien concepts to fill gaps left in the evidence which the Cherokees themselves may not have filled.

There are two further institutions utilized by the Cherokees to mitigate liability for homicide that must be mentioned. Comment on one of these, "the setoff," must be deferred until the discussion of international law, for all our examples of its application are found in situations involving foreign nations. To describe it briefly, the Indian nations often maintained peace by setting off murders, letting unrelated killings serve as commutation one for the other. Suppose, for example, that in June a Cherokee killed a Catawba, and that in July a Catawba killed a Cherokee. Either homicide could touch off a Cherokee-Catawba war, or at least a round of retaliatory killings. If the Catawbas had not taken satisfaction by the time word was received of the July homicide, emissaries of the two nations might adjust matters by agreeing to set off the two killings; to regard them both as things done in the dark which should be buried forever, and not allow their memory to stain the path of peace or to rust the chain of friendship.

It is arguable, indeed likely, that interclan homicides could be adjusted in the same manner, all interested parties agreeable. Should two Cherokee clans owe each other one life apiece, they might agree on a setoff and wipe clean the mutual debt. We may even imagine that in such an event the clans, for once, had the means to enforce their collective agreement—for if the brother of one victim objected to the setoff and threatened to carry out his right of retaliation, he might be persuaded to desist by the counter-threat that the other clan would select him as the object of vengeance for the blood debt still owed to it. Perhaps we would be wiser if we associated the setoff not with mitigation of liability but with the privilege of retaliation, which permitted the clan of a homicide victim to take the manslayer's life without fear of further retaliation. Again we may be postulating questions too sophisticated for the primitive legal mind, nonetheless our understanding of the law of homicide would be enhanced if we knew which notion was stronger in Cherokee jurisprudence: the notion that retaliation by the avenger of blood was a privileged killing, or the notion that the death of the manslayer was not avenged by his clan because it was set off by the original homicide.

The final institution used by the Cherokees to mitigate liability for homicide must be approached with extreme hesitation, for it has been enshrouded in myth and made the subject of much unhistorical supposition. It is the "city of refuge," which in legal theory provided the manslayer with a place of sanctuary where he was immune from retaliation by the avenger of blood.

Traditions regarding the city of refuge must be accepted cautiously, for no other institution has been seized with such eagerness by investigators intent on proving that the American Indians were descendants of the ancient Jews, the Ten Lost Tribes of Israel.[41] As early as 1723, a would-be missionary to the Cherokees, Francis Varnod, reported that the Cherokees were divided into ten tribes, their language was very guttural, and they spoke a few Hebrew or Phoenician words.[42] Later students of Cherokee customs became so obsessed by this theory that it clouded their search for evidence and even determined not only what they looked for, but what they found. Such seems especially true of the John Howard Payne manuscripts, which were gathered during the 1830s by Payne (who hoped to write a history of the Cherokee nation), and which are one of the chief sources of material for Cherokee ethnology. One of Payne's informants believed that the Jews had had four cities of refuge offering sanctuary to manslayers,[43] and his investigation of Cherokee law was rewarded when he discovered that the Cherokees had four.[44] The informant also believed that if a Jewish manslayer escaped to within the sight of a high priest, the avenger of blood could not retaliate—[45] and by a happy chance he learned that if a Cherokee manslayer contrived "to get within the *Ookah's* view, that person was absolved from stain among the rest and could not be punished." [46] Finally the informant believed that should a Jewish manslayer reach the door of any priest's house, he was legally entitled to refuge,[47] and thus we are not surprised that he found that among the Cherokees every priest's dooryard was holy ground, on which the avenger of blood could not touch the manslayer.[48]

The Payne manuscripts provide a remarkably detailed account of the law of refuge and seem to be the chief authority upon which are based most ethnological and historical accounts of that law. In brief, the law of refuge may be summarized as follows: The houses and dooryards of Cherokee priests or "white chiefs" and the "four white towns" of refuge, were holy grounds upon which no blood could be shed, nor could blood be shed before the eyes of the "white chief." [49] Should a manslayer flee the scene of the homicide and reach any of these places of sanctuary before being overtaken, the avenger of blood must not touch him. The priest or "white chief" blew his trumpet or sent a messenger to call the town into council either to declare the manslayer acquitted,[50] or to determine his "guilt" by ordering "a regular trial" [51] before "a regular court," [52] or by having the two interested clans conduct "a hearing" and arrange a settlement.[53] If the manslayer was judged "guilty," the avenger of blood still could not harm him; rather, he was placed in a situation where he would be killed, usually in the front ranks during the next battle.[54] If not killed, he might exonerate himself by slaying or capturing an enemy, renewing "the attempt in each succeeding war, till he was successful, or till he died; never being free from the city of refuge on any other condition." [55]

We cannot dismiss this version of Cherokee law out of hand for, confused as it is, it has been accepted by too many scholars. We can only ask for sustaining proof, for evidence gathered from primary sources, and this is not available. Everything we know points against its authenticity, for it is too elaborate, too institutionalized to fit consistently with substantiated principles of Cherokee jurisprudence. The Cherokees had no "regular courts," and there is no evidence that they possessed adjudicatory machinery for determining "guilt," or even a legal theory defining it. If they had the machinery for judging the "guilt" of a manslayer who had reached the city of refuge, we might suppose they had the machinery for judging any manslayer's "guilt," and hence would have needed neither places of sanctuary nor the blood feud itself.

There is but one fact of which we may be reasonably certain—there was a city of refuge in Cherokee law. It is with much less certainty that we can discuss what refuge meant in terms of rights and duties, or how sanctuary was granted, maintained, and lifted.

It seems likely that the Cherokees had but one city of refuge, Chota, the "beloved town" of the nation and the principal village of the Overhills. James Adair, who was firmly convinced that the Cherokees were transplanted Jews, states flatly that Chota was "their only town of refuge," [56] and most reliable evidence tends to agree.[57] Adair tells the tale of a trader who killed a Cherokee in defense of his property, took refuge in Chota, and was told he was safe as long as he remained in town.[58] It is interesting, however, that in the one recorded instance of this type, the case of Samuel Benn who in 1757 killed in self-defense the Cherokee near Natalee, the trader made his escape from Natalee not to Chota, but to Fort Loudoun a few miles from Chota. He went to Chota only at the insistence of the fort's commander, who sent along the physician to point out Benn's injuries to Old Hop, perhaps as proof Benn had acted in self defense. It may be that Benn knew he was safe in Chota, but the only reassuring word mentioned in extant documents is that Old Hop promised he would be safe because the towns of Chota and Tennessee would protect him. No reference was made to legal sanctuary.[59]

A white man who apparently was told that he was in a city of refuge, however, was William Richardson, a missionary, who was in Chota two years after the Benn affair and who may have gotten his information from white men, as he could not understand Cherokee. Richardson, a timorous man, was thoroughly frightened in January, 1759, when word reached Chota that a Cherokee had been killed by a white man while the two were hunting together. The relatives of the victim, he learned, were determined to have satisfaction, but were apparently being urged by the Overhill headmen not to kill the first white man they encountered. Richardson noted in his diary "that it is dangerous to stir abroad at present," yet he was safe as long as he remained in Chota "for it is a beloved Town, a City of Refuge & no blood is to be shed in it nor any put to death in it." [60] That at the first opportunity Richardson fled Chota and the nation, not stopping until safely in British jurisdiction, may be less a commentary on the strength of Cherokee law than on his confidence in what he was told.

There was a tradition among the Cherokee of the late nineteenth century that the city of refuge gave the manslayer sanctuary until the annual greencorn dance, when a general amnesty was proclaimed and he was "at liberty to leave, his life being no longer in danger." [61] We must doubt the authenticity of this legend as again there is no evidence to substantiate it. An earlier generation of Cherokees seems to have believed that a manslayer was free only if he killed or captured an enemy in battle,[62] and James Adair, our one contemporary authority, implies that a manslayer could never leave Chota in safety unless he paid commutation to wipe away the tears of the victim's relatives.[63] Perhaps the later Cherokees were influenced by the biblical rule that the Jewish manslayer was immune if he stayed in the city of refuge until the high priest died,[64] or perhaps they borrowed a Creek tradition granting immunity to an adulterer (though not a manslayer) who escaped his pursuers until the annual *Boos-Ke-Tau* festival.[65]

We cannot even be certain who could claim sanctuary in the city of refuge. Again, later tradition is in conflict with contemporary evidence, for in the nineteenth century it was believed that only a manslayer who had killed accidentally was safe—[66] but James Adair insisted that Chota protected even "a wilful murtherer." [67] Nineteenth-century investigators, seeking parallels to biblical times,[68] tell us that foreigners and prisoners of war were as safe in the city of refuge as were Cherokees,[69] which may have been true of Hebrew law but was not true of Cherokee law. Indeed, we may wonder whether Chota offered much safety even for the Cherokee manslayer. While he probably could not be driven out, once he reached the town limits, the people of Chota were known to raise a guard and prevent a manslayer from entering their town.[70] And even though eighteenth-century white men believed that a prisoner of war could be executed only if he was taken to another town,[71] the Cherokees themselves seem to have been unfamiliar with such a rule for they not only killed captives in Chota, they also tortured them there.[72]

We must not forget that if a manslayer did reach Chota, he became safe from the avenger of blood—but his clan kin did not. Unless a settlement was quickly arranged, a manslayer could not remain in Chota without sacrificing a relative, perhaps his brother, to pay the blood price for which he was responsible. Thus, we are told, the manslayer would leave Chota and take the penalty himself.[73] This supposition is, in fact, one of the best arguments we have for believing that the Cherokees did indeed have a law of compensation. For if the avenger of blood was able to persuade the average manslayer to surrender by threatening his clan kin, what would have been the purpose of the city of refuge but to offer a short period when passions might cool, and a settlement be negotiated?

The answer to this question may well expose the true legal function of the city of refuge: not so much as a place of sanctuary as a place of respite —a place where a manslayer could bargain for his life, and an avenger of blood might be led to consider the elements of the homicide, to balance accident against malice and vengeance against compensation.

CHAPTER TWELVE

A SOCIAL PERMISSIVENESS

—THE LAW OF MARRIAGE

Matrimony is the most difficult Cherokee institution to place within a definable framework of law. We know matrimony existed in some form yet it appears amorphous, straining to the limit our tolerance with comparative jurisprudence. We have already seen that the basic function of clanship, in addition to avenging homicide, was regulating marriage, but this discovery tells us more about our law than about Cherokee law. The question may be raised whether the average Cherokee, had he been asked, would have said the clan structure existed to regulate marriage rather than to prevent incest. Indeed, we may even wonder if he would have recognized matrimony as a legally viable institution.

Early travelers to the nation assumed that matrimony among the Cherokees resembled the European marriage, and were primarily interested in recording the wedding ceremony. We might be grateful for their efforts, had not each reported something different. One account has the groom sending the bride "a ham of venison in pledge of ample food supply," she in return giving him "an ear of corn in pledge of tending the fields and winning bread." [1] According to a second version, the young man cut some wood and laid it at the girl's door; if she took the wood, made a fire, and cooked him food, the marriage was "confirmed." [2] A nineteenth-century missionary reported still a third ceremony, the exchange of clothes and goods between the groom and the bride's brother. If the brother put on the clothes, the girl was apparently married.[3] A fourth ceremony has the groom approaching the bride's mother, and if she consented, "the bridegroom without much further conference with the bride, was then told where she lay, and thenceforward admitted to her bed." [4]

If we should think these four accounts of the Cherokee wedding confusing, we need not try to disentangle them. They merely prove that when our early informants on Cherokee law looked hard enough, they could find what was not there. Better had they not made the effort. "There is no kind of rites or ceremonies at marriage," a British army officer wrote in 1761, "courtship and all being . . . concluded in half an hour, without any other celebrations, and it is as little binding as ceremonious." [5]

All notions of betrothal and contract in the Cherokee law of marriage must also be dismissed. Nineteenth-century missionaries who report that consent by both sets of parents was legally necessary,[6] or that a girl could not reject a suitor selected by her parents,[7] or that a purchase price was paid,[8] are reporting evidence presupposed rather than observed. Had third parties contracted, it would have been the two clans;[9] fathers who had no rights to enforce would not have been consulted.[10] But we must not think of "contract." Cherokee marriage was not binding on either husband or wife, and to imagine that a girl could be compelled to wed ignores the fact that no relative—neither her mother, her uncles, nor her brothers—exercised compulsory authority over her. The only suggestion that third-party "consent" was necessary comes from a vague myth, "The Man Who Married the Thunder's Sister." But the consent sought was the Thunder's, not the consent of a mortal man.[11]

Perhaps it is misleading to use the common-law definition of contract, as the Cherokees could have had rules of their own. But the fact remains that there was no enforcibility, no elements of *causa,* and no consideration. The bride did not become a member of her husband's clan, nor did he gain any rights over her or her property. When she became a mother, his clan had no interest in her children, and if she became a widow, she looked for support to her brothers—not her brothers-in-law. She was never under the guardianship of her husband's family or her husband's clan, nor did she receive from them either protection or care.

The husband received even less from marriage; the children were not his, they belonged to his wife's clan. Cohabitation may have offered some consideration, but not coition for that was available without marriage; it was freely bestowed by the Cherokee female, as there were no legal (and apparently no social) restraints on fornication or adultery.[12] We cannot say the Cherokee woman lacked virtue; perhaps the girl who found it possible to refuse her favors to the fewest men was accounted the most virtuous. We can only say that premarital chastity was exceedingly unusual,[13] and connubial probity less than the social norm.

It is almost a universal rule that among primitive people adultery is a civil wrong, punishable by some authority—the husband, the wife's clan, or society itself [14]—and so it is not surprising to find historians writing that adultery was a Cherokee crime.[15] Every scrap of available evidence, however, indicates that such was not the case. "The Cheerakee," James Adair wrote with some disgust, "are an exception to all civilized or savage nations, in having no laws against adultery; they have been a considerable while under petticoat-government, and allow their women full liberty to plant their brows with horns as oft as they please, without fear of punishment." [16]

Adair was not only revealing his predilections as a civilized man by defining adultery as a female offense, but he was showing his predilections, as a subject of the common law, by condemning female equality. This was a discrimination no Cherokee would have made, to say that women were given license because they behaved the same as men. While permitting themselves sexual freedom, Cherokee men, to be consistent with Cherokee political theory, had to permit as much to Cherokee women. The promiscuity of their women may have caused Cherokee men to be held in contempt by the British, but there was at least one time that it earned them the goodwill of some Indian neighbors. During 1750, Governor James Glen sent William Sludders into the Creek nation to scout prospects for ending a Creek-Cherokee war. Sludders found support among all ages of Creeks. The older men favored peace because Cherokee warriors had closed the trade path to Charles Town, cutting off supplies and improvising Creek towns. The reasons of the younger men were less patriotic. "[T]here is no [Cherokee] Law for medling with their women," Sludders explained, "which fills all the Young Fellows Hearts with Joy." [17] Since Sludders mentions Cherokee law, and not the charms or the greater permissiveness of Cherokee females as the attraction, it seems that the young bucks had either fornication or adultery on their minds. There is some evidence that fornication was proscribed in the Creek nation,[18] but the best view is that Creek women, before marriage, had freedom to dispose of their bodies as they pleased,[19] while adultery was a serious crime, visiting upon the adulteress a frightful punishment [20] and perhaps even exposing the adulterer to the risk of having his ears cut off.[21] The Cherokee law which filled the hearts of young Creeks with joy at the thought of peace, therefore, was probably the law of adultery, as it meant more women were available in the Cherokee nation than at home. The fact that the neighboring Creeks believed Cherokee female license extended even to foreigners is our most convincing evidence that the Cherokees had no laws prohibiting adultery among their wives.

To find that the Cherokees, almost alone among their neighbors,[22] saw no legal wrong in adultery does not mean they thought it a social right, or that they let it pass unnoticed. For the sake of presents or merely to be hospitable, Cherokee husbands might look the other way when their wives lay with white traders,[23] but when there were no presents or no consent they often reacted as if they had been personally aggrieved, sometimes complaining and on rare occasions threatening reprisal.[24] There is even a possibility that some Cherokees disapproved of adultery on moral principles. Cherokee "priests," for example, were said by Adair to attribute the smallpox epidemic that killed nearly half the nation in 1738 to the rise of adultery among young couples, blaming the pestilence on "their unlawful copulation in the night dews." [25] Adair also reports an instance where a wife was punished for adultery, though oddly by her husband's male clan kin.

> [O]nce in my time a number of warriors, belonging to the family of the husband of the adulteress, revenged the injury committed by her, in her own way; for they said, as she loved a great many men, instead of a husband, justice told them to gratify her longing desire —wherefore, by the information of their spies, they followed her into the woods a little way from the town, (as decency required) and then stretched her on the ground, with her hands tied to a stake, and her feet also extended, where upwards to fifty of them lay with her, having a blanket for a covering.[26]

That one adulteress received a talionic meed in such decisive numbers indicates that adultery could bring shame to the husband and create animosity in society. Thus, we may imagine that on occasion adultery, at least if publicly flaunted, could lead to private confrontations capable of producing bloodshed. Should this occur, homicide—not adultery—was the offense which the law considered, and even *flagrante delicto,* while it may have mitigated the liability, did not make the homicide privileged. An absconding wife and her philanderer could be pursued only with great risk, not merely because the killing of either would invoke the blood price, but also because the wife had a legal right to leave her husband whenever she chose. Cherokee women, Adair complained, were "like the Amazons, they divorce their fighting bed-fellows at their pleasure," [27] a fact which Adair used to prove the inferiority of Cherokee men, but which better demonstrates the equality of Cherokee women.

Again we encounter a rule of law which appears too absolute, but again there is no doubt of its validity. Both husband and wife were free to separate at any time [28]—additional evidence, should we need it, that marriage was not a binding contract. We may suspect that a Cherokee man divorced his wife by leaving her house, and that a Cherokee woman divorced her husband by putting him out or by taking another man in his place. There was no need for a formal declaration, certainly no need for a hearing; the clan structure settled problems which otherwise might arise. The children went with the mother and her brothers assumed the task of protection, a task they were performing anyway, as well as the duty of support.[29] Property was not jointly owned, and so there were no squabbles on that score. Indeed, clan law not only made divorce a simple matter but the ease of divorce helped to simplify clan law. Since a wife could freely leave her husband, Cherokee jurisprudence never had to develop customs defining the rights of brothers to protect their sisters from marital cruelty and abuse, a cause of tension and conflict which troubled Indian nations with more stringent restraints on divorce.[30]

It may be wondered whether "divorce" is an accurate term. "Abandonment" in the common-law sense of removal with an intention never to return is more literal, if it is understood that a Cherokee spouse abandoned no legal duties or responsibilities. Whatever obligation a husband had to support his wife was paid for by admission to the connubial bed on a day-to-day basis, terminating when he or she "abandoned" the bed.

No matter whether we call it divorce, abandonment, or something else, it was the marital norm, the prevailing custom among the primitive Cherokees.[31] Monogamous marriages were of remarkably short duration,[32] many men and women shifted spouses as frequently as three or four times a year.[33] Christian Priber, a French or German idealist who found sanctuary in the nation during the late 1730s, drafted an abortive scheme for a Cherokee republic which included the constitutional right of women "to change husbands every day." [34] Undoubtedly Priber was emphasizing the equality of women, not codifying current marital practice, but there is little doubt he was not proposing new law. Women had the liberty of switching husbands daily, if "husband" is the right word, and some were so inconstant that one early nineteenth-century visitor to the nation concluded that Cherokee females were little better than whores.[35]

While objecting that judgments of comparative morality tell us little, it must be admitted that observable conduct such as promiscuous sexual practices provide obstacles when reconstructing certain Cherokee marital institutions, a reason why there is controversy concerning the existence of polygamy. Some historians, for example, have concluded that the high divorce rate, with its continual rearrangement of spouses, gave the Cherokees the mere aspect of practicing polygamy when in fact they were shifting through a succession of monogamous marriages.[36] In later times, amateur anthropologists among Christian missionaries conveniently discovered that as the sun had but one spouse, the moon, so the ancient Cherokees supposed it improper for a man to have more than one wife,[37] and Cherokee tradition manufactured the myth that polygamy was unknown until introduced by white men.[38] All such arguments are without foundation in fact. Polyandry and polygyny were legal, and may even have been common during certain periods and in certain places, such as frontier towns where women outnumbered men as much as ten to one.[39]

The best proof that polygamy was an established practice among the Cherokees is furnished by subsequent legislation. In 1819, at a time when polygamy was reported prevalent among the Cherokee West living in Arkansas,[40] the Cherokees east of the Mississippi passed a law which provided: "it shall not be lawful for any white man to have more than one wife, and it is also recommended that all others should also have but one wife hereafter." [41] There is an air of compromise surrounding this statute, and within six years it was repealed. In its place the legislators enacted a blanket prohibition covering Cherokee citizens as well as white noncitizens, making it unlawful in the future "for any person or persons whatsoever, to have more than one wife." [42] Although the authorities seem to have made an effort to enforce the statute, indicting at least one man for bigamy,[43] a visitor in 1845 reported that polygamy was occasionally practiced, "and the ruder classes among them all, I believe, sometimes still take any number of wives, and divorce them, at pleasure." [44] As this assertion was made at a time when some Cherokees were terminating monogamous marriages by petitioning the two houses of the national legislature for private bills of divorcements,[45] we may suppose that despite enacted law, the more conservative elements in the population were retaining the old marital customs—testimony to the strength polygamy had once enjoyed.

It is not surprising to find polygamy more common among the conservatives than among progressive Cherokees during the 1840s for a conservative may best be described as one who clung to the clan system, and to a large extent it had been the clan system which made polygamy, especially polyandry, possible during primitive times. The law of clan relationship, with its emphasis on the consanguineous to the virtual exclusion of the connubial family, permitted a woman to mate with any number of men without raising the social and legal problems of parentage which might arise in other societies. Even if the mother was a common prostitute, it would not matter how many men lived with her, as all children belonged to her clan and the identity of each father was immaterial. It is quite possible, as one English visitor wrote in 1817, that some children "never know their fathers with certainty, nor fathers their children," [46] although it must be questioned whether this was ever the general rule. After all, numerous references to "sons" in extant records, as well as the appearance of fathers seeking satisfaction for sons killed by white men or by foreign Indians, implies that some Cherokees (at least the headmen in contact with the British) knew their male children and took an interest in them. Moreover, it is said to have been "usual" for a Cherokee man in advanced age to adopt the name of his son,[47] and as this practice probably prevailed more among the rank and file than among headmen, who had fewer motivations for identifying with another person, we may assume that many of the average Cherokees also knew their children and looked upon their sons either with a sense of pride or as a source of strength.

We must accept the conclusions that polygamy was legally permissible in the Cherokee nation, and that polyandry was as viable an institution as polygyny, yet we may doubt if either were widespread. It is a general rule that monogamy is the usual practice, even in societies which have no restraints on plural marriages,[48] and historians agree that the Cherokees form no exception. The reasons given are social and economic: the monogamous pull of matrilocal residence (which made polygyny difficult except with women of the same family)[49] and the expense of maintaining several households, which was both beyond the financial means of the average hunter, and also unnecessary as the labor of a second wife was seldom needed even for the task of skin dressing.[50] A sounder explanation is that those very legal institutions of unrestricted divorce and sexual license which made polygamy possible also rendered it unnecessary for either a man or a woman to enter into multiple marital relationships, rather than a series of successive alliances. Matrilocal residence may have been a factor weighing against the prevalence of polyandrous unions, if the Cherokees possessed social mores regarding privacy and jealousy similar to western man. The economic argument that the average Cherokee husband could afford not more than one wife, however, is convincing only if the husband was required to support his wife.

We might guess that the Cherokee husband was not required to support his wife, but that he usually did. To suggest he was free to stop furnishing her with goods any time he pleased is another way of describing the ease of divorce. Having ruled out the possibility of legal responsibility, we would be faced with the question whether marital support was arranged by private agreement or regulated by social custom, were it not for a further consideration—the duty of the wife's brother. Did the brother of a married woman have the obligation to support his sister? We may suspect he had some obligations for after all he was her protector and the guardian of her children, and their relationship was the closest in society. A Creek man used the word "home" only to describe the house of his sister,[51] and a Cherokee may have thought in similar terms; yet we may doubt whether he regarded it as the sole place for his meals or the sole depository of his hunting. Whatever his obligations, they cannot be translated into legal concepts, and the only safe conclusion we can draw is to suggest that the economic burden falling upon husbands was not a factor necessarily limiting polygyny, while reliance upon brothers could have encouraged polyandry.

All authorities agree that residence among the Cherokees was matrilocal,[52] yet there is no evidence of a matrilineal extended family in the sense of married sisters living together, or of married daughters building houses adjacent to their mother's.[53] Matrilocality is the least we might expect of their concept of marriage, and were we to insist upon English words, it might be better to think of a man's "family" as his close-clan kin and to refer to his wife and children as his "household." [54] The household may look like the European family and socially it may have been similar, especially when a man married a woman in a distant town, and matrilocal residence removed him physically from his close-clan kin. Yet the "household" was not his family as the word is defined in English, it did not command his primary loyalty; rather, it was a separate, distinct unit of society which stirred emotions and loyalties all its own. When a man did leave his "family" to live with a tramontane woman, he may have found himself connected with a section of his clan containing no genealogically recognizable clan kin.[55] For such a Cherokee his household could substitute for his family, the legal incidents of two blending one into the other, increasing ties to the first group, decreasing them to the second. Thus, the importance of the household as the center of a man's attention could depend on social factors other than affection for his wife, or the endurance of their marriage. The proximity of sisters, and isolation within an ulterior clan section, may have affected a Cherokee's personal attitude toward his household but never altered the mutual rights and obligations arising within the family.

From what we have seen of the Cherokee institution of matrimony, it follows that the Cherokees had no custom requiring sexual abstinence by widows during a specified mourning period, as did their neighbors the Creeks and Chickasaws,[56] no law of *deuterogamy,* no principles of *levirate* or of *sororate.*[57] Sororal polygyny may have been socially convenient,[58] but was neither required nor restricted by law.

Indeed, the lack of rules requiring conformity to any matrimonial standard raises the question whether we can speak of a Cherokee law of marriage. Does the word "marriage" have meaning in a Cherokee context or would it be better to use some other term such as "cohabitation" or "consortium"? Lewis H. Morgan, the scholar of consanguinity and affinity systems, has seriously contended that the American Indian in his native state was below the passion of love, a fact Morgan thought sufficiently proven by the custom of divorcing females without telling them.[59] Some white men who knew or worked among the Cherokees came to the same conclusion, especially after discovering that they had no word for "husband" or "wife," that a woman referred to her husband as "he who lives with me" or "my supporter," [60] an expression "equally applicable to three or four men at the same time." [61] Thus an anonymous visitor to the nation in 1817 wrote:

> There is no synonym in their language for love, and there cannot be imagined a more contemptuous profanation of its most sacred rites, than the uniform habits of the nation in both sexes. The relation of husband and wife, consecrated in our minds by habitual reverence, hallowed by the most imposing solemnities of religion,—the holy and mysterious tie which unites in indissoluble union the moral elements of the world, which sustains and invigorates our tenderest sympathies and most exalted sentiments—cannot be said to exist at all among the Cherokees.[62]

Evidence gathered from rules of law, from observations regarding the structure of social institutions, and from etymology may tend to support arguments of comparative morality when one uses the standards of his own society as the norm, but they furnish an uncertain paradigm for fathoming the degree of conjugal amorousness or the adhesiveness of hymeneal loyalty characteristic of a particular people. That the Cherokees thought little of adultery does not mean they thought little of their spouses. That divorce was unrestricted does not prove that successive monogamous unions or multiple polygamous arrangements lacked the emotional ties which western man identifies with familial love. "No people are more warm in their affection than the Cherokees," a friend of the nation wrote in 1818,[63] and most contemporaries agreed.[64] Three generations earlier, a British army officer deplored the looseness of Cherokee marital bonds. "Notwithstanding this," he concluded, "the Indian women gave lately a proof of fidelity, not to be equalled by politer ladies, bound by all the sacred ties of marriage." [65] He might have added that many Cherokee husbands were as devoted to their women, a case in point being a headman named Moytoy who in 1730 spurned the political prestige associated with a trip to England and a meeting with King George, saying he did not wish to leave his sick wife.[66] Some historians even argue that most marriages were "long sustained" and "stable" rather than merely companionate.[67]

Rules of law, therefore—at least when received only from the perspective of jurisprudence without the tempering evidence of human conduct—may provide misleading impressions concerning the durability of an institution such as marriage, or the conjugal values of a primitive people. The Cherokee law of matrimony probably proves less concerning loose family ties or permissive adultery, than it does about the consistency to which the Cherokees carried constitutional doctrines governing the freedom of personal choice and the equality of women.

CHAPTER THIRTEEN

AN OCCUPANT'S TENURE

—THE LAW OF PROPERTY

Perhaps it is wrong to stress female equality. No Cherokee would have done so. Yet the equal status of Cherokee women is worth our attention, if for no other reason than the contrast it offers between Cherokee primitive law and the law of eighteenth-century Europe. The point is best illustrated by noting that Cherokee married women could own property over which their husbands had no control, and that most European married women could not. But before asking how we know that Cherokee married women owned separate property, or which spouse owned which type of property, there is a preliminary question to be settled. Can we speak of "ownership" and "property" in Cherokee law?

The question might not have to be posed were it not for the contention, which once had some currency, that the Cherokee hunting economy was too marginal to support a system of private property, that goods had to be divided in common, and that by the law of necessity no one could be permitted exclusive rights of possession, even to the fruits of his own labor.[1] Tenable as this argument may seem when we think of the customs of primitive people in general and of the scarcity of Cherokee goods in particular, it is, William Bartram pointed out, "too vague and general," [2] as it confuses economic conditions and social attitudes with legal actualities.

Admittedly, there are many Cherokee concepts of property which must escape us. Most elusive of all are the rules that governed the sharing of property. Like most savages the Cherokees, at least during the eighteenth century, were generous, sharing whatever they possessed with an open-handedness that amazed Europeans, leading some visitors to believe they had stumbled upon an idyllic state of primitive communism. James Adair is but one of several white men to remark on Indian hospitality. "As they were neither able nor desirous to obtain any thing more than a bare support of life," he wrote of the southern nations, "they could not credit their neighbours beyond a morsel of food, and that they liberally gave, whenever they called." [3] Yet to acknowledge generosity in sharing private property does not tell us whether the custom of hospitality placed limits on ownership rights. To learn the answer, we would have to know under what circumstances a guest or stranger, for example, could appropriate food unbidden.[4] When Cherokee warriors were given presents by the British for service in wartime, they were known to share their gifts with the colonial soldiers and other Indians who had taken part in the fight.[5] Yet colonial soldiers, when on a joint expedition, complained that the Cherokees expected to share their food, that when a white man shot a deer, the Cherokees without asking would walk up to the carcass and cut off a portion for their own use.[6] The Cherokees may have assumed permission. More likely they were exercising a customary right of sharing which we would not dare define.

Perhaps the right to appropriate certain property was more a shared notion concerning natural law than one of positive law; at least such is implied by an apologue the Cherokees employed in later years to illustrate American greed for land.

> The Cherokees used to affirm that they had often come upon the panther, in the woods, lying at rest between two deer that he had just taken and killed. And they invidiously compared him, when thus situated, to the white man, who, they said, instead of being satisfied, like the Indian, with enough for his present necessities, and no more, was covetously eager, as the cougar, to pile around him far more property and substance than it was possible for him to consume upon himself.[7]

While it will not do to over-analyze this tale, other evidence indicates that the Cherokees used it to make a natural-law argument, not to explain positive law. Their law of property recognized that the panther, the hunter, had vested rights of dominion over his kill, their ideal was that the owner share his wealth. Greed was a social sin, but private ownership was the legal norm. Adair made this point clear when he noted that the southern Indians thought white men "covetous," since they did not share their possessions with poorer relatives. The Indians, he said, "wish some of their honest warriors to have these things, as they would know how to use them right, without placing their happiness, or merit, in keeping them, which would be of great service to the poor, by diffusing them with a liberal hand." [8] Adair is stressing the ideal conduct of the "honest warrior," an ideal which he and other authorities tell us was often practiced. But even if the ideal was not the exception, it still proves the rule that there were poor people among the southern Indians; good evidence that property was not communistic. Certainly among the Cherokees distribution of wealth was uneven, and the ideal of sharing often had to be channelled through organized charity, especially during times of famine and war, as in 1761 when a British army officer witnessed a method of sharing which had become both a ritual and a form of entertainment.

> When any of their people are hungry, as they term it, or in distress, orders are issued out by the headmen for a war-dance, at which all the fighting men and warriors assemble; but here, contrary to all their other dances, one only dances at a time, who, after hopping and capering for near a minute, with a tommahawke in his hand, gives a small hoop, at which signal the music stops till he relates the manner of taking his first scalp, and concludes his narration, by throwing on a large skin spread for that purpose, a string of wampum, piece of plate, wire, paint, lead, or any thing he can most conveniently spare; after which the music strikes up, and he proceeds in the same manner through all his warlike actions: then another takes his place, and the ceremony lasts till all the warriors and fighting men have related their exploits. The stock thus raised, after paying the musicians, is divided among the poor.[9]

Property as a social concept need not be associated with psychological factors such as covetousness or avarice, just as property as a legal concept need not depend upon judicial machinery to define its limits or to ensure its enjoyments. The fact that wealth was not evenly distributed, and therefore that there were poor Cherokees, indicates that property was privately owned, no matter what privileges the right of necessity may have given a starving or impoverished man to help himself to his neighbors' excess goods. We may be reasonably certain that the Cherokees recognized private property as a bundle of rights and duties, the rights being rights of ownership vested in individuals, and the duties, shared concepts governing obligations to be generous. We can never be certain whether they thought of ownership as a relationship between individuals, or merely as a fact established by possession. The records are clear, for example, that guns were privately owned. Many Cherokees are reported to have lost "my" gun and to have begged the British for another. The warrior who traveled to Charles Town and asked the governor for a gun, knew the gift he received was his personal property. Whether by custom he was required to share its use with his brother or his wife's brother we cannot say, although it does not matter so far as the concept of personal ownership is concerned. What rights others possessed in the gun—even if equal to his—existed by virtue of their relationship to him. Communal property was not a factor. The gun which the warrior brought back from Charles Town did not belong to the nation or to his clan, it belonged to him, and rights were derived from him.

Undoubtedly, notions such as need or fair use entered into the definition of private property as much as did possession, purchase, capture, trover, prescription, abandonment, or inheritance, yet property could be personal and rights in property could be individually owned. When Cherokees were robbed of deerskins by white men, they complained as individuals and asked that restitution be paid to them as individuals, rather than to the nation.[10] They did the same when robbed by fellow Cherokees. In 1758, for example, the Little Carpenter and a band of followers, waiting at Keowee for supplies from Charles Town, helped themselves to the corn of the Great Tistoe and the Wolf, both of whom were away at war. When the Great Tistoe and the Wolf returned to Keowee, the Little Carpenter had departed and as he had gone to fight for the British, they thought the British should pay for the corn, at a price they fixed by demanding a double bounty on the scalps they brought home.[11] The British army officer who paid the bounty implied to his superiors that he thought the corn was private property—and it is certain that scalps were, for the Cherokees often bargained for higher prices by pleading that as individuals they could not afford to leave their families and fight the French unless paid more for the scalps which they sold.

Cherokee concepts of private rights in property were well enough entrenched to include the goods of non-Cherokees in the nation, even white traders whom the Cherokees sometimes robbed, though usually with a sense of guilt. A revealing incident occurred during 1752. The provincial government of Georgia, hoping to take over the Cherokee trade by driving out traders from other colonies, commissioned a trader named Brown to arrest Daniel Murphy, who had settled with his slaves at Aurora intending to open a Virginia trade. When Brown and his men got to Aurora and found Murphy had returned to Virginia for supplies, they attempted to seize his slaves, but the Cherokees "said it was like stealing and would not let him have them till Murphy should return Home, and then it was what he would with them." [12]

The British in turn recognized private Cherokee ownership, dealing with the Indians as individuals whenever they possessed something worth buying, such as deerskins, scalps, or Frenchmen. South Carolina, for example, in mortal fear of what could happen if the black and Indians ever joined forces, at times made it a matter of national policy to keep black slaves out of the nations.[13] Yet, when a Cherokee acquired black slaves, Charles Town authorities did not talk of purchasing them from national headmen or from the town to which they were taken. It was the owner who was approached, for they were his property, and the British assumed they had to be bought from him by private bargain and not by putting pressure on the nation.[14]

Slaves, scalps, and corn sold to the British may prove that the Cherokees practiced private enterprise when dealing with white men, but tell us little about their domestic law. For that we must look to their own institutions, not an easy task as the variety of goods over which Cherokee individuals could enjoy rights of ownership was limited to items available in their mountain homeland—a severe limitation which, along with primitive Cherokee generosity, hampered the growth of property law.[15] One item of some value was clothing for women at least possessed fine garments for ceremonial if not for every-day use,[16] and it must be concluded that they "belonged" to the wearer, whether man, woman, or child. Guns which were introduced between 1673 and 1700 were owned by the men.[17] A revealing light would be shed on Cherokee law were we to discover which spouse "owned" which species of goods. It has been stated as a general rule among the American Indians that the implements for cultivating the soil, preparing food, dressing skins, and making clothes were the property of the wife—[18] but would that we knew who owned the pelts and skins. It might be objected that this question could not have troubled the Cherokees, but when we consider the high incidence of divorce, we cannot be sure. Before the advent of the white traders, we suspect the wife was owner, that pelts were trapped and skins were hunted for her handiwork. Once skins became the chief item of subsistence, however, it is difficult to believe that a departing husband cheerfully left them behind. It is significant that Cherokee men furnished much of the work of skin-dressing; unlike farming, it was not exclusively a female chore.[19] Labor may have been the criteria, and a plausible rule in cases of controversy is that what a person earned by his industry or skill belonged to him.[20]

Aside from guns, the most important form of property which the Cherokees acquired from the Europeans was the hog, and it is possible that in times of peace nearly every household possessed swine.[21] Cattle were less numerous (probably because the Cherokees did not have the competence to fence their corn fields, and because herding cattle with enemies lurking in the woods was dangerous), but the claim that there were no cattle in the nation until after the American Revolution is not true.[22] In 1757 Judd's Friend not only owned but rented two milch cows to the Carolina garrison at Fort Loudoun,[23] an indication that a primitive Cherokee could contemplate enjoying benefits from ownership, while relinquishing immediate possession.

Horses, on the other hand, were kept in "immense droves" as wild and free as the deer;[24] not however in large private herds, for as late as 1775, probably no Cherokee owned more than twelve.[25] Even headmen often had no more than one—for example, the Warrior of Tommothy who in 1754 told Governor Glen that he was late arriving at a council because "a white Man living in the Town of Sticoe had his Horse and detained him from him, and he could not borrow another." [26]

The nucleated-settlement pattern, the availability of water transportation, and mountainous terrain giving the horse marginal value in warfare, together with a social system which did not base status on possession, explain why the accumulation of private herds did not become a source of economic competition among the Cherokees, as it would among the Plains Indians.[27] Yet the horse which a man owned was a highly-prized item not easily replaced. During the 1750s, a Cherokee headman complained that the traders were seizing horses to satisfy debts owed by men killed in war —horses which could "be of Service to the Living" [28]—and a Carolina agent stopping in the town of Ioree reported that "there was hardly a Day but some or other complained of white Men's stealing their Horses." [29]

The Cherokees also stole horses, usually from white people and usually to sell back to them, for horses were a major item of trade with the colonies.[30] So too was Cherokee bacon, which the British preferred to their own,[31] and other foodstuff grown during good years in surplus in the Cherokee country,[32] as well as a few crafted products like blankets [33] and clothesbaskets.[34]

As vending gives us our best clue to ownership among the Cherokees, the important point is not what was sold, but rather, who sold it. While living in the nation both Carolina traders and British troops, depending on the Cherokees for supplies,[35] knew where and from whom to buy. In 1756 Raymond Demere, in charge of constructing Fort Loudoun among the Overhills, reported that the Cherokees were "coming to us both by Land and Water with Eatables &c. to sell to the People which they do in such Numbers that this Place already begins to have the Appearance of a Market." [36] Demere probably intended only to describe the wealth of the Cherokee country, but his statement that as soon as he arrived in the nation, he found Indians anxious to sell farm products reveals as much about their commercial laws as about their economic condition. His dispatches to superiors in Charles Town make clear that he dealt with the Cherokees as individual vendors selling privately-owned property, and that most of the sellers were women. When hunting was poor, he was unable to find anyone who would sell him pork,[37] but the products which he and the white traders did buy, such as corn, chickens, wild fruit, and swine were sold by women.[38] The unmistakable conclusion is that the women, the ones who did the farm work, owned what they raised and could dispose of it as they pleased—evidence supporting the supposition that the product of labor belonged to the laborer.

Another conclusion seems even more certain: the Cherokees did not learn from Europeans the law of barter and sales. From antiquity they had been a trading people, dealing among themselves and with other Indian nations, exchanging the steatite deposits of their country and their skill at manufacturing fine pipes for seaboard goods and salt, an item they always had in short supply.[39] It is possible their economy even supported a professional class of traders, a fact which may explain why they so avidly accepted the white trader,[40] but also raises the question why they did not become middlemen, as did the Iroquois in the northern British colonies [41] and their own neighbors the Occaneechi.[42] In addition to native traders, the primitive Cherokees seem to have paid for the services of other specialists such as conjurers, eagle hunters, musicians, and perhaps myth tellers. Moreover, it is not impossible that on rare occasions they may have compensated these men in currency, for they understood the concept of negotiability. When William Byrd of Virginia sent the first white traders into the nation during 1691, he obtained wampum from New York to be used as the medium of exchange, a sensible move if then, as later, the Cherokees had the same word for "money" as for "beads." [43]

One negotiable product which Europeans certainly did not have to introduce to Cherokee law was the human being. The Cherokees bought, sold, and exchanged captives and scalps among themselves long before they encountered black slavery. As early as 1716, a Cherokee purchased from his captors a Frenchman taken in battle, paying "a gun, a white duffield matchcoat, two broadcloth matchcoats, a cutlash and some powder and paint." He then apparently gave the Frenchman to his sister as she took him to Charles Town and sold him to the British—turning a small profit for, in addition to being reimbursed in strouds for the value of the goods her brother had paid, she received "a suit of Calicoe Cloaths for herself and a suit of stuff and a hat for her son." [44] Throughout colonial history the British acted on the legal assumption that French captives, like Negroes, had to be bought from their "masters," not from village headmen.[45]

Human beings and scalps were, of course, personal property and in common law fall in a category different from real property. In English law there would be no need to distinguish between personal and real property, were it not for historical peculiarities arising from substantive and procedural aspects of the writ system.[46] So too, there would be no need to separate personal and real property in Cherokee primitive law, were it not for the misconceptions that have arisen regarding the manner in which American Indians held land. Rather than history, it is subsequent scholarship and subsequent Indian domestic law which separates real from personal property. The assumption has been that Indians held land in common, never in severalty, that they did not recognize individual rights even over an occupant's demesne. R. S. Cotterill, writing of the Five Civilized Nations during the era of their primitive law, summed up the common theory of landownership:

> The Indians did not have, and have never willingly accepted, any conception of private ownership of land. They insisted that the land belonged to the tribe as a whole and could not be engrossed by individuals, towns, or districts. Custom permitted or recognized the control of each town over the adjacent fields and over their annual allotment to families for cultivation. It permitted private

ownership of the crops raised by private effort subject to a reserve
for public use.[47]

This statement, at least when applied to the Cherokees, is based more
on nineteenth-century theory than on eighteenth-century fact. During the
nineteenth century, the Cherokees, while new-modeling most of their legal
doctrines along American patterns, eschewed the common law of real
property, and evolved a land law communal in principle but private in
practice. It was the theory, however, not the practice, which caught the
attention of white lawyers and of no other Cherokee legal institution was
so much made and so little understood. In general it was thought to be
communistic, and so it was described by one federal judge who, faced
with the task of defining it, held that the Cherokee doctrine of communal
property was a bundle of mutually-shared individual rights-in-common,
by which each Cherokee owned an equal part in the nation as a whole.

> The distinctive characteristic of communal property is that every mem-
> ber of the community is an owner of it as such. He does not take
> as heir, or purchaser, or grantee; if he dies his right of property
> does not descend; if he removes from the community it expires; if
> he wishes to dispose of it he has nothing which he can convey;
> and yet he has a right of property in the land as perfect as that of
> any other person; and his children after him will enjoy all that he
> enjoyed, not as heirs but as communal owners.[48]

As an outline of constitutional principles, this contemporary description of late nineteenth-century communal ownership is valid. As an explanation of Cherokee private-property law, implying that there were no
personally-owned rights to the soil, it is mere theory. Cherokee communal
property is no exception to the general rule that, when tested by the
norms of private law, communal property becomes merely an aggregate
of personal rights.[49]

During their later history, when the concept of communal property was
fundamental to their constitution and was cherished by their national
leaders, the Cherokees did not think of themselves as tenants-in-common.
The nation "owned" the lands, they "owned" rights in the nation,[50] but
as individuals they "owned" indefeasible rights to the improvements
which they made on the land they occupied, they merely could not alienate
the soil.[51] Thus, in 1881, Principal Chief Dennis W. Bushyhead, address-
ing himself to a hostile United States Congress, defended the concept of

communal property among the Cherokees by explaining its basic principle and its public policy.

> The statements made to you that we, or any of the Indians, are communists, and hold property in common, are entirely erroneous. No people are more jealous of the personal right to property than Indians. The improvements on farms may be, and often are, sold; they may descend in families for generations, and so long as occupied cannot be invaded, nor for two years after abandonment. These farms and lots are practically just as much the property of the individuals as yours are. He who does not wish to keep can sell to all lawful citizens. The only difference between your land system and ours is that the unoccupied surface of the earth is not a chattel to be sold and speculated in by men who do not use it.[52]

Borrowing common-law terms, we might say that the nineteenth-century Cherokee landowner held an occupancy estate in his demesne by communal tenure—"estate" referring to interests in the land, "tenure" to the right of holding the soil subordinate to the nation's title in fee simple.* The principle of Cherokee communal property, therefore, was occupancy, and the public policy supporting it, at least by the time Chief Bushyhead wrote, was prevention of monopoly.[54]

The historical difficulty with the public policy expressed by Principal Chief Bushyhead is that it was a recent, a polemical afterthought, formulated to justify communal property to the American government but unrelated to its origins or to the reasons why it first evolved. A different public policy underlay earlier Cherokee political theory—a public policy stated not only in the constitution and laws, but also in many of the deeds by which the nation conveyed to its citizens land in severalty, such as the following which was issued in 1857:

> To have and to hold the afore granted premises to the said F. H. Nash and his heirs, to his and their use forever; subject nevertheless, to the express condition of the law of the Cherokee Nation in this case made and provided, that this deed shall be deemed and held as an occupant title only to the premises above bargained and sold; and that the lot or land conveyed or intended to be conveyed by this deed, shall never be sold, assigned, or transferred from the

---

* The Cherokees, when removed to the Indian Territory, became one of the few Indian nations to hold their land under a patent in a fee simple granted by the United States government.[53]

possession of the said F. H. Nash, his heirs, executors or adminis-
trators, to any person or persons not citizens of the Cherokee Nation.
As otherwise this deed shall become null and void, and of no effect
or virtue in law.[55]

As this deed implies, the original public policy supporting the theory
of communal property was not to prevent monopoly among Cherokees,
but to prohibit alienation to non-Cherokees. This public policy is why the
Cherokees evolved a law of communal property. From the constitutional
rule that no landowner should sell to a foreigner, especially to a white or
black man of American citizenship, the Cherokees were led quite logically
to an estate in occupancy rather than fee simple. The fact that in later
years, under a radically different economy, the legal concept of occupancy
could be used to discourage speculation and proscribe monopoly was an
accident—convenient but unforeseen.

During the era of their primitive law, the Cherokee doctrine of communal property was both indigenous and latent. It was indigenous because
with a surplus of land, an incomplete notion of the law of inheritance,
and little incentive for accumulating possessions, the eighteenth-century
Cherokees practiced in economic fact what they would later turn into legal
theory. It was latent because until non-Cherokees sought to purchase
Cherokee land, the nation did not need the doctrine of communal property to prohibit the sale of rights in the soil to foreigners.[56] In point of
law, land among the primitive Cherokees was both communal and privately owned, and the most valuable parts seem to have been privately
owned.

The question of selling national lands became acute during the decades
just before and after the American Revolution, but the law governing
sales was as old as the national council. For a purchase to be valid the
consent of the entire nation was necessary.[57] Should South Carolina wish
to acquire a tract for a fort, or an agent for Josiah Wedgwood seek to dig
the fine white clay of the Cherokee country, it was the headmen meeting
in council and speaking for the nation in its corporate entity who made
the sale or granted permission.[58] In this sense and for this purpose only,
the land was communal, or to be more exact, was nationally owned. But
in Cherokee domestic law, the concept of communal property had little
importance, with one exception—the hunting grounds.

New dimensions regarding property seem to have been introduced to
Cherokee legal notions with the accentuation of a venatic economy after
the opening of the Carolina trade; property dimensions which taught them

to value their hunting grounds, that vast, unoccupied expanse of mountain ranges rising on all sides of their national homeland.[59] In international law, these property dimensions gave the Cherokees an economic motivation for claiming in sovereignty regions they had previously regarded only as marchlands for warfare. In domestic law, stress on pursuit of the deer caused them to recognize two types of property rights: the skins were individual property, and the hunting grounds communal. Of course there may have been no occasions in domestic law to notice the distinction, yet it was mutely acknowledged in international law after Carolinians began to stalk Cherokee hunting grounds. Asserting the new concept of sovereignty, the Cherokees viewed as illegal intruders the whites who came to hunt the deer, while those who came to trap beaver or kill buffalo were either ignored or treated as mere trespassers.[60]

The Cherokees had every reason to esteem their hunting grounds, for the great altitudes of their Appalachian highlands yielded the thickest, most valuable deerskins in the American south.[61] Perhaps the realization that they possessed a rich national asset first led the Cherokees to claim sovereignty to regions over which they could never hope to exercise exclusive domination—more than 40,000 square miles,[62] stretching far beyond their towns, from the back settlements of South Carolina to the Mississippi [63]—or, Governor James Glen wrote, "all the Lands on each Side down Tennessie River as far as Mississippi, and all from Tennessie to the Ohio or the fair River." [64] We may wonder if the Cherokees appreciated what they were claiming. We may wonder too whether competition for hunting grounds figured in warfare with other Indian nations. Historians disagree,[65] and the point must be deferred for further consideration with the law of war. However, it should at least be noted that the Cherokees claimed Middle Tennessee as national hunting grounds after they and the Chickasaws drove out the Shawnees in 1715,[66] and on at least two occasions, peace was established with neighbors by drawing a line between hunting grounds: with the Catawbas at a date in prehistory, when the line was drawn at a river,[67] and with the Creeks during 1751 when, as the Raven of Hywassee explained, "we have parted the Ground that we are to hunt in, on both sides." [68]

Whether the Cherokees "parted" their own national hunting grounds is doubtful, although the words of a treaty signed in July, 1777, imply that the Middle Settlements had separate hunting grounds from the Overhills. We cannot be certain what to make of this evidence; the best guess is that the treaty described vicinity rather than occupational proprietorship,[69] as every other bit of information indicates that no individual, clan, town, or region could claim exclusive rights in severalty or allotment to any hunting ground. The fruits of the hunt, on the other hand, belonged to the hunter. British traders competing for deerskins knew they were to be purchased from individual owners. The failure of some hunters to kill the number of deer necessary to redeem their credit while other Cherokees succeeded, is a fair indication that debts were personal and the catch private property. Thus the Cherokees combined in one sector of their economy aspects of both private and communal property, one governed by the natural law of labor, the other by the natural law of equal use, neither causing controversy nor requiring definition.

Despite the importance of hunting to the acculturation of Cherokee institutions, from the view point of the average Cherokee property-owner, hunting probably should not be emphasized. Before the Carolina trade began, the Cherokee economy was agricultural rather than venatic, town-centered rather than dispersed in hunting camps, and as this pattern of social life remained constant throughout the era of primitive law, the ownership of houses and planting fields surely played a greater role in the lives of the people than did ownership in common of the hunting grounds.

Cherokee town living was a defensive necessity and the houses, besides being "Muskett proof," [70] were substantial enough to gain the admiration of white men, including Lieutenant-Colonel James Grant who called them "neatly built" and regretted he was under orders to burn them during the War of 1760.[71] Although one historian's assertion that seventeenth-century Cherokee houses were "better than many white homes that today occupy their old lands" [72] is farfetched, the evidence furnished by William Bartram, an educated and observant eyewitness, is that the houses of some towns were not only adequately inhabitable but each had its own garden, orchard, hogpens, and hothouse.[73] Bartram visited the nation just before the outbreak of the American Revolution, yet his description probably reflects property conditions throughout the eighteenth century. Between 1700 and 1775, the average Cherokee's standard of living in terms of possessing goods of white manufacture undoubtedly improved, but the economy remained the same except for the emphasis on hunting as a method of obtaining purchasing power, the introduction of hogs, the cultivation of peach trees, and the universal adoption of British manufactured clothes.[74] Such items, especially if bought, would have reinforced the concept of ownership already present, they would not have required new law.

The important question is ownership of the houses. There are four possibilities as to how houses and town lots were owned: either by the nation as were the hunting grounds, by the towns themselves, by clan sections in each town, or by individual occupants. The possibility of national ownership is the easiest to eliminate, for no matter what theory may have later evolved regarding communal property, during primitive-law times the nation lacked constitutional machinery for enforcing public rights over houses and could have exercised no control which would have had practical meaning in terms of private law.

Leonard Bloom is the only student of Cherokee institutions to suggest that land was controlled by the town, an assertion which is rendered some-what nebulous, at least to a lawyer if not an anthropologist, by his further suggestion that ownership was a matter of occupancy.[75] Undoubtedly the town as a corporate unit "owned" the council house and the ball-play field; they were common property belonging equally to each resident. Yet there is only one recorded instance where Cherokees, speaking for a town, claimed the privilege of disposing part of their town's demesne. During 1767, Thomas Griffiths went to the Lower Cherokees and asked permission to dig clay for his principal, Josiah Wedgwood, an English manufacturer of china. A group of national headmen, including Overhills and Middle Cherokees who happened to be in council at the time, gave their consent. Acting on this authorization, Griffiths dug in an abandoned pit near the town of "Ayoree" *

> but on the fourth day, when the pitt was well cleand out, and the Clay appeared fine, to my great surprise, the Cheif men of Ayoree came and took me prisoner, telling me I was a Trespasser on these lands and that they had Rec'ed private instructions from Fort George,** not to suffer their pitt to be opened on any account; and as to any consent of the head men of the Nation, they minded not, nor would they let any clay be dug under five hundred weight of Leather for every Ton.[76]

This case is difficult to explain. It implies that the men of Ayoree, acting on behalf of the town council, were authorized to exercise proprietorship over vicinal lands, yet it could as easily have been a bold try for tribute, a testing of legal grounds in a new situation by a number of headmen, not sure of their authority but confident of their strength, to see if the town could turn a profit. Unhappily Griffiths does not tell how he settled the

* Ioree.
** Fort Prince George, the site of the council.

controversy. Perhaps he paid some price, for he made an arrangement and shook hands with the Ayoree men, who permitted him to take five tons of clay out of the region by pack animal.

Most of the few historians who have given thought to the question assume that houses and town lots were owned by the clans.[77] This conclusion is tenable, especially if we draw comparative analogies to some other civilizations, but were we to depend solely on Cherokee institutions, there is no supporting evidence. In later years no statutes will be passed ending clan ownership. The only comparable law is one making children the heirs of their fathers, presumably an attempt to abolish avuncular or clan-right succession.[78] Had the clans owned the land, we would expect that, like most changes ending ancient clan law, holding in severalty would have been introduced by legislation. Had sisters in earlier times tended to construct their houses in clusters, we might conclude that a degree of ownership by the clan in a corporate sense, while unproven, was not remote— but this would be as far as we could go. There is no record of clan buildings or clan property used by the clan for clan functions, and there is certainly no indication that the clan was constitutionally equipped to function as the owner of property. True, when a British trader wrote that he was buying a house from a Cherokee, he may have meant he was dealing with a clan agent; yet the records all imply that he thought he purchased from an individual owner.

When it is reported that a Cherokee owned a house, we cannot be sure whether the house is one we might call his wife's, or his sister's, or his alone. We can only assume that by his relationship to someone or by his own right, he possessed an occupancy of that house, and that his occupancy was exclusive enough that the British associated occupancy with ownership. During 1756, an advance party of eight colonial soldiers arrived in the town of Tomatly to begin construction of Fort Loudoun, and the Little Carpenter quartered them in what was described as his own house.[79] Two years later, it was reported that a soldier from the fort had robbed the Little Carpenter by breaking into "his house & is run off with Things of considerable value." [80] That same month William Richardson, a clergyman who hoped to preach among the Overhills, was at Fort Loudoun, planning to move to Chota "as soon as he can get a House." [81] Richardson does not tell us from whom he rented, only that he "hired a House for 4 months for 100 shillings Virginia money which I paid down for their custom is to receive paym't immediately." [82] We may never be certain, but by the tone of the records, by an analogy to the planting fields, and by subsequent legislation, it seems reasonable to conclude that Richardson paid his 100 shillings to an individual owner; that is, he rented the house from its occupant.

The best evidence that houses and town lots were privately owned is gathered from what we know of the planting fields—the most valuable form of real property in the nation. A Spanish Jesuit writing in the 1560s described the Cherokee fields as producing a life of "plenty," [83] and 200 years later, Lieutenant-General Oglethorpe said the Cherokees "are more accustom'd *to labour and live upon Corn,* then to procure their Sustenance by hunting." [84] Colonel Grant reported that when his army reduced 15 Cherokee towns during the War of 1760, it destroyed over 1,400 acres of crops, or about 100 acres per town.[85] So vital a part of the economy, upon which labor had to be invested on a daily basis, was certainly not left undefined, and when we examine the evidence it is difficult to conclude that it was not private property.

The only evidence tending to disprove individual ownership of the planting fields comes from suppositions concerning communal labor and a common storehouse. The argument is that the Cherokees worked their town fields by communistic labor and placed the harvest in a town granary. From these facts it is concluded that the lands themselves, as well as the crops, surely belonged to the town as public property.

The most convincing proof that the fields were held in common stems from evidence that the townspeople, called together by a headman each morning, worked in the fields as a unit.[86] But this custom need not prove communism. More likely it arose from the danger of enemies, the safety of numbers, and the desire of every Cherokee to be surrounded by neighbors while in the middle of his cornfield. James Adair thought the custom arose from the need to make the idle grow their share of crops, to force the delinquent and improvident into the fields so that they would perform some labor. As it cannot be believed that police coercion made the people come out, the force of which Adair speaks probably came from the desire not to be left alone in town, and the scorn of neighbors shaming them into work. Be that as it may, Adair makes clear he is speaking of a labor regulation, not a property law, for even as the people worked "in one body," "their fields are divided by proper marks, and their harvest is gathered separately." [87]

Oddly enough, William Bartram gives nearly the same interpretation, yet his use of the terms "King's Crib" and "Town Plantation" has been cited as the chief evidence to support the notion of common property.[88] But Bartram may have been describing only the Creeks when he wrote of the public granary or King's Crib,[89] and on inspection his "Town Plantation" becomes just an open field located near the town, where custom dictated common labor but not common ownership.

> This is their common plantation, and the whole town plant in one vast field together, but yet the part or share of every individual family or habitation, is separated from the next adjoining, by a narrow strip, or verge of grass, or any other natural or artificial boundary.
>
> In the spring, the ground being already prepared, on one and the same day, early in the morning, the whole town is summoned, by the sound of a conch shell, from the mouth of the overseer, to meet at the public square, whither the people repair with their hoes and axes, and from thence proceed to their plantation, where they begin to plant, not every one in his own little district, assigned and laid out, but the whole community united, begins on one certain part of the field, where they plant on until finished, and when their rising crops are ready for dressing, and cleansing, they proceed after the same order, and so on day after day, until the crop is laid by for ripening.[90]

While Bartram is writing primarily about the Creeks who seem to have had more authoritative town government than did the Cherokees, he makes two points which may bear on Cherokee law. First, fields were held in severalty and second, the crops were private property. Even the "King's Crib" was voluntary—"each family carries and deposits a certain quantity, according to his ability or inclination, or none at all if he so chooses." [91]

There are also indications in the records that the planting fields were private property. During 1725 while in Keowee, Colonel George Chicken was disturbed to discover that the headmen, in order to entertain his party, depended on voluntary contributions from the people. Chicken advised the headmen to build a store house, in which to keep public supplies gathered by taxing each family one bag or basket of corn. Although we may doubt if any action was taken, that Chicken should have made the proposal and the Cherokees are reported to have agreed, implies there was no customary common granary.[92] Thirty-five years later Colonel Grant wrote that when he invaded the nation he found "every where astonishing magazines of corn," [93] a reference apparently not to public but to the private storehouses, raised on posts and plastered with clay, in which Cherokee households kept their corn.[94]

We must not deceive ourselves into thinking that we can reconstruct all of the Cherokee law of property. A common fund of taught custom governing occupancy, possession, and borrowing was surely part of the legal consciousness of every Cherokee, too elusive for the historian's search and lost in undocumented time. Far too many matters which a Cherokee could have defined must now be left to conjecture, or passed over in ignorance. One guess which seems reasonable (but is merely a guess) is that ownership of a section in the planting field was an incident of tenure by occupancy in a town house. Based on arguments drawn from the practice of matrilocal residence, and the fact that women exercised the domain by providing most of the labor and by selling the produce, we may conclude that both house and field were usually "owned" by the women,[95] with perhaps a tendency toward matrilinear succession.[96] This supposition is reinforced by subsequent Cherokee legal history, for the Cherokees and the other southern nations never adopted common-law restraints upon the rights of married women to own separate property, preferring instead to retain their customary law. Separate-property rights of married women remained an absolute rule in the post-primitive economy despite the pressure of common-law analogy,* equally binding upon white men married to Cherokees as to Cherokees themselves,[98] and providing nineteenth-century American courts with a rare lesson in comparative jurisprudence [99] and American legislatures with a model for the emancipation of white married women.[100]

There are, to be sure, many rules of Cherokee property law, in addition to those governing occupancy, possession, and borrowing, which cannot now be reconstructed. We have no idea when questions of ownership could create conflict, except perhaps in situations of divorce or theft. Nor do we know whether the occupancy of a house could be abandoned or forfeited, and under what conditions. The extent and limits on property rights, as well as such concepts as mutual ownership, must remain as much of a mystery as the question whether some occupations enjoyed monopolistic privileges. It is certain, for example that the eagle hunter alone could hunt eagles—it was taboo for anyone else to do so—but was this privilege a property right giving him the legal means to prevent poaching? And did the myth tellers enjoy property rights in their stories? These are but some of the questions we cannot answer.

The best that can be hoped for is to know the outline of this law, not its details. In broad outline the Cherokee law of property, divided like the

---

* E.g., in 1843 the nation was constrained to enact that the property of one spouse could not be seized to satisfy the debts of the other spouse.[97]

common law into two parts though not between realty and personalty, provided that one type of ownership, in the hunting grounds, was communal, and another type, in house lots, planting fields, and chattels, was individual—and that occupancy of realty and possession of personalty were the tests that determined which Cherokee owned which item of property.

CHAPTER FOURTEEN

A NEPHEW'S RIGHT

—THE LAWS OF INHERITANCE AND STATUS

The conclusion that the Cherokees recognized individual rights of ownership in private property may not make it inevitable that they also had a system of inheritance, but the implication that they did is strong. Thus, it has been suggested that as their households were matrilocal, there may have been a tendency for land to pass in a matrilinear fashion.[1] This supposition is logical, yet must be approached with extreme caution as it assumes certain values regarding succession and heirship that the Cherokees may not have felt. Among the Eastern Band of Cherokees, during the earlier years of the twentieth century, the homestead often passed to the person who had "taken care" of the owner. As this person was often the youngest son, a general rule of ultimogeniture prevailed by custom. Yet anyone, even a stranger, could acquire tenure by "taking care" of the old occupants.[2] A right of succession based on a test such as service, rather than kinship, is a legal doctrine reasonably consistent with primitive Cherokee property law and suitable to the primitive Cherokee economy, but should we project it back to the eighteenth century, we must do so with reservations. One reservation is that "succession" may not be the proper concept. In a society of matrilocal residence, it was most likely one of the daughters, perhaps the youngest, who remained at home. Even if on the death of her mother she became the owner of the house and fields, it would be difficult to say that she was acknowledged the owner by reason of inheritance, or by reason of having "taken care" of her mother. Rather, the operative fact, had the Cherokees been capable of legal abstractions, might have been her occupancy of the premises. The other daughters or nieces, living away, probably had homes of their own and little interest in contesting title even had they thought their relationship to the deceased gave them rights despite her occupancy. A Cherokee might have said she was the owner for the same reason other people were owners of their houses, because she occupied it; she had an occupant's tenure and therefore it was hers.

The distinction may be fine, but it is a question of Cherokee attitudes. If they thought a daughter owned her dead mother's house because she remained in it, they did not think in terms of inheritance. The same was true if they thought a nephew owned the gun he had shared with a deceased uncle because he retained possession of it. Much property probably passed in this manner. Then, too, there must have been occasions when a man designated who should receive his gun after his death. Perhaps the word "inheritance" can be applied in such cases, though if a matter of personal choice, we cannot expect to find rules defining which relative was an "heir." Although it is unlikely that houses passed in any way but by right of occupancy, it is possible that for personalty the early Cherokees formulated no rules, even for those situations in which property was not shared and the deceased had designated no heir. We know that the Cherokees buried their dead,[3] and the earliest visitors to the nation furnish some evidence that personal possessions were buried with them [4]—a custom not to be confused with religious beliefs concerning necessities for the after life, as it often is secular in origin, intended to avoid controversy between potential heirs.[5] Eighteenth-century Englishmen report that this was the purpose of the Cherokee practice: to prevent avarice and hereditary acquisitions,[6] by removing any temptation of parents "to hoard up a Superfluity of *Arms and domestic Conveniences, their chief Treasures,* for their children." [7] Even if the existence of this custom is accepted, we still may doubt a nineteenth-century Cherokee informant who claimed his ancestors buried even the horses and guns of a deceased.[8] Such items were simply too valuable. As noted in the last chapter, during

1753 a Cherokee headman remonstrated to Governor James Glen against traders who satisfied Cherokee debts by seizing the horses of dead hunters. What "is left" by the deceased, he argued, "would be of Service to the Living." [9]

It is possible that the headman was speaking after the custom of interring a deceased's property had been abandoned, and no possessions, even those of slight value, were being buried. By the 1750s, according to James Adair, "the nearest of blood" was recognized as heir.[10] Adair believed British traders had persuaded the Cherokees to adopt filial succession,[11] a fact which, if true, would be the first legal manifestation of the acculturation process which lay ahead, and also one which cannot be substantiated from contemporary evidence.

Perhaps Adair did have proof that after the 1750s filiation was the Cherokee norm of succession, but a strong doubt is cast by the nation's first published statute enacted in 1808. This law dealt partly with inheritance and ordered the lighthorse* "to give their protection to children as heirs of their father's property, and to protect the widow's share whom he may have had children by or cohabited with, as his wife, at the time of his decease." [12] The statute may have codified current custom, but as it contains a mandate of force directing the lighthorse to protect the rights of children, it bears the earmarks of police regulation if not of innovative legislation. From whom were the children to be protected in most cases if not from the claims of their father's brothers or nephews, claims based on a custom other than lineal inheritance.

Because of the scarcity of direct evidence, dogmatic conclusions must be avoided but if the Cherokees did have a law of succession, considerations of their most basic social institutions—clan right, uncleship, and brotherhood—make it difficult to imagine that property not already shared by common possession or joint occupancy passed in any manner other than by fraternal, avuncular, or related rules, as was the general practice among the American Indians.[13]

It is not necessary to leave the Cherokee law of inheritance uncertain merely because there is no direct evidence how, and to whom, property passed. Succession to property is but one side of the law of inheritance. Succession to office is another. Logically, there should have been no rules governing succession to public office in the Cherokee nation because there were no offices to which an heir might succeed. Cherokee headmen were self-made, and to think of public office being handed down from genera-

* A troop of men who combined the functions of police and trial judge.

tion to generation, or from brother to brother, is to distort the Cherokee political system.[14] But the British did not know this. Thinking that the Cherokees had "kings" and "chiefs," they assumed that these kings and chiefs held their offices by virtue of hereditary right, and that on their deaths their heirs were crowned in their places. Thus South Carolina, believing that sons succeeded fathers, often upset the normal process of Cherokee politics by distributing to sons presents once given to fathers, expecting them to exercise the same influence their fathers had enjoyed.[15]

By misunderstanding the source of a headman's influence, and by assuming the universality of monarchial succession familiar to eighteenth-century Europe, the British introduced into Cherokee thinking the idea of both public office and hereditary right. In a sense, the force of British pressure upon Cherokee political institutions in this respect may be said to mark the start of the Cherokee acculturation of European concepts of government, just as the beginning of trade began their economic accultura-tion, and the introduction of canons of inheritance may possibly have begun their legal acculturation. It would be erroneous, however, to think that this process was swift or to believe, as some historians do, that the British succeeded in substituting patrilineal descent for matrilineal suc-cession during the eighteenth century.[16] Yet British pressure was great. As early as 1715, for example, Carolina's governor, apparently acting on the premise that sons succeeded fathers, asked "the Emperour of the Cheri-quois" to send his son to Charles Town for an education.[17] More likely than not, "the Emperour" had no idea what the governor had in mind. Thirty-three years later, the astute Raven of Hywassee understood at least part of what was involved for he wanted his son to meet the leaders of South Carolina in order, he said, to prepare the boy to succeed him.[18] It might be thought that the Raven hoped the boy would learn how to conduct himself with the British, and so is proof that the Cherokees had linear succession. Such an interpretation, however, is dubious. The Raven's desire that the boy be introduced to Charles Town leaders is evidence less that the Cherokees had adopted a law of hereditary right to office, than that the Raven appreciated that the concept of headmanship, as a political office, could be separated from the individual holding the office, and that he was aware of some of the incidents supporting that office. The Raven may have recognized that part of the influence he en-joyed in national politics and an important incident to his position as a Valley headman, was due to the presents he could distribute to his followers, presents received from British favoritism. He may have had in mind transferring this favoritism to his son, hoping that the son, by succeeding to his presents, would succeed to his influence and thus succeed to his "office." Political metamorphosis of this sort is hardly surprising. Over the years, Cherokee politics came more and more to depend on British favor and as the British believed the Cherokees had political offices, their belief was bound to have some effect. What is surprising (if we can trust the translator) is that the Raven of Hywassee spoke of his son, and not his nephew.

Comparisons drawn with other southern nations indicate the Raven of Hywassee would have conformed more to general Indian values, had he been sponsoring his nephew. Possibly among the Creeks and probably among the Chickasaws, a man's heirs were his sister's sons or his own brothers, not his own sons.[19] The Chickasaws are thought to have been the first to adopt a headchiefship,[20] an office which, R. S. Cotterill writes, "took the odd, un-Indian turn of becoming hereditary, being handed down, according to Indian custom, from ruler to brother or nephew." [21]

It is difficult to say positively that the Chickasaw principle of succession would have also been the Cherokee norm, had the Cherokees developed constitutional offices that were passed by hereditary right. Few Cherokees formulated ideas about succession, and hence few discussed the subject. One who did was Old Hop, in a conversation with John Stuart during 1756, just a year or two after he had become, in the eyes of the British, the nation's leading headman. Stuart reports that Old Hop wanted one of two men, the Great Warrior or the Great Warrior's brother, to be thought of as his potential successor. In other words, after he died, the British should deal with one of them as they were then dealing with him. Referring by name to two of his own nephews, and also mentioning his own "sons," Old Hop said he could not "tell how they may turn out, but he knows the others." [22] Whether Stuart asked about the sons, and whether Old Hop would have considered them had he not been speaking to a white man, is something we will never know. What we do know is that he had at least one "son," [23] but whether one or several, none of his sons ever became significant in the affairs of the nation. It was Old Hop's nephews who sat with him in the Chota town council, it was his nephews who carried his talks to the British and the French, and it was especially one nephew, the brilliant Little Carpenter, who made his talks "good talks," contributing as much to Old Hop's success as a headman as did Old Hop himself.

Willenawah and Standing Turkey were also Old Hop's nephews and these four men—Old Hop, the Little Carpenter, Willenawah, and Standing Turkey—constituted a majority of the seven headmen whom the

British believed dominated Overhill politics during the latter half of the 1750s.[24] Two of the remaining three were the Great Warrior and the Chota King.* Why Old Hop thought of sponsoring two non-clan kin ahead of his closest relatives is a mystery. One possible explanation is political expediency. The British did not fully trust the Little Carpenter, and Old Hop, knowing his words would not make much difference anyway, may have been talking just to please Charles Town. Jealousy is a second explanation. The British believed the Little Carpenter wanted to succeed Old Hop without waiting for his death,[25] and Old Hop may have thought the same. The important point is that Old Hop was undercutting either the Little Carpenter or Standing Turkey, not his own sons. When Old Hop died, Standing Turkey, with the apparent support of the Little Carpenter, succeeded to his uncle's influence, frustrating the ambitions of the Great Warrior.

There are two conclusions that can be drawn from this evidence. First, the fact that Old Hop, perhaps asked by John Stuart who would take his place after his death, could give no certain answer and only suggest candidates, indicates that the Cherokees during the 1750s, having no offices to which to succeed, had no definite rules regarding succession. Second, the fact that Standing Turkey did succeed Old Hop indicates the opportunities of a nephew to "inherit" his uncle's influence. Persons close to the seat of influence often enjoy its benefits, and in Cherokee society no one was closer to a headman than his brothers and nephews. If we think of Standing Turkey as having "succeeded" Old Hop, we must attribute his selection more to politics than to law. He was acknowledged headman of Chota (possibly as a compromise between the Little Carpenter and the Great Warrior) partly because he had been associated with Old Hop, and it is difficult to doubt that one important reason why Standing Turkey had been associated with Old Hop is that he was Old Hop's nephew.

Perhaps it is possible to say that Standing Turkey's case demonstrates a vague sense of nephew-right. But this right was not absolute; it was qualified by the fact that a nephew's continued influence depended not on being his uncle's heir, but on his own merit and ability to survive the machinations of Cherokee politics. While we must not discount affiliation completely,[26] and admitting that the Cherokees had no doctrine of hereditary right,[27] it may be asserted that there was an inheritance of influence from maternal uncle to sister's son primarily because political association—

_____

* The Great Warrior's brother.

an association which the social realities of clan relationship may have forced on a nephew—made inheritance possible.

There is no better word than "tendency" to describe uncle-nephew succession and, if accepted, the remarkable fact that during the late 1750s, most of the leaders among the Overhills were close-kin may be easily understood. Two clans alone furnished at least six of the seven "greatest men," and each man was fraternally or avuncularly related to at least one other of the six. As we know that Old Hop was the uncle of three of them, we can be sure he and they belonged to the same clan for the term "uncle" was applied only to a clan kin; a father's brother was not an "uncle." The Great Warrior and the Chota King were brothers,* [28] and as the Little Carpenter once spoke of an unidentified Cherokee as a "Relation" of the Great Warrior and not his own relation,[30] we may conclude that the Great Warrior and his brother belonged to a different clan than Old Hop and his nephews.

One troublesome question remains. Can the fact that two of the seven Cherokee clans furnished most of the leadership of the Overhills at a time when the Overhills were the leaders of the nation be attributed solely to Cherokee politics, or did these clans enjoy special prestige and even certain privileges giving their members rank or status above those of the other five? If so, Cherokee equality was not as perfect as we have been led to believe. James Mooney asserted that Cherokee clans were as equal as Cherokee individuals, that no family had a right to power,[31] but at least one historian, Henry Thompson Malone, has concluded that the Wolf clan was more important than the other clans,[32] a fact which could explain the ascendency of Old Hop and his three nephews. We are told that Nancy Ward was a Wolf.[33] As Nancy Ward is believed to be the daughter of the Little Carpenter's sister [34] and therefore a member of the same clan as he, it follows that the Little Carpenter, Old Hop, Willenawah, and Standing Turkey were also Wolfs. Aside from the political prominence of certain Wolfs, the chief evidence supporting Malone's contention is a chance remark by François André Michaux, a visitor to the nation in 1802, who said that "among the Creeks and Cherokees there exists a superior class to the common of the nation." [35] Michaux does not explain what he means, but the context in which his words appear implies strongly that he was speak-

---

* As cousins called one another "brother," we cannot be certain they were blood brothers, but British records imply they were. Historians disagree whether Willenawah was the Little Carpenter's "cousin" or "brother." [29]

ing of the large percentage of half-bloods who then dominated Cherokee economic life. The very idea of political rank or privileged status is so contrary to the general trend of American Indian constitutional norms that the burden should be on those making the assertion. A few tribes did have an aristocracy of birth, for example, the Kiowa and the remarkable Natchez,[36] but most nations practiced perfect political as well as social equality—even the Iroquois League whose war culture one might expect to have been based on rank.[37]

Had the Cherokees less than perfect legal equality, had they a hierarchy of privilege, it would have been reflected in the law of homicide. Yet we encounter no substantial evidence that the lives of some men were worth more than others, or that a manslayer might escape vengeance if he belonged to an important clan and his victim was a member of a less significant clan.[38] It is true that on one occasion when a headman while in liquor killed a white packhorseman, "a silly drunken Fellow," and the British demanded his arrest, the Cherokees protested "that there was no Equality betwixt so great a Man as he, and the Man he had killed." This argument, however, seems to have been little more than a plea for forgiveness, not a legal defense recognized in Cherokee domestic law. Satisfaction was rendered; the manslayer was executed by "one of his own Relations." [39]

It is also true that some nineteenth-century Cherokees believed their ancestors once weighed the comparative worth of manslayers and victims. As the *Cherokee Phoenix* explained, "If the murderer (this however is known only by tradition) was not as respectable as the murdered, his relative, or a man of his clan of a more respectable standing was liable to suffer." [40] This statement has the coloring of nineteenth-century theorizing rather than eighteenth-century reality, and its notions are the reverse of those applied in our one known example—the case of James Vann in which the manslayer persuaded the avenging clan to select Vann as the object of vengeance on the grounds Vann was insignificant, not that he was respectable.[41] Nevertheless, the rule, if true, does not imply status by virtue of clan membership, but status by virtue of individual merit. It is a social status, not a legal status, and does not alter the general principles of Cherokee homicide law. The avengers of blood, who have the free choice of selecting the sacrifice from the clan of the manslayer, are said by this rule to make the selection according to the social status of the victim. The manslayer is not said to have a legal status giving him the right to provide a substitute, should the avengers decide to kill him.

Finally we must disregard the arguments of historians that it was impossible for the Cherokees to satisfy British demands for vengeance when the manslayer "belonged to a strong clan," but easier when he "was an unimportant member of a weaker clan." [42] It is not surprising that on one occasion the headmen, including the Little Carpenter, told the British they could not effect the arrest and surrender of a manslayer belonging to the Great Warrior's clan, or that the British thought the Great Warrior was shielding the manslayer. This problem resulted from deficiencies inherent in Cherokee law—the lack of any coercive force vested in the headmen, and the fact that homicide was a matter of private right—not because some clans were stronger than others. Of course the Great Warrior may have been instrumental in protecting the manslayer. Every Cherokee had a duty to defend fellow clan members from unlawful harm, at least by avenging them, and the arrest of the manslayer would have been unlawful harm as it was not authorized by Cherokee custom. The Great Warrior's role was more effective than that of most men for the same reasons: that in any political situation his role was likely to be more effective, not because his clan was immune from vengeance.

It must be concluded that there is no evidence proving a system of political or legal privilege in the nation, giving either individuals or the members of favored clans a status above those of their fellow Cherokees. Office and influence might be "inherited," but only in the same sense that a person "inherited" a house that he had been occupying at the time of its owner's death. If this conclusion seems unsatisfactory for a people with such strong notions of private property, it must be attributed to the fact that without judicial tribunals to designate an heir, and with slight economic or political reasons to contest "inheritance," the Cherokees could afford to leave the problems of succession to the operation of natural law.

CHAPTER FIFTEEN

A WAY TO WAR

—THE LAW OF THE NATIONS

Warfare was such a central factor in the culture of the American Indians, so great a part of their daily lives, that we might expect it to be the source of many Cherokee legal institutions. Yet except for rules governing adoption, war seems to have contributed little to domestic law. Even captives and scalps taken in battle were subject to the general principles of private-property law, they belonged to an individual owner, not to the war party in a corporate sense. Cherokee public law owed no more to warfare than did private law. As martial glory was not a guarantee of influence or office in town or tribe, war titles were largely honorary, with little political significance. A headman might be a notable warrior, but being headman called for more than military leadership. It is only in international law, the law of the American nations, that war determined doctrine and defined principles. For war, or at least the declaration and commencement of war, was a matter largely of international law.

Retaliation was the chief cause of war between the Cherokees and their neighbors. It is doubtful if any of the southern Indians thought war a sport or a social necessity,[1] although it was surely their chief occupation. Nor was plunder, except perhaps for slaves, a traditional motive for war.[2] Territorial expansion may have been a factor on a few occasions, as in 1714 when the Cherokees and Chickasaws combined to drive the Shawnees from the Cumberland valley,[3] or later when pressure from the east pushed the Cherokees into neighboring hunting grounds, leading to intensive war with the Creeks [4] and sporadic clashes with the Chickasaws [5]—but on the whole there is little evidence that the need for land led to conflict.[6] The legal duty or social requirement that deaths be avenged, however, was a frequent cause of war. When James Adair wrote that the southern Indians were "revengeful of blood, to a degree of distraction," [7] he was speaking as much of their international law as their domestic law.

The basic principle of Cherokee international law was the same as that underlying the blood feud—revenge—and an important, if not the most important motivation for war, was the shared idea that vengeance had to be exacted whenever a Cherokee was slain by a foreigner.[8] General Oglethorpe, writing of the Cherokees during 1762, explained that their wars were started as often by accident as by design. A hunting party far from home would encounter hunters from another nation, a member of the party might be killed, and the Cherokees would demand satisfaction. If refused, "they make Reprisals upon the first they can take of the Nation that committed the Injury." [9] International revenge, not being privileged, might result in war.

The rule that an international killing led to war was so well established that quite often the victim's nation did not wait for satisfaction. A single incident might start a conflict. When he heard that Judd's Friend had "cut off" a number of Shawnees on the Virginia path, the Little Carpenter assumed war had begun and announced plans to lead an expedition against the Shawnee villages.[10] The next year the Raven's Son of Chatuga, "a young brave resolute Fellow," for no apparent reason killed three Chickasaws,[11] thus endangering the traditional Cherokee-Chickasaw peace.[12] That same month two other natives of Chatuga, hoping to appease the British by countering the pro-French diplomacy of neighboring Great Tellico, told the commandant of Fort Loudoun that they intended to start trouble with the French Indians, explaining that "when there is a Stroke once given all the other Towns must follow their Example even in their own Defence." [13] The legal theory was that a deliberate act of hostility involved the entire nation, Great Tellico included.

During July 1757, the Little Carpenter's brother led a reconnaissance against a French outpost on the Ohio river, killing a French army officer.

"According to my Opinion," Captain Raymond Demere told Governor Lyttelton, "that killing French People under the Walls of their Forts, is declaring War against them to all Perfection." [14] There is no doubt that Demere was correctly interpreting Indian international law. In 1725, for example, when the Upper Creeks were in council debating whether to make peace with the Cherokees, word came that a Creek raiding party had killed a white man living in the Cherokee nation. The council was immediately adjourned, the Creeks saying it was useless to continue as they "Expected Nothing Less then a Warr" with the British.[15]

The Creeks did not understand British law as well as the British understood Indian law. There was an important distinction between the two. The killing of a British subject did not usually lead to war. Satisfaction was, of course, absolutely necessary for, Governor James Glen explained, the homicide of a white man by an Indian was "a thing that cannot possibly be put up with, or even postponed." [16] But Glen was speaking of British satisfaction, an entirely different concept than southern-Indian satisfaction. In southern-Indian law, any member of the manslayer's nation could serve as satisfaction. In British colonial law, only the manslayer would do. The distinction is of vital importance for it disproves some popular misconceptions regarding the law of the American nations.

One misconception is that the Europeans introduced the idea of corporate responsibility by treating the Cherokees as a political entity for purposes of satisfaction.[17] In fact, the opposite is true. It was southern-Indian law which held the manslayer's nation collectively liable; British law sought to punish the manslayer as an individual. Time and again, the government of South Carolina tried to persuade the Cherokees that it wanted "satisfaction only from the guilty person, because no man ought to be punished for what another does, for if it was so, a few bad men by one rash action would have it in their power to bring mischief upon a whole nation." [18] The British, by giving the Cherokees a choice between surrendering a specific individual or risking a war, may have forced the headmen to contemplate for the first time the implications of corporate liability but they were contemplating an Indian, not a European legal principle.

Another misconception regarding southern-Indian international law is that the advent of sibless Europeans disrupted the traditional blood feud, causing it to degenerate "into revenge upon helpless or inoffensive whites." [19] The truth is that the southern Indians treated whites in the same manner they treated foreign southern Indians. The doctrine of clan liability was not part of international law. National liability was the basic principle. If a Mohawk of the Turtle clan killed a Cherokee of the Bird clan, the Cherokees exacted the blood price against any Mohawk; they were not limited to the Turtle clan any more than they were limited to the manslayer himself. It was not a question of taking "revenge upon helpless or inoffensive" Mohawks but upon members of the liable nation.

A related misconception is to think that when a member of the Cherokee Bird clan was killed by a foreigner, only the Birds demanded vengeance; that warfare was an extension of domestic clan law. At least one anthropologist has suggested that Cherokee wars were conducted by the clans, that one clan might be fighting one enemy and a second clan a different enemy, while a third clan remained neutral.[20] If this remarkable martial arrangement ever existed, there are no records to indicate it. There was no clan machinery for planning or carrying out offensive actions, no clan leadership for ordering vengeance, and no national clan structure for uniting the clan sections in various towns against a clan enemy. War may have been a form of blood vengeance, but it was conducted to avenge the death of fellow Cherokees or fellow townsmen, rather than fellow clansmen. James Adair indicates that the question of war or peace was determined by the town or its headmen,[21] and almost always the killing of an individual was an affront which aroused the entire town to action, rather than just a section of the town. This point was underscored from the opposite perspective on those few occasions when other Indian nations, knowing in which Cherokee town killers of their countrymen lived, blamed that town for breaking the peace, and not the Cherokees as a whole.[22]

Of course the relatives of the victims had a strong social interest, just as they did in a domestic homicide, but this does not mean they had as strong a legal interest as they had in domestic law. We may suppose they often raised the avenging parties and cried loudest for blood;[23] the forces they raised however were not clan parties so much as town parties, and townsmen probably cried for blood as loudly as clansmen. In the records at least, if not in anthropological theory, vengeance seems to have been thought the duty of the victims' town. During 1752, the Creeks killed a number of people from Ioree who were visiting in South Carolina. The British sent word to Ioree that they had rescued some survivors. "We give you Thanks for the Care of our People that was left," the headmen of Ioree wrote back. "We hope that they won't forgett to see they have Satisfaction." [24] Moreover, the frequent instances of fathers seeking vengeance for the slaying of sons, or of sons seeking vengeance for fathers, almost always relate to international homicides. "I would not have you think we began first to kill the Northern or French Indians," an Upper Creek headman, the Red Coat King of Oakfuskee, wrote Governor Glen, "for as they killed my Son we must have Blood for Blood, and we met with two of the Northerns at Augusta on our own Ground which we killed for Satisfaction." [25] Had international retaliation been a matter of clan right, the Red Coat King might have had little to say about vengeance for his son. But as it was a matter of national right he, as an important headman, had much to say.

The Red Coat King explained another doctrine of southern-Indian international law: liability for homicide attached to the nation of the manslayer, and Indians not belonging to that nation were not liable. He at first thought the Cherokees had killed his son and seems to have been planning an attack on them, before persuaded by "all Circumstances compared with one another, that the said Murder was not committed by any Cherokee but Northern Indians." [26] After killing the two Northerns, the Red Coat King wrote, "I am sinsible my Son was not killed by the Cherokees, therefore I require no Satisfaction of them." [27]

The Red Coat King's original intention to attack the nonliable Cherokees demonstrates the great risk in southern-Indian international law. There was always a chance the wrong nation might be blamed, and a war that neither side wanted could result. This danger may seem a defect equally inherent in the domestic law of homicide, but the consequences of mistake could be more serious. It is likely, too, that whenever an international homicide occurred, passions ran higher and proof was more difficult to obtain, a fact demonstrated several times in Cherokee history when the nation escaped war by sheer good luck. During 1758, for example, a Cherokee war party was returning from a campaign against the French when it encountered a Chickasaw hunting camp. The Cherokees warned the Chickasaws that French Indians were in pursuit and left, but the Chickasaws decided to remain. When the French Indians arrived, they killed or took prisoner all the Chickasaws except one who had gone hunting while the Cherokees were still there. He did not know about the warning and when he returned to find his friends scalped, he assumed the Cherokees were responsible. He hastened to his nation with the news, and a Chickasaw war party was sent out against the Cherokees. A few days later, one of the Chickasaw prisoners escaped from the French Indians and returned home to tell the true story. A runner was immediately dispatched to bring back the avengers of blood, thus averting a Chickasaw-Cherokee war.[28] In July, 1763, a similar event occurred. Three Catawbas arrived in Charles Town to complain that some Cherokees had kidnapped a number of Catawba women. They even identified the leader of the raid, a Cherokee named Red Horse. The Cherokees denied responsibility and we may imagine the Catawbas would have retaliated, had not one of the women escaped to tell her people that the kidnappers were not Cherokee, but Shawnee and Mohawk.[29]

Accident was but one hazard to the law of the southern nations. An even more glaring structural weakness was the fact that third-party instigators could manipulate the law at will and start wars either by killing the members of one nation under circumstances which made it appear that members of a different nation were liable, or (and this was especially true of white men) by paying a few warriors of one nation to kill members of another nation. To stop Cherokee aid to the Chickasaws in 1740, the French precipitated a Creek-Cherokee war,[30] and British officials were well aware that traders in the nation could cause wars and sometimes did.[31] There was, of course, little a nation could do as the warriors were breaking no law, and if they insisted on starting a war they could not be stopped. On one occasion, however, the Creeks utilized their domestic law to prevent war with the Cherokees. In 1760, Governor Henry Ellis of Georgia, "by promises of considerable rewards," [32] attempted "to engage a party of the Creeks to cut off some of the Cherokees," hoping to "create a rupture" between the two nations.[33] Learning of Ellis's plans, "the main body of the nation sent a running embassy" to the Georgians, "requesting them immediately to forebear their unfriendly proceedings, otherwise, they should be forced by disagreeable necessity to revenge their relations blood if it should chance to be spilt contrary to their ancient laws." [34] The Creeks, James Adair explained, were referring to a doctrine of domestic clan law "by which he who decoyed another to his end, was deemed the occasion of his death, and consequently answerable for it." [35]

Usually British machinations were less overt, and the Indian nations were helpless to control events. Sometimes the results were not even sought, as when the British offered scalp bounties and some Cherokees decided to put private profit above national interest. Bounties, to be sure, were paid only for the scalps of French Indians with whom the nation was supposingly at war. But it was difficult to identify the nationality of a clump of hair, and many Cherokees thought nothing of killing any non-Cherokee for the bounty, even friendly Indians.[36] When five Chickasaws were killed for their scalps in 1757, the Little Carpenter, powerless to punish the manslayers and fearful lest the practice lead to a war, took the only step a Cherokee headman could take to prevent similar occurances. He proposed that the British stop paying bounties.[37]

It is with the concept of legal coercion that Cherokee international law and Cherokee domestic law blend one into another, the international law turning on consequences inherent in a domestic public law defined by private rights. Had the Little Carpenter and other Cherokee headmen authority to proscribe antisocial conduct and enforce obedience, their international law might not have left the nation's fate so much at the whim of free enterprisers, or in the hands of foreign governments. Typical of their difficulty was the recurring problem posed by alien Indians entering the nation to sow seeds of sedition or to stir up trouble. During 1757, for example, the Overhills were swarming with Shawnees spreading pro-French talks, a fact the British found inexplicable but which Overhill headmen explained by saying they could do nothing. Frustrated and angered by seeming Cherokee indecision or deliberate vacillation, the British proposed that they themselves kill some of the Shawnees and the headmen, caught in a vise between two belligerent groups, had no choice but to regard it as a thing done in the dark. They resigned themselves to the legal consequences of conduct they were constitutionally, politically, and practically unable to prevent, yet for which the Shawnees would hold their nation liable. When the British persuaded two Cherokees to join their ambush and succeeded in killing several Shawnees, the die was cast. Two Overhill towns, Great Tellico where the Shawnees were visiting, and Chatuga which was the home of the two Cherokees who aided the British, were especially involved. The Tellicos complained bitterly to Captain Raymond Demere, that before he killed the Shawnees they, the Tellicos,

> had a free Path, to walk clean and neat, and without any Danger, but now that I had sent the white People in it, and hooped and hollowed in it, they had made it dirty and all bloody, and very dangerous for them to go any where, without being in Danger of losing their Scalps.[38] . . .

Demere had no doubt what the Tellicos meant. The Shawnees, he wrote, "will do what ever they can, for to revenge themselves," and the Tellicos would have to abandon their intrigues with the French as they "must inevitably take up the Hatchet against the Savannahs [Shawnees] in their own Defence, for the Savannahs will give them no more Quarters, than to us, where ever they find them." [39] Tellico warriors were soon at Fort Loudoun begging for ammunition and war paint. They blamed the British for causing the Shawnee war, but added that "as they were parties to it they were determined to pursue it Vigorously." [40]

Shawnees and other visitors to the nation were not in a completely helpless position. Besides friends upon whom they could count to warn of danger, there was at least one legal restraint discouraging indiscriminate bloodletting—the certainty of retaliation. True, no Cherokee could avenge their death without running the risk of the domestic blood feud, but their country men could, often without leaving home for there were usually as many Cherokees visiting foreign nations as there were alien Indians in the Cherokees—sure candidates for sacrifice, if the Cherokees committed hostile acts. Their relatives alone could be expected to discourage international homicides. Before the British staged their ambush, a Tellico headman named the Lame Arm had considered killing the Shawnees but decided against it "as some of our Men are still among them, it would have been Blood for Blood." [41] It is conceivable but by no means certain that had the Lame Arm acted, he would have been held liable by the clans of any Cherokees killed in retaliation for, after all, he would have been the cause of their deaths. After the British killed the Shawnees, the people of Great Tellico seized a Shawnee woman as hostage for the life of a young Cherokee then in the Shawnee towns. If the Shawnees were to kill him, Demere observed, "I suppose she will run a Hazard to undergo the same Fate." [42]

Public censure was a second restraint on aggressive action which might cause either international retaliation or an unpopular war. Belligerent headmen who defied national opinion would surely be toppled from leadership. James Adair says they might be punished "as enemies," [43] referring, of course, not to physical punishment in the European sense but to the southern-Indian punishments of withdrawal and disfavor. Yet any Indian who wished to start a war had a good chance of succeeding. So too did any Indian who wanted to prevent peace. He could be scolded and ostracized after the act, but not enjoined or restrained before it. In 1754 the Upper Creeks were in council debating the terms of a Cherokee peace. The Gun Merchant, a headman with pro-British sentiments, proposed that the two nations cement their new alliance with a joint war against the Choctaws. A pro-French headman, the Woolf, checked the Gun Merchant's plans by threatening that if the Creeks and Cherokees attacked the Choctaws, he would start another Creek-Cherokee war; all he had to do was kill some Cherokees. The chief Cherokee negotiator appeared surprised by the Woolf's threat, telling the Upper Creeks "that he hoped it would never be in the Power of one Head Man to create a War betwixt their two Nations." [44] The Cherokee should have known better; headmen in his own nation often exercised personal veto over foreign policy by employing exactly the same tactics. During the late summer of 1759, the Lower towns were preparing for a war with South Carolina which the Middle settlements opposed. While the Lower towns were celebrating the annual Green Corn dance, Round O, headman of Stickoee and a leader of the Middle Cherokees, arrived in Estatoe and delivered a "tough lecture." He warned that if the Lower towns did not mind what he said about leaving the British alone, he would immediately kill all the Creeks and Northern Indians in their midst, starting a war so extensive the Lower Cherokees would be unable to attack the Carolinas.[45]

The only recourse which the majority had was to threaten counter action of a like kind. Thus in the autumn of 1760, after the war with South Carolina had commenced and the British had surrendered Fort Loudoun, the Little Carpenter sought to terminate the conflict and to effect the safe release of all the white prisoners. His plan was to kill any French emissaries who came into the nation, and to start a Creek war by having his followers attack the Creeks.[46] When French ambassadors arrived, the anti-British faction conducting the war against the colonies, nipped the Little Carpenter's scheme by telling him that if he touched the French, they would kill the very English prisoners he hoped to save. Unable to force his will on the nation, the Little Carpenter withdrew into the woods.[47]

CHAPTER SIXTEEN

A GIFT OF SCALPS

—THE LAW OF VISITORS
AND RETALIATION

Rival factions and contrary policy makers did not furnish the Cherokees half as many international complications as did the presence of foreign Indians in the nation. The Cherokees' responsibility to and for these visitors was ill-defined in the law of the nations, yet it was a problem which plagued them more than most nations, perhaps because of the size of their territory and its central location. There seems to have been no time when one or another region was not host to a number of foreigners,[1] especially the Shawnees, an Algonquian nation divided into two parts, one living to the southeast and the other to the northwest of the Cherokees.[2] An even larger contingent of visitors came from the north. Vaguely identified in contemporary accounts as "Northerns" and "Northwards," they were generally in alliance with France, although the pro-British Senecas were sometimes included.

"Something akin to tribute entered Cherokee relations with the Northern Indians," William Shedrick Willis writes. "To escape from their attacks the Cherokee permitted these Indians to pass unmolested in their raids upon the Catawba and Creeks. The Cherokee also provided them with munitions and food." [3] Indeed, despite the danger Indian wars created for South Carolina and Georgia, some British colonial officials may have encouraged their Indians to regard the Cherokee nation as a way station to and from war. Lieutenant-Governor George Clarke of New York, for example, negotiated the Cherokee-Iroquois treaty of 1742, permitting the Six Nations to use the Cherokees as a base for raids upon the Catawbas and Creeks.[4] The idea probably was to keep the war paths west of British back settlements, a policy which protected white frontiersmen but jeopardized the Cherokees.

Once in the nation, the visitors were almost totally free from Cherokee control. Cherokee and trader alike were at their mercy. The Northern Indians, an experienced trader wrote in 1755, came into the Cherokee towns to "eat and drink and take their Wives before their face, and when they go off kill them, whom they meet in the Woods or go upon another Town, and the second time they come into the Nation be received as friendly as ever." [5] Bad as the situation was on the domestic front, it entailed dire consequences in the international area. Even the British were not immune from outrages, and they had the military capability to hold the Cherokees responsible. There was a monotonous repetition to events. The Shawnees would rob a Carolina trader,[6] or the Senecas would kidnap a back-country settler and bring him through Keowee or some other village,[7] the British would ask satisfaction and the Cherokees would plead helplessness. If Carolina traders hired the men of one town to retake a white prisoner, another town, fearing reprisals by the visitors, might threaten to kill the traders if the rescue should be attempted.[8]

The problem of pro-French aliens who were not subject to effective Cherokee control, and who were often bent on causing mischief between the Cherokees and their neighbors was one reason why South Carolina decided to build a fort among the Overhills and why the Cherokees wanted the fort.[9] Yet when Captain Raymond Demere stopped at Keowee on his way to start construction near Chota, he was warned not to send an advance party of small size into the mountains. Shawnees living in the Overhills, he was told, would kill his men, "And as they are at Peace with the Cherockees, they will not prevent their offering us any Violence." [10]

There probably was no precise rule whether the Cherokees were responsible in international law for the actions of aliens. Events may have depended upon the degree of aggravation suffered by the injured nation, and the participation in the acts of hostility by the Cherokees. A theory somewhat akin to common-law conspiracy may have been followed, turning on whether the Cherokees encouraged and aided the attacks of their visitors on neighboring tribes, or merely played a passive role. The Catawbas were apt merely to complain when they thought the Cherokees harbored and entertained their enemies, but when they suspected that individual Cherokees actually joined raiding parties, they seemed to have threatened war.[11] The Creeks insisted in 1753 that the chief reason for their long, bloody war with the Cherokees was that the Cherokees not only allowed the Senecas to pass through their nation on the way to the Creeks, but supplied them with arms and ammunition.[12] James Adair agreed to an extent, claiming that "the true and sole cause" of one Cherokee-Creek war was that some Shawnees in the Cherokee country killed two Chickasaw hunters who were adopted relatives of the Creeks.[13] The Cherokees protested that the Northerns either came while they were away hunting, or were so well armed they could not resist them,[14] but the Creeks did not accept this excuse.

The Lower Chickasaws adopted a legal theory similar to the Creeks'. In 1752 the Lower Cherokees made overtures to the Lower Chickasaws not to break their peace merely because Shawnees living in the Lower-Cherokee towns had committed acts of hostility. Speaking for his nation the Squirrel King replied that the Chickasaws

> cannot well think the Cherokees are desirous of being in Friendship with the Checkesaws while they entertain and encourage the Savannahs to live among them in order to come and war against the Chickesaws, nay, and the very Cherokees came with them. If the Cherokees are so very desirous of maintaining a good Understanding with the Chickasaws, the only speedy Way of showing it is by driving away or killing the few Savannahs among them. But particularly the Fellow who killed a Chickasaw named Chinaby. . . . Upon the Cherokees speedy performing these Things there will always remain a firm Peace between them. . . .
>
> But if the Cherokees do not . . . kill the Savannah Fellow above-mentioned, or drive them all away from their Nation (because while the Cherokees suffer them to live there they will be always stealing [onto] the Path to kill the Chickesaws, which will always occasion a Misunderstanding), the Chickasaws say they will not leave off, because they cannot think them their real Friends till they comply with these just Demands.[15]

The Squirrel King's legal theory is plain enough. He would have made the Cherokees vicariously responsible for their visitors' actions, at least those visitors receiving a welcome and whose evil intent or past crimes are known. Moreover, he was willing to underscore this legal theory with force. Under Chickasaw law, he possessed authority to control events to a much greater extent than did a Cherokee headman and perhaps he believed Cherokee headmen could be made to respond to pressure. His people had already taken ten Cherokee scalps in retaliation for the one death, and within a month after his letter they would take at least 20 more. The Chickasaws were then in desperate straits as the long war with France was wearing them down, and they could ill-afford to lose the friendship of the Cherokees, their chief allies. Yet they wanted the Shawnees banished before they would restore peace.[16] It was a legal stalemate. The Chickasaws insisted the Cherokees were responsible for their visitors; the Cherokees, not knowing how to police or expell them, insisted they were not.

To exonerate themselves of responsibility there were several measures, short of policing or expelling the Northern Indians, that the Cherokees could adopt. A month before the Squirrel King's letter, a band of six Senecas passed through Watuga with a Chickasaw female prisoner and one Chickasaw scalp. Fearing pursuit, they stayed but a short time. A few days later six Chickasaw avengers appeared, and the headman of Watuga persuaded two of his men to guide them toward the fleeing Senecas. A British trader said that this action freed the Cherokees of suspicion they had aided the Senecas and avoided a Chickasaw war.[17]

A more convincing step would have been to seize the prisoners or scalps, and return them to their nation. The Cherokees maintained they were powerless to do so, and while we suspect they were afraid to act, it is possible they believed they had no right to act if the prisoner, even a white man, was captured during a legitimate raid beyond their borders. The one clear case on record in which the Cherokees freed a captive occurred entirely within their towns. During July, 1754, a party of 30 Catawbas (returning from a raid to the Northwards with three Northward prisoners) passed through the nation and sent a young warrior to a village for supplies. In that town were nine Northwards who, according to a trader, "lived some Years Over the Hills and [were] almost naturalized" Cherokees. The Northwards seized the Catawba and immediately retreated from the town, arriving after five days at Settico, the Overhill village where lived the Northward who first laid hands on the Catawba and by Indian law claimed him as "a slave." Hearing of the event, the Little Carpenter, the Great Warrior, and several other headmen went to the house of the Northwards and cut the Catawba free, telling the Northwards they could not carry away any friends of the Cherokees. Taking the Catawba to one of their homes, the headmen, as was the Cherokee custom, "washed, painted, and new cloathed him" before sending him back to his friends.[18] Whether we should place stress on the fact that the Catawba was captured in a Cherokee town, or that the Northwards were "naturalized" Cherokees, is uncertain. There is no indication that the Cherokee headmen acted in this situation because they had more physical power than they possessed at other times when they claimed they were powerless to act. Yet they did act, and we must conclude that they did so to avoid a Catawba war, that they knew the Catawbas would hold them responsible if their countryman was not released.

It may not have been a rule of law but as a practical matter, aliens in the nation were just about immune from liability for international misdeeds. There is, however, a possibility that Cherokees aiding visitors could be held accountable for what they did. In 1750 a party of about 25 French Indians was met by a Cherokee at the headstreams of the Monongahela, some distance north of the Overhills. He guided them through the nation into the Carolina backcountry, where they fell on a village of settlement Indians while the men were hunting and only women and children were at home. Pursued by the men who had been aroused by a white Carolinian, they were overtaken and defeated. The survivors blamed the white man for the disaster and when safely in the Lower-Cherokee towns they wanted to take revenge by ambushing James Adair and a companion who were journeying up the path from South Carolina. "But," Adair explains, "their Cheerake guide prevented them from attempting it, by telling them, that as his country was not at war with us, his life must pay for it, if they chanced to kill either of us; and as we were fresh and well-armed, they might be sure we would fight them so successfully, as at least one of us should escape and alarm the towns: with this caution they forbore the hazardous attempt." [19] When the guide said he would be killed, he meant that the British would demand satisfaction, and that the headmen might persuade his relatives to surrender him. That he thought he would be blamed is an indication that under Cherokee domestic custom, a confederate of aliens might be responsible for their homicides. Surely such a doctrine would be consistent with Cherokee notions of causation. The guide would have been the cause of the homicides even if the visitors, immune from retaliation, had done the killing and taken the scalps.

Of course the Cherokees might have acted directly to prevent other nations from using their towns as staging areas for raids. Had they dared take the risk, they might even have expelled the visitors or tried to control them. But conditions would have had to be ideal, the people united against the foreigners and no one working with them. Surely there were times when the headmen discussed doing something. On one occasion eight "Northward Indians" arrived in Stecoe, a frontier town, intending, they said, to move on to Hywassee from hence they would raid the Creeks. When the Raven of Hywassee heard they were coming, he decided to kill them but with luck they went to Tallessee instead. The Raven's plans are what interest us. He would have given the Northwards "a Convoy sufficient to show them the path under pretence to assist them against their Enemies but that when they were at a Convenient Place, none should come back to tell who hurt them." [20] Secrecy was essential. By killing the Northwards, the risk of a Creek-Hywassee war would be avoided. By selecting a secluded spot where no one would know what had happened, blame could be shifted to the Creeks and the certainty of a war with the Northwards might also be avoided.

Perhaps some headmen did what the Raven of Hywassee had planned to do, but as they had to keep it quiet there are no records. Those less bold could protect their towns by at least two other methods. One was to pay the visitors to go home. In 1754 Chota turned back 20 Northern Indians planning to attack the Creeks by giving them a number of scalps.[21] Sometimes the Northerns could not be bribed, such as a party which arrived in Keowee during 1753 intent on raiding the Creeks. The people of Keowee adopted another means to escape censure from the Creeks. They told the Northern Indians that if they persisted, a Keowee runner would be sent to warn the Creeks they were coming. The Northerns went home.[22]

Whether direct or vicarious, the responsibility of one nation for killing people of another nation was the usual cause of Cherokee wars. Yet a killing did not have to lead to a general conflict. The victims' nation wanted revenge and in theory could be satisfied by taking the same number of lives as it had lost. Some Chickasaw headmen expressed this theory in 1725, when they told the Cherokees they had made and kept a peace with the Choctaws only until they had an opportunity to kill as many Choctaws as the Choctaws had killed Chickasaws some while earlier.[23] An ideal version of this legal rule, perhaps used to teach children international law as well as to inspire them with a tale of Cherokee courage, is contained in a myth recorded during the nineteenth century. A number of women and children from a town on the Cheowa were killed by a Seneca raiding party. Men from towns on the Hywassee and the Cheowa trailed the enemy to a Seneca village where they heard shouts in the townhouse, and knew the women were dancing over Cherokee scalps.

> The avengers hid themselves near the spring, and as the dancers came down to drink the Cherokee silently killed one and another until they had counted as many scalps as had been taken on Cheowa, and still the dancers in the townhouse never thought that enemies were near. Then said the Cherokee leader, "We have covered the scalps of our women and children. Shall we go home now like cowards, or shall we raise the war whoop and let the Seneca know that we are men?" "Let them come, if they will," said his men; and they raised the scalp yell of the Cherokee. At once there was an answering shout from the townhouse, and the dance came to a sudden stop. The Seneca warriors swarmed out with ready gun and hatchet, but the nimble Cherokee were off and away.[24]

The tale is of Cherokee valor, but valor is displayed after the legal obligation is performed. Implicit is the rule that the Cherokee avengers were "covering" only the scalps of the dead. It was up to the Senecas to decide if the war would be extended.

We cannot guess how far the ideal was carried. Perhaps the Cherokees felt that retaliatory killings were justified, for the records tell of headmen who sent the enemy word they had taken only as many lives as were owed. They must have thought that war could be stopped, but surely not that the killings were privileged. The avengers acted secretly and always fled. It was a sense of righteousness, perhaps of savage honor, that made them refrain from taking more lives than were owed, not the belief they were privileged to kill only that number.

Even if retaliatory killings were not privileged in international law, the Cherokees could benefit by taking only as many lives as were owed. If the other nation admitted its responsibility, a general war might be avoided. Southern-Indian diplomacy utilized several legal principles to prevent counter-retaliation when both sides desired peace. The nation against which vengeance had been taken usually made the choice, and no method was more effective than the "set-off." In 1750, for example, the Upper Creeks sent as their ambassadors to the Overhills a party of Shawnees instructed to acknowledge Creek responsibility for an attack on an Overhill hunting camp, during which four Cherokee men were killed, seven women taken prisoner, and the camp plundered of twelve horses and five deerskins. Later, the Cherokees and their allies killed or captured eight Upper Creeks, a set-off which the Upper Creeks argued put the two nations "much upon a Ballance." [25]

Even the Europeans acknowledged the legality of the set-off, sometimes carrying it to extremes, as in 1772 when John Stuart, the superintendent of Indian Affairs for the southern colonies, demanded satisfaction from the Upper Creeks for killing three white men. The Creeks had previously claimed that one of their men had been beaten to death in Augusta the year before. Stuart insisted the Creek had died accidentally, falling from a canoe while drunk, but was willing to set-off his death against the death of one of the three whites. In addition, a Creek had been killed by Georgians while stealing horses, and although the Creeks had been warned they would be pursued if they stole, Stuart agreed to set-off this death also. Thus, Stuart argued, there was "one Murther unattoned for" and he wanted satisfaction. [26]

Another way to avoid war was to obtain forgiveness. In June, 1758, the Little Carpenter asked South Carolina to overlook a number of killings on the frontier, which had been provoked by white men killing Cherokees. "Some of my People has been Rogues," he admitted, "but I hope that you won't remember it for we lost some of our People as well as our Brothers [*i.e.,* the British.]" [27] A year later the Great Warrior tried to negotiate peace solely on the basis of mutual forgiveness. [28] South Carolina refused, yet we may assume that had it been in her interest to forgive, war could have been prevented. Just a few months later, when the colonies were attempting to draw the Creeks into the conflict against the Cherokees, several Georgia traders were killed near Augusta by a party of Creeks, an event which the governor of Georgia knew was "traditionally the equivalent of a declaration of war." Satisfaction, he decided, had "to give Way to Prudence," and he overlooked the affair by pretending that the French—not the Creeks—were responsible. [29]

The surest way to avoid war was, of course, to provide satisfaction by surrendering or executing a manslayer. It cannot be doubted that satisfaction was an Indian doctrine long before the arrival of the British. John Archdale, governor of Carolina during the 1690s, described one of the earliest documented cases of international homicide from the Cherokees' part of the continent in words that imply he believed he was reporting Indian law:

> Two *Indians* in drinking Rum Quarrelled, and the one of these presently kill'ed the other; his Wife being by, immediately, with a

Knife, smote off his Testicles, so as they hung only by a Skin: He was
pursued by my Order, I happening to be then that way, being about
16 miles from Town, and was taken in a Swamp, and immediately
sent into Custody into Charles Town; and the Nation to whom the
slain *Indian* belonged unto, was acquainted with it, whose King, &c.
came to the Governour, and desired Justice on that *Indian;* some of
the *Indian's* Friends would have bought him off, as is usual; But
nothing but his Life would satisfie that Nation, so he was ordered
to be shot by the Kinsman of the murthered *Indian.* Before he
went to Execution, the *Indian* King to whom he belonged, told him,
that since he was to die, he would have him to die like a Man:
and farther he said, I have often forwarn'd you of Rum, and now
you must lose your Life for not taking my Council; I hope it will be
a warning to others.—When he came to the Tree, he desired not
to be tyed to it, but to stand loose, for, said he, I will not budge
or stir when he shoots me; so he was shot in the Head, and immediately died. Now the Manner of the *Indians* in such Cases, is to War
one Nation against the other to revenge any Blood-shed; and being
ordered Satisfaction this way, no war ensued.[30]

The Catawbas were a tribe which especially seemed willing to avoid
war by accepting satisfaction,[31] or by offering it to such powerful neighbors as Virginia,[32] the Creeks,[33] and the Cherokees. During 1744, for
example, a Cherokee was killed while in the company of two Catawbas
and two Chickasaws. The head warrior of the Catawbas immediately wrote
to the Cherokees "promising them satisfaction in case it should be found
the Cherokee was killed by one of the Catawbas, and desiring them not
to break out war with them, till they had met." [34]

The Catawba headman or "king" had authority to punish wrongdoers in
his nation,[35] and was able to offer and accept international satisfaction.
Cherokee headmen, without power, seldom provided satisfaction. On occasion they promised it to the British, but when the manslayer or his close-
clan kin refused to cooperate, they were forced to admit helplessness.
To other Indian nations they may have never given satisfaction, preferring
instead to negotiate peace by using a third method for mitigating international homicide—compensation. The presents exchanged among nations,
a characteristic feature of Indian diplomacy, were often given in compensation for a killing.[36] Between 1756 and 1758, the Cherokees several times
averted war with the Chickasaws by timely compensation.[37] In 1757, for
instance, the intractable Mankiller of Great Tellico attempted to win
British favor by leading a war party against the French. Reluctant to at-

tack his friends, he killed a Chickasaw and presented the scalp to the British as that of a French Indian. When the Chickasaws in the nation learned what had happened, they may have threatened war—for the Cherokees presented them with a Chickasaw who had been a Cherokee "slave" for a number of years, and a Chickasaw recently rescued from the French Indians by an Overhill war party. The gifts satisfied the Chickasaws.[38]

When Cherokees were killed by white settlers, the British expected the nation to accept commutation in place of specific performance, and even tried to make compensation mandatory. Yet when Virginia promised compensation for the death of a number of Cherokees during 1765, and the Cherokees (after waiting three years in vain for payment) killed five Virginians in retaliation, the killings were excused as justified, and counter satisfaction was not demanded in return. The Cherokee killers, John Stuart explained to Virginia officials, "were authorised by the custom of their country to act as they did, and their plea of never having received any satisfaction was undeniable." [39]

Stuart was not arguing that the British were bound by Cherokee law, or that the Cherokees were free of liability because their actions had been privileged. He was merely offering Virginia an excuse to avoid war, should it be in her interest to do so. Compensation as a means of settlement was always more effective between friends than between traditional enemies; it was employed somewhat frequently between the Cherokees and the Chickasaws, only occasionally between the Cherokees and the Catawbas, and apparently never between the Cherokees and Creeks. Like the law of visitors and the law of international retaliation, compensation, set-off, and forgiveness depended to a large extent upon attitudes, for they were not binding rules of law which had to be obeyed. Rather they provided legal peace-keeping machinery, which could be used when both sides were of a mind to use it. They were rules of law only if neither party wanted a war, and hence were laws to the same degree as the rules of today's international law, the distinctive mark of which even among civilized nations is voluntary acquiescence. An agreement between American Indians to accept compensation and forego retaliation was as binding as any treaty between sovereign powers. Its force depended upon the self interest of the parties.

CHAPTER SEVENTEEN

A BLOODY HATCHET

—THE WAR MACHINE

Not all Indian wars started by accident. Some were declared. In 1725 the Chickasaws sent runners to Great Tellico announcing that they had "declared open Warr" on a tribe of French Indians, after the tribe killed their "king." [1] We do not know how they informed the French Indians. The usual method was to leave evidence near a corpse so there would be no mistake who the killers were, a gesture so taunting that the enemy had to retaliate. When Governor Ellis of Georgia tried to start a Creek-Cherokee war in 1760, his plan was to hire a few Creeks "to cut off some Cherokees, and leave their national symbols with the dead bodies." [2] Whatever the symbols (often hatchets), they were known to the other side and were surely painted black and red, the colors worn by a warrior in battle.[3] Red stood for bravery,[4] black for war; another way to declare war was to send the enemy a belt of black wampum.

Black wampum declaring war was a "gift" as well as a challenge. If white beads were mixed with black, the gift could signify peace [5] and was probably sent by a nation to say it would remain neutral in a conflict. All gifts—bloody hatchets, colored wampum, bark-girted pipes, and fresh scalps—were part of a universal symbolic language which every southern Indian understood, and which the nations used when communicating to one another.[6] In 1859, at a time when few Cherokees could recall the the old language of the forest, a delegation from the Iroquois of New York petitioned Principal Chief John Ross to incorporate their people into the Cherokee nation, and presented him with wampum as a symbol of friendship. Forwarding their request and the wampum to the national council, Ross explained how the wampum had been interpreted to him.

> That the strings of Beads, represents the friendly compliments of the Chiefs, men, women and children of the whole Iroquois Tribe to the Chiefs, men, women, and children of the Cherokee People— and that, the Wampum Belt is presented in token of the permanent peace and friendship which now exists between the two tribes— and that the tomahawks which were once uplifted in war have been buried at the root of the tree *so deep* under ground, as can never again be reached and raised in hostilities.[7]

In the eighteenth century, such obvious symbols as white wampum and buried hatchets did not have to be explained to a Cherokee. He did not even have to understand the words of the Indian delivering the gifts, for the symbols overcame language barriers. During the spring of 1748, the Cherokees and Nottoways, members of the Iroquois linguistic family, sent the Chickasaws living in the Creek nation, a Catawba scalp, a bloody French hatchet, and two Chickasaw pipes girt together with red-painted bark. They were calling on the Muskhogean-speaking Chickasaws to join them in a war against the Catawbas.[8] Nine years later, a Cherokee headman delivered to the Catawbas a red-painted hatchet, which King Haigler of the Catawbas told the governor of South Carolina was "for to kill the french with." [9] Asked by a Virginian what would happen if the Catawbas did not pick up the hatchet, the Cherokee headman replied that "the Cherokees would look upon it as a Breach of the Peace that then subsisted between them, and resent it the first opportunity." [10]

It is unlikely the headman meant to speak for more than his town or for the Overhill region. A Cherokee town or region may have declared war, at least with signs left beside a dead enemy, but it is doubted if the nation as a whole ever did. To have committed all the Cherokees to a decision of belligerency required a concerted policy, a unity of action beyond the grasp of national politics. Only an impulsive stroke—either an irrevocable gesture so dramatic it aroused passions to a frenzy, or one so insulting to the enemy as to endanger all the towns—could cause the entire Cherokee population to adopt a war talk. The most dramatic instance in recorded history occurred during January, 1716, at the height of South Carolina's Yamasee War. When the war broke out, the Cherokees, like the other southern tribes, had killed a few British traders, but otherwise took little part.[11] South Carolina, struggling for survival against great odds, needed Cherokee allies and had to overlook the "murders." Later in 1715, as the fortunes of war hung in the balance, Colonel Maurice Moore led the first company of British troops ever sent into the nation, a diplomatic mission rather than a military expedition, intended to persuade the Cherokees to take the warpath against Carolina's enemies. According to Charles Town's plan, Creek envoys were to join Moore and propose a Creek-Cherokee alliance against the Yamasee nation. Once he arrived in the Lower towns, Moore not only found Cherokee leadership divided into pro-British, pro-Yamasee, and neutral factions, but the Creeks playing a double game. When the Creek ambassadors appeared at the council held in the town of Tugaloo, they told the Cherokees that between 200 and 500 Creek warriors were waiting in the woods, to join in a general massacre of the British troops. While the debate raged and the fate of Carolina hung in the balance, the pro-British Cherokees "fell upon the Creeks and Yamusees who were in their Towns and kill'd every man of them." [12] The nation was now committed to the British; [13] runners carried the red sticks of war throughout the towns, rallying warriors to Carolina's cause.[14] Whether the result of calculated policy or of sudden impulse, killing the ambassadors was so rude a blow to the Creeks that it amounted to a declaration of war which even the pro-Yamasee Cherokees had to accept and, in the estimation of Governor Craven, assured a Carolinian victory over the Yamasee.[15]

The Cherokee entry into the Yamasee War was unique, as it seems to have been engineered by men from all sections of the nation. The only other occasion when the eighteenth-century Cherokees commenced a conflict with the various regions so united was against South Carolina in 1760. When the southern Indians spoke of a general war, they seldom meant a war involving the entire nation. It is doubtful if at any one time, even 1760, more than half the Cherokees ever took "the war talk." [16] The usual pattern, especially of wars with non-Europeans, was for one region or cluster of towns to be at war, even on the defensive or threatened with defeat, while another region, perhaps fighting a different enemy, tried to maintain peace or at least to appear neutral.

When a town went to war, we would expect its governmental structure to be reorganized for the town council and powerless headmen were not convenient instruments to direct strategy, provide for defense, or achieve victory. Yet the Cherokee war machine seems to have been based on the same principles as those governing domestic or peacetime activities. The one discernible difference was that the war leaders often had titles— Great Warrior, Mankiller, or Outacity, the Raven, and the Slave-Catcher were the most prized.[17] Perhaps Skiagunsta was another, or it may have been synonomous with Raven.[18] It is also possible that "Wolf," "Owl" and "Fox" were titled warriors or battle scouts, the Wolf scouting to the right, the Owl to the left, and the Fox to the rear of march.[19] Certainly these names were awarded for achievements of valor,[20] but it is questionable whether they were war ranks in a command structure, as some anthropologists believe.[21] There may or may not have been a war priest and war chief in every town, or a speaker for war, a surgeon, a flag bearer, and a seven-man council appointed to lead every war party.[22] Again we need not ask for proof that such men existed in fact, rather than in later fancy. As in civil government, the test is not whether men were called by this title or that title, or whether they were elected to serve this or that function, but whether they had the power to command obedience, and whether they were obeyed.

The first point which tells against any command structure is that war parties, even those setting out to avenge killings on behalf of an afflicted town, were private enterprises. Any headman with the initiative to organize and the influence to inspire men could recruit a war party, and to think of him as holding an official post or exercising designated power is to stretch western concepts, and probably is unrealistic by Cherokee concepts. It is equally unrealistic to accept the tradition that if he lost too many men he was killed.[23] Who would have killed him? Undoubtedly he would have lost prestige, making it difficult to raise another war party, but surely he would not have been killed.

A second reason for doubting that Cherokee war parties had a command structure is their size. Tradition tells of great Indian battles involving over a thousand men. In 1731 the Cherokees and Catawbas are said to have lost 1200 warriors in a two-day battle with the invading Iroquois near present-day Clarksville, Tennessee.[24] Earlier, the Cherokees and the Chickasaws drove the Shawnees from the Cumberland, and during the 1760s the Chickasaws dealt the Cherokees a crushing defeat at Chickasaw

Old Fields. Perhaps the best known tradition, repeated by most Cherokee scholars, is the battle of Taliwa fought in 1755 by 500 Cherokees under the leadership of Oconostota, the Great Warrior of Chota, which drove the Creeks forever from north Georgia, and opened the lowlands to Cherokee colonization.[25] Engagements of this size and national importance surely called for central direction, yet the records are silent regarding any enterprise approaching such magnitude. Lieutenant Timberlake reported that a war party of 165 men was excessive, and even 30 appears to have been a great number, if for no other reason than the danger of the enemy tracking a larger group.[26] Ideal conditions for raising sizeable parties occurred during the French and Indian War; the British guaranteed the warrior's pay, the men bivouaced in Virginia, and then marched forth as auxiliaries for white militia. In 1751, for example, the Little Carpenter and Tassetty of Settico went through all the Cherokee towns trying to recruit about 100 men,[27] yet seldom did leaders depart for Virginia with anywhere near the number promised. More typical was the experience of Judd's Friend in 1757. "[Y]ou thought that I Should have a great many men," he wrote Old Hop from Virginia, "but you and I was mistaken, for I have but thirty men." [28]

A third reason why it is improbable that the Cherokee had a command structure in war was that there was no one for commanders to command. Every warrior was a volunteer; the decision to join a war party was entirely up to the individual.[29] Even when on the path, stalking an enemy village, or engaged in battle, every man could act as he pleased, fight as he pleased, and leave when he pleased. The war chiefs, Timberlake wrote, "lead the warriors that chuse to go, for there is no laws or compulsion on those that refuse to follow, or punishment to those that forsake their chief." [30] Major Andrew Lewis, a Virginia frontiersman with much experience commanding mixed companies of Indians and provincials, complained that the Cherokees were "like the Devil's Pigg; they will neither lead nor drive." [31]

General John Forbes, when preparing his forces for the final, successful assault on Fort Duquesne, found the chaos of the Cherokee war machine more than a British regular should properly tolerate. "[O]ur greatest Dependance is upon them," Forbes wrote to William Pitt of the Cherokees; yet "they are capable of being led away upon any Caprice or Whime that seizes them." As a result he was "obliged by every Artifice to amuse them from returning home, they being rather offended at not seeing our Army and Artillery assembled." [32] To keep the Cherokees in camp, Forbes disregarded the warning of American Indian experts, raised the amount of presents paid the warriors and when they continued to complain, promised even more gifts. Some Cherokees received so much booty that they first asked for rooms and strong chests to store it, then decided to go home, saying there was no reason to stay as they could carry no more goods, but promised to return. Their leader, Round O, tried to persuade them to remain, but even his warning that Fort Duquesne might be taken without their aid fell on deaf ears.[33]

Usually Cherokee warriors did not wait for such a sensible excuse to quit. Speaking of the southern Indians in general, James Adair said that

> if their dreams portend any will, they always obey the supposed divine intimation and return home, without incurring the least censure. They reason that their readiness to serve their country, should not be subservient to their own knowledge or wishes, but always regulated by the divine impulse. I have known a whole company who set out for war, to return in small parties, and sometimes by single persons, and be applauded by the united voices of the people.[34]

Even the shrewd Little Carpenter could dream bad dreams. In October, 1756, he surprised the British by starting on an expedition and returning within a week. "They intended to have continued out for three Months," Captain Raymond Demere wrote, "but their Conjuror's prognosticateing that they should loose some of their Warriours as well as kill some of the Enemy they thought it the best to return and preserve the Lives of their people." [35] Demere does not say whether the warriors abandoned the Little Carpenter or if he had bad dreams too, but usually a war leader watched his following melt away. Tired of the march, deciding he would just as soon not risk his life, or merely disenchanted with the expedition, a warrior needed no legal excuse to go home, but if he sought a face-saving reason, a bad dream was as handy as any.[36] Thus, a successful captain's main task was not to direct activities, but to sustain the martial fervency and bellicose mania which (at least when personal vengeance or British presents were not a factor) alone kept the men on the warpath. The need to establish a high pitch of enthusiasm, later to counter flagging spirits, explains the war songs of the would-be leaders reciting past exploits when raising their parties.[37] The three-day purification rituals impressed on the men the idea they had sanctified themselves for battle,[38] and the fierce, passionate war dance was an example of how well American Indians bent on starting or continuing a conflict understood mass psychology.[39]

Even when a war party reached the enemy village, it was seldom co-ordinated and acted on no specific plan.[40] Captain Raymond Demere, in June 1757, even believed it a Cherokee custom that as soon as a war party shed blood, it broke off the engagement and immediately returned home.[41] Either Demere was exaggerating or he may have seen a letter which Judd's Friend, while on the warpath the month before, wrote to Old Hop in Chota: "I Shall make all the hast Possible, as soon as I have killed or taken any French or Indians, I shall return as Soon as Possible." [42]

It is not unlikely that Judd's Friend knew he could not keep his warriors together, once they took a scalp. They would want to go home to dance and celebrate, to boast to the women of brave deeds, and to hear the praise of the old men. Perhaps he did not even bother to try. The great characteristic of Cherokee war leaders was that they lacked enter-prise. A second was that they were remarkably incompetent, a third that they were cowardly. These judgments may be unfair, for they were operat-ing under severe handicaps. War leaders like Judd's Friend might have shown more initiative and devised better tactics, had they thought there was a reasonable chance that someone would obey. They were, moreover, no more cowardly than their men. Consider, for example, one report of a typical Cherokee war party. It was written by a British trader to the Chickasaws during 1753, when the Cherokees were aiding the Chickasaws against the French and their Choctaw allies.[43]

Forty-six Cherokees came here in order to go to war against the Chocktaws. They came down the River in Canoes and coming down the Falls or Breakers, the Rapit running of the Water oversett four of their Canoes with at least twenty Fellows in them. They lost all their Guns, Blankets, and Boots, and had two Men drownded, and the Rest got out with great Difficulty. They came into this Nation [the Chickasaws] in a Manner naked, and stayed but a little while here before thirteen of them fitted out for the Chocktaws, but did not gett to that Nation before they where engaged with about twenty Chock-taws who came upon them about the Midle of the Day. They killed three of them the first Shott, and wounded one. The Rest, after throwing away their Guns, run off. The wounded Man was shot throw the Arm, and him they took alive, and carryed him to the Choctaws, throw several of their Towns, whiping him at every Town for three Days, which is their Custom with Slaves. The fourth Day he was to have been burnt, and they thinking him by this Time secure, they untied his Hands. In the Middle of the Night he made his Escape, and in three Days gott safe here, notwithstanding he was persued by at least a hundred Fellows, and says he was many Times in the Midst of them. The Rest of them are returned to their Land, he only remains here under the Doctor's Hands. Their coming here has been attended with bad Success, and I am apt to think they will hardly attempt War with the Chocktaws any more. The Chocktaws say they think but little of them since they find they are so easily started.[44]

This account was recorded in the journal of a British trader, and as most white men shared the Choctaws' contempt for Cherokee fighting ability, the account may be a bit biased, although the writer seems to have had no reason to color the facts. It is more difficult to obtain meaningful evaluations from the Cherokee side, as most of their statements were self-serving and made after the event. We have, however, one campaign report written by the Little Carpenter during late December, 1757 or early January, 1758, perhaps the only extant field dispatch from an eighteenth-century war leader. From its contents, apparently he and the Great Warrior of Chota took a party through the Creek nation and attacked the so-called Alabama Fort, a French garrison stationed on the Choctaw side of the Creeks.

> We went down the River and could see nobody till we came opposite the Breed Nation. There we espied a white Flagg, which gave us all great Pleasure. We all stripped and painted for Battle. When we came up to the Place, we found a red Pipe and some Tobacco and three Boats marked upon a Tree. We did not meet with our Prey there, but pursued till we came to the Mouth of a small River. There we held a Council of War. The Great Warrior went off with 19 Men and pursued towards the French Fort. About 2 Miles above the Fort, we came up with a French Lieutenant and five Soldiers. We killed them first, and then went and way laid the Fort. We saw 4 great Guns. We took two Prisoners there and came off two Days' March of this Side.[45]

Perhaps we should not seek definitive evaluations of the Cherokee war machine. A reasonable general conclusion is that the Cherokees were not equipped to wage a European-type armed conflict with land occupation, mass annihilation, and sustained warfare.[46] This statement, however, could be made about any southern-Indian nation. In later wars against the Americans during the 1770s and 1780s, especially along the Cumberland valley,

Cherokee leaders again appear both incompetent and cowardly; yet it is difficult to tell what part of their failures was due to their personal faults, and what part due to the handicap of operating under a military law that made every warrior a generalissimo. The appearance of a lone white scout in the woods, or the barking of a dog just before an attack, could send the entire company running home. As other Indian war chiefs were more successful despite similar legal handicaps, Cherokee leadership cannot escape ridicule. Yet the law was largely to blame.

It might be concluded that the voluntary composition of war parties explains why there was no authoritative command structure even during battle. Yet the home front was no better organized, a fact which returns us to the two dominant realities of Cherokee legal life: the constitutional right of equality and the absence of a law of physical coercion. Cherokee headmen could not control events even when their towns were threatened with attack. Their leadership was a leadership of the moment, for they could not plan strategy or devise tactics.

During the late spring and the summer of 1725, Colonel George Chicken of South Carolina was sent to the nation partly to warn the Cherokees that the Creeks and Choctaws were assembling a large army of invasion. Charles Town had learned that over 500 Choctaws were to aid the Creeks in a war to annihilate the Cherokees, and all through the summer months, dispatches from agents in the Creek nation repeated the alarm.[47] Colonel Chicken's orders were to persuade the Cherokees that war was best fought by taking the offensive, and he advised them to raise an army which would meet the Creeks and Choctaws in the woods. By drawing a force of ten men from each town, Chicken told the Lower Cherokee headmen meeting in council, "you would be able to give the Creeks such a Blow that they would forever after dread you." The Lower Cherokees said they would think about it, but Chicken expressed the fear that they would not listen to his advice.[48] It is a commentary upon how little the British understood Cherokee institutions that Chicken, one of Carolina's most experienced Indian experts, assumed the Cherokees had the legal capability to act had they wanted to.

Continuing on his mission into the Overhills, Colonel Chicken urged a second council to order out a force of fighting men. The Creeks were reported near the town of Estatoe, yet the Cherokees told Chicken they would first have to send for the head warriors of all the towns, and after they had gathered together "they would Consult about it." [49] Later, when they had met, they sent him their thanks for his advice but said

the Method they designed to take is for to lett them come to their
Towns, but not undiscovered, for they design to keep out lookouts
every way and be ready to give them a Smash in their Towns First
and then to gather all their Strength and follow them when they are
upon their retreat with their Wounded men.[50]

By now Chicken should have realized that this strategy—really non-
strategy requiring no planning and calling for no discipline—was the
best the Cherokees could devise. Earlier, Chicken had asked the Head
Warrior of Great Tellico why he permitted his men to go to war against
the Upper Creeks at the very time Great Tellico was entertaining a
peace emissary from that nation. The Head Warrior replied "That they
were Young Men and would do what they pleased." [51]

Chicken received the same answer when he returned to the Lower towns
and asked King Crow, the headman of Keowee, why his people were
so slow repairing their fort when everyone knew the Creeks were in the
vicinity and likely to attack at any moment.

He informed me that the people would work as they pleased and go
to Warr when they pleased, notwithstanding his saying all he could
to them, and that they were not like White Men.[52]

With so lackadaisical a command structure, it seems improbable that
any knowledgeable European thought the Cherokees capable of military
strategy. Yet in 1742, Jean Baptiste Le Moyne, Sieur de Bienville, governor
of Louisiana, and founder of New Orleans believed the Cherokees were
raiding his outposts in order to pressure French Canada to stop the attacks
of the northern Indians. The security of Louisiana, Bienville held, depended on a Canadian-Cherokee peace.[53] Among the British, credit of
Cherokee leadership usually turned upon whose colony was threatened.
South Carolinians could flee in panic at rumors that the Cherokees were
listening to French war talks, yet treat with scorn any alarm sounded
by Virginia. In 1761 the Carolinas believed the nation was planning a
general invasion of their backcountry and asked Virginia for military
assistance. Williamsburg refused, saying that the Cherokees would abandon the Lower Towns and Middle Settlements to the Carolinians, unite
in the Overhills, and destroy Virginia. Believing Virginia only wanted
an excuse to beg regular troops from Lord Amherst and throw the
expense of war on the Crown, South Carolina's agent was bitter. "The
reasoning they [the Virginians] give to the Indians," he wrote, "is a

Policy beyond them, as they have no coercive laws, the whole body can never act on one plan." [54] Many years earlier, King Crow had made the same point when asked what the power or office of headman "Signifyed" if the people in times of threatened invasion "would not mind what was said to them" [55]

> You see (says the King) that they'll promise you to go to Warr (but its when they please) and that they will have their own way of Warring and that it would be good if the English would let them alone and see what they will do of themselv's and by that means they may grow better.[56]

Colonel Chicken's frustration was not unique. The compliant resignation of Indian headmen such as King Crow often exasperated Europeans trained to act and to command. But their resignation should be put in Cherokee perspective. It was not merely the result of a domestic law which made headmen so constitutionally impotent they could not overcome the indifference of their people. It was also the result of military law —not just the military law of the Cherokees but of the southern Indians in general. King Crow's people could afford to be indifferent because they knew the Creeks and the Choctaws also lacked the legal and martial machinery to mount the massive invasion which Charles Town reported was on the way. The British might panic but the Cherokees had no cause for alarm. Of the 300 warriors who set out from the Creek nation, all but 40—exercising their prerogatives as southern Indians— changed their minds and (dreaming bad dreams or thinking of better things to do) had returned home after only one day on the path.[57]

The Cherokees of 1725 were a primitive nation, which could afford the resignation of its leaders and the indifference of its people because its enemies were also primitive. But the day was coming when these attributes would pose a dilemma both for them, and for the other American Indians. If we appreciate the full implications of this dilemma, we learn much, not merely of the Cherokee law of coercion or the Cherokee war machine, but of the mind of the average Cherokee and the options of leadership that his headmen possessed. King Crow's knowledge that the Creek army of invasion would dissipate in the woods created a luxury of civic indifference, for which future generations would pay a heavy price. When the American people were ready to march across the continent, they would easily push aside the Indian because the Indian was easily pushed. An enemy who could not organize his resources or marshall his strength may have been an enemy who momentarily halted the advance of civilization, an enemy undoubtedly menacing and terrifying in isolated places or for brief periods of time, but he was never a permanent barrier.

The Cherokees of Keowee and the Overhill towns, knowing the invasion army from the south would never appear, could easily laugh at the warning brought them by the white men from the east. But while theirs was the first laugh, they would not have the last. When the invasion came from the east, they would not know how to fight.

CHAPTER EIGHTEEN

A BELOVED OCCUPATION

—THE LAW OF CAPTURE AND ADOPTION

One might suppose that with so inefficient a war machine, their propensity for losing battles, and the contempt in which their martial abilities were universally held by Indians and Europeans alike—"old Women" the Shawnees called them with good reason [1]—the Cherokees would have eschewed warfare. On the contrary, they sought it. True, they do not seem to have regarded it a sport. It was a test of manhood perhaps, but not a means to social status or political influence. Rather, warfare to the Cherokees was a business, a grim, dangerous, exciting business so important to their way of life that its mores and values dominated their culture.

In the early part of the eighteenth century, Cherokees took the war path to reap vengeance, to seize slaves for sale at Charles Town, or because, as their uncles had done the same before them, it seemed to be the thing to do. In 1725 Colonel George Chicken found the men of one

Cherokee town "going out to Warr daily against the Creeks." [2] In later years, some Cherokees probably earned more presents collecting British scalp bounties than by hunting, and the rivalry between France and Britain made war, at least defensive war, absolutely necessary for national survival. War, moreover, was the reason for the Cherokee's widest rangings. Forays against the Senecas, the Mohawks, and the Delawares took them above the Ohio, sorties against the French tribes and the Choctaws took them to the Mississippi, raids on the Catawbas, the Cheraws, and the Uchees took them to the tidewater country of Carolina, and sallies against the Creeks introduced them to the territory which one day would form the heartland of their nation. [3] "We cannot live without war," the Cherokees told British emissaries urging them to bury the hatchet with a neighboring nation. "Should we make peace with the Tuscaroras with whom we are at war, we must immediately look out for some other, with whom we can be engaged in our beloved occupation." [4]

Surely to contemporary Europeans, war appeared the "beloved occupation" of the Cherokees, indeed of all American Indians. Writing to his brother in Scotland, William Fyffe probably expressed the view of most Carolinians when he made warfare the key to Cherokee cultural life, shrewdly calling it a "trade."

> War is their principal study & their greatest ambition is to distinguish themselves by military actions . . . even the old men who are past the trade themselves use every method to stirr up a martial ardour in the youth. The women (as among the whites know how to persuade by Praises or Ridicule the young men to what they please) employ their art to make them warlike. . . . Their young men are not regarded till they kill an enemy or take a prisoner. Those houses in which there's the greatest number of scalps are most honoured. A scalp is as great a Trophy among them as a pair of colours among us. [5]

Some of Fyffe's arguments were exaggerated. As often as urging the young to war, for example, the old men were cautioning peace, and as much as a Cherokee might take pride in a scalp, he was ever ready to sell it for a price. It is true, however, that no boy proved his manhood until he had successfully been on the warpath, and "Mankiller" or "Slave-Catcher" were titles any Cherokee would have proudly claimed. As late as 1859, more than a generation after the last battle and long after the last Catawba war, there was a member of the Eastern Band of Cherokees named "Catawba Killer." [6]

There are many legal oddities connected with the Cherokee war culture, but none is more puzzling than the office of *Ghi-ga-u,* a word variously translated as "Beloved Woman," "Pretty Woman," or most commonly "War Woman." As might be expected, so colorful a title has caught the imagination of popular historians, and more myths have been spun around the War-Woman legend than any other Cherokee institution.[7] Even the most conservative claims attribute to the War Woman power to pardon national enemies condemned to death. It would be easy to scoff at the notion of a female official entrusted with an authority surpassing that of any headman, were it not that both nineteenth-century Cherokee tradition[8] and reputable scholarship[9] believed the War-Woman legend and at least one War Woman is identified in the records. She is Nancy Ward, the Little Carpenter's niece, and she is credited with saving at least one person from the stake: an American named Mrs. Bean, during the Revolutionary War.[10]

We must consider the office of War Woman in some detail, for if it did possess the constitutional authority to pardon captured enemies condemned to torture, some of our ideas regarding Cherokee government have to be modified. At least we would be faced with the possibility that the power to command obedience could be vested in a single individual, even if only for a limited purpose.

The first point that must be conceded to the legend is this: the Cherokees did have the title "War Woman," but there is no evidence that it was any different from the military titles of men such as "the Raven"; it was bestowed upon Cherokee females for valorious achievement in wartime.[11] Nancy Ward, for example, is believed to have won fame and perhaps the title when she took the place of her slain husband, Kingfisher, in a great battle with the Creeks and helped the Cherokees carry the day.

It is an entirely different question whether power went with the title. Undoubtedly influence and prestige did; the War Woman surely ranked high in Cherokee councils and her words were received with respect. But there is little evidence that she could save anyone from the stake, or order the young men not to torture a prisoner. There are stories in Seneca manuscripts telling of two Cherokee women who decided the fate of captives, which may relate to the War-Woman legend.[12] But these women apparently decided upon the method of torture, not whether there should be torture, and Seneca tales must be accepted with caution as they may have been influenced by the Senecas' own customs. They were members of the Iroquois League, which delegated many decisions of this type to the women.[13] Our best evidence is that Nancy Ward saved Mrs. Bean. Again we must be skeptical. She is said to have spared Mrs. Bean partly because she was pro-American and opposed the war against colonies, yet she did not save a boy who had been captured with Mrs. Bean and who was tortured. Also she prevailed by arguing that Mrs. Bean was more valuable alive to the Cherokees than dead, as she could teach the women to spin cloth—an indication that she depended on her powers of persuasion and her influence, not on a constitutional right to pardon prisoners.

It is better to disregard the undocumented traditions about the War Woman's power to pardon prisoners, and to examine independent evidence. When we do so, it becomes apparent not only that the War Woman had no absolute authority to pass judgment, but that the Cherokees had no rules governing the question of torture. First of all a second myth must be laid to rest. It is not true, as has been asserted, that the southern Indians, or at least the Creeks, did not burn and torment captives.[14] In 1745 the Creeks burned a Cherokee boy whose father was white and mother a half blood, despite "pressing entreaties and very high offers of the British traders" to purchase his life.[15] Nor is it true, as has been claimed, that the Cherokees never tortured white men.[16] Although it is possible that burnings at the stake, like lynchings in civilized society, occurred only when passions were high,[17] there are several recorded instances of white men and women tortured and burnt by the Cherokees,[18] including the boy captured with Mrs. Bean whom Nancy Ward did not rescue.[19] John Downing, a trader at Tuckaseegee who was captured during the War of 1760, was taken to Estatoe, had his feet cut off, and was burned at the stake.[20]

William Fyffe wrote a description of the Cherokee method of torturing a prisoner.

> They begin at his Extremities one pulls out his Nails by the Roots, another puts his fingers in his mouth & chews it a third puts the mangled Stump in the Bole of a tobacco pipe made red hot & smoaks it. Others in the meantime do the same with his Toes snapping the Tendons cutting the Nerves & Cartilages about the Joints cutting out pieces of flesh & stopping the Blood with cauterizing Irons lest He shou'd bleed to Death & not allow them time to continue their tortures.[21]

We may be certain that the Cherokees tortured prisoners, but we cannot be certain how the fate of captives was decided. The best evidence indicates that there was no law governing the question. British traders, who occasionally tried to save prisoners and who often demonstrated their opposition to torture by withdrawing from the scene,[22] supposed that authority had to rest somewhere but disagreed as to who exercised it. Two of the most knowledgeable were Cornelius Daugherty and Ludovic Grant. Daugherty said that the headmen made the decision, an assertion which seems doubtful. Grant said it was made by the person who had captured the prisoner, subject to a veto by the headmen.[23] There is also another contemporary reference to the veto—this time vested in the War Women [24] —but again we must be careful before accepting such evidence, especially any inference that the veto was binding as a matter of law. Captain Raymond Demere, for example, also believed that Cherokee headmen decided whether and how a prisoner should be tortured; yet the very year he made that assertion he reported a case which indicates that when theory was tested by practice, no person or group had the final word. A party of about 40 Cherokee warriors returned to Chota with a young Indian prisoner whom they tied to a stake. "Some of the Indians," Demere wrote, "were of Opinion that he should be immediately burnt, and others that he should not, the Majority was that he should not be burnt, upon which he was untied, when immediately a young Fellow struck him through the Back with his Hatchet and killed him on the Spot." [25]

Whether the "young Fellow" acted "legally" is a difficult question. If he was the captor and the prisoner belonged to him, he was probably within his rights. If he was not the captor and acted from spite because he did not have his way, we might say that he did "wrong" but he apparently broke no law (even though he shed blood in Chota, the city of refuge). The lesson of this case is that no one decided the fate of prisoners in an orderly, decisive manner. It was left to passion, chance, and luck. If a War Woman was present and persuaded the people not to torture the prisoner, we might say she "vetoed" the torture, but anyone like the "young Fellow" could override her veto.

To doubt whether there was a tribunal or authority which decided the fate of prisoners is not to doubt that there were laws governing the disposition of captives. In fact, one of the best arguments for discounting War Women as supreme judges is that prisoners were private not public property, belonging by the rights of war either to the person capturing them, or to the person who acquired them by purchase. There is said to have been one exception to the right of ownership by capture; the close-clan kin of men slain in battle are supposed to have had the privilege of adopting a prisoner in the place of their dead relative. When describing this practice, William Fyffe implied it was a right which vested in them absolute ownership, for if they did not choose to adopt the prisoner possession did not revert to his captor; rather, the prisoner was put to death. According to Fyffe the prisoner belonged to the close-clan kin or "family" of the deceased

> every family getting an Offer of one or more according to the Number they've lost in the War the Person who took Him Prisoner conducts Him to the Door of the House where He's to be deliver'd & with Him offers a String of wampum. The family view the Prisoner & if He's ugly weakly or they thirst for more Revenge they reject the Prisoner by throwing away the String of wampum this is passing Sentence of Death or rather of Torture on Him.[26]

One white man who was rejected by the close-clan kin of a slain Cherokee and who survived to tell his tale was David Menzies, a Carolina surgeon. Menzies was captured during the War of 1760, about 100 miles from the nearest Cherokee town, at an Oconies River plantation where he had gone to care for some sick slaves.

> In proceeding to the town I understood (having some knowledge of their tongue) that these Cherokees had in this expedition lost one of their head-warriors, in a skirmish with some of our rangers; and that I was destined to be presented to that chief's mother and family in his room: At which I was overjoyed, as knowing that I thereby stood a chance not only of being secured from death, and exempted from torture, but even of good usage and caresses. I perceived however that I had over-rated much my matter of consolation, as soon as I was introduced in form to this mother of heroes; she sat squat on the ground, with a bear's club in her lap, as nauseous a figure as the accumulated infirmities of decrepitude undisguised by art could make her, and (instead of courteously inviting her captive to replace, by adoption, her lost child) fixed first her haggard blood-shot eyes upon me, then, riveting them to the ground, gargled out my rejection and destruction.[27]

After some torture, Menzies escaped.

It is likely that Fyffe learned his law from Menzies—he wrote shortly after Menzies returned to South Carolina—and that Menzies misunderstood what he was describing. It is doubtful if rejection meant death. Whether or not the close-clan kin of a deceased Cherokee had the right to claim for purposes of adoption a prisoner belonging to the nation which had killed their relative, one fact is certain: title in the prisoner did not automatically vest in them. This practice or custom was not an exception to the general rule, that a captive belonged to the person who captured him. The adopting clan had to purchase the adoptee from his owner, often at a very high price. As Woolenowaugh, the Great Warrior of Tennessee, explained three years before Menzies was captured, when the Cherokees "took a Slave and carried him to the next Relative of any Person who had been killed by those to whom such Slave belonged they had 200 and sometimes 300 weight of Leather for such Slave." [28] Woolenowaugh was not talking about the law of capture. He was telling the British that Cherokees sometimes paid higher prices among themselves than Charles Town was offering for Frenchmen, and hinting that the British would have to raise their offers. But he does suggest to us that prisoners were tendered to close-clan kin of recently-dead warriors, because for some reason of reciprocity—to replace their loss—they were the most likely purchasers. The captor had probably already decided he did not want to keep the captive. If the close-clan kin did not want him, and he was killed, it was not because he was rejected by those who had a legal right to decide his fate, but because no one would purchase him.

The general rule, therefore, was that prisoners belonged to the man who first seized them. It was this man who normally decided if the prisoner should be killed, held for ransom, sold, or set free. One European who learned what it meant to be captured, to be owned, and to be sold was a French soldier, named Antoine Bonnefoy who, during August, 1741, left New Orleans in a large convoy. On November 15, the party was ambushed on the Ohio River by about 80 Cherokees. Three Frenchmen were killed and the remainder taken prisoner. Immediately upon being secured, slave collars were placed on the necks of the captives, apparently by the Cherokees claiming them.[29] The French knew they belonged to certain warriors not only because they wore that warrior's collar, but because they were fed by him, getting a portion of meat and rum equal to their owner's.[30]

The Cherokee owning the prisoner might keep or sell him. When Bonnefoy's party was still more than a month's travel from home, he was purchased by a man "of prominence" who struck a bargain with his owner.

> I was adopted as brother by a savage who bought me of my master, which he did by promising him a quantity of merchandise and giving me what at that time I needed, such as bed-coverings, shirts, and

mittens, and from that time I had the same treatment as himself. My companions were adopted by other savages, either as nephews or as cousins, and treated in the same manner by their liberators and all their families.[31]

This transaction, negotiated on the war path far from the Overhill towns, may be the only documented instance of an executory Cherokee contract during their primitive-law era. The purchaser received immediate possession of Bonnefoy, the seller received the promise of future payment. Two months later Bonnefoy witnessed the execution of the contract, and his description of the ceremony, while a bit contrived, is important not merely as an example of how a prisoner was purchased. If Bonnefoy was correctly reporting an established custom for settling debts it is reasonable to suppose the method was also used on other occasions such as the payment of compensation in homicide cases.

> The savage who adopts a captive promises a quantity of merchandise to the one to whom he belongs at the moment when he buys him. This merchandise is collected from all the family of the one who makes the purchase, and is delivered in an assembly of all the relatives, each one of whom brings what he is to give and delivers it, piece by piece, to him who sold the slave, and at the receipt of each piece he makes the rounds of the assembly, constantly carrying what has been given to him, it being forbidden to lay down any piece on the ground, for then it would belong to whoever touched it first. The collection of my ransom was made on *the 9th* and *10th* and the ceremony on *the 11th*.[32]

Bonnefoy used two terms when describing his status—"slave" before he was purchased, "adopted brother" following his purchase. The distinction is obvious to us and may have been obvious to the Cherokees, but just what the terms meant in domestic law is a question somewhat clouded by the fact that Europeans tended to refer to every captive in the nation as a "slave."

Slaves were an important part of the booty of war, belonging to their individual captors.[33] At one time they were sold to the British,[34] but after the colonial governments outlawed Indian slavery, they may have been kept primarily as hostages or to be exchanged. Their value as laborers —grounding corn and tilling fields—was probably marginal in the Cherokee economy. Whether slaves had legal rights is problematical. The British supposed that they had none, a reasonable conclusion for it seems that at least their owners could treat them as they pleased.

A case in point occurred during 1747. A number of French and Shawnees, having failed in their mission to persuade the Cherokees to break their alliance with the British, were preparing to leave the nation. With them was a Shawnee, who had been captured in war by a Cherokee headman named Black Dog and made a slave. Black Dog was on his way to a meeting when he passed the place where the Shawnees were gathered and ordered the slave to accompany him. The slave refused, declaring that he intended to go home "down the river" with his fellow tribesmen. Black Dog, seizing his tomahawk, sunk it into the slave's skull, grabbed the corpse by the heels and flung it into the river, saying that if the Shawnee wanted to go to his countrymen he could go, and to tell them the others would be coming the same way if they so much as spoke a cross word. The French and Shawnees lost no time leaving.[35]

It was incidents such as this one that persuaded the British that Cherokee slaves had no rights. The Black Dog had killed his slave with impunity therefore it followed that a slave could be killed with impunity. It is unlikely that a Cherokee would have explained the same case in terms of personal status. To a Cherokee, the Black Dog's slave lacked legal rights not because he was a slave, but because he did not belong to a clan. The Black Dog had been able to kill him with impunity, for the same reason he could have killed any non-Cherokee in the nation. There was no one with the duty to avenge him. A Cherokee probably would have taken the same approach, if asked to explain the difference between the status of a slave and the status of an adoptee. No matter what the social distinction may have been—and there is no reason to think a slave was regarded as an inferior person—the legal distinction was that an adoptee was a member of a clan and a slave was not.

Were it not for clan law, it would be impossible to distinguish between captives mentioned in the records. Perhaps the most famous Cherokee captive was a man named French John who lived among the Overhills. He was a Canadian whom the British thought a French agent, and whom they wanted either delivered to Charles Town or killed. French John had been purchased from his captor by Old Hop, who claimed he paid 142 weight of leather to save the Canadian's life.[36] The British referred to French John as Old Hop's "slave," but must have known they were not using the word in a legal context. They complained that Old Hop treated him like an equal, and when they thought of executing him, they dared not regard him as a person without rights. Unable to hire a Cherokee willing to kidnap or kill French John on the sly, Captain Raymond Demere told Governor Lyttelton that he himself could not act directly. "I could not have him killed," he explained, "it would have been the same as if I had killed one of them." [37] If Demere was correct, French John had to be protected by clan law, and his relationship to Old Hop was more than that of master and slave. The conclusion is that French John enjoyed a different status than had the Black Dog's slave, a status which in terms of law may have been equal to that of Old Hop.

Antoine Bonnefoy, the French soldier captured on the Ohio in 1741, understood that once his purchaser received him from his captor, he was no longer a slave but an equal. When the war party returned to the Overhills, Cherokee custom required that the prisoners for a brief time, even though adopted, be treated as captives. Their slave collars were returned, and they were forced to entertain each town through which they passed by singing in the council house. But once the amusement was over the collars were again removed and they were free.

> I followed my adopted brother who, on entering into his cabin, washed me, then, after he had told me that the way was free before me, I ate with him, and there I remained two months, dressed and treated like himself, without other occupation than to go hunting twice with him. We were absent thirteen days the first time and nine days the last.[38]

Bonnefoy said that he was a "brother," and that the other Frenchmen captured with him were adopted as "nephews" or "cousins." It has been suggested that the correct designation should be "particular friend" or "special friend," [39] but the word "friend" would have had no meaning in law while "eldest brother," the phrase the Little Carpenter used to describe Captain John Stuart after purchasing him,[40] explains why Stuart, even though in the nation at the height of the War of 1760 and surrounded by enemies who wanted to kill him, was relatively safe.

Just what it meant in positive-law rules for John Stuart to be the Little Carpenter's "eldest brother" is conjecture. The tone of all the evidence—that men feared to harm him, and that by making him his brother the Little Carpenter intended to protect him—indicates that adoption placed Stuart within the blood feud, that he was the Little Carpenter's brother for purposes of the law of homicide. But what if he wanted to marry the Little Carpenter's sister, or suppose he accidentally killed the Little Carpenter? Was he still the Little Carpenter's "eldest brother"? More serious and more likely—if John Stuart killed a Cherokee of a different clan, was every member of the Little Carpenter's clan liable for that death? We shall never know the precise answers given in Cherokee positive law to these questions, but it is probable that an adoptee was regarded a member of the adopting clan as completely as if he had been born into it. Such a rule at least is suggested by general principles of the law of adoption shared by many of the eastern Indian nations.

> From the viewpoint of the primitive mind adoption serves to change, by a fiction of law, the personality as well as the political status of the adopted person. For example there were captured two white persons (sisters) by the Seneca, and instead of both being adopted into one clan, one was adopted by the Deer and the other by the Heron clan, and thus the blood of the two sisters was changed by the rite of adoption in such wise that their children could intermarry. Furthermore, to satisfy the underlying concept of the rite, the adopted person must be brought into one of the strains of kinship in order to define the standing of such person in the community, and the kinship name which the person receives declares his relation to all other persons in the family group; that is to say, should the adopted person be named son rather than uncle by the adopter, his status in the community would differ accordingly.[41]

The evidence that adoption gave Stuart the protection of the blood feud indicates that his clan brothers would have had to pay the blood price, had he been a manslayer. Thus, adoption could be a serious step in which the entire clan had a legitimate interest. If a Cherokee wished to adopt a non-Cherokee and make him a member of his clan, thereby creating a relationship binding on every member of the clan, one might expect the entire clan, a town-section of the clan, or at the very least the close-clan kin of the adopter to have the right of rejection. We have, however, no evidence that the clan or any part of the clan had anything to say on the question of adoption.[42] On the contrary, unreasonable as it may appear to us, Cherokee law apparently permitted an individual to adopt just about anyone he pleased and to bind his fellow clansmen to the adoptee by the most fundamental relationships known to their society, entailing both legal duties and legal perils. Such a rule is certainly consistent with Chero-kee constitutional principles governing freedom of choice, and was law in other American Indian nations.[43] In the cases of both John Stuart and Antoine Bonnefoy, the adopting Cherokee seems to have made the decision on his own. Indeed, Bonnefoy was adopted on the warpath far from the nation, and Bonnefoy's purchaser may even have pledged the goods of his clan kin to pay the purchase price. Conceivably the clansmen helping him execute the contract may have been present and have given their word when the bargain was struck. But just as likely, the Cherokee adopting Bonnefoy acted on his own and bound his clan brothers not only in clan ties to Bonnefoy, but also to help pay the purchase price.

We would know more about Cherokee law if we knew more about Indian rules of adoption in general, for adoption was a universal custom among the southern nations—perhaps among all Indians east of the Mississippi [44]—so well understood that it gives the appearance of international common law. An Indian captured by his enemies might not be able to anticipate whether he would be tortured, enslaved, held as a hostage, or adopted, but if adopted he probably understood without being told what his status was, and what treatment he might expect. That adopted citizens did not believe their condition precarious is shown by the large number who did not try to run away. Many of course did escape, yet there are frequent references in the records of Indians, sometimes called "slaves," who remained for years with the people who had taken them in. The Little Carpenter, for example, had once been adopted by a French tribe which captured him in battle, and he stayed with it long enough to rise to the rank of headman.[45] In 1794 a Cherokee who had been kidnapped as a boy was a Seneca chief, and as late as 1847, the Senecas could identify the members of their nation who were grandchildren of Cherokee captives taken in bygone wars.[46]

Adoption undoubtedly made Indian warfare more humane, but there is disagreement whether it helped or hurt the Cherokees. Lieutenant Timberlake believed it harmful as adopted Cherokees, returning to their original tribes, carried with them intelligence of Cherokee invasion routes, of Cherokee defensive weakness, and of Cherokee military tactics.[47] John R. Swanton, on the other hand, has argued that the law of adoption could strengthen a nation, pointing out that it "was in a large measure responsible for the rise to power of the great Iroquois Confederation." [48] Timberlake and Swanton may have been speaking of two different aspects of adoption, and Timberlake was certainly correct when he said that some individual adoptees, especially white men not prone to remain in savagery, could bring disaster to the Cherokees by leading parties through mountain passes with which they had become familiar while living in the nation. General James Robertson's forces were able to inflict the last great defeat suffered by Cherokees: the destruction of the Chickamaugas at Nickajack in 1794, because they had as their guide through unknown country a white boy who had been captured by the Chickamaugas and adopted by a Nichajack family. Swanton may be speaking of a different type of adoption, that is, adoption by the nation of whole peoples or tribes.

One of the most remarkable yet universal legal institutions shared by eastern Indians was the adoption of alien nations. The Iroquois especially followed this practice with notable success, adopting various neighbors, such as the Tutelo, the Sponi, and the Nanticoke.[49] On occasion, individual nations within the Iroquois League adopted alien people, as in 1649 when the Senecas adopted the Tohontaenrats, one of the four Huron tribes.[50] The practice was also common in the south. Following their defeat in the Yamasee War, for example, the Yuchi were merged into the Creek Confederacy, one body of Yuchi preserving its distinct identity for many years.[51]

It might be thought that adoption of entire nations or sizeable sections of nations would more accurately be described as "incorporation," but generally in Indian law it was regarded as adoption differing in detail and procedure, but not in theory, from adoption of individuals. The details and procedure are a mystery, at least as regards the Cherokees, for we have no hint how a national adoption was negotiated, and whether the adopting agency could be one town, a region, or all the towns. The theory, on the other hand, was the same as if a single person was adopted, a fact best demonstrated by the method used to effect the most famous national adoption in American history, that of the Tuscaroras by the Five Nations during the 1710s. The Tuscaroras, driven from North Carolina by a British-Catawba-Cherokee alliance, were sponsored by the Oneidas as the sixth constitutive member of the Iroquois League.[52] Political difficulties arising from the war made it inexpedient to recognize the Tuscaroras as equals, at least not immediately. Thus the Oneidas employed a legal fiction said to have been common in individual adoptions, a fiction permitting them to give asylum to the Tuscaroras without offending their late enemies.

A fictitious age might be conferred upon the person adopted, since age largely governed the rights, duties, and position of persons in the community. In this wise, by the action of the constituted authorities, the age of an adopted group was fixed and its social and political importance thereby determined. . . . Therefore the Oneida made a motion in the federal council of the Five Nations that they adopt the Tuscarora as a nursling still swathed to the cradle-board.

> This having prevailed, the Five Nations, by the spokesman of the
> Oneida, said: "We have set up for ourselves a cradle-board in the
> extended house," that is, in the dominions of the League. After due
> probation the Tuscarora, by separate resolutions of the council, on
> separate motions of the Oneida, were made successively a boy, a young
> man, a man, an asistant to the official woman cooks, a warrior, and
> lastly a peer, having the right of chiefship in the council on an
> equal footing with the chiefs of the other tribes.[53]

We do not know if the Cherokees used stages of political status anal-
ogous to the ages of human growth, when adopting alien tribes *en masse*.
All we know is that they, too, offered sanctuary to neighbors defeated
in war and no longer able to defend themselves. Perhaps they did not
adopt so much as protect, for they seem to have permitted other tribes to
settle within their midst yet remain in separate towns. The end result,
however, was not confederation but assimilation.

When the Chickasaws, worn down by continual wars against the French,
applied to the Cherokees for a place of refuge, the British urged the
Cherokees "to give an Invitation to the Chickesaws to settle amongst
them." [54] Later the British thought better of the scheme, and a Carolina
agent warned the Chickasaws that moving to the Cherokees would cost
them their domestic law.

> You may be sure whenever you leave your Lands and settle in other
> Nations you will be no more a People. Besides you'l lose your
> antient Rights and Customs, and be confined to comply with the
> Laws and Customs of other Nations whom you live amongst, who
> perhaps may use you hardly, and you will get no Satisfaction.[55]

This warning was not an accurate statement of Cherokee law. The once
powerful Natchez, who had earlier been adopted by the Chickasaws, more
recently had moved to the Cherokee nation where they were permitted an
independent existence. They maintained their own town, chief, and council,
not marrying or mixing with the Cherokees, a separation they continued
until about 1800. There were even a few survivors, speaking their native
language among the Cherokees in Oklahoma, when the Cherokee nation
came to an end.[56] Size, rather than law, was the moving force toward
assimilation, as illustrated by the Taskigi, a small tribe of unknown origin
who joined the Cherokees in an early period and were nearly extinct as
an identifiable group by 1819.[57]

During the next century, when Cherokees were more politically sophisticated and more aware of potential difficulties, they would adopt or incorporate alien tribes only after protracted negotiations in which rights were defined and duties acknowledged.[58] But during their primitive-law era, the issues of national adoption do not seem to have troubled them. There is no indication that they gave thought to the problems that might arise, even to such obvious questions as whether the Natchez clans were incorporated into domestic law for purposes of the blood feud, or to rules regulating marriage between full-blood Cherokees and the children of Taskigi mothers and Cherokee fathers.

The conclusion that an adopted nation was able to maintain a separate status in domestic law until socially assimilated is supported by the international law of the southern nations, which often distinguished between native and adopted citizens. In 1725, for example, the Upper Creeks lived in such "a great Dread" of Chickasaws in the Cherokees that Creek men were afraid to go from one of their towns to another without arms. We may infer that the Creeks regarded the responsible Chickasaws as adopted or incorporated into the Cherokee nation and not merely visitors, because they do not seem to have blamed the main body of Chickasaws still living in their ancient homeland. That they also did not blame the Cherokees is significant, although it is possible the distinction was based less on law than pride, for the Creeks implied the Cherokees alone could never terrorize them. "[T]he Chickasaws are men," they explained, "but the Cherokees are old women." [59] A quarter of a century later, there were Chickasaws incorporated in the Creeks and other Chickasaws living just outside the nation. Some members of the latter band killed a Cherokee named Black Dog, a "true friend" of the Raven of Hywassee. The Raven was careful to distinguish between the two bodies of Chickasaws. "[T]he Chickasaws who live by the Creeks shot him," he said, "and not those of the Nation," [60] implying that if satisfaction was sought, the Cherokees would recognize that the Chickasaws in the Creek nation belonged to a body politic not responsible for the homicide.

Whether the Cherokees would have started a war with the Creeks, had the Chickasaw manslayer belonged to that nation, is a different question. We may suppose that under international custom the adopting nation could be held responsible, for otherwise the Oneidas might not have been so cautious when adopting the Tuscaroras. If the independent Natchez committed an offense, they alone may have been blamed, and retaliation could have been limited to them without involving the Cherokees—or at least the Cherokees could have argued they were not responsible on much the same grounds that they argued they were not liable when mere visitors in their nation breached the peace. But if the guilty party was a member of a small group such as the Taskigi, who were relatively assimilated or who could not have existed but for the protection given them by the Cherokees, we may imagine the Cherokees were held liable.

Undoubtedly no rule prevailed, only attitudes. If the injured nation was small, it would react differently than if it were large, and if it wanted war it needed no legal excuses. The law existed not to settle questions, but to furnish arguments. A nation seeking satisfaction rather than war might take note that a manslayer belonged to an adoptee group, rather than to the native-born part of the nation; expecting that to avoid trouble, the nation would put pressure on the dependent tribe to surrender the manslayer, as the Creeks had threatened to expell the Chickasaws if the Chickasaw manslayer was not killed or delivered to the British.[61] Again, we must not ask for answers more definite than international law is able to provide.

CHAPTER NINETEEN

A PATH SWEPT CLEAN

—THE MAKING OF PEACE

The Cherokee war machine was so often in operation that it is doubtful whether the nation experienced complete peace at any time between the beginning of its recorded history and the last defeat of the Chickamaugas in 1794. In almost every year the Cherokees were at war with one or another of their traditional enemies, often with several at a time. In 1725, for example, they were fighting the Creeks, Choctaws, Senecas, and the French tribes, and probably were raiding the Chickasaws as there were Chickasaw prisoners in several of their towns. Of course some of these opponents—the Chickasaws and Choctaws surely, the Creeks and Chocktaws perhaps—were at war with each other. Yet even when their enemies were not united, or were distracted by other foes, the Cherokees were hard pressed to repell so many raiders. There was, therefore, no aspect of international relations more vital to their survival than the making of peace.

It is not easy to define what a southern Indian understood by the word "peace." For a Cherokee it probably meant to be free from raids, although it is doubtful if the nation ever experienced peace to the degree that all towns were free from the fear of attack. Using this limited definition—the only practical definition—it can be said that the assertion sometimes made that the southern Indians had no peacemaking machinery is fallacious.[1] The Cherokees and their neighbors were not doomed to perpetual war. They had the means to end conflict. Their problem was not to negotiate but to maintain peace.

The Cherokee method of negotiating peace is demonstrated by their relations with the Creeks, not so much because these two nations were constantly at war, but because they were constantly trying to make peace. Many of their negotiations are reported in British records, partly because the British sometimes were responsible in bringing the parties together,[2] and partly because colonial officials tried to claim credit whenever a war was ended.[3] The usual practice, however, was for the Cherokees and Creeks to deal independently of Charles Town or Savannah, and to do so by utilizing what seems to have been a customary law of international negotiation.

Even when employing customary diplomatic procedures the Cherokees, at least during recorded periods, were seldom free of British influence. Traders were always present, either in the Creek nation or in the Cherokees, and they frequently exerted pressure by giving advice, by bribing parties, or by purporting to speak for some colonial official, particularly for the governor of South Carolina. Moreover, the traders impose themselves upon us—even when they were merely spectators, taking no part in the proceedings—because they wrote most of the extant reports of peace negotiations upon which history must rely. As they were white men, they described what interested or seemed important to white men, and we may doubt whether the points they stressed would have been stressed by a southern Indian. Their standards were European standards, not Cherokee standards, and as they probably defined "peace" differently than an Indian defined it, their reports were surely colored by expectations different from those of the negotiators.

There were also times when the British were asked to play a role within the structure of traditional Indian diplomatic procedures, without influencing the result. On one occasion, for example, the Creeks refused to receive Cherokee ambassadors unless a white man accompanied them.[4] Just what the Creeks had in mind is uncertain—unless the white man was to be evidence of the Cherokees' good faith—for usually it was the contacting, not the receiving nation which sought third-party assistance. A major obstacle in forest diplomacy, after all, was for the people wanting peace to make contact with the other side. Thus in 1753, Skiagunsta of Keowee asked Governor Glen to dispatch a white man with a peace talk to the Lower Creeks, after which he would "send some of my People with Peace Tokens directly to Chigilli among the Creeks." [5] Just as often, the Cherokees hired white packhorsemen, working for Carolina traders in their towns, to carry peace talks.[6] Before the British appeared on the continent, the southern nations probably used neutral Indians, a practice the Cherokees continued until the end of warfare. Chickasaws, for example, sometimes carried Cherokee peace talks to the Creeks.[7]

We might expect that intermediaries were always needed, that no Cherokee would have dared risk his scalp carrying talks into the center of an enemy nation. But in fact, the hiring of neutrals seems to be the exception to the general rule that the Cherokees themselves made the initial contact. In the great majority of cases, the belligerents turned up in the other nation looking for peace. Perhaps they placed some trust in a doctrine of safe conduct. "By common tribal custom," James Mooney writes, "ambassadors of peace were secure from molestation, whatever might be the result of the negotiations." [8] The rule may have been better understood than observed; its application at least was by no means absolute. A nation was never certain how its envoys would be received. When three Upper-Creek ambassadors arrived home in 1749 from a peace mission to the Cherokees, bringing with them five Cherokee commissioners, the Creeks were reported "overjoyed . . . to see their People return safe from the Cherokees." [9] One expediency employed to secure a safe welcome was to send a captive with the envoy, as the Creeks did in 1725 when their ambassador to the Overhills was accompanied by the daughter of the Head Warrior of Great Tellico. She had been kidnapped by the Creeks, and Colonel George Chicken believed her return won the ambassador a friendly hearing at Tellico. Yet his presence was kept secret. Had the headmen of the other Overhill towns known he was at Tellico, they would have killed him.[10] In 1750 Cherokee envoys to the Upper Creeks were accompanied by nine Shawnees and one Chickasaw, obstensibly to guard them on the path.[11] And three years later, as previously mentioned, Skiagunsta of Keowee did not wish to risk sending his men with "Peace Tokens" until Governor Glen made the path safe by informing the Creeks they were on the way.[12]

Sometimes the receiving nation demanded evidence of good faith. When the Red Coat King of the Oakfuskees heard Glen's talk on behalf of

Skiagunsta, he stipulated what "Peace Tokens" the Cherokee ambassadors were to bring. "It is of no Use your sending any Peace Talks here," he wrote, "without three or four Head Men will come from the Cherokees to my Town, and bring two Northern Indians Slaves with them.[13] He wanted one Northern for Oakfuskee, the other for the town of Coweta; the idea, one trader explained, was that "the Creeks might have the burning of the said Slaves, and then they say they will think it is all streight." [14]

Despite these precautions, it cannot be said that the doctrine of safe conduct, even if less than absolute, lacked standing in the international law of the southern Indians. Peace emissaries often arrived unannounced in an enemy nation during a war. Surely they had some reason to expect that they might not be killed, but would be received as accredited diplomats. Perhaps they carried specially painted calumets as credentials or passports; the records do not say. What the records do make clear is that they usually received a cordial welcome. We will never know how many were slain on the path out of sight of the British reporters, but the impression is that most made it in safety, probably because they had some idea of when and where to appear.

During July, 1750, the Upper Creeks were in council at Ockehoys when they heard that two Cherokee men and three Cherokee women from the town of Great Tennessee had arrived with peace talks. Fifteen headmen went to meet them at Abbecutchee but forgetting to bring an interpreter, they took one of the Cherokees back to the council where "we made him King of the Ockchoys and twelve Towns more." The Cherokee, speaking for the Overhill towns, presented the Upper Creeks with beads, tobacco, and a white wing. "[W]e the Upper Creeks Savannas and Chickasaws and Sinkinglings † gave him Beads Tobacco and a White Wing in return." [15]

These gifts—the beads, tobacco, and white wing—indicate the ambassador probably spoke for Great Tennessee, for he quite likely would not have had such items unless they had been furnished by his town council to serve as tokens of friendship. Strings of white beads were especially popular among southern-Indian diplomats. So too was wampum, exchanged not merely as a symbol of harmony but as a reminder of the agreement, as a mnemonic device to record the negotiations once peace was concluded.

If more of these wampum belts had escaped destruction during the

† The Savannas (Shawnees) and Chickasaws acted as interpreters. The Sinklinglings were a Louisiana nation.

American Revolution, we might have a better idea of Cherokee diplomatic procedure. As it is, only one seems to have survived to be officially read at a council during the post-primitive era. It was a wampum belt given the Cherokees by the Iroquois in 1768, which they still possessed when driven across the Mississippi to the Indian Territory west of Arkansas. Assuming leadership among the newly-arrived eastern nations, they called an international conference in 1841 to make peace with the Plains tribes. It was the greatest gathering of Indians on record and of vital importance to the Cherokees for they were civilized now, fifty years removed from the warpath. If the Kansa, the Osage, or the Pawnee were to attack, the Cherokees might have to defend their farms and schools themselves. They had only recently, after much effort, persuaded the Secretary of War to rule that the United States Army had the constitutional authority to help them, and while the military was willing, it was still possible orders could be changed. Thus it was a dramatic moment in the proceedings when a Cherokee spokesman produced the wampum belt given by the Iroquois in 1768 and interpreted it to the delegates for it told the tale of how, following the defeat of France, the eastern nations, once bitter enemies, had made a universal, lasting peace, proving that Indians could live without war.[16] The Iroquois had selected the Shawnees to carry the peace talk to the Cherokees. The Shawnee ambassadors travelled south until they reached a Cherokee village, where they waited in the woods while two of their members went to the house of the Cherokee headman.

> The chief's daughter was the only person in the house. As soon as she saw them, she went out and met them, and shook them by the hand and asked them into the house to sit down. The men were all in the field at work—the girl's father was with them. She ran and told him that there were two men in the house, and that they were enemies. The chief immediately ran to the house and shook them by the hand, and stood at the door. The Cherokees all assembled around the house, and said, Let us kill them, for they are enemies. Some of the men said, No, the chief's daughter has taken them by the hand; so also has our chief. The men then became better satisfied. The chief asked the two men if they were alone. They answered, No; that there were some more with them. He told them to go after them and bring them to his house. When these two men returned with the rest of their people, the chief asked them what their business was. They then opened this valuable bundle, and told him that it contained a talk for peace. The chief told them, I cannot do business alone; all the chiefs are assembled at a place called Cho-qua-ta [Chota],

where I will attend to your business in general council. When the messengers of peace arrived at Cho-qua-ta, they were kindly received by the chiefs, who told them they would gladly receive their talk of peace. The messengers of peace then said to the Cherokees, We will make a path for you to travel in, and the rising generation may do the same,—we also will keep it swept clean and white, so that the rising generation may travel in peace. The Shawnee further said, We will keep the doors of our houses open, so that when the rising generation come among us they shall be welcome. He further said, This talk is intended for all the different tribes of our red brothers, and is to last to the end of time. He further said, I have made a fire out of the dry elm—this fire is for all the different tribes to see by.[17]

Perhaps the major cultural gap to be overcome by an eighteenth-century colonial official first introduced to Indian affairs was the apparent aimless drift in peace talks; the insufferable delays, while orators such as this Shawnee spoke on and on, never coming to the point. The official might wait patiently for preliminaries to be concluded so that both sides could get down to business, but he would wait in vain. The preliminaries for the white man were the talks for the Indian. Today, also, on reading the translation of beads exchanged to commemorate peace talks, we may look for the terms of a concordat to be discussed, the articles of a treaty to be concluded, only to look in vain. The southern Indian was interested in the atmosphere of the talk, not the substance. The agreement was less important than the cordiality; and it is the cordiality, not the agreement, which belts of wampum report. Like this belt given the Cherokees by the Iroquois, they tell of friendly welcomes and of peace talks exchanged around a council fire; they do not relate the provisions of a treaty. If this fact surprises us, it is because we expected them to describe a European peace conference, rather than an Indian peace talk.

It cannot be said that international controversies were never subject to negotiation between the southern Indians. It can only be said that when specific issues were settled during a peace talk, the agreement reached and the terms ratified by the two sides—even on those rare occasions when war could not have been concluded without an agreement—took secondary importance next to the peace talk itself. What counted was the talk. Points in dispute were seldom significant either in fact, or in the thinking of the average southern Indians. Wars, after all, were not fought over questions which could be settled, such as land claims, alliances, or the rights of dynasties. They usually arose by accident, were fought to obtain retaliation, or resulted from age-old animosity. It was not often ambassadors discussed ways of avoiding future wars. There would have been little point doing so. A peace or an agreement was only as lasting as each warrior was willing to observe it. No headman or ambassador could bind an individual Cherokee without his consent, and a Cherokee's consent did not bind him beyond a change of mind.

The task of southern-Indian ambassadors—to terminate the current conflict—could be accomplished only if they succeeded in putting their people and the people of the other side in a peaceable frame of mine. Hence the mnemonic belts of wampum with their words of buried hatchets, and of welcomes for the "rising generation"—not so much historical records, as devices for propaganda carried through the nation so their message of peace could be read in the council houses. It was necessary to show the people of both sides, as Judd's friend put it, "that our hearts are good and strait." [18]

Considering the realities of the Cherokee constitution, peace makers probably did not try to persuade the average warrior to accept their negotiations. They more likely brought their message to the town councils, hoping that if the majority received their peace talk, public opinion would shame individuals into observance. Their chief task was to convince the town to accept it. Even more important was to convince separate regions of the nation to go along. A warrior or party of warriors might be shamed into consent, but not whole towns or regions. Their political independence was the greatest threat posed during peace talks, for countrymen and enemies alike.

During 1725, the Cherokees wanted to negotiate a peace with the Creeks but neither region of the Creek nation, the Uppers or Lowers, would talk. Even had the Upper Creeks been willing, the Lowers said they would continue fighting. "The Upper Creeks may do as they Please," a Lower-Creek headman explained, "but as for me and my People we will hear nothing of a Peace we have not forgott them men yet that was killed there in cold blood when the white People was there † and that remains in our minds and shall so long as one of us is alive." [19]

A tested (but not always successful) solution to the dilemma posed by national divisions was for the peace faction to dissassociate itself from the majority and conclude a separate truce. When the Conjuror of Ufassey arrived on a peace mission in the Upper-Creek town of Oakfuskee two years later, he found the people tired of war. Oakfuskee, on the Tallapoosa

† *i.e.*, the slaying of the Creek delegates in the Cherokee nation during the Yamasee War.

River in present-day Alabama, was exposed to Cherokee attacks while the more belligerent Lower Creeks, shielded by the Upper Creeks, were relatively secure. The headman of Oakfuskee told the Conjurer that if the Lower Creeks would not accept the Cherokees' peace talk, the Oakfuskees would remove their town from the nation and settle somewhere near the Cherokees.[20] They did not move but if they had, no informed Cherokee would have been puzzled by their status. In the international law of the southern Indians, the right of dissociation was a well-established practice. After the Yamasee War, for example, the Creeks were determined to exterminate the Yamasees, yet protected that part of the Yamasee nation which had detached itself from the main body of Yamasees and obtained asylum in Creek towns.[21] The reverse could also occur as enemies might permit a single town to withdraw from the conflict, yet remain geographically where it was. During 1737, the Overhills made peace with the Creek town of Coosa, apparently continuing hostilities against the remainder of the nation.[22]

No town, either Cherokee or Creek, could keep its young men from joining the war parties of other towns, and as a result separate armistices were seldom lasting. The Indians surely realized this fact for when single towns or regions met to talk peace, the negotiators sometimes tried to persuade the other side to speak for its entire nation, even if they themselves could not reciprocate. During 1750 the Overhill Cherokees sent a peace feeler to the Upper Creeks. The Gun Merchant, on behalf of the Upper Creeks, replied by warning the Overhills that a large war party from the Lower Creeks was out against the Lower Cherokees. "Notwithstanding," he is reported to have said, "if the Lower Cherokees would hearken to peace we make no doubt but we could prevail upon the Lower Creeks to comply to a Peace Likewise." [23] When the Overhill ambassador arrived in the Upper Creeks, he was asked if he was authorized to speak for the Lower Cherokees as well. He answered that he was not, but when he had been commissioned to negotiate with the Upper Creeks, the Overhills had sent runners to the Lower Cherokees to inform them of his mission. The best he could offer was the hope that by the time he returned home, the Lower Cherokees would have sent a white wing to the Lower Creeks.[24] Apparently the Upper Creeks pressed him to speak for the entire Cherokee nation because the ambassador admitted he was from "an outside Town," and while "all the outside Towns are mightily for Peace," he implied that towns less ravished by war might not accept any talk he carried back from the Creeks.[25]

A European colony might have declined dealing with a Cherokee representative speaking for such a limited section of the nation. But the Upper Creeks judged diplomatic credentials by the more limited standards of southern-Indian realities. They were anxious to reach an agreement, and "articles of Peace" were arranged. The most revealing item of the Cherokees' half of the bargain was not that Cherokee negotiators undertook to speak for their nation, but that they specifically excepted from the treaty one town (probably Great Tellico) for which they said no promises could be made, as its people were rogues and friendly with the French.[26] We cannot be certain just what the southern Indians meant by excepting a whole town from peace. It was a tactic the Cherokees would successfully use with the Americans to avoid liability for the acts of the Chickamaugas during the 1780s, and which they would employ as late as the 1820s with the Osage in Arkansas.[27] If we draw an analogy to the domestic law of homicide, the Cherokee ambassador may have been saying that Great Tellico, should it offend the Creeks, was no longer under the nation's protection. This legal concept would have been similar to the practice by which clans put individuals outside the operation of the law of homicide. "If Watts goes to war and falls," Unacata said of his brother, "I will not pick him up." [28] In return for the Cherokee promise to stop raids, the Gun Merchant on behalf of the Upper Creeks, agreed to undertake a mission to the Lower Creeks and persuade them to make peace with the Cherokees, a pledge he immediately fulfilled.[29]

As a large percentage of the Upper Creeks were supporting the peace, expectations were high that the Gun Merchant would succeed,[30] but the Lower Creeks rejected his talk. For more than a year they remained at war with all the Cherokees, while the Upper Creeks, apparently free from Cherokee raids, were noncombatant.[31] There is reason to believe that the peace party among the Upper Creeks, led by the Gun Merchant and the Red Coat King, tried to keep the peace but the task was hopeless. With war parties crossing their country in both directions, and some of their young men actively engaged, it was inevitable that before long they would once more be drawn into the conflict. By 1752 if not sooner, the Upper Creeks again had joined the Lower Creeks against both the Lower and Overhill Cherokees. Now it was the Lower Cherokees' turn to seek peace. Continual warfare had destroyed their economy, and most of the people had fled into the mountains. Even the Carolina-border town Keowee had, its headman Skiagunsta reported in July 1753, "so few People in it that it scarce deserves the Name." [32] Skiagunsta learned that the Upper

Creeks were still in favor of peace, while the Lower Creeks wanted to continue the war,[33] and he had hopes that the 1750 treaty with the Upper Creeks could be renegotiated. The Lower Creek headman Malatchi rejected his overtures. The Lower Cherokees, he said, might be sincere in their desire for peace, but the international situation had changed since 1750. The Overhills now were harboring Northern Indians whom the French had sent to attack the Lower Creeks, "and we have good Reason to think that they aided and assisted them by which Means we have lost several of our People since the [last] Peace was agreed to; an Agreement which we hoped would have been binding on boath Sides." [34] Even if the Overhills would join the Lower Cherokees in seeking peace, Malatchi doubted his people could be persuaded to negotiate, for he understood that two of the Cherokee towns "that lay backwards," probably remote from the Creeks and exposed to the Northern Indians, would not agree. "I must think it will be in Vain to make a Peace when any one Town was to be at War," Malatchi concluded, "for unless the whole Nation should be unanimous, a Peace will not be practicable." [35]

We must not attribute too much to Malatchi's words. He was the most intractable anti-Cherokee leader among the Creeks and would employ any argument to keep the Upper Creeks and British from being impressed with Cherokee peace talks. It might appear that Malatchi's words mark a shifting in southern-Indian attitudes: a realization that peace depended upon binding the entire nation, or else an agreement could prove valueless. Such was the interpretation of the governor of South Carolina: that Malatchi thought of the Cherokee nation as a unit which could control its separate parts. But the important question is not what the British thought he meant. The important question is how the Upper Creeks understood his words. It is doubtful if Malatchi was asking that the Cherokees sign a peace backed by the coercion of physical force, instead of public opinion. Rather, he was warning the Upper Creeks that the circumstances of 1753 created a situation in which it was unlikely that the implementation of public opinion necessary to make peace at least minimally effective could be obtained among the Cherokees. Read in the context of the particular problem with which he was dealing, Malatchi's argument that peace was not "practicable" unless every town agreed, may best be interpreted as a recognition of the foreign-Indian problem. It was one thing if the nation made a peace, and some towns remained aloof as in 1750. It was quite another for the Cherokees to try to make peace with the Creeks while a few Cherokee towns continued to shield, supply, and perhaps even be dominated by the Creeks' active enemies. Malatchi knew that with the Northern Indians in control of a few Cherokee towns, the moral persuasion of the majority would be ineffectual. He was arguing that the Northerns be expelled from the Cherokees before the Creeks accept a peace talk.

Third parties, such as the Northern Indians in 1753, were often vital factors in Cherokee peace negotiations. Sometimes they played a positive role: as for example the British who exerted pressure to keep the Cherokees from making peace with French Indians, or to persuade them to make peace with such British allies as the Creeks. At other times their role was negative, as in 1753 when the presence of Northern Indians in the Cherokees not only gave Malatchi an excuse to refuse a peace talk, but caused one Cherokee delegation to fail to keep an appointment with the Creeks because every man was needed at home to guard their towns against the visitors.[36]

On occasion foreign-Indian pressure complicated national decisions. In 1725 the Upper Creeks had offered to make peace with the Cherokees, partly because they had discovered that the Chickasaws, not the Cherokees, were to blame for the killings which precipitated the war,[37] and partly because the Choctaws were killing so many of their people that they could no longer sustain a war on two fronts.[38] The Lower Creeks, on the other hand, were less afraid of the Choctaws and the Cherokees than they were of the Senecas—a nation also at war with the Cherokees. When the Upper Creeks asked the Lowers to join in a peace talk, the Lower Creeks sent a delegation to sound out Seneca reaction. The Senecas warned them not to make a Cherokee peace, "Lest we Deem You our Enemies as we do them; for we have no peoble to warr Against nor Yet no Meal To Eat But the Cherokeys." [39]

It took a good deal of diplomatic ingenuity to overcome some third-party complications. Cherokee envoys were nimble at glossing over difficulties when they could persuade everyone to join forces against a fourth enemy. In 1749, for example, the Creeks refused to consider a Cherokee peace talk because the Cherokees were harboring their enemies, the Nottoways. Here was a serious dilemma for the Cherokees. They could not expel the Nottoways without offending them and risk starting a Nottoway war as the price for a Creek peace. The Cherokee ambassadors tried to maneuver around the Creeks' demand. The Nottoways, they told the Creeks, were not in their nation primarily to make war on the Creeks. They would rather have a Creek peace as they wanted "to turn their whole Force, with all other Nations, that will join them, against the Catawbas in order to destroy them Root and Branch." [40] If the Creeks made war on the Catawbas, they not only could have peace with the Cherokees, but with the Nottoways as well. It was a neat diplomatic package, which solved everyone's problem except the Catawbas'.

To turn an enemy into an active ally fighting someone else was surely a diplomatic triumph for Cherokee negotiators. There was no better way to assure that raids would halt, at least temporarily. After all, most of the nations with whom the Cherokees dealt lacked coercive law and as a result, lacked the means to enforce a negotiated peace. If they could draw the enemy into a second war, they were free of some pressure. If they could draw him into a war as their ally, they could probably count on public opinion in his nation to have some success discouraging raids.

That both sides to most southern-Indian peace negotiations knew neither could bind individuals to the terms of an agreement may make Indian diplomacy appear somewhat nebulous to us, but considerably eased the task of negotiators. As often as not, the parties merely agreed to forgive and forget past injuries; the future was left to take care of itself. At times the nations vaguely promised to overlook future killings. "Where there is blood spilt I will wipe it up clean," the Shawnee ambassador told the Cherokees in 1768, "wherever bones have been scattered, I have taken them and buried them, and covered them with white hickory bark and a white cloth—there must be no more blood spilt; our warriors must not recollect it any more." [41]

Knowledge that peace could not be built on hopes may have caused some headmen to seek only temporary truces, a reasonable approach as the primary purpose of negotiations was to stop raids. A Creek ambassador was sent to the Cherokees in 1725, to ask "about a peace with them for the Summer gone, the Winter coming and the Spring following." [42]

Seldom were specific demands presented as conditions for peace. The chief exceptions in Cherokee history occurred when enemies told them to expel visitors—as the Squirrel King of the Chickasaws did when the Cherokees asked him to stop Chickasaw raids, or as Malatchi did when he made it a condition for starting peace talks. Earlier, in 1749, the Upper Creeks had told the Cherokee ambassadors they would cease fitting out war parties "provided the Cherokees drive away or kill all the Nottowagoes, and other Northern Indians from amongst them." [43] It was to counter this demand that the Cherokee ambassadors lamely proposed they should all join in a Catawba war, destroying them "Root and Branch."

If terms were not always important, words were, for words could be reported back in the nation to put the people in a proper frame of mind. The stress was upon phrases and expressions that had become familiar in Indian diplomacy, and were repeated over and over. The appearance of the same sentences at the same places, in peace talk after peace talk, may explain why Judge Haywood implied that Cherokee peace negotiations were conducted by ritual; they gave the impression that the success depended on such things as the wearing of special ceremonious clothes, by bowing to one another at prescribed times, by mouthing set formulae, or by crowning the messenger of peace.[44]

Of course the Indians were courteous to each other and may have bowed on occasions, and like Thomas Becket representing Henry II in Paris, a Cherokee ambassador did not want to appear in rags. But to suppose an agreement was made binding by ritual is to think differently than a Cherokee thought.

There is no evidence to indicate that any ceremonious gestures had to be performed. Clarity in communication was the object, and actions were designed to be understood and reported. Red paint might be washed from a warrior, a knife might be cleansed of blood, or a tomahawk might be buried—and word would be passed from town to town that the bloody hatchet would be seen no more. On some occasions the symbolism was intended to impress the other side. Early in 1718, the British made peace with the Creek nation at a council held in Coweta. The agents from South Carolina broke a knife to confirm the peace, and the Creeks shattered a bow and arrow. But they kept another bow and a bloody knife to show they were still at war with the Cherokees, apparently to remind Charles Town that it was supplying the enemy with arms and ammunition.[45]

Aside from symbolic acts, it is hard to find evidence of ceremony. Most of our accounts of Cherokee peace negotiations, after all, are from reports of traders and colonial government agents who were not interested in savage customs or diplomatic protocol, but tended to focus on the agreement as if detailing a European treaty. One of the few contemporary descriptions of an all-Indian peace council in which Cherokees participated, and which did not involve negotiations to divert attention from the proceedings, appeared in a colonial newspaper during the summer of 1751. "[O]ne of the Kings of the *Cherokee Indians* with Eight of his Nobels, and about thirty Attendants," [46] was in Williamsburg when word came that a band of Nottoways planned to ambush them on the path home. The Nottoways thought the Cherokees had killed seven of their young

men many years before, and were after vengeance. Somehow they learned
these Cherokees were not the ones they wanted and to restore peace,
entered Williamsburg under a white flag.

> The *Cherrokees* being inform'd of their Arrival immediately gave the
> Signal of War, and were preparing for Battle; but several Gentlemen
> representing to them the friendly Appearance of the *Nottoways,* ad-
> vised them to march out, and meet them in the same friendly Manner:
> At first they were inflexible, but being at last prevail'd on, they
> hoisted a white Flag, and marching by Beat of Drum, met the Notto-
> ways in the Market Place, each Party singing the song of Peace.
> After many of the accustomed Ceremonies, they join'd Hands and
> smoak'd the Pipe of Peace together: But not being able to hold
> any Conference, the Crowd being very great, they repair'd to the
> Court House; where the *Nottoways* being sensible these were not
> the *Indians* who had done them the Injury they complain'd of,
> produc'd a Belt of Wampum, which they had receiv'd of the
> *Cherrokees* at their last Peace, and desired a Continuance of their
> Friendship. The Orator, who negotiates all their Treaties, receiv'd
> the Wampum, and raising it up made a long Speech to his Friends,
> telling them that he himself had many Years ago given this Belt
> as a Token of Peace; that he now found it intire, not a Bead amiss,
> and from thence concluded that their Hearts were strait, and their
> Friendship preserv'd entire; afterwards by the unanimous Consent
> of all his People, he made them a Present of a Pipe of Peace, assuring
> them of his Friendship. All Differences being thus adjusted to the
> Satisfaction of both Parties, they met in the Evening at the Camp
> of the *Cherrokees,* where making a large Fire, they danced to-
> gether around it, and concluded the Evening with Harmony and
> Cheerfulness.[47]

At Williamsburg the Cherokees and Nottoways were not negotiating
but affirming a peace, hence it is not surprising that ceremony dominated
the parley. Yet despite the colorfulness of the dancing and the symbolism
of exchanging gifts, it is difficult not to believe that the significant parts
of the proceedings were the orations and the reading of the wampum. It
would not matter that the words were familiar, that the expressions were
those which had been formulated long ago, so they might be easily
remembered and repeated in the council houses when runners carried the
white wing of peace throughout the nation: to brighten the chain of
friendship and keep it free from rust, to sweep clean and white the path
which is now stained with blood, to bury the hatchet so deep it will not

be found again as long as the grass shall grow, as long as the sun shall shine, as long as the waters run.

The Cherokee speaker in 1841 who interpreted the Iroquois belt of wampum expected the Plains Indians beyond the Mississippi—the Osage, the Comanche, the Quapaw, the Kiowa, the Wichita—to understand the diplomatic language of the eastern woodlands, for he concluded his narrative by having the Shawnee ambassador say to the Cherokee council of 1768:

> I have prepared white benches for you, and leaned the white pipe against them, and when you eat you shall have but one dish and one spoon. We have done everything that was good, but our warriors still hold their tomahawks in their hands, as if they wished to fight each other. We will now take their tomahawks from them and bury them; we must bury them deep under the earth where there is water; and there must be winds, which we wish to blow them so far that our warriors may never see them again.[48]

Words and acts often went together. Symbolic acts were used to emphasize symbolic words, as when the orator handed white beads to a member of the other nation as a sign of the peace between them, or tossed aside black beads to show that his nation had discarded its "bad thoughts." There were many notable Cherokee orators, but few more famous among the whites than Judd's Friend who, in January, 1769, renewed the Overhills' peace with Virginia by asking the colony's commissioners to take his black beads and throw them away.

> Brothers, we are sorry to have it to say that for some time bad blood and evil actions prevailed amongst us, which occasioned a stroke from our Elder Brothers,† but now I have the satisfaction of telling you that our hearts are good and strait, and you may depend on their continuing so, and that you may depend the more on what we say, we take off those black beads from the end of this string, that nothing may remain but what is pure and white, we now put the black beads in your hands, which we call the remains of our Evil thoughts, and desire you may now cast them away that they may never be had in remembrance more.[49]

† *i.e.,* the British in the War of 1760.

CHAPTER TWENTY

A STILL HOT WAR

—THE KEEPING OF PEACE

Peace for the Cherokees was a state of mind calling for an exercise of national will power beyond the capacity of the body politic. A government which functioned only in crises could not implement a policy of disengagement. It was not enough for the headmen to throw away bad thoughts; every Cherokee had to do so, or the nation could never hope to honor a truce. The people had to sensate peace or public opinion would lack the force to check the hotspurs. The best guarantee that raiding parties would remain at home was not a matter of negotiated terms or gifts of wampum, but of national good feelings. More effective than any peace talk was a traditional and historical amity: not international comradeship necessarily, but international harmony such as existed with the Chickasaws, whom Cherokee men do not seem to have regarded as enemies, at least not intuitively.

War bred war among the American Indians, and each generation inherited the enemies of its elders. A Creek peace was more fragile than a Chickasaw peace, for the very reason that there had been too many Creek raids over too many years, leaving too many animosities. In terms of raising the war cry within any Cherokee town, a Creek insult could not have been the same as a Chickasaw insult. The first surely inflamed passions to a higher degree than the second. Both might be resented, but it was the course which resentment took that shaped the international world of the southern Indian.

We may imagine that a lone Cherokee hunter encountering a foreigner in the woods reacted differently if the stranger was a Delaware, a Catawba, or a Mohawk. With the Delaware he might have smoked his pipe and perhaps spent the night. The Catawba he might have cautiously approached, briefly questioned, and, if the answers were not reassuring, quickly left. He would have been foolhardy not to kill the Mohawk on sight.

Those lone hunters in the woods posed an almost inconceivable problem for the southern Indians, one they probably ignored as much as tried to solve. Of all the impediments faced by Cherokee diplomats—making contact with the enemy, trying to speak with authority on behalf of a disunited nation, and persuading their towns to support their pledges—none was more difficult to unravel than the problem of communications. How, for example, to inform the people on both sides that negotiations had begun? Once the parties had agreed to talk, it must have been a herculean task to spread the word throughout the villages extending over hundreds of miles of paths, and to the hunting camps stretched far beyond. Even if the talks were limited to only one town, the job was not easy. Raiding parties already out had to be told to avoid the town, and raiding parties might be out for months.

In 1750 the Cherokees believed they were concluding a peace with the Creeks, when it was learned or rumored that the Creeks had killed many of their people.[1] This news apparently led to retaliatory raids by the Cherokees because four months later, the Upper Creeks accused them of breaking the peace by scalping a Creek hunting party.[2] While these events were occurring, some of the Lower Creeks, who had not participated in the original negotiations, were persuaded by the Upper Creeks to adopt the peace talks. A party of Lower Creeks went hunting, met a party of Cherokee hunters, and confirmed the peace. Later they heard of the killings, went home, and prepared for war anew.[3]

Even headmen promoting peace negotiations might be influenced by rumors or unsubstantiated tales of killing, reverse themselves, and join the cry for blood. Or, learning that someone in their town had been slain, they might feel bound to enforce the international law of retaliation, interrupt negotiations, depart for the warpath, obtain satisfaction, and later return still actively pursuing peace. In 1752, for example, Malatchi of the Lower Creeks and the Raven of Hywassee of the Valley Cherokees talked of peace, and both said they favored a truce. The Raven was sincere, Malatchi probably was not, but the Cherokees, who wanted peace, dealt with him as though he were, and treated him by appearances not by actions. It might be expected that if the Raven and Malatchi both hoped to see an end to hostilities, each would discount idle stories, work to temper passions, and seek to have a slaying overlooked or forgiven. Yet during July, after a peace talk had arrived from the Cherokees, Malatchi announced that he was going "to War for Satisfaction for a Friend that was killed by the Cherokees." [4] It is impossible to be sure because the records are unclear, but it appears that the "friend" was his brother, a fact which explains why vengeance was so important to Malatchi. It turned out that his brother had not been killed,† but Malatchi may not have learned this until after he got his satisfaction.[6] When the Cherokees heard that he and other Creek raiders were scalping their people, they despaired of peace. "[O]ur Hearts were altered," the Raven of Hywassee reported, "and we grew afraid to go out, finding still hot Warr." [7] He meant, of course, that they were afraid to go out and hunt deer. They were not afraid to hunt Creeks, and before long Cherokee warriors obtained counter-satisfaction of their own,[8] an eventuality Malatchi might have anticipated but which apparently caught him by surprise. When he arrived back in his village carrying Cherokee scalps, he professed to believe the path could still be swept white for he persuaded two Creek war parties not to go out, asking them to wait for the Cherokees to confirm the peace. Employing an apriority characteristic of the southern Indian, Malatchi did not recognize himself as the responsible party in a cause-and-effect pattern, but gave the impression of being puzzled as to why the Cherokee ambassadors had left and would not return. "I have sent for them several Times," Malatchi wrote of the Cherokees, "and none of them will come near me." If negotiations did not resume, it would surely be due to Cherokee bad thoughts. "I cannot help thinking they have throwed my Talks away, but if they do not come hear quickly it will not be in my Power to stop the Warriours from going out to kill them." [9]

† Of 21 Creeks killed by the Cherokees over the next few months, however, Malatchi reported that "2 of them was my near Relations." [5]

Malatchi's attitude was not unusual. It was a southern-Indian attitude that we probably will never understand with our different conceptual values regarding war and duty and legal blame. It seemed to surmise that peace talks could be disrupted to obtain satisfaction and then resumed at will. At the very time Malatchi was returning from raiding the Cherokees, the Red Coat King was also working for peace. Surely he knew that Malatchi's party was out, yet also knowing that Malatchi was legally right—indeed legally obligated—to be out, the Red Coat King put the onus on the Cherokees. He hoped peace could be concluded "but that in Case any of his Town's People should be killed he was afraid it would not be in his Power to restrain them from seeking Revenge." [10] This southern-Indian attitude was flaunted to perfection in 1725 by Hobyhawchey, another Upper Creek headman, when he announced that he was postponing Chero-kee peace talks. The Cherokees, he explained, "have lately killed several of the Principal Warriours of our Nation and til we have Satisfaction we will not Rest, as soon as our Corn is hard we design to be with the Cherokees." After they had given the Cherokees a blow, he said, the Upper Creeks would be ready to think of peace. [11]

Anthropologically, the problem might be explained in a number of ways. In legal terms, it comes down to the fact that individual warriors could not be restrained. If a responsible headman like the Red Coat King felt Malatchi had to obtain satisfaction for the death of a brother, it follows that more bellicose close-clan kin of victims could not be held in line. The surprising fact is not that a killing could disrupt peace negotia-tions in progress, but that quite often the talks continued despite a killing. If the two sides wanted a truce, there were at least three techniques they could use to avoid a renewal of war. The offending nation could offer satisfaction, it could ask that the killing be overlooked, or the other side could pretend that a third tribe was responsible.

In 1741 the Northern Indians called upon the Cherokees "to Confirm a Lasting Peace" and Virginia invited delegates from the two nations to meet in that colony. Writing to the Council of Virginia, the Cherokees explained that while they wanted peace they did not dare come in.

> That Since there has been Mischeif done by Some of the Cheraukee Nation to the Loss and Prejudice of those to the Norward they begg to be Excused Sending Deputies thither because they do not Yet know by what means they must make up that Breech and Least it Should be by delivering those by whom the Mischeif was done or as many as were concerned in it, for if, So they fear that while they are in

that Height of Passion as is reasonable to believe they must be if they Should Send Deputies the innocent would Suffer and therefore they desire that one or two of those Persons Injured would go to their Nation and Demand a Sattisfaction that is no more than Just and will readily Comply. And in order for a future Security and Lasting Confirmation of that Peace they will send 8 or tenn of the Head men to Albany to meet his Honour the Gov'r of New York & perform what he has Promised on their Parts.[12]

It must be suspected first, that the Cherokees were making excuses not to appear and second, that they asked a trader to write this answer for the offer of satisfaction was not part of their customary international law, and the reference to the fact that "the innocent would suffer" was not yet representative of their legal psychology. They usually did not propose satisfaction (probably because it was a promise they could not keep), although as previously noted, there are recorded instances of other southern nations not only offering would-be enemies satisfaction but rendering it.[13] The usual Cherokee practice was for the headmen conducting negotiations to overlook the killing. In 1725 a peace envoy from the Creek town of Coosaw † was at Great Tellico when news came that the Creeks had cut off a Cherokee village. The ambassador fled "in the Night," but not before the Head Warrior of Great Tellico told him "that there were Several of his people out at Warr and that if they killed any of the Coosaws or if the Coosaws killed any of his People that it must not be thought of." [14]

To overlook or "not think of" a killing was a more effective technique than we might imagine. In 1753 the Cherokee-Creek wars had about run their course, and although a few Creek headmen like Malatchi had strong reservations about Northern Indians resident in the Cherokees,[15] propitiators on both sides could afford to be conciliatory without losing their political influence. For the Cherokees, Skiagunsta of Keowee advocated the boldest measures. Some of his men had been killed by the Creeks, he said, yet "we did not seek Revenge for them" as perhaps the Creeks "were out and did not hear of the Peace." [16] At the same time, the Red Coat King of the Oakfuskees and Malatchi (who had just returned from obtaining personal satisfaction for the death of his "friend") persuaded the warriors of their towns not to send out revenging parties against the Cherokees in retaliation for Creek deaths.[17] The Red Coat King could arrange only a temporary respite. The Oakfuskees would wait three months, and if peace
† Also Coosa.

were not concluded by then, "we will stay no longer in going to war with the Cherokees." [18] Malatchi, on the other hand, quieted his people by promising they could yet have satisfaction. If peace with the Cherokees was confirmed, they still "might go out and kill the Northward Indians." [19]

A third device employed by a peace faction was to blame killings on someone else. Early in 1750, the Cherokees violated a truce with the Upper Creeks. Hearing that the Overhills still favored peace, the Gun Merchant sent word to the Overhills "that we shall not Suffer any of our Warriours to go to War against them unless they kill some of us and if any of our People should happen to be killed we shall Blame the Nottaweegas for it." [20] Three months later, when Overhill deputies were negotiating at Oakfuskee, a prominent man of that town was killed on the outskirts. Some Creeks accused the Cherokees, others the Nottoways, and as there was talk of killing the Overhill delegates, the headmen moved the council to another town and continued the negotiations.[21]

It may be chiefly conjecture but it is difficult to avoid the conclusion that most Creek-Cherokee peace talks ended with the promise that future killings would be overlooked—a theory which must remain speculative, partly because the nations rejected British offers to draft formal articles of agreement. The Creeks once protested that they wanted no writing when making peace with the Cherokees, for "it is a thing they cannot understand." [22] Yet the information we have indicates that on those occasions when they tried to deal with future events, they were limited to four choices. They either had to pledge that they would forgive a killing, that they would blame someone else, that they would await satisfaction, or that they would limit retaliation to the manslayer or his town. In 1754, for example, the head of the Cherokee delegation informed the Upper Creeks that his nation, resolving to avoid war, had agreed to adopt two rules of conduct and asked the Creeks to do the same. First, if a Cherokee was found dead in the woods, the Creeks would not be suspected or accused even if Creek tokens were left, but killings would always be blamed on the French or Northward Indians. Second, when it was known that the Creeks were responsible for mischief, the Cherokees still would not go to war "but would send and complain of the Injury and seek Satisfaction from the Nation or they would take it of the particular Person who committed the Offence or at least his Town, but that they would never involve the two Nations in a War." [23]

We must realize that the primitive Cherokees were not naïve; they did not think peace could be secured by exchanging promises to overlook killings or to blame someone else. Rather, they were part romanticists who hoped good talks would purge their enemies of bad thoughts, and part realists who saw little point in negotiating guarantees that neither side could enforce. It is an obvious consequence of their legal premises; yet again we encounter the prolepses, or anticipated conclusions, of post-primitive investigators. They did not understand the options of Cherokee jurisprudence, assumed that there must have been more to the Cherokee peace-keeping machinery than meets the eye, and reported at least three traditions of how the Cherokees prevented the renewal of war—traditions which can be dismissed when critically examined by the twin tests of positive law and historical proof.

The first tradition has more to do with war containment than with peacekeeping—"an amusing piece of military etiquette" it has been called —and is so amusing it is farcical. It would have us believe that an early treaty between the Iroquois and Cherokees made the Tennessee River the limit of pursuit against fleeing war parties; the insulted nation might stage a counter raid, but could not molest the camp of the retreating raiders.[24] The Tennessee was far closer to Cherokee than Iroquois towns, and the arrangement would have been decidedly in favor of the other side. What Cherokee headman would have dared offer the enemy a sanctuary so near the homeland, and how many Cherokee warriors in hot pursuit of those who had attacked their village and killed their neighbors would have honored it? The force of custom was strong among the American Indians, but custom of this sort could not be legislated or negotiated.

The second Cherokee peacekeeping tradition concerns their relations with the Delawares and fancies a mediatory town between the two nations where conflicts were settled.[25] The only evidence to substantiate the existence of such a town is the fact that the Delawares and Cherokees seem to have avoided war. But the Cherokees got on at least as well with the Chickasaws, with whom they kept no mediatory town, and their success with the Delawares may as easily be attributed to the same international good feelings. They called the Delawares "grandfathers" and in the nineteenth century would incorporate them into the nation. Surely a conciliation town is a possibility, a place where, when war threatened, headmen could gather to exchange good talks and relax tensions. It is not necessary to accept or deny its existence, if we remember what would have been the legal realities of such an institution. At the most, it would have been a mutual meeting ground, and whatever was decided there would have had no more force in positive law than a treaty with any other nation. The legal tenets would have been the same: personal consent and public opinion. The only factor making a difference would have been a social custom or tradition persuading the average Cherokee that an agreement reached in a mediatory town was somehow hallowed. Depending on the strength of the custom, personal consent might more easily have been obtained—if the custom were strong enough, consent might even have been certain—and by degrees, an agreement of this type would have approached inviolability. However, it would never have been binding—in the sense that a person who did not share the awe of custom could be forced to honor it against his will—except by public opinion.

A third (and more tenable) tradition regarding the peacekeeping machinery of the Cherokees tells us that some of the treaties of the more powerful southern nations included a provision designating a specific strip of marchland which, "though claimed by both, was practically considered as neutral ground, and the common hunting ground of both." [26] The idea seems to be that the parties were creating a no-man's land where everyone was free to roam, and where no one would be attacked as an intruder. The difficulty with this interpretation is its implication that southern-Indian wars could be started by claims to territorial exclusion. If the Cherokees told the Creeks to keep out of an area and backed the order with force, there would have been a killing and a war. But it is unrealistic to think of the Cherokees making such a claim. The southern Indians killed one another for retaliation or because they were already at war or because they wanted to kill. They did not kill each other for being trespassers, nor is it likely that out in the woods the concept of trespass could be a factor. A foreigner caught stalking a village might be killed in its vicinity, and with good reason. He was a dangerous intruder whose nearness to the village, not his violation of territorial rights, made him a menace.

If the Cherokees and their neigbors marked off a "neutral strip" in the woods between their towns, the purpose was probably to designate an area in which the chance of accidental encounters was great, and where they promised to be on their guard against unintentional killings—an area where they would meet in friendship rather than suspicion. Such a precaution is certainly consistent with what we know of their two chief peacekeeping methods: the practice of hunting parties meeting in the woods to confirm the peace, and of exchanging visits between headmen and delegations.

The Cherokees and the other southern nations, knowing they could not enforce mutual promises, followed the line of least legal resistence. The peacekeeping customs which they developed avoided the impossible chore of trying to prevent hostilities. Rather, they were designed to encourage restraint. Such, surely, was the purpose of a neutral strip if, as suggested, it was not a border but an area of special caution. So, too, were the practices of hunting parties confirming a peace when meeting in the woods, and of exchanging visits between peace delegations. These three peace-keeping devices seem to have been summed up in one descriptive sentence in 1754, by a Scot who lived in the Upper Creeks, when he wrote that the Cherokees and Creeks had "met in the hunting Ground, eat, drank, and smoaked together, and a few Days ago there was several Head Men and Warriours set out from this Nation for the Cherokees in order to confirm the Peace." [27]

Just what the southern Indians had in mind when they said hunting parties met in the woods and confirmed a peace is not clear. It was, however, a common practice (at least between Cherokees and Creeks), which must have followed a customary procedure designed to relax the tensions of a chance encounter, to allay the suspicions rife between recent enemies, and to prevent the friction that could produce a new war.[28] Perhaps also it was a method of relaying news of a treaty. In 1753 the Warrior of Estertoe† was hunting when a Creek appeared at his camp to announce the two nations were at peace. "At which the Estertoe Warrior thanked him, and promised to send through the Nation and forbid his People to go any more to War, and withall gave the Creek Warriour Presents as usual amongst Indians, Pipes, Beads, and Tabacco in Token of Peace, and desired he should give them to his Warriours and beloved Men." [29]

If we define peacekeeping not as policing the two sides but as encouraging restraint, the most obvious and useful peacekeeping method evolved by the southern Indians was to confirm a truce by exchanging visitors between the nations themselves. A party negotiating peace in a foreign land almost always asked that ambassadors be sent to its towns. At the very least, headmen urged to accept a truce wanted to meet the enemy face-to-face. On July 5, 1753, Skiagunsta of Keowee, who was in Charles Town, told Governor Glen that he was glad to receive a Creek peace talk "but I should be better satisfied to see them here." [30] Twenty-one days later, the Red Coat King of the Oakfuskees refused to listen to talks transmitted by Carolinian agents. "It is of no Use your sending any Peace Talks here without three or four Head Men will come from the Cherokees to my Town," he wrote Governor Glen, "and if the Cherokees are gone from Charles Town before this comes to your Hands I expect you will send somebody up immediately, and acquaint them that no Talks will do but

† Also, Estatoe.

their own Presence here. If they will not come now, this will be the last Talk we will send to them." [31]

Even after peace was concluded, mutual visits were a standard procedure, neither side feeling secure unless some of the former enemy were in their midst. Asked in Charles Town by Glen whether a Cherokee peace was "firm," Malatchi was unable to answer until he learned whether Cherokees had gone into the Lower Creeks to confirm the peace. When he arrived back in his village, he wrote to Glen:

> There was 8 of them came into my Town, three is returned Home, and the rest is here still, and there is some of my Townspeople now in the Cherokees. They have sent to me to assist them against the Nottawages. My People is all out a hunting, but when they return I intend to send them to warr against the Northward Indians. I now believe it a firm Peace between the Cherokees and us, for my People and them has met together in the Hunting Ground and eat and smoked together.[32]

One visit was not enough, a series was needed to confirm peace. At about the time Malatchi wrote to Glen, three more Cherokees arrived in the Upper Creeks and it was agreed there should be at least four mutual visits between the nations. After a long stay, the three Cherokees returned home accompanied by ten Creek warriors including two important headmen, the Red Coat King's Son and the Handsome Fellow.[33] They remained in the Cherokees for a lengthy visit, and when they went home, brought with them 15 Cherokees, some of whom were principal headmen and who called a council to urge the Creeks to join forces against the Choctaws on behalf of the Chickasaws.[34] While the 15 Cherokees were among the Creeks, the Gun Merchant, a leader of the Upper Creek peace party, went to Chota and Great Tellico, where he apparently remained for several months.[35]

It might be thought that visits were a risky method for insuring peace, that Chota would not want former enemies like the Gun Merchant around where any disgruntled member of the war faction could kill them and bring down on the town the certain vengeance of the whole Creek nation. But on the contrary, the risk for the Cherokees was worth taking. When they were hosts, they were the side which benefited from the visits. Not only were their own people put in a more peaceable frame of mind by seeing the Gun Merchant walk their streets, but they could feel reasonably certain the Creeks would not raid a Cherokee town while the Gun Merchant or any other Creek was at their mercy. If the keeping of peace was, in fact, largely a matter of restraining trouble makers, the practice of visits put more restraint on the nation sending the visitors than on the host.

As for the Gun Merchant, his position was not completely precarious, he was not at the mercy of individual passion. He could depend on international law to protect him from the whim of a Cherokee killer wanting to start a new Creek war, and he may have counted on domestic Creek law to keep his own people from jeopardizing his life by slaying a Cherokee. While he was in Chota, the good will of Overhill headmen was of course important, as was public opinion, both of which shielded him from harm. There was also the international custom of a friendly welcome to an invited guest, which, if violated, caused shame to his hosts and particular shame to the wrongdoer. There may have even been the sanction of the domestic blood feud, although we cannot be sure. Eastern Indians have been known to commit suicide when their nation violated their pledged word in international affairs,[36] and possibly a Cherokee headman would do the same. Suppose some Cherokee warrior killed the Gun Merchant and a headman, the Raven of Chota, for example, feeling shame, committed suicide. Would the manslayer have been thought the cause of the Raven's death, and could the Raven's brother take satisfaction against him? We have no evidence, but an affirmative answer is a possibility—though how strong a possibility cannot now be calculated. Much more likely, the Gun Merchant counted on a similar doctrine in Creek domestic law to restrain would-be killers of Cherokees among his own people. Had he been sacrificed in revenge for the killing by a Creek of a Cherokee, his brother may well have been privileged under the law of homicide to execute the Creek manslayer of the Cherokee. The manslayer, after all, was the cause of the Gun Merchant's death.

It may be a fine point, but the southern Indians seem to have distinguished between peace visitors and hostages. The Gun Merchant was not a hostage, nor did the Cherokees think of him as such. He was a volunteer whose purpose was to assure the Upper Creeks that a former enemy could be trusted and to demonstrate his people's good faith to the Cherokees. Of course it is possible to compare him to a hostage. When the Gun Merchant was in Chota, the Overhills knew the Upper Creeks were unlikely to renew hostilities. His life in a sense was held in forfeit. But he was not in Chota for this purpose. Had trouble started, our evidence indicates that the Chota headmen would have spirited him out of the nation. Peace visitors like ambassadors seem always to have survived. A hostage, on the other hand, was held specifically as a guarantee of peace. Many eastern

Indian nations demanded hostages as the price for ending a war—the Iroquois would ask of the other side the same number of hostages as Iroquois captured and killed [37]—but there is no documented evidence that the Cherokees followed this custom. On the contrary, as a condition for making peace they may have required that all Cherokees held prisoners be released, and sometimes they took the initiative of returning captives to their nation as a method of showing good faith and of starting peace negotiations.[38]

On the whole, it can be said that due to the Cherokee constitution which gave to each warrior the power if not the right to declare war, the ending of raids, the drafting of terms, and the adoption of the agreement seldom were as difficult to accomplish as the keeping of peace. Without a law of physical coercion, there was no sure means to enforce a treaty. The best method devised by the southern Indians was a method of restraint: a method which called for little more than a series of mutual visits by brave men determined to secure peace at the risk of their own lives. It was largely a matter of faith brushed with a touch of hope and based on the optimism, seemingly shared by all Indians, that if only enough people would think good thoughts, all the bad thoughts would be thrown away. As the Upper Creeks said in 1750:

> We all agree to be at Peace and Live like Brothers with the Upper Cherokees and where they and we shall meet at any time in our Hunting to eat and drink together like Brothers and not to think of anything that has pash [sic] between us in our former differences.[39]

CHAPTER TWENTY-ONE

A SCOLDING HOUSE

—THE CHEROKEE LEGAL SYSTEM

Reconstructing the Cherokees' legal system and Cherokee jurisprudence is a more difficult and perilous task than discussing the substantive rules of their primitive law. When dealing with values and ideas, we must be even more careful not to force primitive facts into current theories or to use contemporary legal categories to rearrange primitive concepts. The Cherokees, Lieutenant Timberlake wrote in the 1760s, practiced freedom of religion.[1] But how does one apply the principle of religious liberty to a society which could not contemplate either a theological dispute or a state-imposed system of doctrine? These difficulties are real, yet they must not deter us from asking questions concerning Cherokee legal thought. "The history of law must be a history of ideas," writes Frederic William Maitland. "It must represent, not merely what men have done and said, but what men have thought in bygone ages." [2] Still, we must acknowledge the risks and accept the shortcomings.

The challenge is not to return to Cherokee patterns. The challenge is to escape our own. We are as much the product of our law ways as the

Cherokee was of his, and by inclination if not necessity, we are all legal comparativists. The problem is not that the Cherokee thought on a different level than we, it is that he thought different thoughts. "Primitive man is not radically different from modern man," Jacob Henry Landman has pointed out. "Fundamentally, the difference lies neither in his anatomy, nor in his mentality, but in his mass of knowledge. Culture must not be confused with intelligence." [3] If his cultural law ways are vague, we must be content to leave them vague. To seek a semblance of clarity for the Cherokee legal system by adopting a tone of false lucidity is both unscientific and unhistorical.[4] Maitland has taught us that the haze should be allowed to remain hazy. "In dealing with ancient communities," he writes, "our words and thoughts are too modern, too sharp, too unqualified." It is too late for us to be primitive Cherokees.[5] Our legal theories are too civilized, our legal distinctions too institutionally oriented to be applied to facts in a manner that would have interested the eighteenth-century Cherokee. What can we learn by asking whether the wrong revenged by the Cherokee law of homicide was a "crime," a "tort," or a "delict"? The answer would tell us no more about the Cherokee legal mind, than were we to know if the Cherokee law of marriage was the same as that of the Ibo of West Africa. Comparative legal anthropology is a science separate from legal history.

If our legal values and standards are uncertain guides for reconstructing the Cherokee legal system, the values and standards of other primitive societies are little better. Actual solutions of factual problems by a neighbor may tell us how the Cherokee would answer a question when legal principles were the same, but they tell us nothing more. We can fill in gaps with missing cases, we cannot fill in gaps of theory. Comparative legal ethnology has the advantage of raising issues we might otherwise overlook, such as whether the Cherokee attached liability for accidents resulting from unguarded weapons. Without specific cases, we cannot answer those questions. Comparative legal anthropology, like comparative jurisprudence, deals with generalities which rebel against concrete application without specific cases to lend them authenticity. Our problem is not to "think primitive" or to "think Indian." Our problem is to "think Cherokee."

If we are willing to "think Cherokee," and not "Indian" or "primitive," there is no need to ask if the Cherokee legal system comes under one or the other of the many definitions of "law" which have been excogitated by jurisprudents and anthropologists alike. Minimum definitions of "law" are relevant to comparative studies of legal systems, but they add little to the study of a single legal system.[6] Nor are the efforts to distinguish between "law" and "custom" of any practical value. Ethnologists may puzzle over the difference; legal historians can learn nothing from it.[7] Yet it must be recognized that the records upon which the legal historian depends are themselves sometimes tinged with judgments based on such comparisons, as for example, contemporary accounts which purport to mention no Cherokee law because the writer (influenced by his preconceived notions that all law must resemble common law) concludes that there is no Cherokee law to report. The Cherokee government was so "full of Liberty," William Fyffe wrote in 1761, "they can't be said to have any Laws being guided by the Customs of their Ancestors." [8] Timberlake made much the same point when he said the Cherokees "have no laws, and are both judges and executors of their revenge." [9] As a result, he concluded that homicide was the only "crime" and it was "more properly revenged than punished." [10] Most contemporary commentators seem to have used a similar definition of law, even men who should have known better. Benjamin Hawkins, the experienced and compassionate agent to the Creeks and Cherokees during the Federalist era, once protested to an official of the War Department that the government did not understand Indian ways. "If you in the course of your researches have found out the secret of making Indians fulfill their public engagements where there is no law and it belongs to individuals to take personal satisfaction, and to the family of the individual to avenge the wrong, and you will communicate that secret to me, I hereby bind myself and my successors in office to send you six princesses in full dress." [11]

These men, Fyffe, Timberlake, Hawkins, and their contemporaries, thought European, they did not think Cherokee. For them law meant the coercive state, and it followed that the Cherokees had no "law." A Cherokee would not have appreciated their standards. He observed the white man's ways and saw no value in courthouses and jails.[12] For the Cherokee, a legal system functioned successfully if it maintained social harmony through mutual submission to customary procedures exercised by clearly defined groups, such as the clans. There was no need to produce that harmony by coerced submission to sovereign authority channelled through judicial institutions.

The Cherokee might think institutionalized justice unnecessary but for some jurisprudes the judiciary is the lodestar, the essence, the embodiment of law, the measure of legal formulary for all times and all societies. Many common lawyers may be expected to agree with William Seagle's statement "that the test of law in the strict sense is the same for both primitive and civilized communities: namely the existence of courts." [13] It may be assumed that nineteenth-century investigators were influenced by this test when they reported that the primitive Cherokee legal system had had courts, judges, and punishments; [14] believing that courts existed everywhere, they looked for them among the Cherokees and what they looked for they found. Some anthropologists have accepted these legends, even giving the supposed courts the aspect of inquisitorial tribunals, with the accused defending themselves and judgment being followed immediately by public execution. [15] The only reliable contemporary evidence is furnished by James Adair's description of a Cherokee oath, which he uses not to show that the Cherokees had judicial tribunals, but that their words and their procedures "of adjuring a witness to declare the truth" were similar to those employed by their ancient ancestors, the Hebrews of Biblical times. [16] If the Cherokees had such tribunals or even the tradition that such tribunals had once existed, why were they not adapted during the 1790s when the nation was vainly searching for the means to impose state-decreed physical sanctions? A court empowered to hand down final, absolute judgments would not only have been alien to the Cherokee legal system prior to 1800, it was not needed—and a society which does not need Nemesis will not honor her. The Cherokees had no adjudicatory system, no method of ordeal, no remedial procedures or concepts, because Cherokee jurisprudence did not contemplate public wrongs or adjudicable private disputes. Should a Cherokee wife refuse to perform the customary ritual of bathing at prescribed intervals, her husband did not quarrel with her and bring her to court. If he was offended, he left her.

Perhaps the nineteenth-century researchers were looking for the wrong kind of courts. Justice could not be institutionalized in the Cherokee nation but surely there were adjudicable disputes. Men accused of homicide might deny that they were the perpetrators, that they were the cause, or that they were liable. Defenses are to be expected. Men, after all, do deny their guilt, and their clans would want them to have a hearing. But there is no need to postulate an inquisitional system. The very most the Cherokee legal mind could have contemplated would have been tribunals of mediation—not even of arbitration—with conciliation and the restoration of harmony the chief objects. During the opening two decades of the nineteenth century, when the growth of commercial activity within the nation made state-sponsored adjudication necessary, the first Cherokee courts leaned heavily on reconciling the antagonists; they tried to give something to each side. If the eighteenth-century Cherokees had "courts," they surely were of a different type. The word "court" can, for example, be loosely applied to self-help when it is not private or secret, but is "adjudicated" at the "bar of public opinion." As E. Adamson Hoebel writes: "When vigorous public opinion recognizes and accepts the procedure of the plaintiff as correct and the settlement or punishment meted out as sound, and the wrongdoer in consequence accedes to the settlement because he feels he must yield, then the plaintiff and his supporting public opinion constitute a rudimentary sort of 'court,' and the procedure is inescapably 'legal.' " [17] Another Cherokee "court" was the clan, at least when asked to decide on causation, to offer forgiveness, or to accept compensation. "Given the complete absence of central authority," Robert H. Lowie observes, "the kinship group becomes the judicial body—one that confronts all like bodies in the tribe as one sovereign state confronts the next." [18] Surely these two "courts" acted in conjunction, the clan's decision often being influenced by society's desire for peace or compromise expressed through public opinion.

The Cherokees may have lacked forensic institutions, but they recognized certain rules of right conduct and knew the consequences that resulted from their breach. Whether they had a word for "law" does not matter, for appreciation of these rules and the procedures governing their enforcement controlled their lives—just as the average colonial backsettler, who could not distinguish between a writ of "trover" and a writ of "replevin," knew he could not appropriate his neighbor's property without running afoul of process servers and courts. Regularity as an element of law need not mean absolute certainty regarding the result;[19] it need only permit "the application of physical force by an individual or group possessing the socially recognized privilege of so acting." [20] A Cherokee manslayer could predict the consequences of a killing. Either he or some member of his clan would have to pay the blood price, provide compensation, obtain forgiveness, or plead a set-off. Once the feud was set in motion, each actor knew the role he was to play. Everyone in the town could have told us what each succeeding step might be.

So far, then, as Cherokee law is tested by the norms of regularity and predictability, the adjudicatory unit of the Cherokees legal system was the clan. Cherokee law was not a law of individual responsibility but of clan relationships: a law which consisted largely of procedural rules defining who could act, when he could act, and what form his action should take. It was procedural but not archaic. It did not stress technicalities or formalities but duties, rights, and obligations. Clan membership conferred upon a Cherokee his right to share the property of the nation, his right to be present in town councils, his right of protection from the nation or the town, and his right to adopt an alien. Clan membership impressed upon a Cherokee the obligation (1) not to marry within his clan nor his father's clan; (2) the obligation to avenge the deaths of fellow clansmen; (3) perhaps the obligation to contribute a share of the indemnity when a clan-kin was a manslayer and the blood price was commuted to compensation in goods; and (4) possibly the obligation to obtain a prisoner to replace a clansman slain in battle.

Clan relationships determined every side of Cherokee life except perhaps a person's role in war and his conduct in battle. From the clan structure of national society stemmed the taboos, privileges, and customary social controls which we might not think of as coming under the definition of "law," but which to the Cherokee were probably as much "law" as were the rules governing homicide and incest. These determined with whom he could jest, whom he had to respect, to whom he deferred, whom he might assault under what circumstances, and how he addressed each individual. These norms of clan and interclan relationships were in turn enforced by counter taboos, privileges, and social customs which gave to the other party the right to rebuke or to prohibit any sign of resentment.[21] The contemporary European paid slight attention to these rules of conduct. Had he noticed them, he might have catalogued them along with his own table manners, as customs perhaps but not "law," for their infraction (unlike homicide and possibly incest) did not cause the entire clan to function as an enforcement agency. Yet it was these rules of conduct which held together the clans, and it was the clans which made the Cherokee legal system a viable civic organism. It was from the respect and loyalty of their members that the seven clans received their strength, and it was from the strength of the clans that Cherokee laws received their force and energy.[22]

Only in the area of international law was the Cherokee legal system independent of the clans. Retaliation was not a clan function, and war parties were not clan groups. The Little Carpenter and the Great Warrior of Chota, members of different clans, would take the war path together. Yet the analogy to the clan structure was marked. Although a Cherokee who retaliated against a foreign manslayer for the death of a fellow Cherokee may not have thought of the nation as a larger clan, the idea was in the air. The legal premises upon which he acted were borrowed from the domestic law of homicide, from the law of clan privilege and clan duty.

It might be argued that activities which the clan relationship did not encompass were not the concern of domestic law; that in the Cherokee legal system there could be only clan wrongs, there were no public or individual wrongs. It is difficult to imagine what public wrongs could have existed outside the clan system. As there was no religion, there could be no crime of sacrilege and without a state, there was no sedition, which leaves witchcraft as the most likely possibility. It may be that witchcraft was regarded as a public wrong, and that killing a witch was a privileged act.[23] But the determination would still have involved the clan. For how would the killing of a witch become privileged except by persuading the victim's clan that he or she was a witch, and by having the clan withdraw its protection, declaring him outlawed? Witchcraft could have been a public wrong, but it could be corrected only by ensuring that the correction did not create a clan wrong.

It is possible, on the other hand, that individual wrongs as distinguished from clan wrongs may have existed. We know little about the constitution of hunting parties, but as they ranged over a hundred miles from home and were out for two or three months, some customary organizational apparatus could have been recognized, perhaps even imposing on members reciprocal rights and duties.[24] But as hunting itself was a matter of individual skill and private enterprise, Cherokee hunters do not seem to have needed police units similar to the soldier societies among the Plains Indians to coordinate the group.[25] Disputes as to who made a kill and owned a carcass may have arisen, but it must be supposed that they were mediated. There is no reason to guess that the hunt leader acted as judge or even that there was a hunt leader.

Theft or deliberate injury seem the only civilized wrongs likely to have been treated as individual rather than clan wrongs by Cherokee law. The difficulty is that we cannot be sure they were wrongs at all. The Hurons had a method of compensation for bloody wounds, and the right of self-help for the victim of a robbery, both of which seem to have been related to clan right and clan enforcement.[26] The Cherokees may have also, but it is unlikely.[27] An individual may have resented an injury or insult and he may have used self-help to recover stolen property. It was a personal choice, however; he could not expect clan support.[28] In 1742 a Pennsylvanian was attacked by an Iroquois who broke his jaw. The Iroquois was arrested by the British and jailed. The Iroquois asked Governor George Thomas to release the prisoner, saying that as the white man had recovered they hoped the British "would not expect any further Punishment." Thomas told them that English laws "obliged the Assailant to make good all Damages, besides paying for the Pain endured," and as the Indian had no money, he should stay in jail. To this argument the Iroquois speaker replied: "The Indians know no Punishment but Death; they have no such

Thing as pecuniary Mulcts; if a Man be guilty of a Crime, he is either put
to Death, or the Fault is overlook'd." [29]

The mores of the Cherokee legal system also expected that an injury be
overlooked. Public opinion might aid the injured party who sought self-
help, but public opinion discouraged self-help that would disrupt the
harmony of society. There were taught moral values, both social and legal,
which contributed to the avoidance of face-to-face encounters between
individuals. From the social side came the tradition of sharing property,
and the attitudes that made avarice and the accumulation of goods a disgrace.[30] Traders often complained that they and their property were unsafe
among a people who did not believe in God and hence had no conscience
to keep them honest.[31] Yet they believed their goods were more secure in
the care of Cherokee employees than white employees,[32] and it was claimed
by the first superintendent of the southern Indians that Cherokees increased in virtue in direct proportion to their distance from the English.[33]

No social value made a greater contribution to the function of the
Cherokee legal system than the shared tradition that harmony was the
measure of moral excellence.[34] It meant that many domestic injuries would
be overlooked, forgiven, or mediated; the honorable man did not seek
revenge, he sought harmony.[35] To be sorry for having committed an
offense by displaying shame was correct conduct for a wrongdoer, and for
the injured party to harbor resentment was bad taste. The wrongdoer
might show contrition by performing an unrelated act such as going "to
the Woods to War that he might die by the hand of the Enemie." [36]
These social values could result in strange legal doctrines, such as the
principle that two wrongs set off against one another became a right if
quarrels were avoided. In January, 1762, a Cherokee delegation, headed
by the Little Carpenter, was returning from Charles Town when its horses
were stolen on the path by Carolinians retaliating for earlier Cherokee
thefts. Charles Town furnished new mounts, some of which were also
stolen. When he arrived at Fort Prince George, the Little Carpenter sent
word to Lieutenant-Governor William Bull that he would overlook the
incident, as he knew there were rogues in both nations. He was trying to
excuse the continual stealing of back-country cattle by Cherokees and avoid
possible unpleasantness with the British.[37] There were undoubtedly many
felt legal attitudes which could be used by an injured party, and which
society expected him to use to prevent conflict. Two doctrines mitigating
theft—substitution of goods and an argument of good use—are suggested
by a story borrowed from an older southern Indian myth which the Cherokees told during the nineteenth century.

When Sequoya, the inventor of the Cherokee alphabet, was trying to introduce it among his people, about 1822, some of them opposed it upon the ground that Indians had no business with reading. They said that when the Indian and the white man were created, the Indian, being the elder, was given a book, while the white man received a bow and arrows. Each was instructed to take good care of his gift and make the best use of it, but the Indian was so neglectful of his book that the white man soon stole it from him, leaving the bow in its place, so that books and reading now belong of right to the white man, while the Indian ought to be satisfied to hunt for a living.[38]

The felt traditions of social harmony buoying the Cherokee legal system were summed up by Fred Gearing when he described the eighteenth-century Cherokee culture as "a consistent pattern of moral thought which disallowed face-to-face conflict." [39] Over the generations, he added, "the directive to avoid conflict came finally to pervade the group life and came to be the overriding measure of a good man." [40] Good Cherokees in the 1700s employed three methods to avoid conflict: first, by asserting their rights or interests cautiously and respectfully; second, by turning away from impending conflict; and third, by withdrawing from men who openly clashed with their fellows.[41]

A Cherokee with rights or interests to assert did not make demands or offer threats; he may even have mentioned the subject only with a sense of embarrassment. If he was owed a debt, the ultimate step would have been to distrain the creditor's chattels, but James Adair doubted if many southern Indians would go so far.

These instances indeed seldom happen, for as they know each other's temper, they are very cautious of irritating, as the consequences might one day prove fatal—they never scold each other when sober—they conceal their enmity be it ever so violent, and will converse together with smooth kind language, and an obliging easy behaviour, while envy is preying on their heart.[42]

Adair was suspicious of Indian motives and likely to attribute to craftiness or guile, conduct which they thought natural and normal. The Cherokee ethos viewed as aggression any act or attitude "giving offense," [43] and to be aggressive was a cardinal sin in the Cherokee social order. Even Carolinians who misunderstood Cherokee values and attributed their social harmony to mutual fear of "barbarous Revenges" admitted that there was "rarely any quarreling among them." [44] The Cherokee legal system did not have to be institutionalized, partly because their ethical values and social attributes gave the Cherokees a predisposition to turn away from an unpleasant situation. [45] The need to be free of bad thoughts, and to close their ears to bad talks was stressed again and again by the Cherokees whenever difficulties arose between them and the British. When Samuel Benn killed the "cousin" of the Cock Eye Warrior who was trying to rob him on the path, [46] and the headmen feared trouble, Old Hop sent the Cock Eye Warrior a "physic" so "he might be cleansed from all bad thoughts." [47] The Cherokees often complained that horses belonging to traders in their nation trampled down their cornfields, and they asked British officials to make the traders be more careful. When told that if they killed the horses, the traders would learn to respect their property, they replied they were not "willing to Shoot any White Mans horse." [48] It has been supposed that the traders intimidated them, but it is just as likely that as good Cherokees, they were avoiding a quarrel. [49]

Much of the Little Carpenter's success as a Cherokee headman can be attributed to his genius for avoiding quarrels. When Captain Raymond Demere and John Stuart were leaving the nation in August, 1757, at a time of anti-British tension, they planned to travel the familiar path taking them through Great Tellico, the center of pro-French intrigues. On the day they left, the Little Carpenter arrived at Fort Loudoun and guided them through the mountains by a route which bypassed Great Tellico and potential conflict. [50] A few years earlier, the British had suspected the Little Carpenter of being a French agent and had demanded his arrest. [51] Later, when he appeared at his first council with Governor Glen, and Glen tried to make him defend himself, the Little Carpenter avoided a quarrel by getting Glen to smoke a pipe.

> GOVERNOR (looking on the Little Carpinter). I have been 10 Years here and never saw this Man before. (To the Interpreter) Tell him I have heard great Complaints about him, and that he is a Disturber of the Peace, but as he is now come down, I doubt not but that he will clear himself of these Reports, and will deserve my good Opinion of him.
>
> LITTLE CARPINTER (taking a lighted Tobacco Pipe in his Hand). This Pipe was sent by Old Hop at Chote, and desired that it might be delivered to your Excellency and your beloved Men, that you may all smoke of it. (Another Indian Fellow who had a Cross of Brass hanging at his Ear, gives the Pipe to the Governor. He and

all the Council and Others smoke out of it, then the Indians all of them).

GOVERNOR. We have now smoaked out of one Pipe; this is a Token of Peace, and that we are all Friends with your Nation.[52]

Only on one occasion did the Little Carpenter press an argument to the point that he almost quarrelled with Governor Glen. The British had arrested a number of Shawnees, and the Cherokees wanted them freed in their custody.[53] Glen said it was not their affair but the Cherokees thought it was, for if the Shawnees were not released they might blame the Cherokees and either start a war with them or, by killing Carolinians in the nation, touch off a Cherokee-British conflict. The Little Carpenter was so alarmed that he persisted. "I do not vindicate the Shawnees," he told Glen, "but it is for the Sake of the white People [traders] that come among us, for if these Indians are punished the Path will be made bloody, and no white Man will be able to come to us. As for you, and those about you (pointing to the Governor) you are safe, but many straggling white Man will lose their Lives." [54] To argue was such unorthodox Indian behavior that Glen was shocked. "You surely observed in what an impertinent Manner they spoke to me in their last Talk," he asked a trader the following day. "I did," the trader replied.[55] Perhaps the Cherokees became ashamed for they returned 48 hours later and apologized. Long Jack was their spokesman:

> Two Days ago when we had the last Talk with your Excellency we acknowledge that we were very faulty in speaking what we did about the Prisoners below, and we beg your Excellency would forgive it, but as it was for the Good of the white People for Fear they should take Revenge upon them, we hope your Excellency will pardon it. For our Parts we have entirely forgot it, and confess our Faults, in Token whereof we present you with this Piece of Tabacco to smoak (lays before the Governor some Tobacco) with Old Hop. Keep it safe as a Proof that we are very sorry for what we have said, and that we ask Pardon.[56]

Perhaps the Little Carpenter had good reason to violate Indian etiquette. As he had predicted, the Shawnees blamed his people for their being locked in the Charles Town jail. Old Hop believed they sent wampum to the Northwards, urging them to attack the Overhills.[57] When the headmen asked for ammunition to defend their towns, they did not beg. The

British owed it to them for it was their fault the Shawnees were killing Cherokees. "[T]he white People imprisoning the Savannahs," they argued, "has caused them to join the French against us because we would not join the Savanahs against the English." [58]

The third mechanism of Cherokee ethos for avoiding social discord was withdrawal. There were at least two aspects of withdrawal that should be noted. Either an individual would withdraw from a situation of potential trouble, or society would withdraw from an individual who threatened the harmony of the group. In 1757 the Little Carpenter refused to attend a Chota council called to discuss correspondence with the French. To say, as one historian has, that his withdrawal "amounted to a veto" is to misrepresent the Cherokee constitution.[59] But to see his withdrawal as a rebuke to the pro-French faction—a rebuke that was keenly felt by his rivals, yet avoided a dangerous confrontation or a possible counter-rebuke—is to understand in part the Cherokee legal system and the Cherokee concept of political harmony. By withdrawing, the Little Carpenter was acting as a good Cherokee should, and at the same time shaming the pro-French Overhills for forcing an issue which they knew would disrupt the harmony of the towns.

Withdrawal also explains why Europeans found it difficult to deal with American Indians. When a Cherokee gave an evasive answer to an unwelcome question, the Englishman thought him untruthful. When he did not answer at all, the Englishman thought him stubborn. From the Cherokee's point of view, the cultural or legal gap was potentially disastrous. Withdrawal was more than a defense, it was a sanction; yet when an Englishman threatened a quarrel (thereby forcing the Cherokee to withdraw), the Englishman did not experience a sense of shame, there was no feeling of guilt. The Cherokee's withdrawal was worse than useless, it could be harmful to his interests for it had failed in its purpose, it was not a sanction. "It seems clear that we deal with the Cherokee ethos," Gearing wrote of withdrawal: "circumspection in council is the ethos recommendation of caution in pursuing one's interests generally; dropping out when one cannot accept the crystallizing group sentiment is the ethos recommendation to avoid open confrontation." [60]

The effectiveness of withdrawal depended on circumstances. During the War of 1760, when the nation was under stress and emotions ran high, the Little Carpenter underscored his opposition to the war by again withdrawing from the Chota council and going for a time to live in the woods. His tactics were not as successful as they had been in 1757, for he could hardly have been expected to shame the militant faction. Yet even under

such adverse circumstances, withdrawal might serve a pragmatic purpose—
more political, perhaps, than legal. When the tide of war turned against
the Cherokees and dissatisfaction among the people became apparent, other
headmen joined the Little Carpenter's withdrawal, and it was to him that
the nation eventually turned to negotiate peace with South Carolina.

> Men came to councils with conflicting interests. No matter how
> circumspect Cherokees might have been, some had to yield to others.
> It seems also clear that the option to drop out of the proceedings
> could not in fact have been exercised for every causal difference. The
> system of persons and roles in councils is here seen as a kind of tool
> which, when used, caused influence to flow in nonrandom ways and
> which provided some measure of assurance that villages would suc-
> cessfully reconcile interests, for most members, most of the time.[61]

The other side of Cherokee withdrawal was for the group to withdraw
from an aggressor; withdrawal which, if the offender persisted, might
develop into ostracism.[62] This form of withdrawal was the chief sanction
outside the clan law utilized by the Cherokee legal system to discourage
antisocial behavior. Whether it should be termed a "legal" sanction may
be a matter of dispute. Some theorists hold that law must be predicated
upon the external application of sanctions;[63] that the fundamental *sine qua
non* of law is the legitimate use of physical coercion;[64] and that only organized sanctions, dependent on a centralized authority, are "legal." [65] As we
have seen, the Cherokees had no law of physical coercion; the Cherokee
nation was not a state possessing even minimum police powers. Yet it
cannot be said that there were no legal sanctions in Cherokee jurisprudence. The Cherokee legal system functioned because it was supported by
sanctions such as social withdrawal, and from the point of view of Cherokee law these sanctions certainly were legal.

Legal sanctions need not be formal or coercive (for example, state-
imposed punishments) nor need they be religious, another form of sanctions which the Cherokee legal system does not appear to have employed.[66]
There are also moral or ethnical sanctions (such as disapproval) and
satirical sanctions (such as ridicule) as well as private sanctions approved
by the group (for example, the election of vengeance). As explained by
A. R. Radcliffe-Brown:

> The sanctions existing in a community constitute motives in the
> individual for the regulation of his conduct in conformity with usage.
> They are effective, first, through the desire of the individual to obtain

the approbation and to avoid the disapprobation of his fellows, to win such rewards or to avoid such punishment as the community offers or threatens; and, second, through the fact that the individual learns to react to particular modes of behaviour with judgments of approval and disapproval in the same way as do his fellows, and therefore measures his own behaviour both in anticipation and in retrospect by standards which conform more or less closely to those prevalent in the community to which he belongs. What is called conscience is thus in the widest sense the reflex in the individual of the sanctions of the society.[67]

Should it be objected that sanctions designed to control private conduct would more accurately be labeled "moral" than "legal," it must be recalled that in a primitive society such as that of the Cherokees, rules of law are rules of private as much as public conduct. They are, therefore, necessarily surrounded by an atmosphere of morality.[68]

Aside from private sanctions (largely limited to clan-law enforcement), the Cherokee legal system depended upon satirical and ethical sanctions to maintain harmony and order. Cherokee ethics did not contemplate corporal punishment, even within households or clans to restrain or discipline the young. To be whipped was considered no disgrace;[69] to whip another may have been a serious breach of good conduct. The Great Warrior disapproved of British schoolmasters whom he saw caning students. The Cherokees never beat children with rods, he said, "but pour water upon them or threaten them with Physick which does as well." [70] About the only other bodily punishment was to dryscratch boys. Once some young Cherokees near Tellico threw stones at white hog drovers carrying supplies up the path to Fort Loudoun. Captain Demere protested to the headman, who "found out those that had done it, had them in the Town House, and Scratched them dry and one of them being absent, they took his Brother and Scratched him in the other's Room." [71]

White men marvelled that Cherokee children were never chastised "with blows," [72] and a few so misunderstood the primitive mind as to think the Cherokees looked "on Corporal Punishments as apt to blunt their warlike Disposition." [73] In truth, they simply were treating children as they treated everyone and disciplined them by methods as least as effective as the rod of an English schoolmaster. When a Cherokee uncle poured water over a child, or headmen dryscratched unruly youths in the town's council house, they were holding them up to ridicule, the same satirical sanction used to check antisocial aggressiveness by adults. James Adair called it "only an ironical way of jesting" though he thought it the main form of punishment among the southern Indians.

> They commend the criminal before a large audience, for practising the virtue, opposite to the crime, that he is known to be guilty of. If it is for theft, they praise his honest principles; and they commend a warrior for having behaved valiantly against the enemy, when he acted cowardly; they introduce the minutest circumstances of the affair, with severe sarcasms which wound deeply. I have known them to strike their delinquents with those sweetened darts, so good naturedly and skillfully, that they would sooner die by torture, than renew their shame by repeating the actions.[74]

When we ask, therefore, how the headmen in 1753 kept an anti-Creek Cherokee from killing the Gun Merchant while in Chota on his peace mission, we must remember that the majority of the town would have made life unpleasant for any Cherokee who threatened to start a new war. Men of his own and of his father's clan would have praised him for his love of peace, women of his own and of his father's clan would have pointed him out as a friend of the Creeks, and the children of his own and of his father's clan would have followed him around, asking that he teach them the virtues of patriotism so that when they grew up they, like he, would be known as persons who put the interests of Chota before their own. It was this sanction which led a British governor to remark that the punishments of eastern Indians were "Shame" and "being despised," [75] and which explains why the southern Indians referred to colonial courts as "scolding houses." [76]

If we are unable to believe that such a sanction was an effective deterrent on the anti-Creek warrior who lived in Chota, it is because we are unable "to think Cherokee." We must remember that he "thought Cherokee," and for him public ridicule could be an awful experience. "To meet with universal reprobation on the part of one's neighbors," Robert H. Lowie has written; "to have derisive songs sung in mockery of one's transgressions; to be publicly twitted with disgraceful conduct by joking relatives—these were eventualities to which no Indian lightly exposed himself. They made it possible to dispense largely with a powerful executive and with penal institutions; while the customary law sufficed, rendering new legislation unnecessary." [77] For primitive man in general, as well as the primitive Cherokee, respect for law prevented the chaos one might expect to find in a society without central authority, and law was enforced by the weight of public opinion backed by fear of shame and disgrace.

There was, in addition, one further measure which the majority could exercise to restrain the potentially aggressive individual. The ultimate ethical sanction of the Cherokee legal system was withdrawal by the many from the few—"a loose form of ostracism" [78]—used sometimes against a political dissenter who actively opposed the town's consensus, and most effectively to curb anyone who threatened to disrupt social harmony by being loud, domineering, or aggressive. On very rare occasions it may have involved withdrawing clan protection; usually, however, the offender was merely ignored.[79] If he spoke, his clan-kin might pretend they did not hear or that they could not understand his words. Aggression was not matched by counteraggression, but by silence. The aggressor was left to feel his shame and mend his ways. The misbehaving child soon learned that silence could be as painful as harsh words or blows.[80] Ostracism, not behests, taught him the rules of communal life.†

Again we must ask if it is possible for us to think Cherokee. "To become the laughing-stock of his daily associates for minor misdeameanors and to be completely ostracized for graver offenses are terrific punishments for the native," Lowie argues, "and they have a deterrent force of which the infliction of penalties in our sense is often quite devoid." [82] Perhaps we are too civilized to appreciate the impact of moral and satirical sanctions; they depended on unfamiliar social conditions for their psychological support. It is necessary, therefore, to recall the structure of Cherokee society and to consider the explanation by Dr. Kimball Romney that the matrilineal household helped make withdrawal an effective sanction.

> The world over, he has suggested, punishment by male parental fig-
> ures tends to be physically coercive and punishment by females tends
> to depend on withdrawing affection. Where punishment by males
> does not occur, the child tends to become psychologically vulnerable
> to the threatened withdrawal of his mother's affection and, by exten-

† Conceivably an individual who felt unjustly treated might himself try to shame those who withdrew from him by withdrawing in turn from them—by leaving the group which had made him an outcast. One Cherokee myth tells of a boy "who used to go bird hunting every day, and all the birds he brought home he gave to his grandmother, who was very fond of him. This made the rest of the family jealous, and they treated him in such a fashion that at last one day he told his grandmother he would leave them all, but that she must not grieve for him." [81]

sion as he matures, to similar threats by all members of his face-to-face community. In societies where males are absent from the household during large portions of the year for the hunt, socialization of the child falls almost exclusively to females. Cherokee males were absent from the village almost half of every year. The question remains whether special features of Cherokee village life counteracted the expectable psychological effects on the growing child. If adult Cherokees were, through that socialization, vulnerable to the withdrawal of affection, then withdrawal would be an adequate sanction.[83]

Withdrawal must have been an adequate sanction for it was the chief prop of the Cherokee legal system, and by every indication the Cherokee legal system worked. Certainly it functioned more adequately than the Cherokee political system. On the whole, the Cherokee town experienced internal peace, the harmony of the group was maintained. Coercive sanctions were not needed to restrict the liberty of individuals. "The paradox of anarchy and order is, of course, to be explained by the strength of custom which regulated conduct and disregard of which made the Indian a pariah." [84]

A generation after they abandoned their primitive law, the Cherokees looked back on their ancient customs and called them "savage and barbarous;" their ancestors, they thought, should be pitied for having lived under such a code.[85] Not all of the white contemporaries who knew their ancestors would have agreed. The Cherokee legal system, William Bartram wrote, "produces a society of peace and love, which in effect better maintains human happiness, than the most complicated system of modern politics, or sumptuary laws, enforced by coercive means." [86] Even William Fyffe, who thought the Cherokees savage and ungovernable, marvelled at their social harmony.

> Their Government is not supported by Laws and Punishments as among us. They believe their old men who tell them the Customs of their ancestors & punctually follow these Customs. . . . They are so regular that Quarrels or Murders their almost only vices among themselves happen very seldom. Without Laws & punishments to force them they adhere punctually to what their Fathers practiz'd before them, our numerous Laws enforced by Punishments & join'd to Religion can't keep us in half the Order they observe voluntarily.[87]

CHAPTER TWENTY-TWO

A WAY OF DREAMING

—THE CHEROKEE LEGAL MIND

It may be too late to think Cherokee, nonetheless we must try. It is not enough to know what the Cherokees did, we must also know how and why they did it—knowledge that will always remain just beyond our reach.

It might be suggested that because we know a good deal about Cherokee law, we also know a good deal about the Cherokee legal mind. In truth, there are many matters about which we cannot even make a sound guess. An area of mystery which we would have to unravel, should we wish to know how a law-conscious Cherokee thought, is the role of the peace pipe in Cherokee jurisprudence. Their international transactions with the British are well documented and Cherokee headmen, either as individuals or as speakers on behalf of groups, often expressed ideas on the nature and force of international obligations; yet we do not know what the frequent smoking of the peace pipe meant in either international or domestic law. Were we to limit ourselves to Cherokee evidence and not draw analogies to other Indian nations—analogies too easily drawn, and for which there is no scientific justification—we might say that the peace pipe meant nothing, that it was mere ceremony, a symbol which the Cherokees shared with other American Indians but which had no appreciable significance in their law. After all, everything we know of Cherokee law indicates that only consent—never ceremony or symbology without consent—could create an obligation which an individual would regard as binding on himself. We cannot be sure, however. In 1765, when trouble threatened to erupt between the nation and the colonies, Alexander Cameron, the first resident British agent in the nation, called a meeting of the headmen to persuade them to smoke the peace pipe. When some demurred, Cameron reported to his superiors, he made them "smoke" it by forcing the pipe into their mouths.[1] Why he did so he does not say. If a peacemaker got a pipe between the teeth of a Kiowa or a Sioux, for example, the smoker felt himself legally bound to keep the peace, but it is difficult to believe a Cherokee experienced any sense of legal obligation. Yet Cameron thought it important to make the Cherokee headmen smoke, and he must have understood it signified something to the Cherokees. The most reasonable explanation which can be offered is that the peace pipe was similar to the "physick" that headmen sent to wrongdoers or to people with grievances against wrongdoers, telling them to purge themselves of bad thoughts. Perhaps the pipe (like the physic) was chiefly a psychological measure, and if the Cherokee who was forced to smoke it was a good Cherokee, it was legally effective even when shoved into an unwilling mouth.

There is one aspect concerning the Cherokee legal mind which is closely related to the Cherokee concept of a proper legal system. As noted in the last chapter, the average Cherokee abhorred violence, aggressiveness was the cardinal offense against his social order because it threatened violence, and the mark of a good man was a willingness to withdraw from conflict and to think "good. thoughts." The Cherokee legal mind, therefore, while it may have lacked logical sequence and control of events, was dominated by a faith in the present arrangement of affairs and by a fear of disturbing the current social peace. Perhaps this fear explains why the Cherokees often expected that a legal problem could be solved merely by stating how serious that problem was. Time and again, we find the headmen ignoring the causes of peril and anticipating that if everyone could be persuaded of the potential dangers which might result if bad thoughts were not thrown away, everyone would agree to forgive and forget. "We are a poor People and can make Nothing ourselves, nor have we Anything but what we get from the white People," the Raven of Hywassee once said when seeking to avert a crisis with South Carolina. "Therefore I promise there never shall be any more bad Talks if I can help it, and as you have formerly supplied us with Goods, I hope you will continue to send among us Traders as you have done, and not stop the Trade." [2] Carolina had threatened to withdraw the traders unless certain wrongdoers were punished, but as both the attempt to punish and the ending of trade would have disrupted Cherokee harmony, the Raven expected the British to forgive and forget. The proper legal solution was self-evident to any Cherokee, who was able to eliminate the possible alternatives as too disruptive to the harmony of society.

The key to the Cherokee legal mind was the Cherokees' desire for social harmony and their resentment toward acts of hostility.[3] If we encounter a sense of frustration in our inability to answer specific questions or to explain apparent gaps in Cherokee law, we must not assume that the eighteenth-century Cherokee was also frustrated. To say that he would not have appreciated the questions or understood the gaps is no explanation. For the Cherokees' answers were not necessary, or perhaps better, they were satisfied with whatever solution events turned up, especially if it was a solution which could be avoided. Not the predictability of that solution, but the fact that a solution was needed, troubled the Cherokee. Harmony, not jurisprudence, was his legal concern. "In a simple and stable human community such as a Cherokee village," Fred Gearing has observed, "most of group life is ordered by moral sentiments. In such a social order, the recurrent presence of relations not ordered by notions about decency is, I must suppose, a source of some measure of uneasiness. Cherokees would perceive such behavior as un-Cherokee. It would produce discomfort because it could not be handled in the accustomed manner." [4]

As Gearing suggests, the Cherokee legal mind was limited to issues and premises traditional to the maintenance of harmony in his own social order and did not contemplate the need for exact standards. James Adair tried to explain this attitude—not too satisfactorily—when he wrote of the legal values of the southern Indians, of the Creeks, Chickasaws, and Catawbas as well as the Cherokees. What he says must be taken with reservations for Adair had several encounters with South Carolina law, and the feeling that he had been robbed by dishonest officialdom, manipulating the judicial process to suit themselves, colors the arguments which he attributes to the Indians. Yet despite the fact that he is speaking his own private thoughts, Adair manages to tell us much about the Cherokee legal mind.

> As their own affairs lie in a very narrow circle, it is difficult to impress
> them with a favourable opinion of the wisdom and justice of our

voluminous laws—They say, if our laws were honest, or wisely framed, they would be plain and few, that the poor people might understand and remember them, as well as the rich—That right and wrong, an honest man and a rogue, with as many other names as our large crabbed books could contain, are only two contraries; that simple nature enables every person to be a proper judge of promoting good, and preventing evil, either by determinations, rewards, or punishments; and that people cannot in justice be accused of violating any laws, when it is out of their power to have a proper knowledge of them. They reckon, that if our legislators were not moved by some oblique views, instead of acting the part of mudfish, they would imitate the skilful bee, and extract the useful part of their unwieldly, confused, old books, and insert it in an honest small one, that the poor people might be able to buy, and read it, to enable them to teach their rising families to avoid snares, and keep them from falling into the power of our cunning speakers—who are not ashamed to scold and lie publicly when they are well paid for it, but if interest no longer tempted them to inforce hurtful lies for truth, would probably throw away all their dangerous quibbling books.[5]

Undoubtedly Adair's last point had much substance. The Cherokee legal mind, confined within the narrow limits of its own needs and experiences, could not understand why the British colonies tolerated lawyers. The Cherokees, as individuals, never encountered lawyers professionally until after the American Revolution, but a hint of how they might have treated attorneys can be gathered from their attitude toward a related gender, the Protestant evangelist. Lawyers who relied upon "quibbling books" to discover what nature taught other men † had at least a role to perform in the scolding houses when paid to scold and lie, but preachers seemed to be utterly useless. John Martin, the first English-speaking missionary among the Overhills was an ordained Presbyterian minister who apparently attempted to propagate a gospel somewhat along the line of the old-time

† Adair implies that the southern Indian distinguished between natural and positive law, but again he may have been attributing to them his own thoughts. When prosecuted for violating trading statutes, he wrote in his own defense to the South Carolina Executive Council "[W]e showed you the desire we had of conforming to the Indian Trading Laws but as the Laws of Nature and general Reason Supercede the Municipal and possitive Laws of Nations we possibly could not be fettered by such Unequal Laws to this or that when at the same time the disorderly trader Lived and triumphed in our Ruins without any evident Punishment." [6]

religion which would ring through the Cherokees' mountains after the
Indians were supplanted by white people. Martin is said by Lieutenant
Timberlake to have preached the scripture "till both his audience and he
were heartily tired." Perhaps the Cherokees mulled over his message;
Timberlake does not say. Either by intuition or after thoughtful reflection,
they concluded that Martin was unenlightening and informed him "that
they knew very well that, if they were good, they would go up; if bad,
down; that he could tell no more; that he had long plagued them with
what they no way understood, and that they desired him to depart the
country." [7] In the legal world of the primitive Cherokee, no man needed
another to tell him how to behave.

When seeking to understand the Cherokee legal mind, it is not enough
to ask, as Adair did, what the Cherokees thought of the English legal
profession or of the multiplicity of laws in the British colonies. We must
raise questions about their attitudes toward their own laws, and of no
Cherokee law do we know more than of their law governing homicide.
From our point of view, therefore, no aspect of Cherokee jurisprudence
would tell us more about the Cherokee legal mind than if we were to
know how the Cherokees conceptualized the payment and acceptance of
compensation in lieu of the talionic blood price. What did the Cherokees
mean by "covering the bones of the dead," of "quieting the claim"? Did
they regard what later investigators have called "compensation" as recompense, remuneration, indemnification, commutation or emendation? The
Cherokee legal mind and the Cherokee legal system would both assume
sharper dimensions for us if we knew, as we may suspect, that they would
have called the payment neither "compensation" nor "mitigation" but
"composition." Yet could the Cherokees possibly have thought of it as
"exculpation"? In terms of jurisprudence—in terms of penetrating the
Cherokee legal mind—there is a world of difference between "exculpation" and "composition." "Exculpation" would imply that they were
freeing the manslayer of his guilt, a notion which appears to have been
alien to the Cherokee legal mind. "Expiation" may be closer to what some
anthropologists have in mind when they speak of the manslayer "atoning"
for his "crime," but again atonement suggests "guilt," and there is no
reason to suspect a Cherokee manslayer had to atone. He had to pay—one
way or another—as he was absolutely liable for the blood price, but he did
not have to atone. When we consider the mores of the Cherokee legal
system, the word "composition" seems to be the only suitable term. For
the Cherokees, payment of compensation was a method of maintaining
social harmony, of avoiding counter violence, so it is not difficult to

imagine that society encouraged the clan kin of a victim to negotiate a settlement. Surely the victim's relatives were not disgraced when they accepted peace rather than blood. They were disgraced only if they dared not enforce the law of homicide in some manner. Yet was not the ideal Cherokee the man who did so without undue aggressiveness?

We might also be able to gauge the "progress" of Cherokee jurisprudence, at least in terms of comparative legal anthropology, were we certain how they conceptualized noxal liability. The best guess is that they had no theory of noxal responsibility, an interesting point when it is remembered that they placed animals within a rational frame of reference. Yet it seems that liability always attached on the human side. The Cherokee who killed any beast but a bear had to beg its pardon to avoid retaliation; the animal that killed a Cherokee was not hunted by the victim's brother seeking blood vengeance. Harm done by domesticated animals could sometimes be a matter of vicarious responsibility, although it is doubtful the Cherokees thought of transferred liability. If the Catawba Killer lent his horse to the Slave Catcher of Tennessee and the horse threw and killed the Slave Catcher, the Catawba Killer was the object of vengeance from the Slave Catcher's clan—not the horse as would have been the case, not only in many primitive societies but in Greece, Rome, and perhaps Anglo-Saxon England. The same is true for inanimate objects. Cherokee mythology attributed animation to many of nature's wonders, the sun and wind for example, but they did not translate animation into domestic legal responsibility. In the myths, the wonders of nature—such as the thunder—might exercise retaliation but in Cherokee law, vengeance was never exacted against the object or instrument causing harm—a knife used in a slaying was not buried, a tree whose falling branch struck and killed a passing man was not destroyed. If the progress of mankind is from complete liability to noxal surrender,[8] the Cherokee legal mind had yet a way to go in its quest for social harmony. How a Cherokee man who left a loaded gun where a child might find it was called to account by the law of homicide, we cannot say. All we can be confident of is that if there was any liability, he and not his gun was liable.

Such questions as the descriptive word for compensation and the theory of noxal liability were not too sophisticated for the eighteenth-century Cherokee legal mind. They concern primitive-law doctrines, not doctrines of later law, and moreover they raised the sort of issues that might have interested the law-conscious Cherokee who had a propensity for splitting juristic hairs. During the coming years of the nineteenth-century, the era of legal, social, and economic acculturation, the Cherokee legal mind would display four distinctive characteristics: a fondness for legalism, a respect for the law, an abhorrence of state-sanctioned punishments, and an adaptability permitting it to adjust to new challenges, jettison old customs, and absorb new ways. All four of these traits, to varying degrees, were evident also in the legal mind of the primitive Cherokee, and none was more pronounced than what may be called Cherokee literal legalism.

All throughout their recorded history, the Cherokees have displayed a tendency to dwell upon fine points and technical issues when arguing legal matters with each other or with foreigners. One knowledgeable Cherokee scholar referred to this characteristic recently when he wrote of "the 'narrow literalness' of the Cherokees, the Indians that have had more litigation with the Government than any other tribe." [9] Of course a legalistic turn of mind would more readily be demonstrated, were we to consider their post-primitive history. During the primitive era we have less documentation. One example from their public law which we have previously considered was the office of national speaker. The Cherokees limited the speaker to his instructions, he was authorized to speak only within those instructions, and when he strayed beyond them he spoke as an individual, not as national speaker. The year after the Overhills told the Reverend Martin to leave the nation, the Presbyterians sent a second missionary named William Richardson, who asked the Chota council for permission to preach. He told them he had come to teach what God would have them do, and "they were so foolish as to ask when I came from heaven." [10] Richardson thought the Cherokees should be pitied for such nonsense, not realizing it was their legal mind which prompted the question. They asked Richardson for his credentials and when he could show them no authority to speak for God, they told him he could not preach.

The discernible legalism of the primitive Cherokees often assumed a narrower turn than an emphasis on legality, for they also had a fondness for drawing close, literal distinctions and for hiding behind technicalities. While not involving a legal point, an illustrative story is told of Oconostota, the Great Warrior of Chota, who in his later years enjoyed recalling the military exploits of his youth. Once he and Thomas Price, an old trader, were reminiscing about an expedition against the Shawnees when Price reminded him that the Cherokees had been beaten and had had to flee. "True, Thomas," the Great Warrior replied, "I confess that we had the worst of it; but they did not make us *run;* we only *walked very fast!*" [11]

The Cherokees of the nineteenth century often asserted their rights against the United States government by taking advantage of every technicality, every delaying tactic that turned up during negotiations, a trait they inherited from their primitive ancestors. In 1763 the peace of the nation was threatened when the Catawbas' settlement was raided by a war party which they said a Cherokee named "Red Horse" had led.[12] The Little Carpenter apparently tried to gain time so passions might have a chance to cool, by pretending that the party accused was named "Red dog." "[W]e have no man of that name in all our Country," he replied, "but there was a Nittiwagar fellow, that Lived at Wattago in the Middle Settlements that was called the Black Horse, and lived Severall years in our Country and learnt our tongue, we all think that it was him and his Gang that did the Mischief for none of our people have been to war this Year." [13]

The compounding of the name from "Red Horse" to "Red dog" to "Black Horse" was no error. The Little Carpenter knew how to manipulate small technicalities. Even among the Cherokees he was a master at forensic maneuvering. It was a faculty—this Cherokee aptitude for legalism—which he displayed at the very first recorded council in which he served as speaker for the Overhills. The council was held at Charles Town during July, 1753, at a time when relations with South Carolina were strained to the breaking point, and Governor James Glen was determined to force upon the Cherokees several programs they were reluctant to accept. Among other matters, Glen wanted the nation to make peace with the Creeks for trouble between France and Great Britain was in the air and Carolina, needing the assistance of both the Cherokees and Creeks, could no longer risk antagonizing either side in a Creek-Cherokee war. The governor had two arguments with which to support his demands: he threatened to stop the Carolina trade, an action which would have dealt a serious blow to the Cherokee economy, and he cited the treaty of London of 1730 in which, he said, the Cherokees had pledged to make peace with nations in alliance with King George II. In reply the Little Carpenter had counter arguments which he used with consummate skill. He was not authorized to negotiate a Creek peace, and he and Old Hop had started talks in Williamsburg hoping to break the Carolina monopoly with a Virginia trade, a possibility which caused more alarm in Charles Town than even the Creek-Cherokee war. Moreover, the Little Carpenter had been in London in 1730, he had met King George and had been present at the signing of the treaty and did not have to acknowledge (as other speakers might have) the right of Glen to interpret it. He could say, and did say, that he knew what both King George and the Cherokee delegates had intended. Thus, the Little Carpenter opened the proceedings on the second day of the council by relying on his own memory of the treaty and questioning Glen's authority under the treaty to make peace.

"I remember when I was in England," the Little Carpenter asserted, "we were told by the great King George to vindicate ourselves against all our enemies Indians, and that we should have Amunition to fight against the Southern Indians, and I want to know if you have any Orders from the great King George to make Peace between us and the Creeks." [14]

"You was very young at that Time, and must have forgot the Talk," Glen answered. "I have the great King's Talk, and the Paper in my Custody, where the great King desires that all the Indians who are Friends with the English should be at Peace with one another." [15]

The Little Carpenter would not concede the central issue and not only questioned Glen's understanding of the treaty † but argued that as the Creeks had recently killed Carolinians, the Cherokees, by warring on the Creeks, were fulfilling their treaty obligations and were entitled to British military assistance. "The Great King," he said, "when I was in England, desired us to revenge the Lives of his White People, whose Bones lay white upon the ground [of the Muskogee—*i.e.,* the Creeks]. The Creeks [killed?] the white People, but our Nation did not, for we aided and assisted them." [17]

Glen could not deny that the Creeks were responsible for several recent deaths as yet unsatisfied, but at the same time he could not permit to go unchallenged the dangerous precedent which the Little Carpenter was asserting—the right of an Indian to interpret an agreement. "What I say is the great King's Talk," he told the assembled Cherokees. "You are not to mind anybody else." [18]

The Little Carpenter knew there was a higher authority, yet avoided un-Cherokean aggressiveness and a direct confrontation with Glen by hinting at his right to appeal. "I shall be glad if you will let me go to

---

† The next day the Little Carpenter even attempted to nullify the advantage which Glen, by virtue of his ability to read English, enjoyed and suggested that the governor might not know the terms as he did not have a copy of the treaty.

"When I was in England," the Little Carpenter told Glen, "two papers were given by the great King George, one for the Cherokees, the other, I suppose came to the Province of South Carolina. I have not seen these Papers and I suppose they are lost."

"That Paper," Glen replied, "though it cannot at present be so readily come at, being among a great Heap of other Papers, is not lost. I shewed you it in print the other Day in a Book."

The Little Carpenter then cited the ultimate argument in primitive law for interpreting an agreement—his own memory. "This is the third Time I have been here," he said, "and I remember the great King's Talk." [16]

England in the Spring," he said. "I want to talk with the great King George myself." [19]

The governor was not about to finance a Cherokee delegation to London and appeared to be annoyed by the Little Carpenter's suggestion of an appeal, but managed to maintain a conciliatory tone by being both evasive and complimentary. "It may be that in two or three Years hence, when all Things are made easey, you may have leave to go," he replied, "but your Nation is at present so engaged with your Enemies that it would be wrong so useful a Warriour as you are should be taken away from assisting your Country." [20]

"There are other Countries and Places to go to England from besides this," the Little Carpenter answered,[21] referring to Virginia.†

"The great King will not see any from this Country, but when I send them," Glen told him.[23]

The Little Carpenter then brought the discussion to a close by bluntly informing the governor that he had no instructions regarding the Creek war. "I should be glad to hear your Excellency's Talk about your white People, and our Trade," he concluded, "but as to the making Peace, we have no Directions about that." [24] At this point Glen apparently lost his patience. He did not understand, he said, why the Little Carpenter had come to Charles Town without "full Powers" to conclude a Creek peace when he had known that was the purpose for which South Carolina had called the council, and he accused the Little Carpenter of being "a Disturber of the Peace." [25] As mentioned in the last chapter, the Little Carpenter then gave him a peace pipe sent by Old Hop, and Glen had to smoke.[26]

We may admit that the Little Carpenter was more intelligent and more nimble than the average Cherokee, but as a legalist he was by no means unique. American constitutional history is replete with instances of Cherokee headmen employing similar arguments to defend their people's interests: arguments stressing rights, debating methods of interpretations, and dissecting the terms of a treaty. The Cherokees' tendency to dwell upon fine points, to insist upon technicalities, and to demand that agree-

† This remark was the closest the Little Carpenter came to insolence as he was reminding Glen of the Overhills' talks with Virginia, talks which the governor said violated their commitments with South Carolina. To answer Glen's charge, the Little Carpenter again relied upon the treaty of 1730. "It was on account of the Trade that we went to Virginia," he said. "When I was in England I was told that I might go any Way for Goods when I could get them the cheapest." [22]

ments be loosely construed when in their favor, narrowly construed when against them, appears again and again in nineteenth-century records when the nation fought for its survival by relying upon law rather than arms. It was a tendency which characterized not merely their diplomacy but also private dealings conducted between themselves. Speaking of the Eastern Cherokees during the 1850s, a small band isolated in the North Carolina mountains (retaining many of the old primitive values and with few contacts outside their own group), researchers have recently uncovered what they described as "new proof that there is something immutable in Cherokee psychological makeup"—"That legalistic turn of mind, with its tenacity for proprietary and monetary rights." [27] Certainly this quality—this "legalistic turn of mind" which Cherokees employed to gain private rights and financial advantages over business associates—was evident during the primitive-law era, as may be seen by considering their attitude toward contractual obligations.

"The sanctity of the given word among them led to sophistry, craftiness, and narrow literalness," writes David H. Corkran of the eighteenth-century Cherokees, "for the Indian realized that his insistence upon the inviolability of the word made him also vulnerable." [28] Corkran is right about the Cherokees' narrow literalness, but we may doubt if the primitive Cherokee thought himself vulnerable. If he held any word inviolable it was his pledgee's, not his own.

A headman striving to maintain his influence may have had to keep his word and he certainly was expected to make others keep theirs. In 1755 the Little Carpenter negotiated a treaty which required that South Carolina prohibit the export of rum to the Cherokee towns. When Governor Glen and the colonial assembly enacted the appropriate legislation to enforce the treaty, John Elliott, the trader at Chota, decided to challenge the law. He loaded a hundred kegs on packhorses which, as he may have anticipated, Captain Raymond Demere seized as soon as they crossed into the nation near Keowee. Elliott had consulted a Charles Town lawyer before buying the rum, and had been advised that the South Carolina government did not have authority to forbid the sale of rum to Indians. He had, however, no intention of testing the statute in a court of law. After all, he was an Indian trader and Indian traders had little use for the provincial judiciary or the law which they enforced. Rather, Elliott devised an ingenious scheme for using Cherokee law to nullify the statute. He bided his time until Demere, needing corn for his soldiers and unable to purchase any in the nation, turned to him for help. Elliott obtained the corn and hired Cherokees to deliver it, paying them with orders made out to Demere for rum.

Probably to create additional embarrassment, Elliott purchased horses from some headmen including the Great Warrior, also giving them receipts for rum. When the Great Warrior and his men arrived at Fort Loudoun, Captain Demere refused to honor the drafts, reminding the Great Warrior of the Little Carpenter's treaty. As a Cherokee headman asserting Cherokee law, it was incumbent upon the Great Warrior to obtain what may be called his people's equitable rights. They had performed their half of a bargain, and it was not their problem but Demere's to worry about the treaty.

"I did not think you would refuse me so reasonable a request," the Great Warrior told Captain Demere. "The rum is justly due us. The white people expect the Indians to pay their debts, but now we will take care not to pay any of them. Goods for the fort from Charles Town must come by Tellico, and I will now go to the Tellico people and tell them to take everything that comes, and in particular, all rum." [29]

The Great Warrior's argument is a typical instance of the Cherokee legal mind as it functioned during the eighteenth century. The desire for rum is of course a factor and had another product been involved, he might not have been so aggressive. Yet his threat to seize other property in retaliation for a violated bargain—a bargain he was forcing Demere to acknowledge not only because of the rum but because it was a good bargain in Cherokee law—was not an isolated thought expressed in the heat of passion. It represented a concept well entrenched in Cherokee law and reflected a primary value in their legal ethics: a value which may be summarized either by the phrase that "two wrongs could make a right," or that "one bad turn deserved a counter bad turn and together, balanced one against the other, they made everything smooth." The Great Warrior had accepted, or was forced by his followers to accept, certain premises which most Cherokees would have acknowledged as legally valid. The first was that the rum belonged to them. They had sold the horses and rendered the service of transportation, and for Demere not to pay them would have created a wrong. The second premise we must guess at and while admitting that rum had a special attraction, it is evident that the Cherokees had not yet developed to the political or legal level where they thought a treaty could supersede a private bargain. The individual was free to make his own contracts and even the Little Carpenter, when he bargained for or was promised rum as an individual, would demand delivery no matter what national policy he espoused as a diplomat. The third legal premise is that the Cherokees believed they had a right—even if they and the British knew they lacked the courage—to seize any British property in retaliation for the broken bargain. They could, as the Great Warrior said, stop the next train to enter the Overhills, whether the goods in that train belonged to Elliott, Demere, or some other Carolinian. The legal doctrine may be explained as a blow for a blow. The legal principle may be explained as equity.

In 1724 the Cherokees were at war with the Creeks and believed that by treaty the British were obliged to assist them. South Carolina, which was at peace with both nations, denied any commitment to take sides. When Creek raiders attacking a Cherokee town plundered the store of a Carolina trader named John Sharp, the Cherokees stood by and refused to defend him. Charles Town, they explained, had reneged on its promise to aid them with soldiers against their enemies; [30] there was no duty on their part to aid Sharp against the same enemies. Their sense of equity was exacting and somewhat revengeful, but to them it was equity.

Captain Demere gave in to the Great Warrior's demands. He had to. For him it was a matter of international politics, not a question of law. He might say there was no binding contract for him to surrender the rum; the Great Warrior said there was, and pressures of the situation gave the Great Warrior the final word. He merely insisted that debts must be paid, a rule valid in both English and Cherokee law. If we have difficulty with the question of how Elliott's agreement with the Great Warrior obligated Demere to make payment of the rum, we must realize that a debt and a bargain meant one thing to a European and another to a Cherokee. So too did the obligation arising from a debt. The Cherokees who contracted with Elliott to deliver the corn to Demere considered Demere bound to pay them once the corn was delivered, but while delivering it they probably felt no duty to make the delivery and did so only in anticipation of the rum. Had they been asked, while on the way to Demere with the corn in their canoes, they probably would have said that should they change their minds and no longer want the rum, they had the right to throw the corn overboard and return home.

We must not conclude that the Cherokee sense of honest dealing was different from the European's. When the Raven of Tuxo tried to sell the British an Englishman's scalp, saying it was that of a French Indian, the Little Carpenter warned the British they were being tricked and told them not to pay.[31] His sense of equity was broad enough to allow a non-Cherokee to cancel a commitment with a Cherokee when that Cherokee proved to be a cheat. What we can say is that the Little Carpenter and other Cherokees did not regard a bargain as binding, even when they had executed their part. It was always legitimate to demand more than the stipulated consideration. The Little Carpenter may have disapproved of Cherokee cheating but he approved of what we might call Cherokee extortion. For him and for other Cherokees, a contract seems to have been valid only if a better agreement could not be wheedled or coerced. He felt it wrong when the Raven of Tuxo tried to sell a fraudulent scalp, but when the scalp was genuine, he saw nothing wrong with putting pressure on the British to pay more than they had agreed to pay. When a party led by his brother returned from an expedition with the scalp of a French officer, the Little Carpenter demanded that despite the original contract, every man be given a match coat, a pair of boots, a flap, a shirt, a knife, a pound of powder, and two pounds of bullets. In addition, the warrior who had actually killed the officer was to get a gun.[32] The British had only agreed to pay a fixed price to each man who came back with a scalp. They had not said they would compensate everyone. By taking advantage of his influence and perhaps implying the British might find it difficult to recruit more war parties, the Little Carpenter did not bargain for better terms in the future. He forced the British to pay this particular war party more than they had planned to pay and left the future to take care of itself.

One fact is clear. The Little Carpenter's demand was in keeping with Cherokee legal concepts. What is less clear is whether we can say that the Cherokee legal mind regarded no bargain as inviolable. The danger is that "bargain" and "inviolable" may be European concepts which had no meaning in Cherokee law. We may say with more certainty that the Cherokees felt that any bargain or agreement could be altered, and that any means were legitimate which forced the other side to grant better terms than those originally stipulated.

Early in the eighteenth century, before the path was wide enough for horses, British factors in the nation hired Cherokee "burtheners" to carry deerskins to the nearest Carolina settlements. The Cherokees would demand and receive prior payment. Later, when about halfway down the path, they might throw off their loads and threaten to return home unless paid again.[33] It was not merely ordinary Cherokees but also headmen who thought such conduct proper and undoubtedly legal. The emphasis was on what a man could obtain, not on what he was obliged to render. All throughout the colonial era, it was a common occurrence for headmen to contract with the British to go to war, to accept presents to do so, and when the time of departure came, to change their minds. They would tell the British recruiting agent "that several bad Omens had appeared in their Conjurations and they were threatened with Sickness and Death to many and vast Fatigue to the Whole if they went in, and possitively refused to go till the Fall and wanted me to wait till then." [34]

Perhaps the Cherokees believed that bad dreams altered a situation and freed them of their obligations, but it is not surprising that such conjuring usually occurred after they had been paid their *quid pro quo* and were hoping for more presents. Their way of dreaming was less an excuse to break a contract than a means to force the British to raise the price beyond what had already been paid. "The Keowee Indians dreamed last night that they must have a Cagg of Rum before they go to War or they shall have no Success," the commander of Fort Prince George reported in 1758. "I am pretty well acquainted with their Way of dreaming, for they have dreamed me out of a good many Pounds of Beef and Salt since I came here, and I am afraid they'l dream for some of this fresh Pork ere they go to War." [35]

We must be cautious about drawing definitive conclusions from this evidence. Cherokee attitudes regarding bargains may have been one thing when the agreement was with non-Cherokees and quite another when dealing among themselves. Even the white men who knew them best, and who had many dealings with them were not sure how to explain the Cherokee legal mind in this regard. Some Carolina traders felt that the pledged word of a Cherokee had slight value. "It is hard to affirm what these People say for Truth," Ludovic Grant observed, "for they talk commonly for the sake of talking, without any regard to Reality, and it is no great Wonder seeing they are subject to no Law, and seldom the Checks of Conscience, which if that happens, is quickly stiffled by them." [36] James Adair agreed, but with one important qualification. "They are ingenious, witty, cunning, and deceitful," he wrote, yet they were also "very faithful indeed to their own tribes." It was only to "Europeans and christians" that Adair thought the Cherokees "privately dishonest and mischievous." He was not sure why they kept promises among themselves. "Their being honest and harmless to each other," he suggested, "may be through fear of resentment and reprisal—which is unavoidable in case of any injury." [37]

We might conclude that the Cherokee ethics of honesty did not extend to foreigners, yet this explanation may be too simple. The very traders who would not rely on their pledged word trusted them with personal property and commonly extended to the Cherokees a great deal of economic credit, expecting they would be repaid. When hunters tried to escape their obligations, they did not refuse to pay but pleaded the excuse that some event had intervened which released them, such as that they had lost time fighting for the British, and South Carolina was now responsible for their debts. From a legal point of view the best explanation seems to be that the Cherokee system of social sanctions did not fix shame on a man who bettered his position in a bargain. No one scolded the "burtherner" who returned from South Carolina after making the white man pay double wages. Whether he would have been ashamed to drop the packs of a Cherokee is a question we cannot answer. Adair implies that he would have been, but another possibility may be that few Cherokee contractors were so foolish as to pay their countrymen in advance.

Should we seek clues to the Cherokee legal mind by comparing it to the legal mind of the eighteenth-century European, there is no issue which provides greater contrasts and of which we have more documentation than that involving concepts of guilt and attitudes toward punishment. Whenever a Cherokee committed an act of violence against a Carolinian, British policy was to demand that the nation punish the offender.[38] It was an impossible request, not merely because the Cherokees lacked a law of physical coercion, but because of the gulf separating the Cherokee and British legal minds. Culpability was a relative value in Cherokee law. Perhaps due to the influence of clan law, individual liability could be transferred under some circumstances and perhaps due to premises traditionally applied in international law, collective liability could be narrowed to one section of the body politic, seemingly by the unilateral decision of the party accused.

These two doctrines have been suggested in earlier chapters and need be illustrated by but one example each. James Mooney explained the first. "The shifting of responsibility for the killing to a vicarious victim," he observed, "is a common feature of Indian formulas for obtaining pardon, especially for offenses against the animal tribe or the spirits of the dead." [39] By "a vicarious victim" Mooney means "a vicarious slayer." A Cherokee eagle killer, for example, obtained forgiveness of a slain eagle by telling its spirit that a Spaniard was to blame. The doctrine of narrowed collective liability is demonstrated by the troublesome case of Great Tellico during the 1750s. When Great Tellico's pro-French intrigues had gone beyond the point where they could be "overlooked," yet had not reached the stage of contrition so they might be "forgiven," the British sought to hold the entire nation collectively responsible for what they regarded as Great Tellico's "treason." The headmen of the other villages "withdrew," telling Charles Town that Great Tellico's acts were not their acts, that

Tellico was "but one town." The British, with different standards of national responsibility and different concepts of what constituted guilt, misunderstood the Cherokees' legal position.[40] They expected the other towns either to acknowledge responsibility for Great Tellico's acts or to punish Great Tellico's guilt. Neither possibility occurred to the Cherokee legal mind. The only Cherokee alternatives were to overlook, to forgive, or if all else failed, to withdraw and disassociate themselves from Great Tellico.

A confrontation between the European and Cherokee legal minds employing contrary concepts of guilt arose in 1751, when Charles Town demanded the surrender or execution of certain Keowee or Lower Cherokees who had killed a Carolinian at the Oconees within the area of white settlement, yet near the path to the Creeks with whom the Cherokees were at war. The Overhills, the first to respond to Charles Town's request, tried to shift the onus onto the victim who, by being in an area of potential trouble, had been the cause of his own death.

> That we are lately come in from War with the Chactaws and are very sorrow to hear of the white Man being killed on the Creek Path by the Keewohee People, however, that we hear it was his own Fault, for that he joined and assisted their Enemies and encouraged them in the Creek Tongue against them. That he was in a House at this Time, and they could not see him to distinguish him, though they could hear him well enough. That another white Man that was there and a Negro they seen run off from the House, whom they never ran after nor hurted, though they had six of their People at the same Time wounded, as they, the Keewohee People, have sent to relate it to us.[41]

The British, to be sure, could not accept the idea that a victim who defended himself from attack was the cause of his own death merely because he was mistaken for a Creek. Perhaps the Lower Cherokees realized this fact for when they wrote to Charles Town, they employed the defense of mistake not to prove lack of causation but to suggest that no one should be blamed, that the affair should be overlooked.[42] Mistake, the Lower Cherokees argued, was justification to forgive and forget, exactly the opposite from what the British, who thought in terms of responsibility and guilt, intended. "We wrote to you before concerning some white Man that was shot in his House through Mistake," the Lower-Cherokee headmen told Governor Glen, "and we assure you we did not know there was a white Man in the House. But as soon as wee saw white people come out of the House, we all called out, let go, and not hurt them, so hope you'll excuse all that's past." [43]

Of course the Cherokees did not want to surrender the manslayer and forgiveness ("I hope the Governor will be as easie as he can to pardon Everything," was how the Raven of Hywassee explained the legal doctrine) [44] would have been a happy solution. But the problem went deeper than a national reluctance or inability to deliver a fugitive. There was a gulf between legal concepts for the Cherokees understood but could not appreciate why the manslayer had to be a fugitive, why he was blamed, and why the British wanted him punished. The abyss which can separate the legal minds of two people may be placed in sharper focus by considering the British assumption that the Cherokees punished wrongdoers, and that the demand for a manslayer's surrender or execution could be justified on the grounds of reciprocal justice. "Is it fit that the Authors of this Murder and Mischief should live," Governor Glen asked a Cherokee delegation, "or can we forgive such Wrongs and Injuries, would not you yourselves have expected Satisfaction from us if any of your People had been killed by some of ours, and would not you have thought yourselves as much injured if we had delayed or denied bringing the Murderers to Justice?" [45]

It would be difficult for anyone, even another British colonial governor less informed of Cherokee ways, to have been more wrong in the application of legal premises than was Glen. The Cherokees asked for vengeance in domestic law, they asked for retaliation in international law, or they asked for composition, but in the sense that Glen used the word they never asked for "punishment." Indeed, there is every reason to believe that they did not understand the purpose of punishment and that when they encountered it among the Europeans, they did not approve of it. A legal system which depended solely on social and ethical sanctions—on withdrawal and irrision—could have little occasion to contemplate the uses of either physical or economic punishment. Surprisingly, the Cherokees also seem to have shared an inbred feeling that punishment lowered the dignity of man. It was treating a prisoner honorably to test his courage by prolonged torture, but it would have been demeaning to have incarcerated that same prisoner, or to have used torture not to dignify but to punish him. Most of all, the Cherokees' distaste for punishment was influenced by the emphasis which their legal system placed on forgiveness as a means for restoring harmony to society. In a small community such as a Cherokee village, physical punishment would have fostered disharmony by creating further resentment and reminding the people of the original violence which was being punished.

From the perspective of the Cherokee legal mind a distinction may be drawn between punishment and vengeance, for vengeance was talionic, immediate, and final. It was not extended over a period of time, and while it may have left a nephew without an uncle or a wife without a husband, it did not leave constant reminders of social disharmony such as a man crippled physically by flagellation or mentally by extended isolation from his fellows. We must not overlook the fact that talionic vengeance in Cherokee law was limited to homicide, and we may suppose that other types of vengeance—even perhaps self-help in cases of theft—were discouraged because of the disharmony that would have followed in their wake. Forgiveness and talionic vengeance represented similar social values in Cherokee jurisprudence, while punishment would have been their antithesis.

The case of rebellious, pro-French Great Tellico offers an illustration of the Cherokees' attitude toward punishment and of their emphasis on forgiveness. The Mankiller of Great Tellico and his fellow Tellico headmen did not intrigue with the French merely because they were dissatisfied with the Carolina alliance. They were challenging the influence among the Overhills of the Chota council by offering an alternative to the leadership of Old Hop and the Little Carpenter. To the average Overhill Cherokee, the machinations of Great Tellico probably had more to do with internal Overhill politics than with international affairs. Charles Town, of course, did not see matters in the same light. British officials thought of Great Tellico in terms of sedition and believed that the Tellicos had to be punished, or "treason" might spread to other regions of the nation. The remainder of the Overhills responded to Carolina pressure by withdrawing from Great Tellico, which they said was "but one town." The British and Cherokee legal minds thus reacted differently to the problem; yet it was later, when the effects of withdrawal were felt and the Tellicos asked forgiveness, that the British were completely mystified by Cherokee legal attitudes. Charles Town would have continued the punishment by withholding presents from Great Tellico until the Mankiller and his henchmen were repudiated by their people. The Cherokees on the other hand saw no need for punishment. They forgave Great Tellico and it was the Mankiller's political rivals—the headmen of Chota, Old Hop and the Little Carpenter—who personally pleaded the case for Great Tellico and asked the British to remove their economic sanctions.[46] Great Tellico was sorry, and no Cherokee could appreciate the value of retribution when forgiveness would smooth away all bad thoughts and restore harmony to the body politic.

If British officialdom did not comprehend the Cherokee legal mind, Carolina traders did. Or at least they knew how to take advantage of it, for they counted upon the Cherokees to forgive their offenses and knew that Cherokee reluctance to punish a man provided them a means to escape even the sanctions of colonial law. One of the worse offenders against the trading statutes was John Elliott of Chota, who seems to have consistently swindled the Cherokees by using short measures or by overcharging them for goods. The headmen complained about his abuses [47] and when no corrective action was taken, the Great Warrior seized his measuring sticks which the Little Carpenter carried to Fort Loudoun as proof that Elliott was cheating them.[48] Yet when the British authorities were about to revoke Elliott's license, he prevailed on the Little Carpenter not only to forgive him but to go to Charles Town to plead his case.[49] We cannot be sure that the Little Carpenter believed Elliott when he said he was sorry and would have no more bad thoughts. Possibly the question would not have mattered to the Little Carpenter. Having asked forgiveness, Elliott may have been entitled to it and sincerity was not a probative issue.

A few years earlier two Cherokee headmen, Chucheche and Tossitee, had complained to Governor Glen of a trader named Branham. Glen ordered Branham arrested and removed from the nation yet when his agent, James May, sought Cherokee assistance, neither Chucheche nor Tossitee would help. Chucheche told May that he was thankful Glen was not neglectful of Cherokee interests, "but he talked to Branham and he has promised to be good and there should be no more bad talks of him." More revealing was the explanation given by Tossitee. He claimed that he no longer believed the accusations he had made against Branham but apparently he did, for he said that if any horses were stolen from either white men or Cherokees he, Tossitee, would personally check Branham's range and return them.[50] We cannot doubt that both headmen still believed Branham had been guilty and that at least Tossitee did not expect him to reform, but Branham had asked forgiveness and as Chucheche put it, "there should be no more bad Talks of him." Cases such as this one, in which the forgiven person was not a member of Cherokee society and whose punishment—exile—would not have disrupted social cohesiveness, cannot be explained by saying Chucheche and Tossitee sought to preserve harmony in their community. Rather, it must be conjectured that the social value of forgiveness had become so much a part of the Cherokee legal psyche that it was automatically bestowed upon anyone who said he was ashamed of his aggressive actions. Even though Branham, the subject of the punishment, was an alien, forgiveness was the one solution that a Cherokee could contemplate and with which he could be at ease.

It is the Cherokee mood regarding punishment—regarding execution, incarceration, and whipping—which illustrates the truth that we are too late to think Cherokee. We may understand the legal theory, but to do so is not enough. We would have to know how a Cherokee thought as well as what he thought, and twentieth-century man is too civilized to comprehend the abhorrence with which the Cherokee legal mind (indeed the legal mind of most primitive men) viewed punishment. It was an abhorrence manifested in such unrelated events as the Great Warrior's shocked discovery that colonial schoolmasters caned their students, and the Little Carpenter's refusal to send a French soldier to a Charles Town jail against his will. Perhaps we come closest to comprehending the Cherokee attitude toward punishment when we realize that Cherokee legal norms were subjected to their severest test, at least when challenged by European legal standards, on those occasions when the Cherokees were asked to capture and return escaped felons and bondsmen, or to surrender French prisoners who wanted to stay in Cherokee towns. The promised rewards were undoubtedly sufficient to attract the Cherokees, especially as they could render service at slight risk to themselves. Yet they were always reluctant to force a man to do something he did not care to do, a reluctance which extended even to enemies whom they might have killed on the slightest whim without a sense of remorse or a feeling of guilt.

In 1758 the Little Carpenter arrived at Fort Loudoun on his way to Charles Town and was asked why he did not have with him a French captive whom he had promised to deliver. "He answered that the young Man was not willing, that he never would force his Inclinations, and that as soon as he tired to stay with him then he would dispose of him." [51] The Cherokee constitutional precept of freedom of choice was of course an operative factor in the Little Carpenter's answer, but so, too, was the Cherokee abhorrence of incarceration. We might be tempted to see these two legal values as interrelated aspects of the Cherokee love of liberty were it not for the supposition that abhorrence of punishment sprang from a desire for social harmony, which as a legal value is the opposite of absolute freedom of choice.

Even if these legal causes are thought to be interrelated, it can be asserted that the dominant motivation explaining the Little Carpenter's reluctance to surrender the Frenchman was a dislike of punishment, rather than a love of liberty. As proof, we need look only at the reasons Cherokee headmen gave for hesitating to capture and return British army or militia deserters. They did return them because the British were their allies and may have paid them to do so, but they were dismayed by the knowledge that the men would be flogged. It was difficult for a Cherokee to understand the meaning of desertion. It was perhaps even more difficult for a Cherokee to understand why a man had to be whipped.[52] "I desire that you may not make his Flesh smart by beating of him," Old Hop wrote the commander of Fort Loudoun after capturing a runaway soldier. "I am Governor and will bring him Home myself, so desire that he may not be beaten." He asked the British not to "make me ashamed by a Refusal," but to forgive the man "for he has promised not to run away any more."[53]

Apparently there had been several desertions at that time for on the same day that Old Hop wrote this plea, the Great Warrior of Chota reported that he also had captured two English soldiers. "[W]e Warriors that carry People and have People under our Charge we love these People so I hope you forgive them this one Fault," he asked. "I am very Glad to see them come back, For we Warriours when we are at War, if we lose a Man, we are uneasy and when he comes back we are very glad, so hope that you will be glad likewise. I desire that you may not hurt their Flesh in no Place, for we are all of one Flesh and Blood and Children to the King our Father."[54]

The deserters may have prevailed on Old Hop and the Great Warrior to make these pleas, for the soldiers apparently knew of the Cherokee distaste for punishment. The most important deserter was an officer, Lieutenant Robert Wall, who robbed a store in Keowee and was within ten miles of the French fort in the Creek country when arrested by Carolina agents. Even before he was returned to Charles Town, Wall wrote a letter to a friend in the Cherokee nation, asking him to tell a Cherokee named "Nancy" of his troubles "and also beg that you and she may use all the Interest you possibly can with some of the principal Indians and engage them to petition the Governor to release me."[55] It is likely the British intercepted this letter for the headmen do not seem to have interceded for Wall, but both the Lower Creeks and the Overhills did plea that South Carolina forgive the man who was captured with him.[56] We may suspect that had Nancy received the message, she would had had little difficulty getting petitioners. While a captive in the Creek nation, Wall not only persuaded some of the Creek headmen to accompany him to Charles Town, he persuaded the most important of the Lower

Creeks, the headmen of Coweta (one of whom the British thought was "emperor" of the Creeks) to go with him. They did not succeed in having him set free, but they did force the governor to promise that no matter what Wall had done, his life would be spared.[57]

We must not confuse the Cherokees' dislike of punishment with tenderness, compassion, or mercy. It must be explained by considering their legal mind—their primitive-law concepts and their search for social harmony—for it was a legal, not an ethical manifestation. What troubled them was the disruptive effect punishment might have on the tranquillity of society, not the personal hardship it might impose on the punished individual. The Cherokees' world was a cruel world, and they were not easily stirred to pity. They would work to remove bad thoughts from the community but personal suffering did not shock them. The British deserter whose pardon they obtained might, if captured by them in war, be subjected to a long, excruciating, and ingenious torture. The Cherokee legal mind placed men in categories, and the average Cherokee conducted himself according to those categories. For enemies he had no mercy. In 1747 a French agent who was on a diplomatic mission to the nation was shot by the Indians, probably Shawnees, who were escorting him. He begged Robert Kelly, a Carolina trader, to get him the "famous Cherokee Doctor of that Town." So did the Shawnees who said "they were answerable for his returning in safety that their wives & children were all at the mercy of the French Fort." Kelly went for the physician, who not only refused to come but "expressed great surprise" that Kelly wanted him to treat a Frenchman "and said he could do no more for a friend but that as he was his Enemy he ought either to let him dye like a Dog or lend a helping hand to hasten it." Kelly offered him a large fee but to no avail.[58] Cherokee medical ethics in this case are consistent with the Cherokee legal mind. The physician probably would have declined to aid Kelly in arresting the French agent so the British might imprison him, but no one could have convinced the physician that it was his duty or even that it was right for him to treat that same Frenchman in distress.

CHAPTER TWENTY-THREE

A PEOPLE OF LAW

—THE FUTURE

When we consider the primitive legal mind, we may not think the Cherokees' attitude toward punishment either unusual or remarkable. What is remarkable is the tenacity with which the Cherokees clung to the doctrine of forgiveness in the totally different legal world which they were to construct during the nineteenth century. Long after the Cherokees abandoned their primitive customs and sought social harmony through state-imposed sanctions by adopting a penal system based on courts, fines, and imprisonment, their legal mind would continue to rebel against the concept of punishment. Economic penalties were often remitted,[1] and even convicted murderers were as likely to be pardoned as executed. Surely one of the most time-consuming tasks associated with the office of principal chief during the nineteenth century was to evaluate and act upon petitions for clemency, which seem to have followed the conviction of most felons.[2] Until these petitions are studied we will not know to what extent they depended upon traditional clan sentiment, for even though the clan system by then was much weakened, it is possible that petitioners were

271

largely fellow clansmen. More likely, however, the pleas for clemency stemmed from the anti-punishment tradition for they purport to come from neighbors of the wrongdoer, not from relatives. While this evidence is not conclusive, it tends to confirm the impression that forgiveness remained a Cherokee legal value despite acculturation, and that punishment continued to be at best a necessary social evil.

The survival of the Cherokee distaste for punishment from primitive-law to civilized-law times must be termed remarkable because it is one of the very few known exceptions to the most pronounced characteristic of their legal mind—adaptability. If the Cherokee stress on legality, with its resultant narrow literalism and appearance of sophistry, may be said to have weakened nineteenth-century Cherokee jurisprudence by emphasizing technicalities and fine distinctions, then the score was more than balanced by a strength that the Cherokees seem to have possessed to a larger degree than any other important Indian nation—an ability to accept new law and forget old ways. During the early decades of the nineteenth century, they would discard all their primitive customs, turn their back on their legal past, create a new judicial system borrowed almost entirely from their American neighbors, and do so with a success that would make them both the leaders and the envy of their fellow Indians.

Of course they did not change completely. In jurisprudence they retained a strong distaste for coercion and despite an economy keyed to nineteenth-century interstate commerce, they maintained vague traces of communal property. In substantive law a few reminders of their primitive past also survived. Adultery, for example, never became a crime in the Cherokee nation, and as late as 1845, the penalty for rape was more than twice as harsh as the penalty for infanticide.[3] These are odd anachronisms which go against the rule. The outstanding feature of the Cherokees' legal acculturation was not how much they adopted, but how little they retained.

When we seek examples of the adaptability of the Cherokee legal mind during primitive-law times, they are of course difficult to find. It is, in fact, a contradiction of sorts to speak of adaptability and primitive law for the very essence of primitive jurisprudence is resistance to change. The primitive legal mind cannot stray far from its original concepts and patterns of conduct, or it will encounter challenges beyond its comprehension. By its very definition the primitive legal mind should not adapt to change, or it ceases to be primitive. Still, if we look hard enough we can find hints of things to come for the eighteenth-century Cherokee could accommodate to legal innovations when necessary. Consider the office of national speaker which, if never vested with what we could call political or legal power, at least evolved enough so that the Cherokees had a rudimentary apparatus for dealing with European governments. Then, too, there is the notion of liability. It would not change much until the 1790s but all through the eighteenth century, the British were slowly forcing the Cherokees to realize that a man's acts could harm the commonweal, and that for such acts he should be accountable to the nation. When we search for adaptation or accommodation of substantive-law rules, they are almost impossible to find, but Lieutenant Henry Timberlake may have uncovered one during the 1760s when he noted that the Cherokees overlooked acts of aggression committed by a drunken man, that "no one will revenge any injury (murder excepted) received from one who is no more himself." [4] We might think that the Cherokees were beginning to recognize the element of intent—that a person who lacked the guilty mind should not be blamed for his actions—and perhaps from our point of view they were. But from the Cherokees' own perspective, they were simply adapting an old legal concept to a new problem. The old legal concept was that an aggressive man was a man "not himself." The novel situation was the introduction of rum by Carolina traders. The Cherokees ostracized an aggressive person by treating him as a man "who is no more himself" and by shaming him into better conduct. Timberlake was correct when he said no one revenged an injury from such a person, at least not in the sense that Timberlake meant "revenge." But a sanction was applied and the new problem of the drunken wrongdoer was handled by an old method; he was made to feel shame for his faults.

It is well to end our search for the primitive laws of the Cherokees by considering their capacity to adopt new ways and abandon the old, for it was that capacity which made it possible for the nation not only to survive but to prosper during the first four decades of the nineteenth century. We cannot be sure just why the Cherokees were so adaptable; scholars do not agree on an answer. The best explanation seems to be that the psychological pull of the ancient aboriginal culture was never as strong among the Cherokees as among most other American Indians.[5] The Cherokees were not a nativist people, they had no religion to tie them to tradition, and in social values, economic ways, and especially in law they were progressive while most Indians generally were conservative. Illustrating this point is the fact that Cherokee cultural memory was remarkably short. "They forgot their own traditions and history with a facility that seems amazing in a primitive people," Donald Davidson explained. "Although not fundamentally unlike other Indians in customs and beliefs, they dropped off and simplified where others, through sheer accretion, got involved in accumulations of myth and taboo." [6] Eighteenth-century colonials remarked the fact that the Cherokees appeared to be the only eastern nation to have no tradition of a migration, that they did not believe they had wandered from place to place as had other tribes, but that their ancestors had come out of the ground.[7] During the early nineteenth century, the Cherokees themselves,[8] as well as such white men as France's Louis Philippe,[9] bemoaned the fact that the nation had no history, only a few myths and traditions which were quickly being forgotten.[10]

Cherokee legal memory was as short as Cherokee cultural memory. Few of their myths surviving among their old men into the second half of the nineteenth century were concerned with legal lessons. Some of course were—the story of the Rattlesnake's Vengeance, for example, which may have been intended during the primitive-law era to teach youth its duties and rights—but a nation which seems to have had no traditions of its ancient wars [11] also seems to have had little interest in its ancient customs.

What legal memory the Cherokees possessed even during the eighteenth century was largely pragmatic, designed to remember specific incidents or promises made in international affairs, and was not concerned with domestic jurisprudence. Like the other American Indians, they came in great numbers to treaty councils not merely because the individual consent of every Cherokee was required or to obtain more presents, but to have witnesses who in later years would recall the agreement. "I bring this little Child," the Little Carpenter said, taking a boy by the hand at the Cherokees' first important land cession, "that, when he grows up, he may remember what is now agreed to, and that he may tell it to the next Generation, that so it may be handed down from one Generation to another for ever." [12] By the 1760s and 1770s, the Cherokees were preserving in their archives the talks and treaties they made with the British. They could not read these documents, but they sensed their value,[13] and the knowledge that went with that sense represents a gigantic psychological step between the primitive and the civilized legal mind. Law and rights, they now realized, need not depend on customs or be secured by traditional procedures. They could be created by agreement, and if the nation retained the agreement it might protect itself against the British and the Americans.

A generation later, the Cherokees would take the next tentative step and begin to recognize the binding force of the sovereign's will. It would not be a sudden leap forward but one pursued cautiously by a people who realized that times had changed, and that necessity demanded new ways and new laws. During most of the eighteenth century, they had lived in splendid isolation in their mountain fastness on the marchland of three European empires, and while contact with the British, French, and Spaniards shaped their politics and altered their economy, it did not influence their domestic law. The Cherokees were too remote, too powerful, and too independent. But after the defeat of France, the opening of the western headwaters, and the American Revolution, they were soon surrounded on all sides by white settlers and could no longer afford the luxury of their ancient law of blood; they could no longer permit each man to be a government unto himself. Should a white hunter accidentally kill a Cherokee, the old law required that the victim's brother retaliate, if not against the manslayer himself, at least against some other American. The price of vengeance was now too high, retaliation led to war and the nation faced annihilation if men were not held in check. Starting with hesitant promises during the 1760s that they would build a stronghouse to imprison wrongdoers, and during the 1780s that they would make close-clan kin whip horse thieves, Cherokee headmen tried to solve their dilemma with only moderate success until the first decade of the nineteenth century, when they were able to break free of their legal past by abolishing the right of clans to exact the blood price. Thus the Cherokees converted their nation into a state. After this achievement, change was rapid. In the 1820s they adopted a constitution which was as coercive in concept and as efficient in operation as that of any American state, and the future lay before them.

The future of the Cherokees was to be a future of law, a future that was both a triumph and a tragedy. It was a triumph when they acquired both prosperity and peace by adhering to the rule of a new law and placing their faith in courts, rather than in arms. It was a tragedy when that same rule of law failed to protect their nation. They would be uprooted and driven west, not because they had lost in war but because after winning in constitutional litigation and vindicating their legal rights through the judicial process, they found that law alone was not enough. They would be exiled from their ancient homeland and herded across the Mississippi, despite John Marshall's ruling that the State of Georgia had no legal right to seize their nation. Andrew Jackson was President of the United States, and for him the realities of politics took precedence over the rule of law. John Marshall might make his decision but Andrew Jackson would not enforce it.

When we consider the primitive law of the Cherokee Indians, we may discern the origins of both that triumph and that tragedy. The primitive

Cherokees were a law-abiding people, their ancient customs served them well and despite their size, their geographical divisions, and the problem of their three dialects, they maintained social harmony in their towns and a sense of common ethnic identity. We cannot say that during the primitive era they understood the importance of law; more likely, law was taken for granted by the Cherokees. Yet later, when those ancient customs became obsolete and their survival depended upon the adoption of a new system of jurisprudence, the Cherokees demonstrated a remarkable national trait. They reached back into the very past they were discarding, into their strength as a people, and developed a law consciousness surely rare in history, not merely because they were giving their allegiance to a foreign law but because of the degree to which they pledged their commitment. It was not only the elected chiefs and the educated councilors but also the average Cherokee—the common man living on his isolated farm—who expressed an unqualified, naïve faith that the American judiciary would save the nation from destruction, who trusted their rights, their fortunes, and their future to the rule of law. The Cherokees' triumph was that they turned to American common law, converted it to their own use, and made it work. Their tragedy was that not all men shared their respect for the rule of law.

ABBREVIATIONS

Identification of sources: six frequently cited authorities have been abbreviated and are as follows:

1. CHEROKEE LAW

The statutes of the Cherokee nation are to be found in many printed and manuscript sources. After 1840, for example, session laws were printed every legislative year and several times the national authorities compiled the operative statutes in books resembling codes. The chief collection of the earliest enactments is *Laws of the Cherokee Nation* (1852) which employs a chronological arrangement. The *Cherokee Phoenix* during the 1820s and 1830s also published the early laws.

2. LYTTELTON PAPERS

are manuscript letters and documents in the Governor William Henry Lyttelton Collection, Clements Library, University of Michigan, Ann Arbor.

3. PAYNE PAPERS

are the collected documents gathered from a number of contemporary investigators by John Howard Payne during the early 1830s and are deposited at the Newberry Library, Chicago. As they are catalogued in a series of volumes and sometimes paginated, they are so cited—4 *Payne Papers* 92, for example, refers to the fourth volume and the 92nd page of the typescript copy.

4. S. C. COUNCIL JOURNAL

refers to a series of manuscript volumes, some in photostat, variously titled (e.g., "The Journal of the Proceedings of the Honorable Governor and Council, 29 May 1721 to 10 June 1721") and located in the South Carolina Archives Department, Columbia. Entries are cited by the date on which the entry was made on the minutes. Where manuscript volumes are numbered, the numbers are provided in brackets and when possible the manuscript page is cited following the brackets.

5. SECOND S. C. INDIAN BOOK

refers to a publication by the South Carolina Archives Department entitled "Documents Relating to Indian Affairs May 21, 1750—August 7, 1754 (William L. McDowell, Jr., ed., 1958) and containing books 2, 3, and 4 of the so-called "Indian Books" (mss.) located in the Archives, Columbia.

6. THIRD S. C. INDIAN BOOK

refers to the published volume of the final three of the seven "Indian Books" in the South Carolina Archives, Columbia (William L. McDowell, Jr., ed., 1970).

NOTES

NOTES FOR CHAPTER ONE

1. *Cherokee Phoenix,* Aug. 24, 1833, p. 2, col. 3.

2. Samuel Cole Williams, *Early Travels in the Tennessee Country, 1540–1800* 246 (1928).

3. Kilpatrick (ed.), "The Wahnenauhi Manuscript: Historical Sketches of the Cherokees," *Bulletin 196 Bureau Am. Ethnology* 179, 183 (1966).

4. Muriel H. Wright, *A Guide to the Indian Tribes of Oklahoma* 57 (1951).

5. Gilbert, "The Eastern Cherokees," *Bulletin 133 Bureau Am. Ethnology* 194 (1943).

6. Mooney, "The Cherokee River Cult," 13 *J. Am. Folk-Lore* 1, 3 (1900).

7. Wilma Dykerman, *The French Broad* 41 (1955).

8. Bloom, "The Acculturation of the Eastern Cherokee: Historical Aspects," 19 *N. C. Hist. Rev.* 323 (1942).

9. Anon., *An Enquiry into the Origin of the Cherokees in a Letter to a Member of Parliament* 20 (1762).

10. 1 Frederick Webb Hodge, *Handbook of American Indians North of Mexico* 363 (House Doc. 926, 59th Cong., 1st Sess., 1906).

11. *The Travels of William Bartram* 307 (Francis Harper, ed., 1958). See also Bartram, "Observations on the Creek and Cherokee Indians." 3 (Part I) *Transactions Am. Ethnological Soc'y* 11, 28 (1853).

12. See e.g., "The Battle of *Wa?doh:gi* Mound," in Kilpatrick & Kilpatrick, "Eastern Cherokee Folktales," *Bulletin 196 Bureau Am. Ethnology* 379, 434–35 (1966).

13. Letter From Ludovic Grant to James Glen, April 29, 1755, *Third S. C. Indian Book,* 13; Letter from Tobias Fitch to Francis Nicholson, Oct 15, 1725, *S. C. Council Journal* [3], 152.

14. William Shedrick Willis, *Colonial Conflict and the Cherokee Indians, 1710–1760* 198 (unpublished doctoral dissertation, Columbia University, 1955); Swanton, "The Indians of the Southeastern United States," *Bulletin 137 Bureau Am. Ethnology* 691 (1946). But see [Dr. Milligan], "A Short Description of the Province of South Carolina . . . ," in 2 *Historical Collections of South Carolina* 519 (B. R. Carroll, ed., 1836).

15. C. Hale Sipe, *The Indian Wars of Pennsylvania* 35 (1929).

16. 1 Theodore Roosevelt, *The Winning of the West* 55 (1897). But see Grace Steele Woodward, *The Cherokees* 31–35 (1963); 5 J. A. Doyle, *English Colonies in America* 299 (1907).

17. Dale Van Every, *Disinherited: The Lost Birthright of the American Indian* 11 (1966); W. W. Abbot, *The Royal Governors of Georgia, 1754–1775* 36 (1959); Alden, "The Eighteenth Century Cherokee Archives," 5 *Am. Archivist* 240 (1942).

18. Henry Thompson Malone, *A Social History of the Eastern Cherokee Indians From the Revolution to Removal* 4–5 (unpublished doctoral dissertation, Emory University, 1952).

19. *Indians of the Southern Colonial Frontier: The Edmond Atkin Report and Plan of 1755* 49 (Wilbur R. Jacobs, ed., 1954).

20. David Duncan Wallace, *South Carolina: A Short History, 1520–1948*

21. Alden T. Vaughan, *New England Frontier: Puritans and Indians 1620–9* (1961).

1675 28–29 (1965); David H. Corkran, *The Cherokee Frontier: Conflict and Survival, 1740–62* 3 (1962).

22. Verner W. Crane, *The Southern Frontier, 1670–1732* 69 (1928).

23. Swanton, supra note 14, 114.

24. Ibid.; John H. Logan, *A History of the Upper Country of South Carolina From the Earliest Periods to the Close of the War of Independence* 207 (1859); Verner W. Crane, supra note 22, 131 n. 91.

25. Henry M. Owl, *The Eastern Band of Cherokee Indians Before and After the Removal* 11 (unpublished master's thesis, University of North Carolina, 1929); Swanton, supra note 14, 114.

26. *Adair's History of the American Indians* 238 (Samuel Cole Williams, ed. 1930); Henry M. Owl, supra note 25, 11; Swanton, supra note 14, 114.

27. "A Treaty Between Virginia and the Catawbas and Cherokees, 1756," 13 *Virginia Mag. Hist. & Bio.* 225, 228 n. (1906); Gilbert, supra note 5, 193.

28. Klingberg, "The Mystery of the Lost Yamassee Prince," 63 *S. C. Hist. Mag.* 18, 31 (1962).

29. Henry M. Owl, supra note 25, 13; see sources cited supra notes 25 to 28; [Dr. Milligan], supra note 14, 519.

30. Muriel H. Wright, supra note 4, 85–86.

31. "Annual Message of the Principal Chiefs," *Cherokee Phoenix,* Oct. 22, 1828, p. 1, col. 3.

32. *Virginia Gazette,* Sept. 19, 1755, p. 1, col. 2. But see Muriel H. Wright, supra note 4, 58.

33. Corkran, "Cherokee Pre-History," 34 *N. C. Hist. Rev.* 455, 458–59 (1957).

34. Webb, "The Prehistory of East Tennessee," 8 *East Tenn. Hist. Soc'y Pub.* 3, 6–7 (1936); Swanton, supra note 14, 31; Frederick O. Gearing, *Cherokee Political Organizations, 1730–1775* 4 (unpublished doctoral dissertation, University of Chicago, 1956).

35. Brown, "Eastern Cherokee Chiefs," 16 *Chronicles of Oklahoma* 3 (1938). But see Robert H. Lowie, *Primitive Society* 132 (1920).

36. Thomas Nuttall, *Journal of Travels into the Arkansa Territory, During the Year 1819,* reprinted as 13 *Early Western Travels 1748–1846* 175 (Rueben Gold Thwaites, ed., 1905).

37. *Adair's History . . .,* supra note 26, 411.

38. Henry Thompson Malone, supra note 18, 8.

39. Wissier, "Material Cultures of the North American Indians," 16 *Am. Anthropologist* 447 (1914); Davis, "Early Life Among the Five Civilized Tribes," 15 *Chronicles of Oklahoma* 70, 73 (1937); R. S. Cotterill, *The Southern Indians: The Story of the Civilized Tribes before Removal* 9 (1954); Bloom, supra note 8, 323.

40. Foreman (ed.), "Notes of a Missionary Among the Cherokees," 16 *Chronicles of Oklahoma* 171, 180 (1938).

41. 1 Theodore Roosevelt, supra note 16, 51. But see Frederick O. Gearing, supra note 34, 84.

42. Kilpatrick (ed.), supra note 3, 184 n. 8.

43. Douglas L. Rights, *The American Indian in North Carolina* 151 (1947); James Mooney, *Myths of the Cherokee* 16 (1900).

44. Fred Gearing, *Priests and Warriors: Social Structures for Cherokee Politics in the 18th Century* 1 (1962); Bloom, supra note 8, 325.

45. Kilpatrick & Kilpatrick, "Chronicles of Wolftown; Social Documents of the North Carolina Cherokees, 1850–1862," *Bulletin 196 Bureau Am. Ethnology* 1, 9 (1966).

NOTES FOR CHAPTER TWO

1. Bloom, "The Acculturation of the Eastern Cherokee: Historical Aspects," 19 *N. C. Hist. Rev.* 323, 325 (1942); *Adair's History of the American Indians* 238–39 (Samuel Cole Williams, ed. 1930).

2. 1 John H. Logan, *A History of the Upper Country of South Carolina From the Earliest Periods to the Close of the War of Independence* 207 (1859).

3. R. S. Cotterill, *The Southern Indians: The Story of the Civilized Tribes Before Removal* 5 (1954); Henry Thompson Malone, *A Social History of the Eastern Cherokee Indians From the Revolution to Removal* 6 (unpublished doctoral dissertation, Emory University, 1952).

4. Samuel Cole Williams, *Early Travels in the Tennessee Country 1540–1800* 246 (1928).

5. Douglas L. Rights, *The American Indian in North Carolina* 152 (1947).

6. John Richard Alden, *John Stuart and the Southern Colonial Frontier: A Study of Indian Relations, War, Trade, and Land Problems in the Southern Wilderness, 1754–1775* 8–9 (1944).

7. Fred Gearing, *Priests and Warriors: Social Structures for Cherokee Politics in the 18th Century* 1 (1962).

8. Letter From Ludovic Grant to James Glen, Feb. 8, 1754, *Second S. C. Indian Book,* 475; Letter From James Glen to Old Hop, Dec. 12, 1754, *Third S. C. Indian Book,* 24.

9. Letter From Timothy Millechamp to the Secretary, Nov. 16, 1741, quoted in Klingberg, "The Mystery of the Lost Yamassee Prince," 63 *S. C. Hist. Mag.* 18, 31 (1962).

10. "Historical Relation of Facts Delivered by Ludovick Grant, Indian Trader, to His Excellency the Governor of South Carolina" 10 *S. C. Hist. & Genealogical Mag.* 54, 55 (1909).

11. *Indians of the Southern Colonial Frontier: The Edmond Atkin Report and Plan of 1755* 49 (Wilbur R. Jacobs, ed., 1954).

12. 1 John H. Logan, supra note 2, 237.

13. 2 Alexander Hewatt, *An Historical Account of the Rise and Progress of the Colonies of South Carolina and Georgia* 4 (1779); *Indians . . .,* supra note 11, 48.

14. Letter From James Beamer to Raymond Demere, July 28, 1756, *Third S. C. Indian Book,* 151.

15. Verner W. Crane, *The Southern Frontier, 1670–1732* 129–30 (1928).

16. Corkran, "The Unpleasantness at Stecoe," 32 *N. C. Hist. Rev.* 358, 364 (1955).

17. Henry Thompson Malone, supra note 3, 6; Muriel H. Wright, *A Guide to the Indian Tribes of Oklahoma* 57 (1951); John P. Brown, *Old Frontiers:*

The Story of the Cherokee Indians From the Earliest Times to the Date of their Removal to the West, 1838 17 n. 5 (1938).

18. Letter From James Beamer to Raymond Demere, July 28, 1756, *Third S. C. Indian Book,* 151.

19. Corkran, "Cherokee Pre-History," 34 *N. C. Hist. Rev.* 455, 461 (1957); Talk from Skiogusto Kehowe & the Good Warrior Estuttowe to James Glen, April 15, 1752, *Second S. C. Indian Book,* 247.

20. Letter from James Beamer . . . , supra note 14.

21. Letter From John Stuart to W. H. Lyttelton, Oct. 25, 1759, *Lyttelton Papers.*

22. Rothrock, "Carolina Traders Among the Overhill Cherokees, 1690–1760," 1 *East Tenn. Hist. Soc'y Pub.* 3, 4 (1929); Samuel Cole Williams, *Tennessee During the Revolutionary War* 263 (1944); J. Stoddard Johnston, *First Explorations of Kentucky* 41 n. 2 (Filson Club Pub. No. 13, 1898); Verner W. Crane, supra note 15, 131.

23. Thomas, "The Mound-Builders Were Indians," 20 *Mag. Am. Hist.* 65, 66 (1888).

24. James Mooney, *Myths of the Cherokee* 207 n. 20 (1900).

25. Corkran, supra note 16, 362.

26. See *e.g.,* Affidavit of the Big Half Breed, *et al.,* Oct. 18, 1833, October Term, Record Book Cherokee Supreme Court (Mss.), John Ross Coll., Tennessee State Archives, Nashville.

27. David H. Corkran, *The Cherokee Frontier: Conflict and Survival, 1740–62* 3–4 (1962).

NOTES FOR CHAPTER THREE

1. Talk of Caneecatee [Old Hop] to James Glen, April 29, 1752, *Second S. C. Indian Book,* 258.

2. Letter From O Tassity [Judd's Friend] to Connecotte [Old Hop], May 26, 1757, *Lyttelton Papers.*

3. Affidavit of the Big Half Breed, *et al.,* Oct. 18, 1833, October Term, Record Book Cherokee Supreme Court (Mss.), John Ross Coll., Tennessee State Archives, Nashville.

4. Minutes of Nov. 17, 1747, *S. C. Council Journal* [15], 9.

5. Letter From Ludovic Grant to James Glen, May 3, 1752, *Second S. C. Indian Book,* 263.

6. Corkran, "Cherokee Pre-History," 34 *N. C. Hist Rev.* 455, 466 (1957).

7. David H. Corkran, *The Cherokee Frontier: Conflict and Survival, 1740–62* 4 (1962). See also Henry Thompson Malone, *A Social History of the Eastern Cherokee Indians From the Revolution to Removal* 55 (unpublished doctoral dissertation, Emory University, 1952).

8. *Adair's History of the American Indians* 85 (Samuel Cole Williams, ed., 1930).

9. Samuel G. Drake, *Early History of Georgia Embracing the Embassy of Sir Alexander Cuming to the Country of the Cherokees, in the Year 1730* 9 (1872).

10. Gilbert, "The Eastern Cherokees," *Bulletin 133 Bureau Am. Ethnology* 356 (1943); Bloom, "The Acculturation of the Eastern Cherokee: Historical Aspects," 19 *N. C. Hist. Rev.* 323, 328–29 (1942); William Shedrick Willis, *Colonial Conflict and the Cherokee Indians, 1710–1760* 245 (unpublished doctoral dissertation, Columbia University, 1955); Henry Thompson Malone, supra note 7, 55–60; Robinson, "Virginia and the Cherokees—Indian Policy From Spotswood to Dinwiddie," in *The Old Dominion: Essays for Thomas Perkins Abernathy* 21, 32 (Darrett B. Rutland, ed., 1964).

11. Wiliam Shedrick Willis, supra note 10, 245.

12. 1 Frederick Webb Hodge, *Handbook of American Indians North of Mexico* 703 (House Doc. 926, 59th Cong., 1st Sess., 1906).

13. See *e.g.,* Corkran, supra note 6, 462; 5 *Encyc. Brit.* 450 (1968).

14. H. A. L. Fisher, *Frederic William Maitland: A Biographical Sketch* 97–98 (1910).

15. Quoted in H. E. Bell, *Maitland: A Critical Examination and Assessment* 39 (1965).

16. Proceedings of the Council Concerning Indian Affairs, *Second S. C. Indian Book,* 398.

17. See *e.g.,* Information of George Johnston, *Third S. C. Indian Book,* 11–12.

18. Corkran, supra note 6, 461 n. 13.

19. Fred Gearing, *Priests and Warriors: Social Structures for Cherokee Politics in the 18th Century* 6 (1962).

20. Corkran, supra note 6, 462 & 464.

21. Ibid., 463–64; James Mooney, *Myths of the Cherokee* 393 (1900); Henry Thompson Malone, supra note 7, 62.

22. William Shedrick Willis, supra note 10, 210–18.

23. *Adair's History . . .,* supra note 8, 85.

24. William Shedrick Willis, supra note 10, 216.

25. Gilbert, supra note 10, 366.

26. Edmund Kirke, *The Rear-Guard of the Revolution* 17 (1886); John P. Brown, *Old Frontiers: The Story of the Cherokee Indians From the Earliest Times to the Date of their Removal to the West, 1838* 32 (1938).

27. Letter From George Turner to W. H. Lyttelton, July 2, 1758, *Third S. C. Indian Book,* 470, 471.

28. Swanton, "The Indians of the Southeastern United States," *Bulletin 137 Bureau Am. Ethnology* 767 (1946).

29. Kilpatrick (ed.), "The Wahnenauhi Manuscript: Historical Sketches

of the Cherokees," *Bulletin 196 Bureau Am. Ethnology* 179, 185 n. 14 & 16 (1966).

30. Douglas L. Rights, *The American Indian in North Carolina* 214 (1947).

31. Spence, "Cherokees," 3 *Encyc. Religion & Ethics* 502 (1922).

32. *Adair's History* . . ., supra note 8, 17.

33. Compare James Mooney, supra note 21, 295, to Swanton, supra note 28, 768.

34. Williams, "An Account of the Presbyterian Mission to the Cherokees, 1757–1759," 1 (2d series) *Tenn. Hist. Mag.* 125, 135 (1931).

35. Davis, "Early Life Among the Five Civilized Tribes," 15 *Chronicles of Oklahoma* 70, 92 (1937).

36. *Indians of the Southern Colonial Frontier: The Edmond Atkin Report and Plan of 1755* 49 (Wilbur R. Jacobs, ed., 1954); *Adair's History* . . ., supra note 8, 238–39.

37. Talk of the Warriours of Estertoe to W. H. Lyttelton, March 20, 1758 and Letter From Lach. Mackintosh to W. H. Lyttelton, March 21, 1758, *Third S. C. Indian Book,* 449–50.

38. William Shedrick Willis, supra note 10, 243–44.

39. Robinson, supra note 10, 25.

40. Letter From George Chicken to Francis Nicholson, April 21, 1725, *S. C. Council Journal* [3], 136; Letter From George Chicken to Arthur Middleton, Sept. 20, 1725, "Colonel Chicken's Journal to the Cherokees, 1725," in *Travels in the American Colonies* 97, 151 (Newton D. Mereness, ed., 1916).

41. Talk of Skiogusto Kehowe & the Good Warrior Estuttowe to James Glen, April 15, 1752, *Second S. C. Indian Book,* 247.

42. Fred Gearing, supra note 19, 86; Robinson, supra note 10, 38.

43. William Shedrick Willis, supra note 10, 255. See generally, Frederick O. Gearing, *Cherokee Political Organizations, 1730–1775* 85–86 (unpublished doctoral dissertation, University of Chicago, 1956).

44. Letter From O Tassity [Judd's Friend] to Connecotte [Old Hop], May 22, 1757, *Lyttelton Papers.*

45. Corkran, "The Unpleasantness at Stecoe," 32 *N. C. Hist. Rev.* 358, 362 (1955).

46. *Virginia Gazette,* Aug. 8, 1751, p. 3, col. 1; Aug. 16, 1751, p. 3, col. 1; Oct. 31, 1751, p. 2, col. 2.

NOTES FOR CHAPTER FOUR

1. Bloom, "The Acculturation of the Eastern Cherokee: Historical Aspects," 19 *N. C. Hist. Rev.* 323, 325 (1942); Grace Steele Woodward, *The Cherokees* 46 (1963).

2. Fred Gearing, *Priests and Warriors: Social Structures for Cherokee Politics in the 18th Century* 3 (1962).

3. D. A. Lockmiller, *Land Grants of the Cherokee Nation* 6 (unpublished master's thesis, Emory University, 1928); Gilbert, "The Eastern Cherokees," *Bulletin 133 Bureau Am. Ethnology* 190 (1943).

4. R. S. Cotterill, *The Southern Indians: The Story of the Civilized Tribes Before Removal* 9 (1954).

5. Henry Thompson Malone, *Cherokee Civilization in the Lower Appalachians, Especially in North Georgia, Before 1830* 37 (unpublished master's thesis, Emory University, 1949).

6. Gilbert, supra note 3, 317.

7. "Historical Relation of Facts Delivered by Ludovick Grant, Indian Trader, to His Excellency the Governor of South Carolina," 10 *S. C. Hist. & Genealog. Mag.* 54, 56 (1909).

8. Fred Gearing, supra note 2, 64.

9. "Colonel George Chicken's Journal (1725)," in *Early Travels in the Tennessee Country, 1540–1800* 97, 98, (Samuel Cole Williams, ed., 1928).

10. Quoted in Henry Thompson Malone, *A Social History of the Eastern Cherokee Indians From the Revolution to Removal* 31 (unpublished doctoral dissertation, Emory University, 1952).

11. David H. Corkran, *The Cherokee Frontier: Conflict and Survival, 1740–62* 31 (1962).

12. Ibid., 26–27.

NOTES FOR CHAPTER FIVE

1. Louis Knott Koontz, *Robert Dinwiddie: His Career in American Colonial Government and Western Expansion* 187 (1941). But see, Douglas Summers Brown, *The Catawba Indians: The People of the River* 1–2 (1966).

2. *United States Constitution,* Art. 1, § 8.

3. *Cherokee Nation* v. *Georgia,* 1 U.S. 30 (1831).

4. John Salmond, *Jurisprudence* 213 (7th ed., 1924). But see Frederick O. Gearing, *Cherokee Political Organizations, 1730–1775* 3 (unpublished doctoral dissertation, University of Chicago, 1956).

5. See Acts of Sept. 11, 1808, April 10, 1810, & May 6, 1817, *Cherokee Laws; Cherokee Phoenix,* March 13, 1828, p. 1, cols. 1–2.

6. Swanton, "The Indians of the Southeastern United States," *Bulletin 137 Bureau Am. Ethnology* 664 (1946). But see Gilbert, "The Eastern Cherokees," *Bulletin 133 Bureau Am. Ethnology* 244 (1943).

7. James Mooney, *Myths of the Cherokees* 212 n. 29 (1900).

8. "Letters and Notes," 4 *Payne Papers* 92.

9. Henry Thompson Malone, *A Social History of the Eastern Cherokee Indians From the Revolution to Removal* 54 (unpublished doctoral disserta-

tion, Emory University, 1952). See also, John Haywood, *The Natural and Aboriginal History of Tenenssee* 427 n. "hh" (Mary U. Rothrock, ed., 1959).

10. See *e.g.,* "Miscellany Notes," 2 *Payne Papers* 43–45.

11. Bloom, "The Cherokee Clan: A Study in Acculturation," 41 (new series) *Am. Anthropologist* 266 (1939); 2 Frederick Webb Hodge, *Handbook of the American Indians North of Mexico* 53–54 (House Doc. 926, 59th Cong., 1st. Sess., 1906).

12. *Cherokee Phoenix,* Feb. 18, 1829, p. 2 col. 5.

13. Arthur Pound, *Johnson of the Mohawks* 62 (1930).

14. "Old Cherokee Customs," Unidentified Newspaper Clipping, Weaver Collection, vol. 8, p. 38, microfilm No. 1V100(2), Fort Smith National Historic Site, Fort Smith, Ark.

15. John P. Brown, *Old Frontiers: The Story of the Cherokee Indians From the Earliest Times To the Date of Their Removal to the West, 1838* 527 (1938).

16. J. P. Evans, "Sketches of Cherokee Character, Customs, and Manners," 6 *Payne Papers* 202. See also, Lewis H. Morgan, *Systems of Consanguinity and Affinity of the Human Family* 135–36 (1871).

17. 1 John H. Logan, *A History of the Upper Country of South Carolina From the Earliest Periods to the Close of the War of Independence* 288 (1859).

18. Alexander Spoehr, *Changing Kinship Systems: A Study in the Acculturation of the Creeks, Cherokee, and Choctaw* 202 (Pub. 583, Anthropological Series Field Museum of Natural Hist., vol. 33, number 4, Jan. 17, 1947).

19. Davis, "Early Life Among the Five Civilized Tribes," 15 *Chronicles of Oklahoma* 70, 100 (1937).

20. Jane Richardson, *Law and Status Among the Kiowa Indians* 65 (1940).

21. Alexander Spoehr, supra note 18, 202; Gilbert, supra note 6, 203 & 324–25; Davis, supra note 19, 90.

22. 1 Paul Vinogradoff, *Outlines of Historical Jurisprudence* 193 (1920).

23. Alexander Spoehr, supra note 18, 206.

24. Ibid., 204.

25. I Paul Vinogradoff, supra note 22, 193; Lewis H. Morgan, supra note 16, 158.

26. Gilbert, supra note 6, 249.

27. "Letters and Notes," 4 *Payne Papers* 13.

28. Jane Richardson, supra note 20, 51.

29. Gilbert, "Eastern Cherokee Social Organization," *Social Anthropology of North American Tribes* 285, 289 (F. Eggan, ed. 1937).

30. Ibid. 295.

31. Fred Gearing, *Priests and Warriors: Social Structures for Cherokee Politics in the 18th Century* 22 (1962).

32. Ibid. 114 n. 8; *Cherokee Phoenix,* Feb. 18, 1829, p. 2, col. 5; "Letters and Notes," 4 *Payne Papers* 270.

33. Bronislaw Malinowski, *Crime and Custom in Savage Society* 79 (1926).

34. *Cherokee Phoenix,* Feb. 18, 1829, p. 2, col. 5; Gilbert, supra note 6, 340; Kilpatrick (ed.), "The Wahnenauhi Manuscript: Historical Sketches of the Cherokees," *Bulletin 196 Bureau Am. Ethnology* 179, 185 (1966); "Letters and Notes," 4 *Payne Papers* 22.

35. Josiah Gregg, *Commerce of the Prairies or The Journal of a Sante Fé Trader,* reprinted as 20 *Early Western Travels 1748–1846* 295 (Rueben Gold Thwaites, ed., 1905).

36. Alexander Spoehr, supra note 21, 206.

37. *Cherokee Phoenix,* Feb. 18, 1829, p. 2, col. 5.

38. "Bro. Martin Schneider's Report of his Journey to the Upper Cherokee Towns (1783–1784)," in *Early Travels in the Tennessee Country 1540–1800* 250, 262 (Samuel Cole Williams, ed., 1928).

39. Gilbert, supra note 6, 208, 238–45, 310; Gilbert, supra note 29, 276.

40. Alexander Spoehr, supra note 18, 205; Fred Gearing, supra note 31, 21; A. R. Radcliffe-Brown, *Structure and Function in Primitive Society* 80 (1952).

41. Gilbert, supra note 6, 246; A. R. Radcliffe-Brown, supra note 40, 79; Gilbert, supra note 29, 289.

42. A. R. Radcliffe-Brown, supra note 40, 101.

43. Gilbert, supra note 6, 208, 238–39, 310; Gilbert, supra note 29, 296; A. R. Radcliffe-Brown, supra note 40, 80.

44. Gilbert, supra note 6, 278–79.

45. Ibid., 238–45; A. R. Radcliffe-Brown, supra note 40, 80.

46. A. R. Radcliffe-Brown, supra note 40, 104.

47. Ibid. 100.

48. Gilbert, supra note 6, 359.

NOTES FOR CHAPTER SIX

1. Edmund Kirke, *The Rear-Guard of the Revolution* 20 (1886).

2. See generally, Gilbert, "The Eastern Cherokees," *Bulletin 133 Bureau Am. Ethnology* 321–22, 348–49 (1943); Henry Thompson Malone, *A Social History of the Eastern Cherokee Indians From the Revolution to Removal* 55 (unpublished doctoral dissertation, Emory University, 1952); David H. Corkran, *The Cherokee Frontier: Conflict and Survival, 1740–62* 4–5 (1962); Corkran, "The Unpleasantness at Stecoe," 32 *N.C. Hist. Rev.* 358, 362 (1955); Bloom, "The Acculturation of the Eastern Cherokee: Historical Aspects," 19 *N.C. Hist. Rev.* 323, 328 (1942).

3. Gilbert, supra note 2, 323.

4. *Adair's History of the American Indians* 460 (Samuel Cole Williams, ed. 1930); Fred Gearing, *Priests and Warriors: Social Structures for Cherokee Politics in the 18th Century* 4 (1962); Davis, "Early Life Among the Five Civilized Tribes," 15 *Chronicles of Oklahoma* 70, 91 (1937); John Haywood, *The Natural and Aboriginal History of Tennessee* 255 (Mary U. Rothrock, ed. 1959).

5. *Adair's History* . . ., supra note 4, 460.

6. Letter From William Fyffe to John Fyffe, Feb. 1, 1761, Gilcrease Institute, Tulsa; Gilbert, supra note 2, 323.

7. Fred Gearing, supra note 4, 39.

8. *Cherokee Phoenix*, Feb. 28, 1828, p. 3. col. 1.

9. Gearing, "The Structural Poses of the 18th Century Cherokee Villages," 60 *Am. Anthropologist* 1148, 1149 (1958).

10. "Message of the Commons House to the Council," Feb. 5, 1736–37, *The Journal of the Commons House of Assembly [S.C.] November 10, 1736–June 7, 1739* 216 (J. H. Easterby, ed., 1951).

11. Talk Between Lieut. Outerbridge and the Lower Creeks, Sept. 3, 1759, *Lyttelton Papers*.

12. Fred Gearing, supra note 4, 63–65.

13. Wilbur R. Jacobs, *Diplomacy and Indian Gifts: Anglo-French Rivalry Along the Ohio and Northwest Frontiers, 1748–1763* 26 (1950).

14. *Lieut. Henry Timberlake's Memoirs 1756–1765* 95 (Samuel Cole Williams, ed., 1948).

15. Letter From William Fyffe . . ., supra note 6.

16. Letter From Raymond Demere to W. H. Lyttelton, July 30, 1757, *Third S. C. Indian Book*, 391, 392.

17. *Adair's History* . . ., supra note 4, 460.

18. Fred Gearing, supra note 4, 39.

19. *Virginia Gazette*, Sept. 19, 1755, p. 2, col. 1.

20. Samuel Cole Williams, *Tennessee During the Revolutionary War* 265 (1944).

21. Thomas Jefferson, *Notes on the State of Virginia* 62 (Peden, ed., 1955).

22. Letter From Thomas Jefferson to John Adams, June 11, 1812, *The Indian and the White Man* 95 (Wilcomb E. Washburn, ed., 1964).

23. Alden T. Vaughan, *New England Frontier: Puritans and Indians 1620–1675* 33–34 (1965).

24. E. Adamson Hoebel, *The Law of Primitive Man: A Study in Comparative Legal Dynamics* 132 (1954).

25. Ibid.

26. John Haywood, supra note 4, 257.

NOTES FOR CHAPTER SEVEN

1. William Shedrick Willis, *Colonial Conflict and the Cherokee Indians, 1710–1760* 229 (unpublished doctoral dissertation, Columbia University, 1955).

2. Letter From Federal & Georgia Commissioners to Chiefs, Headmen & Warriors of the Cherokee Nation, Jan. 20, 1823, *John Ross Papers* [File 23–1] Gilcrease Institute, Tulsa.

3. Minutes of March 15, 1744/45, *S. C. Council Journal* [14], 133.

4. Minutes of April 23, 1745, ibid. 177.

5. James Glen, *A Description of South Carolina* (1761), reprinted in 2 B. R. Carroll, *Historical Collections of South Carolina* 243 (1836). See also Ludovick Grant's comment why he believed this purchase binding under Cherokee law. "Historical Relation of Facts Delivered by Ludovick Grant, Indian Trader, to His Excellency the Governor of South Carolina," 10 *S. C. Hist & Genealogical Mag.* 54, 64 (1909).

6. Journal of Col. George Chicken, Aug. 20, 1725, *S. C. Council Journal* [3], 127; "Colonel Chicken's Journal to the Cherokees, 1725," *Travels in the American Colonies* 97, 126 (Newton D. Mereness, ed., 1916).

7. *Virigina Gazette,* Sept. 19, 1755, p. 2, col. 1.

8. Talk of Skiagunsta, The Warrior of Kewoee, Nov. 26, 1751, *Second S. C. Indian Book,* 193.

9. Ibid. 194.

10. Ibid.

11. See *e.g.,* Act of April 10, 1810, *Cherokee Phoenix,* March 13, 1828, p. 1, col. 2.

12. Art. iii, § 22, 23, *Cherokee Constitution* (1827).

NOTES FOR CHAPTER EIGHT

1. *Colonial South Carolina: Two Contemporary Descriptions* 185–86 (Chapman J. Milling, ed., 1951).

2. John Haywood, *The Natural and Aboriginal History of Tennessee* 254 (Mary U. Rothrock, ed., 1959).

3. Qouted in Harriette Simpson Arnow, *Seedtime on the Cumberland* 176 n. 13 (1960).

4. Frederick O. Gearing, *Cherokee Political Organizations, 1730–1775* 16 (unpublished doctoral dissertation, University of Chicago, 1956).

5. Ibid. 1.

6. Ibid. 25. See also ibid. 17 & 120.

7. Ibid. 20.

8. See post Chapter 21.

9. Frederick O. Gearing, supra note 4, 2.

10. See *e.g.,* Williams, "An Account of the Presbyterian Mission to the Cherokees, 1757–1759," 1 (2d series) *Tenn. Hist. Mag.* 125, 134 (1931).

11. See *e.g.,* Letter From Andrew Duche to James Glen, Minutes of April 9, 1748, *S. C. Council Journal* [15], 211; Minutes of April 16, 1748, ibid. 213; Letter From Cherokee Traders to James Glen, 13 April 1748, Minutes of April 21, 1748, ibid. 218–19.

12. See *e.g.,* the matter of the seven "Savanahs." Letter From John Stuart to W. H. Lyttelton, June 12, 1757, *Lyttelton Papers.*

13. Talk of the Black Dog of Nottally & Long Dog of Nottally to the Warrior of Keowee Fort, Oct. 15, 1758, *Lyttelton Papers;* Letter From Thomas Harrison to James McCay, Feb. 14, 1754, *Second S. C. Indian Book,* 477; Minutes of April 8, 1748, *The Journal of the Commons House of Assembly* [S. C.] *January 19, 1748—June 29, 1748* 175 (J. H. Easterby, ed., 1961).

14. See, *e.g.,* Letter from Ludovic Grant to James Glen, Feb. 8, 1754, *Second S. C. Indian Book,* 475; Letter From the Headmen of the Upper Cherokees to James Glen, Feb. 19, 1754, ibid. 486–87; Frederick O. Gearing, supra note 4, 97; David H. Corkran, *The Cherokee Frontier: Conflict and Survival, 1740–62* 20 (1962).

15. Letter From John Stuart to W. H. Lyttelton, Jan. 29, 1760, *Lyttelton Papers.*

16. "A Treaty Between Virginia and the Catawbas and Cherokees, 1756," 13 *Vir. Mag. Hist. & Bio.* 225, 261 (1906).

17. John Richard Alden, *John Stuart and the Southern Colonial Frontier: A Study of Indian Relations, War, Trade, and Land Problems in the Southern Wilderness, 1754–1775* 116 (1944); Hamer, "Fort Loudoun in the Cherokee War 1758–1761," 2 *N. C. Hist. Rev.* 442, 453 (1925).

18. *Lieut. Henry Timberlake's Memoirs 1756–1765* 89–90 (Samuel Cole Williams, ed., 1948). See also, Brown, "Eastern Cherokee Chiefs," 16 *Chronicles of Oklahoma* 3, 12 (1938); Donald Davidson, *The Tennessee— The Old River: Frontier to Secession* 120–21 (1946); James Mooney, *Myths of the Cherokee* 43 (1900).

19. Hamer, supra note 17, 453.

20. Robert H. Lowie, *Primitive Society* 186 (1920).

21. See post Chapter 13.

22. David Duncan Wallace, *South Carolina: A Short History, 1520–1948* 10 (1961); Bloom, "The Acculturation of the Eastern Cherokee: Historical Aspects," 19 *N. C. Hist. Rev.* 323, 326 (1942).

23. 2 Frederick Webb Hodge, *Handbook of American Indians North of Mexico* 284 (House Doc. 926, 59th Cong., 1st Sess., 1906).

24. Art. I, § 4, 7, *Cherokee Constitution* (1827).

25. Frederick O. Gearing, supra note 4, 45 n. 1.

26. Henry Thompson Malone, *A Social History of the Eastern Cherokee*

Indians From the Revolution to Removal 36 (unpublished doctoral dissertation, Emory University, 1952).

27. James Mooney, supra note 18, 204.

28. Minutes of Feb. 9, 1757, *S.C. Council Journal.*

29. Minutes of Feb. 12, 1757, *S.C. Council Journal.*

30. Davis, "Early Life Among the Five Civilized Tribes," 15 *Chronicles of Oklahoma* 70, 100 (1937).

31. *Adair's History of the American Indians* 152 (Samuel Cole Williams, ed., 1930).

32. See post Chapter 21.

33. Robert H. Lowie, supra note 20, 398.

34. E. Sidney Hartland, *Primitive Law* 138 (1924).

NOTES FOR CHAPTER NINE

1. Powell, "Tribal Marriage Law," *Primitive and Ancient Legal Institutions* 277, 280 (Albert Kocourek & John H. Wigmore, eds., 1915).

2. Gene Weltfish, *The Lost Universe* (1965).

3. Lurie, "Indian Cultural Adjustment to European Civilization," *Seventeenth-Century America: Essays in Colonial History* 33, 46 (James Morton Smith, ed., 1959).

4. *Cherokee Phoenix*, Feb. 18, 1829, p. 2, col. 5.

5. Edmund Kirke, *The Rear-Guard of the Revolution* 20 (1886); James R. Gilmore [Edmund Kirke], *John Sevier as a Commonwealth-Builder* 181 (1887).

6. Gilbert, "The Eastern Cherokees," *Bulletin 133 Bureau Am. Ethnology* 294 (1943). See also, James Mooney, *Myths of the Cherokee* 295 (1900).

7. Gearing, "The Structural Poses of the 18th Century Cherokee Villages," 60 *Am. Anthropologist* 1148, 1150 (1958); Fred Gearing, *Priests and Warriors: Social Structures for Cherokee Politics in the 18th Century* 21 (1962).

8. *Adair's History of the American Indians* 156 (Samuel Cole Williams, ed., 1930).

9. Evans, "Sketches of Cherokee Character, Customs, and Manners," 6 *Payne Papers* 203.

10. *Adair's History* . . . , supra note 8, 156.

11. "Miscellany Notes," 2 *Payne Papers* 43–45.

12. Ibid. 45–46; Ralph Henry Gabriel, *Elias Boudinot Cherokee & His America* 25 (1941); de Baillou, "The Vanns," 2 *Early Georgia* 6 (1957).

13. Letter From William Martin to Lyman Draper, Dec. 1, 1842, Draper Collection, series DD, vol. 14, State Hist. Soc'y of Wis., Madison.

14. Letter From John Ridge to Albert Galatin, Feb. 27, 1826, 8 *Payne Papers* 106.

15. "Miscellany Notes," 2 *Payne Papers* 45–46.

16. James Mooney, supra note 6, 305.

17. Minutes of April 17, 1746, *S. C. Council Journal* [3], 92.

18. Josiah Gregg, *Commerce of the Prairies, or The Journal of a Santa Fé Trader,* reprinted as 20 *Early Western Travels 1748–1846* 311 (Rueben Gold Thwaites, ed., 1905).

19. Thomas Nuttall, *Journal of Travels into the Arkansa Territory, During the Year 1819,* reprinted as 13 *Early Western Travels 1748–1846* 189 (Rueben Gold Thwaites, ed., 1905); Gilbert, supra note 6, 324.

20. *Cherokee Phoenix,* Feb. 18, 1829, p. 2, col. 5; Davis, "Early Life Among the Five Civilized Tribes," 15 *Chronicles of Oklahoma* 70, 89 (1937).

21. Hawkins, "A Sketch of the Creek Country, in the Years 1778 and 1779," 3 *Collections Georgia Hist. Soc'y* 19, 74 (1848).

22. But see the later case of Sam Newton, an uxorcide. *Fort Smith* [Ark.] *Elevator,* Nov. 6, 1885, p. 2, col. 4.

23. See *Niles' Register,* June 21, 1823, p. 248, col. 2; "Judicial Executions of Indians at Fort Smith," 29 *Am. L. Rev.* 468 (1895).

24. Josiah Gregg, supra note 18, 311–12.

25. Second Journal of Thomas Bosomworth, October 1752—January 1753, *Second S. C. Indian Book,* 312.

26. Second Journal . . . , supra note 25, 316.

27. Ibid.

28. Ibid.

29. Talk of James Glen, May 30, 1753, Proceedings of the Council Concerning Indian Affairs, *Second S. C. Indian Book,* 393.

30. Second Journal . . . , supra note 25, 317.

31. *Niles' Register,* June 21, 1823, p. 248, col. 2. See also the cases in *Cherokee Phoenix,* April 5, 1834, p. 2, col. 2–3; Edmond J. Gardiner, *Executing a choctaw under tribal law* 7–8 (1889) (unpublished ms., Gardiner Papers, Gilcrease Institute, Tulsa).

32. Powell, supra note 1, 279.

33. John P. Brown, *Old Frontiers: The Story of Cherokee Indians From the Earliest Times to the Date of Their Removal to the West, 1838* 332 (1938).

34. Ibid. 357.

NOTES FOR CHAPTER TEN

1. Swanton, "The Indians of the Southeastern United States," *Bulletin 137 Bureau Am. Ethnology* 731 (1946).

2. Act of April 10, 1810, *Cherokee Phoenix,* March 13, 1828, p. 1, col. 2.

3. *Cherokee Phoenix,* Feb. 18, 1829, p. 2, col. 5; *Indian Justice: A Cherokee Murder Trial at Tahlequah in 1840 as Reported by John Howard Payne* 67n. (Grant Foreman, ed., 1934).

4. Gilbert, "The Eastern Cherokees," *Bulletin 133 Bureau Am. Ethnology* 324 (1943).

5. Journal of Thomas Bosomworth, Agent of South Carolina to Creek Nation, July-October 1752, *Second S. C. Indian Book,* 279.

6. Jane Richardson, *Law and Status Among the Kiowa Indians* 51 (1940).

7. Act of April 10, 1810, *Cherokee Phoenix,* March 13, 1828, p. 1, col. 2.

8. Gilbert, supra note 4, 325.

9. Powell, "Tribal Marriage Law," *Primitive and Ancient Legal Institutions* 277, 279 (Albert Kocourek & John H. Wigmore, eds., 1915).

10. Ibid. See also Lewis H. Morgan, *Systems of Consanguinity and Affinity of the Human Family* 132 (1871).

11. Letter From William Fyffe to John Fyffe, Feb. 1, 1761, Gilcrease Institute, Tulsa.

12. Letter From William Martin to Lyman C. Draper, Dec. 1, 1842, Draper Collection, series DD, vol. 14, State Hist. Soc'y of Wis., Madison.

13. "The False Warriors of Chilhowee" (Myth #102), James Mooney, *Myths of the Cherokees* 375–77 (1900). It may be noted that one recorded instance when a British official speaks of compensating a Cherokee town rather than individuals concerns the same town of "Chilhowie." See Letter From John Stuart to John Blair, Oct. 17, 1768, "Virginia and the Cherokees, &c.— The Treaties of 1768 and 1770," 13 *Vir. Mag. Hist. & Bio.* 20, 22 (1905).

14. Petition of the Old Thigh, *et al.,* Oct. 18, 1833, October Term, Record Book Cherokee Supreme Court (Mss.), John Ross Coll., Tennessee State Archives, Nashville.

15. *Indian Justice* . . . , supra note 3, 66–67.

16. See comment of General Oglethorpe quoted in *Adair's History of the American Indians* 157 n.57 & 423 n.233 (Samuel Cole Williams, ed., 1930).

17. See *e.g.,* case reported in *South Carolina Gazette,* July 7, 1733.

18. "Letters and Notes," 4 *Payne Papers* 49; Alexander Spoehr, *Changing Kinship Systems: A Study in the Acculturation of the Creeks, Cherokee, and Choctaw* 202 (Pub. 583, Anthropological Series Field Museum of Natural Hist., vol. 33, number 4, Jan. 17, 1947); Gilbert, supra note 4, p. 324.

19. "Judicial Executions of Indians at Fort Smith," 29 *Am. L. Rev.* 468 (1895). In some cases, however, the murderer himself was permitted to appoint his executioner, usually a friend. *Cherokee Phoenix,* April 5, 1834, p. 2, col. 2–3; *The Experiences of a Deputy U.S. Marshall of the Indian Territory* 31 (ms. dated April 19, 1937, Gilcrease Institute, Tulsa).

20. See, *e.g.,* Letter From the Red Coat King to James Glen, July 26, 1753, *Second S. C. Indian Book,* 380.

21. Powell, supra note 9, 278.

NOTES FOR CHAPTER ELEVEN

1. Fred Gearing, *Priests and Warriors: Social Structures for Cherokee Politics in the 18th Century* 23 (1962).

2. Hawkins, "A Sketch of the Creek Country, in the Years 1778 and 1779," 3 *Collections Georgia Hist. Soc'y* 19, 81 (1848).

3. For an account which describes this killing as deliberate, see Corkran, "The Unpleasantness at Stecoe," 32 *N. C. Hist. Rev.* 358, 359 (1955).

4. Talk of Skiyogusta of Kehowe & the Good Warrior Estuttoye [spring 1752], *Second S. C. Indian Book,* 249–50.

5. Letter From William Martin to Lyman C. Draper, Dec. 1, 1842, Draper Collection, series DD, vol. 14, State Hist. Soc'y of Wis., Madison.

6. "Letters and Notes," 4 *Payne Papers* 331.

7. "Miscellany Notes," 2 *Payne Papers* 11.

8. "Letters and Notes," 4 *Payne Papers* 331.

9. Walser, "Senator Strange's Indian Novel," 26 *N. C. Hist. Rev.* 1, 16 (1949).

10. Letter From Daniel Pepper to W. H. Lyttelton, Nov. 18, 1756, *Third S. C. Indian Book,* 254.

11. Letter From Paul Demere to W. H. Lyttelton, Dec. 30, 1757, ibid, 426.

12. Letter From Paul Demere to W. H. Lyttelton, Jan. 5, 1758, ibid, 433.

13. Talk of the Warriour of the Long Savannah to Paul Demere, [March, 1758], ibid., 441.

14. Letter From Paul Demere to W. H. Lyttelton, Dec. 30, 1757, ibid., 426, 430.

15. James Mooney, *Myths of the Cherokee* 263–64 (1900).

16. Ibid. 250.

17. See, *e.g.,* David H. Corkran, *The Cherokee Frontier: Conflict and Survival, 1740–62* 230 (1962).

18. Ibid. 35.

19. "Miscellany Notes," 2 *Payne Papers* 11; *Cherokee Phoenix,* April 1, 1829, p. 2, col. 2.

20. John P. Brown, *Old Frontiers: The Story of the Cherokee Indians From the Earliest Times to the Date of Their Removal to the West, 1838* 76 (1938).

21. Wilbur R. Jacobs, *Diplomacy and Indian Gifts: Anglo-French Rivalry Along the Ohio and Northwest Frontiers, 1748–1763* 17 (1950).

22. James Mooney, supra note 15, 261.

23. L. H. Morgan, *League of the Hodenosaunee or Iroquois* 331–33 (1851); 1 Cadwallader Colden, *The History of the Five Indian Nations of Canada* 2–3 (1922 edition).

24. 1 Frederick Webb Hodge, *Handbook of American Indian North of*

Mexico 546 (House Doc. 926, 59th Cong., 1st Sess., 1906). See also Hassler, "The Real Hiawatha," 1 (no. 2) *Am. Hist. Illustrated* 35, 37 (1966).

25. Francesco Gioseppe Bressani, *A Brief Account of Certain Missions of the Fathers of the Society of Jesus in New France* (1653), reprinted in 38 *The Jesuit Relations and Allied Documents: Travels and Explorations of Jesuit Missionaries in New France 1610–1791* 205, 283–85 (Rueben Gold Thwaites, ed. 1959 edition). See also Jean de Brebeuf, *Relation of the Huron* (1636), reprinted in 10 *The Jesuit Relations and Allied Documents: Travels and Explorations of the Jesuit Missionaries in New France 1610–1791* 216–17 (Rueben Gold Thwaites, ed. 1959 edition).

26. Lurie, "Indian Cultural Adjustment to European Civilization," *Seventeenth-Century America: Essays in Colonial History* 33, 45 (James Morton Smith, ed., 1959).

27. James Mooney, supra note 15, 207 n. 20. See also ibid. 261.

28. Gilbert, "The Eastern Cherokees," *Bulletin 133 Bureau Am. Ethnology* 324 (1943). See also remarks of Return J. Meigs, in "Note," 3 *Mag. Am. Hist.* 199, 200 (1879).

29. Hamer, "Fort Loudoun In the Cherokee War 1758–1761," 2 *N. C. Hist Rev.* 442, 443 (1925).

30. Letter From W. H. Lyttelton to the Lower & Middle Cherokee Headmen & Warriors, Sept. 26, 1758, *Third S. C. Indian Book,* 481; Letter From W. H. Lyttelton to the Lower Cherokee Headmen & Warriours, n.d. [c. 1758], ibid., 479; Letter From John Stuart to John Blair, Oct. 17, 1768, "Virginia and the Cherokee, &c.—The Treaties of 1768 and 1770," 13 *Vir. Mag. Hist. & Bio.* 20, 22 (1905); John P. Brown, supra note 20, 58–59, 131; John Richard Alden, *John Stuart and the Southern Colonial Frontier: A Study of Indian Relations, War, and Land Problems in the Southern Wilderness, 1754–1775* 78–79 (1944).

31. Talk of the Warriour of the Long Savannah to Paul Demere, [March, 1758], *Third S. C. Indian Book,* 440, 441.

32. Bronislaw Malinowski, *Crime and Custom in Savage Society* 115 (1926).

33. Letter from John Stuart to John Blair, Oct. 17, 1768 and Letter From Lord Botetourt to Andrew Lewis, Dec. 20, 1768, "Virginia and the Cherokee . . . ," supra note 30, 22 & 29.

34. William Shedrick Willis, *Colonial Conflict and the Cherokee Indians, 1710–1760* 80 (unpublished doctoral dissertation, Columbia University, 1955).

35. *Adair's History of the American Indians* 165 (Samuel Cole Williams, ed., 1930).

36. Ibid.

37. Petition of the Old Thigh, *et al.,* Oct. 18, 1833, October Term, Record Book Cherokee Supreme Court (Mss.), John Ross Coll., Tennessee State Ar-

chives, Nashville. See also Affidavit of the Big Half Breed, *et al.*, Oct. 18, 1833, ibid.

38. David H. Corkran, supra note 17, 178–79.

39. *Cherokee Phoenix,* April 1, 1829, p. 2, col. 2.

40. Letter From William Fyffe to John Fyffe, Feb. 1, 1761, Gilcrease Institute, Tulsa.

41. See generally, John L. Stoutenburgh, Jr., *Dictionary of the American Indian* 219 (1960). Specifically for the Cherokees see Judge Samuel Cole Williams' "Introduction" to *Adair's History,* supra note 35.

42. Klingberg, "The Indian Frontier in South Carolina as Seen by the S.P.G. Missionary," 5 *J. Southern Hist.* 479, 495 n. 64 (1939).

43. "Letters and Notes," 4 *Payne Papers* 330.

44. Ibid. 145.

45. Ibid. 330.

46. "Traditions of the Cherokees," 1 *Payne Papers* 75. See also "Letters and Notes," 4 *Payne Papers* 49.

47. Ibid. 330.

48. Ibid. 49.

49. Gilbert, supra note 28, 324; "Letters and Notes," 4 *Payne Papers* 144.

50. Ibid. 49.

51. Henry Thompson Malone, *A Social History of the Eastern Cherokee Indians From the Revolution to Removal* 61 (unpublished doctoral dissertation, Emory University, 1952).

52. Gilbert, supra note 28, 324.

53. Fred Gearing, supra note 1, 21.

54. Letter From Johnson Pridget to John H. Payne, Dec. 15, 1835, 4 *Payne Papers* 21.

55. *Cherokee Phoenix,* April 1, 1829, p. 2, col. 2.

56. *Adair's History,* supra note 35, 85. But see also ibid. 166–67.

57. Letter From William Martin to Lyman C. Draper, Dec. 1, 1842 . . . , supra note 5; James Mooney, supra note 15, 207 n. 20; *Cherokee Phoenix,* April 1, 1829, p. 2, col. 2. See also *Cherokee Phoenix,* March 15, 1834, p. 2, col. 3. But see "Note," 3 *Mag. Am. Hist.* 199, 200 (1879).

58. *Adair's History* . . . , supra note 35, 166.

59. Letter From Paul Demere to W. H. Lyttelton, Dec. 30, 1757, *Third S. C. Indian Book,* 426.

60. Williams, "An Account of the Presbyterian Mission to the Cherokees, 1757–1759," 1 (2d series) *Tenn. Hist. Mag.* 125, 134 (1931).

61. Kilpatrick (ed.), "The Wahnenauhi Manuscript: Historical Sketches of the Cherokees," *Bulletin 196 Bureau Am. Ethnology* 179, 184 (1966). See also James Mooney, supra note 15, 207 n. 20.

62. *Cherokee Phoenix,* April 1, 1829, p. 2, col. 2.

63. *Adair's History* . . . , supra note 35, 166.

64. *Numbers* 35: 22–29.

65. Hawkins, supra note 2, 74; Bartram, "Observations on the Creek and Cherokee Indians," 3 (Part 1) *Transactions Am. Ethnological Soc'y* 11, 66 (1853).

66. Letter From William Chamberlain to Calvin Jones, Oct. 10, 1818, Miscellaneous File, Tennessee Historical Society, Nashville, "Letters and Notes," 4 *Payne Papers* 330.

67. *Adair's History* . . . , supra note 35, 165.

68. See *e.g., Cherokee Phoenix*, March 15, 1834, p. 2, col. 3, citing *Numbers* 35:15.

69. "Letters and Notes," 4 *Payne Papers* 331; *Cherokee Phoenix*, April 14, 1832, p. 2, col. 4.

70. *Adair's History* . . . , supra note 35, 165–67.

71. Williams, supra note 60, 134; *Adair's History* . . . , supra note 35, 166–67.

72. See case discussed post page 189.

73. Letter From William Martin to Lyman D. Draper, Dec. 1, 1842 . . . , supra note 5.

NOTES FOR CHAPTER TWELVE

1. Henry Thompson Malone, *A Social History of the Eastern Cherokee Indians From the Revolution to Removal* 37 (unpublished doctoral dissertation, Emory University, 1952). See also Grace Steele Woodward, *The Cherokees* 40 (1963).

2. Alexander Longe, *The Ways and Manners of the Nation of Indians Called Charrikees* 21–22 (c. 1698) (mss. Gilcrease Institute, Tulsa).

3. "Letters and Notes," 4 *Payne Papers* 270.

4. Thomas Nuttall, *Journal of Travels into the Arkansa Territory, During the Year 1819*, reprinted as 13 *Early Western Travels 1748–1846* 188–89 (Rueben Gold Thwaites, ed., 1905).

5. Quoted in Henry Thompson Malone, supra note 1, 38.

6. "Letters and Notes," 4 *Payne Papers* 92 & 270.

7. Gilbert, "The Eastern Cherokees," *Bulletin 133 Bureau Am. Ethnology* 339 (1943), citing Judge John Haywood who was a lawyer, not a missionary.

8. Alexander Longe, supra note 2, 21–22.

9. See Alexander Spoehr, *Changing Kinship Systems: A Study in the Acculturation of the Creeks, Cherokee, and Choctaw* 206 (Pub. 583, Anthropological Series Field Museum of Natural Hist., vol. 33, number 4, Jan. 17, 1947).

10. See Hawkins, "A Sketch of the Creek Country, in the Years 1778 and 1779," 3 *Collections of the Georgia Hist. Soc'y* 19, 73 (1848).

11. James Mooney, *Myths of the Cherokee* 345–47 (1900). And note the

myth related ibid. on pages 398–99 which implies that a girl was free to reject a suitor.

12. Letter From William Fyffe to John Fyffe, Feb. 1, 1761, Gilcrease Institute, Tulsa.

13. Bloom, "The Acculturation of the Eastern Cherokee: Historical Aspects," 19 *N. C. Hist. Rev.* 323, 328 (1942).

14. E. Adamson Hoebel, *The Law of Primitive Man: A Study in Comparative Legal Dynamics* 286 (1954); 13 *Encyclopaedia Britannica* 821 (1968).

15. William Shedrick Willis, *Colonial Conflict and the Cherokee Indians, 1710–1760* 140 (unpublished doctoral dissertation, Columbia University, 1955); Gilbert, supra note 7, 340.

16. *Adair's History of the American Indians* 152–53 (Samuel Cole Williams, ed. 1930). See also 1 John H. Logan, *A History of the Upper Country of South Carolina From the Earliest Periods to the Close of the War of Independence* 292 (1859). Adultery never became a Cherokee statutory offense even as late as 1890. *In re* Mayfield, Petitioner, 141 U.S. 107 (1890).

17. Letter From William Sludders to James Glen, July 11, 1750, Minutes of Sept. 5, 1750, *S. C. Council Journal* [4].

18. *The Travels of William Bartram* 135 (Francis Harper, ed., 1958).

19. Swanton, "The Indians of the Southeastern United States," *Bulletin 137 Bureau Am. Ethnology* 703 (1946).

20. Davis, "Early Life Among the Five Civilized Tribes," 15 *Chronicles of Oklahoma* 70, 100 (1937); William Shedrick Willis, supra note 15, 140; Hawkins, supra note 10, 74; Swanton, supra note 19, 703; 1 Frederick Webb Hodge, *Handbook of American Indians North of Mexico* 364 (House Doc. 926, 59th Cong., 1st Sess., 1906) (but for an exception in Creek law, see ibid., 44). For a Creek statement that the Creeks had a law punishing adultery in 1752, see Journal of Thomas Bosomworth, Agent of South Carolina to Creek Nation, July-October 1752, *Second S. C. Indian Book,* 306.

21. *The Travels of William Bartram,* supra note 18, 135.

22. But see 1 Frederick Webb Hodge, supra note 20, 44.

23. Letter From William Fyffe . . . , supra note 12; William Shedrick Willis, supra note 15, 141.

24. Ibid. 139–40.

25. *Adair's History* . . . , supra note 16, 244.

26. Ibid. 153.

27. Ibid.

28. Alexander Longe, supra note 2, 22.

29. Gilbert, supra note 7, 251; *Lieut. Henry Timberlake's Memoirs 1756–1765* 90 (Samuel Cole Williams, ed. 1948).

30. See, *e.g.,* Jane Richardson, *Law and Status Among the Kiowa Indians* 27, 45–47, 65–70 & 74–76 (1940).

31. William Shedrick Willis, supra note 15, 141.

32. *Adair's History* . . . , supra note 16, 133.

33. Henry Thompson Malone, supra note 1, 38; Grace Steele Woodward, supra note 1, 40; William Shedrick Willis, supra note 15, 142.

34. "Journal of Antoine Bonnefoy, 1741–1742," *Travels in the American Colonies* 241, 249 (Newton D. Mereness, ed., 1916).

35. Anon., "Reflections on the Institutions of the Cherokee Indians," *The Analectic Magazine* 36, 45 (July, 1818).

36. Bloom, supra note 13, 328; William Shedrick Willis, supra note 15, 142.

37. "Letters and Notes," 4 *Payne Papers* 277. In Cherokee mythology the sun and moon were brother and sister, not husband and wife. James Mooney, supra note 11, 256–57.

38. *Cherokee Phoenix*, April 1, 1829, p. 2, col. 2.

39. William Shedrick Willis, supra note 15, 137 & 139; Anon., supra note 35, 45.

40. Thomas Nuttall, supra note 4, 188.

41. Act of Nov. 2, 1819, *Cherokee Laws*.

42. Act of Nov. 10, 1825, *Cherokee Laws*.

43. Case of James Pettit, Oct. 28, 1829, Record Book Cherokee Supreme Court (Mss.), John Ross Coll., Tennessee State Archives, Nashville.

44. Josiah Gregg, *Commerce of the Prairies, or The Journal of a Santa Fé Trader,* reprinted as 20 *Early Western Travels 1748–1846* 310 (Rueben Gold Thwaites, ed., 1905).

45. "An Act for the benefit of Minerva Jane Lea," passed Nov. 12, 1847, *Cherokee Laws*.

46. Anon., supra note 35, 45.

47. Bloom, supra note 13, 328.

48. Robert H. Lowie, *Primitive Society* 40–43 (1920).

49. William Shedrick Willis, supra note 15, 137.

50. Ibid., 135–39; Bloom, supra note 13, 328.

51. Alexander Spoehr, supra note 9, 201.

52. Gearing, "The Structural Poses of the 18th Century Cherokee Villages," 60 *Am. Anthropologist* 1148, 1149 (1958), Davis, supra note 20, 98.

53. Alexander Spoehr, supra note 9, 201.

54. 1 Frederick Webb Hodge, supra note 20, 450–51.

55. Fred Gearing, *Priests and Warriors: Social Structures for Cherokee Politics in the 18th Century* 21 (1962).

56. *Adair's History* . . . , supra note 16, 195. But see Bloom, supra note 13, 328.

57. Alexander Spoehr, supra note 9, 207. But see William Shedrick Willis, supra note 15, 136.

58. See Gibert, supra note 7, 252.

59. Lewis H. Morgan, *Systems of Consanguinity and Affinity of the Human Family* 207 n. 2 (1871).

60. But see Letter From William Chamberlain to Calvin Jones, Oct. 10, 1818, Miscellaneous File, Tennessee Historical Society, Nashville. During the 1930s the Eastern Band of Cherokees still had no word for "husband." Gilbert, supra note 7, 250.

61. Anon., supra note 35, 45.

62. Ibid.

63. Letter From William Chamberlain . . . , supra note 60.

64. See, *e.g.,* Thomas Nuttall, supra note 4, 188. For an evaluation made in the 1780s see Bartram, "Observations on the Creek and Cherokee Indians," 3 (Part 1) *Transactions Am. Ethnological Soc'y* 11, 31 (1853).

65. Lieutenant Timberlake quoted in Henry Thompson Malone, supra note 1, 38.

66. Harriette Simpson Arnow, *Seedtime on the Cumberland* 176 n. 12 (1960); Donald Davidson, *The Tennessee—The Old River: Frontier to Secession* 89 (1946).

67. David H. Corkran, *The Cherokee Frontier: Conflict and Survival, 1740–62* 9 (1962); Corkran, "Cherokee Pre-History," 34 *N. C. Hist. Rev.* 455, 463 (1957). See also 1 John H. Logan, supra note 16, 289.

NOTES FOR CHAPTER THIRTEEN

1. See, *e.g.,* Anon., "Reflections on the Institutions of the Cherokee Indians," *The Analectic Magazine* 36, 40 (July, 1818).

2. *The Travels of William Bartram* 325 (Francis Harper, ed., 1958). See also 2 Frederick Webb Hodge, *Handbook of American Indians North of Mexico* 308 (House Doc. 926 59th Cong., 1st Sess., 1906).

3. *Adair's History of the American Indians* 462 (Samuel Cole Williams, ed. 1930).

4. Robert H. Lowie, *Primitive Society* 207 (1920).

5. David H. Corkran, *The Cherokee Frontier: Conflict and Survival, 1740–62* 120 (1962).

6. Ibid. 66–67.

7. 1 John H. Logan, *A History of the Upper Country of South Carolina From the Earliest Periods to the Close of the War of Independence* 55 (1859).

8. Quoted in Frederick O. Gearing, *Cherokee Political Organizations, 1730–1775* 29 (unpublished doctoral dissertation, University of Chicago, 1956).

9. *Lieut. Henry Timberlake's Memoirs 1756–1765* 92–93 (Samuel Cole Williams, ed. 1948).

10. See, *e.g.,* documents in *Second S. C. Indian Book,* 22–29.

11. Letter From Lachlan McIntosh to W. H. Lyttelton, July 21, 1758, *Lyttelton Papers*.

12. Letter From Ludovic Grant to James Glen, May 3, 1752, *Second S. C. Indian Book*, 262.

13. Petition of the Commons House to the King, Oct. 13, 1743, *The Journal of the [S. C.] Commons House of Assembly September 14, 1742—January 27, 1744* 481 (J. H. Easterby, ed., 1954).

14. Message of the Commons House to the Lieutenant Governor, May 27, 1741, *The Journal of the [S. C.] Commons House of Assembly May 18, 1741—July 10, 1742* 46 (J. H. Easterby, ed., 1953).

15. Swanton, "Aboriginal Culture of the Southeast," *42nd Annual Report Bureau Am. Ethnology* 673, 725 (1928); Bloom, "The Acculturation of the Eastern Cherokee: Historical Aspects," 19 *N. C. Hist. Rev.* 323, 325 (1942); R. S. Cotterill, *The Southern Indians: The Story of the Civilized Tribes Before Removal* 13 (1954).

16. Grace Steele Woodward, *The Cherokees* 38 (1963).

17. James Mooney, *Myths of the Cherokees* 32 (1900); Henry Thompson Malone, *A Social History of the Eastern Cherokee Indians From the Revolution to Removal* 8 n. 4 (unpublished doctoral dissertation, Emory University, 1952); Douglas L. Rights, *The American Indian in North Carolina* 155 (1947); *Adair's History . . .* , supra note 3, 238 n. 114; Bloom, supra note 15, 334–35; William Shedrick Willis, *Colonial Conflict and the Cherokee Indians, 1710–1760* 81–85 (unpublished doctoral dissertation, Columbia University, 1955).

18. 2 Frederick Webb Hodge, supra note 2, 308.

19. William Shedrick Willis, supra note 17, 138.

20. Bartram, "Observations on the Creeks and Cherokee Indians," 3 (Part 1) *Transactions Am. Ethnological Soc'y* 11, 37 (1853).

21. Swanton, "The Indians of the Southeastern United States," *Bulletin 137 Bureau Am. Ethnology* 351 (1946); Henry Thompson Malone, supra note 17, 47.

22. Gilbert, "The Eastern Cherokees," *Bulletin 133 Bureau Am. Ethnology* 360 (1943); William Shedrick Willis, supra note 17, 143; Henry Thompson Malone, supra note 17, 48. But see Bloom, supra note 15, 332.

23. Letter From Raymond Demere to W. H. Lyttelton, June 26, 1757, *Lyttelton Papers*.

24. 1 John H. Logan, supra note 7, 159.

25. Gilbert, supra note 22, 360; William Shedrick Willis, supra note 17, 122.

26. Talk of the Warriors of Highwassee & Tommothy to James Glen, April 15, 1754, *Second S. C. Indian Book*, 506.

27. Knowles, "The Torture of Captives by the Indians of Eastern North

America," 82 *Proceedings Am. Philosophical Soc'y* 151, 152 (1940); William Shedrick Willis, supra note 17, 122–23.

28. Proceedings of the Council Concerning Indian Affairs (July 5, 1753), *Second S. C. Indian Book,* 441.

29. Letter From Ludovic Grant to James Glen, March 4, 1752, ibid. 223.

30. William Shedrick Willis, supra note 17, 122 & 154.

31. Ibid. 120; 1 John H. Logan, supra note 7, 290.

32. William Shedrick Willis, supra note 17, 115.

33. 1 John H. Logan, supra note 7, 307.

34. *Adair's History* . . . , supra note 3, 456.

35. Ibid. 241–42; Wiliam Shedrick Willis, supra note 17, 116.

36. Letter From Raymond Demere to W. H. Lyttelton, Oct. 13, 1756, *Third S. C. Indian Book,* 214, 218.

37. Letter From Raymond Demere to W. H. Lyttelton, Dec. 8, 1756, ibid. 262.

38. William Shedrick Willis, supra note 17, 124.

39. *Adair's History* . . . , supra note 3, 455–56; Bloom, supra note 15, 324; Swanton, supra note 21, 14 & 546; William Shedrick Willis, supra note 17, 106.

40. R. S. Cotterill, supra note 15, 15.

41. Verner W. Crane, *The Southern Frontier, 1670–1732* 23 (1928).

42. Clarence Walworth Alvord & Lee Bidgood, *The First Explorations of the Trans-Allegheny Region by the Virginians 1650–1674* 81 (1912).

43. "Letters of William Byrd, First," 28 *Vir. Mag. Hist & Bio.* 11, 23 n. 6 (1920); 1 Frederick Webb Hodge, supra note 2, 138.

44. Chapman J. Milling, *Red Carolinians* 272 (1940).

45. See *e.g.,* Letter From James Glen to the Little Carpenter, Oct. 14, 1755, *Third S. C. Indian Book,* 75.

46. F. W. Maitland, *Equity, Also the Forms of Action at Common Law: Two Courses of Lectures* 368–72 (1913).

47. R. S. Cotterill, supra note 15, 13.

48. *Charles Journeycake, Principal Chief of the Delaware Indians* v. *Cherokee Nation,* 28 Ct. of Claims 281, 302 (1893).

49. Frederic William Maitland, *Domesday Book and Beyond* 150 (Norton Library edition, 1966).

50. *Brief of the Cherokee Delegates on the Delaware Claim* 4 (submitted to U.S. Congress, Feb. 19, 1898).

51. *Reply of the Cherokee Delegation to Ex. Doc. No. 86* 1 (March 8, 1884), document H11. 86 Gilcrease Institute, Tulsa.

52. *Summary of the Census of the Cherokee Nation. Taken by the Authority of the National Council, and in Conformity to the Constitution, in the Year of 1880* 4 (1881), document H11.67 Gilcrease Institute, Tulsa.

53. In re *Wolf,* 27 Fed. 606 (D.C.W.D. Ark. 1886); *United States* v. *Reese,* 5 Dill. 405, 27 Fed. Case 742, 8 Central L. J. 453 (D.C.W.D. Ark. 1879). See also *Cherokee Nation* v. *Southern Kansas Railway Company,* 135 U.S. 641 (1890); *Cherokee Nation* v. *Southern Kan. R. Co.,* 33 Fed. 900 (D.C.W.D. Ark. 1888); *United States* v. *Rogers,* 23 Fed. 658 (D.C.W.D. Ark. 1885).

54. For "occupancy" see *Brief on Behalf of the Cherokee Nation on the Question Touching Her Jurisdiction* 12 (submitted to Attorney General Charles Devens, May 3, 1879), document H11.49 Gilcrease Institute, Tulsa. For "antimonopoly policy" see *Sixth* [sic *Seventh*] *Annual Message of Hon. D. W. Bushyhead to the Senate and Council of the Cherokee Nation* 18 (Nov. 4, 1885); *Second Annual Message, Second Term of Hon. D. W. Bushyhead, Principal Chief, Cherokee Nation: Delivered at Tahlequah, C.N.* 9 (Nov. 4, 1884); *First Annual Message (Second Term) of Hon. Joel B. Mayes, Principal Chief, C.N.—Delivered at Tahlequah, I.T.* 12 (Nov. 4, 1891). See also Graebner, "Pioneer Indian Agriculture in Oklahoma," 23 *Chronicles of Oklahoma* 232, 237–38 (1945).

55. Deed From Cherokee Nation to F. H. Nash, Feb. 21, 1870 (reconveying land first granted by the nation in 1857), *John Drew Papers* (folder 205), Gilcrease Institute, Tulsa.

56. 2 Frederick Webb Hodge, supra note 2, 283.

57. Alexander Hewit [Hewatt], *An Historical Account of the Rise and Progress of the Colonies of South Carolina and Georgia* (1779), reprinted in 1 B. R. Carroll, *Historical Collections of South Carolina* 65 (1836).

58. Letter From Thomas Harrison to James Glen, March 27, 1754, *Second S. C. Indian Book,* 485; Minutes of Sept. 11, 1747, *S. C. Council Journal;* Thomas Griffiths, *Journal of a Visit to the Cherokees, 1767* (mss.) Treasurer's and Comptroller's Papers, Indian Affairs and Land, Box #1, North Carolina Dep't of Archives and History, Raleigh.

59. William Shedrick Willis, supra note 17, 147.

60. Ibid. 76–78; Bacot, "The South Carolina Up Country at the End of the Eighteenth Century," 28 *Am. Hist. Rev.* 682, 683 (1923).

61. Proceedings of the Council Concerning Indian Affairs (June 2, 1753), *Second S. C. Indian Book,* 407; William Shedrick Willis, supra note 17, 27–28.

62. David Duncan Wallace, *South Carolina: A Short History, 1520–1948* 5 & 10 (1961); Douglas L. Rights, supra note 17, 151; Webb, "The Prehistory of East Tennessee," 8 *East Tenn. Hist. Soc'y Pub.* 3, 4 (1936).

63. *Virginia Gazette,* Sept. 19, 1755, p. 1, col. 2. See also *Cherokee Phoenix,* Aug. 24, 1833, p. 2, col. 3; Donald Davidson, *The Tennessee—The Old River: Frontier to Seccession* 41 (1946); Harriette Simpson Arnow, *Seedtime on the Cumberland* 114 (1960).

64. Talk of James Glen to the Headmen of the Upper Cherokees, n.d. [Summer 1754], *Second S. C. Indian Book,* 519.

65. William Shedrick Willis, supra note 17, 145 n. 1; Frederick O. Gearing, supra note 8, 67 n. 1.

66. John P. Brown, *Old Frontiers: The Story of the Cherokee Indians From the Earliest Times to the Date of Their Removal to the West, 1838* 41 (1938).

67. James Mooney, supra note 17, 381; Douglas L. Rights, supra note 17, 125. See also Deyton, "The Toe River Valley to 1865," 24 *N. C. Hist. Rev.* 423, 436 (1947) and appraisal of authorities in Chapman J. Milling, supra note 44, 231–32.

68. William Shedrick Willis, supra note 17, 147.

69. Fink, "Early Explorers in the Great Smokies," 5 *East Tenn. Hist. Soc'y Pub.* 55, 58 (1933).

70. "Colonel Chicken's Journal to the Cherokees, 1725," *Travels in the American Colonies,* 97, 112 (Newton D. Mereness, ed., 1916); "Colonel George Chicken's Journal (1725)," *Early Travels in the Tennessee Country 1540–1800* 97, 99 (Samuel Cole Williams, ed., 1928).

71. Letter From James Grant to William Bull, June 4, 1760, 29 *The London Magazine or, Gentleman's Monthly Intelligencer* 425 (Aug. 1760).

72. Harriette Simpson Arnow, supra note 63, 302.

73. Grace Steele Woodward, supra note 16, 48; Chapman J. Milling, supra note 44, 12–13.

74. David H. Corkran, supra note 5, 251; Chapman J. Milling, supra note 44, 10–11.

75. Bloom, supra note 15, 328.

76. Thomas Griffiths, supra note 58.

77. Fred Gearing, *Priests and Warriors: Social Structures for Cherokee Politics in the 18th Century* 21 (1962); Davis, "Early Life Among the Five Civilized Tribes," 15 *Chronicles of Oklahoma* 70, 90 (1937).

78. Act of Sept. 11, 1808, *Cherokee Laws; Cherokee Phoenix,* March 13, 1828, p. 1, col. 1.

79. Letter From Raymond Demere to W. H. Lyttelton, Aug. 11, 1756, *Third S. C. Indian Book,* 161.

80. Williams, "An Account of the Presbyterian Mission to the Cherokees, 1757–1759," 1 (2d series) *Tenn. Hist. Mag.* 125, 137 (1931).

81. Letter From Paul Demere to W. H. Lyttelton, Jan. 1, 1759, *Lyttelton Papers.*

82. Williams, supra note 80, 134.

83. Henry Thompson Malone, supra note 17, 5.

84. *An Enquiry into the Origin of the Cherokees, in a Letter to a Member of Parliament* 20 (1762).

85. William Shedrick Willis, supra note 17, 110.

86. Swanton, supra note 21, 637.

87. *Adair's History* . . . , supra note 3, 462. But see Chapman J. Milling, supra note 44, 16.

88. William Shedrick Willis, supra note 17, 105 & 118; Henry Thompson Malone, supra note 17, 43.

89. Bartram, supra note 20, 40.

90. *The Travels of William Bartram,* supra note 2, 325–26.

91. Ibid. 326

92. "Colonel Chicken's Journal . . . ," supra note 70, 109.

93. Letter From James Grant . . . , supra note 71, 425.

94. 2 Frederick Webb Hodge, supra note 2, 461.

95. William Shedrick Willis, supra note 17, 115 & 124.

96. Bloom, supra note 15, 328.

97. Act of Oct. 25, 1843, *Cherokee Laws.*

98. Act of Nov. 2, 1819, *Cherokee Laws;* Foster, "A Legal Episode in the Cherokee Nation," 4 *Green Bag* 486, 487 (1892).

99. See *Davidson* v. *Gibson,* 56 Fed. 443 (C.C.A. 8th Cir. 1893).

100. "Current Topic," 45 *Albany L. J.* 199 (March 5, 1892).

NOTES FOR CHAPTER FOURTEEN

1. Bloom, "The Acculturation of the Eastern Cherokee: Historical Aspects," 19 *N. C. Hist. Rev.* 323, 328 (1942).

2. Gilbert, "The Eastern Cherokees," *Bulletin 133 Bureau Am. Ethnology* 307 (1943).

3. Swanton, "The Indians of the Southeastern United States," *Bulletin 137 Bureau Am. Ethnology* 723 (1946).

4. *Adair's History of the American Indians* 92 (Samuel Cole Williams, ed., 1930); *Lieut. Henry Timberlake's Memoirs 1756–1765* 90–91 (Samuel Cole Williams, ed., 1948); Josiah Gregg, *Commerce of the Prairies, or The Journal of a Santa Fé Trader,* reprinted as 20 *Early Western Travels 1748–1846* 290 (Rueben Gold Thwaites, ed. 1905); "Miscellany Notes," 2 *Payne Papers* 10.

5. See Powell, "Tribal Marriage Law," *Primitive and Ancient Legal Institutions* 277, 279 (Albert Kocourek & John H. Wigmore, eds., 1915). But see *Lieut. Henry Timberlake's Memoirs* . . . , supra note 4, 92.

6. Ibid.

7. *An Enquiry into the Origin of the Cherokees, in a Letter to a Member of Parliament* 21 (1762).

8. "Miscellany Notes," 2 *Payne Papers* 10.

9. Proceedings of the Council Concerning Indian Affairs (July 5, 1753), *Second S. C. Indian Book,* 441.

10. *Adair's History* . . . , supra note 4, 187.

11. Ibid. See also, Henry Thompson Malone, *A Social History of the Eastern Cherokee Indians From the Revolution to Removal* 65 n. 89 (unpublished doctoral dissertation, Emory University, 1952).

12. Act of Sept. 11, 1808, *Cherokee Laws.*

13. Lewis H. Morgan, *Systems of Consanguinity and Affinity of the Human Family* 140 (1871).

14. Swanton, supra note 3, 653. But see Frederick O. Gearing, *Cherokee Political Organizations, 1730–1775* 38 n. 1 (unpublished doctoral dissertation, University of Chicago, 1956).

15. William Shedrick Willis, *Colonial Conflict and the Cherokee Indians, 1710–1760* 239–49 (unpublished doctoral dissertation, Columbia University, 1955).

16. Ibid. 276.

17. Verner W. Crane, *The Southern Frontier, 1670–1732* 180 n. 55 (1928).

18. William Shedrick Willis, supra note 15, 206.

19. Morton, "The Government of the Creek Indians," 8 *Chronicles of Oklahoma* 42 (1930).

20. But see 2 Frederick Webb Hodge, *Handbook of American Indians North of Mexico* 36 (House Doc. 926, 59th Cong., 1st Sess., 1906).

21. R. S. Cotterill, *The Southern Indians: The Story of the Civilized Tribes Before Removal* 12 (1954).

22. Talk of Old Hop to John Stuart, Oct. 27, 1956, *Third S. C. Indian Book,* 235, 237.

23. See *e.g.,* Letter From Ludovic Grant to James Glen, Feb. 8, 1754, *Second S. C. Indian Book,* 474.

24. Letter From Raymond Demere to W. H. Lyttelton, Aug. 10, 1757, *Third S. C. Indian Book,* 396; Letter From same to same, July 10, 1757, ibid. 381. See also, Affidavit of the Little Carpenter, *et al., Journals of the House of Burgesses of Virginia 1758–1761* 263 (H. R. McIlwaine, ed. 1908).

25. Letter From Paul Demere to W. H. Lyttelton, Dec. 7, 1759, *Lyttelton Papers;* Letter From Raymond Demere to W. H. Lyttelton, Oct. 13, 1756, *Third S. C. Indian Book,* 214; Letter From same to same, Dec. 17, 1756, ibid. 271. See also John Richard Alden, *John Stuart and the Southern Colonial Frontier: A Study of Indian Relations, War, Trade, and Land Problems in the Southern Wilderness, 1754–1775* 104–05 (1944).

26. For the force of affiliation in a primitive society with stronger matricolenal ties than the Cherokees (though with patrilocal residence) see Bronislaw Malinowski, *Crime and Society in Savage Society* 100–111 (1926). In the 1780s the Great Warrior wanted the Americans to recognize his son, Tuckasee, as his successor. Samuel Cole Williams, *Tennessee During the Revolutionary War* 209 (1944); Cook, "Old Fort Loudon, The First English Settlement in what is now the State of Tennessee, and the Fort Loudon Massacre," 7 *Tenn. Hist. Mag.* 111, 116 (1921). Again it may have been a

case of undercutting a nephew for the Great Warrior's closest lieutenant had been his nephew, Savanooha. But Savanooha is thought to have been born a Shawnee which may have "disqualified" him. Samuel Cole Williams, ibid. 268. Like the sons of Old Hop, Tuckasee never inherited his father's influence and remained an inconspicuous figure in Cherokee affairs. Ibid. 210.

27. Swanton, supra note 3, 653.

28. Letter From Raymond Demere to W. H. Lyttelton, Oct. 13, 1756, *Third S. C. Indian Book,* 214.

29. Compare David H. Corkran, *The Cherokee Frontier: Conflict and Survival, 1740–62* (1962), to John Richard Alden, supra note 25, 105 n. 7.

30. William Shedrick Willis, supra note 15, 243.

31. James Mooney, *Myths of the Cherokee* 393 (1900).

32. Henry Thompson Malone, *Cherokee Civilization in the Lower Appalachians, Especially in North Georgia, Before 1830* 36 (unpublished Master's Thesis, Emory University, 1949).

33. John Haywood, *The Natural and Aboriginal History of Tennessee* 423 n. "f" (Mary U. Rothrock, ed. 1959).

34. Crane, "Nancy Ward," 19 *Dictionary Am. Biography* 433 (1936).

35. Francois André Michaux, *Travels to the West of the Alleghany Mountains,* reprinted in 3 *Early Western Travels 1748–1846* 107, 263 (Rueben Gold Thwaites, ed., 1904).

36. See generally Jane Richardson, *Law and Status Among the Kiowa Indians* (1940). For the Natchez, see *The American Heritage Book of Indians* 147–52 (Alvin M. Josephy, Jr., ed., 1961).

37. 1 Cadwallader Colden, *The History of the Five Nations of Canada* xxviii (1922 edition).

38. Anon., "Reflections on the Institutions of the Cherokee Indians," *The Analectic Magazine* 36, 42 (July, 1818).

39. Proceedings of the Council Concerning Indian Affairs (May 31, 1753), *Second S. C. Indian Book,* 400; 1 John H. Logan, *A History of the Upper Country of South Carolina From the Earliest Periods to the Close of the War of Independence* 457 (1859). For a remarkably similar 1748 case see Chapman J. Milling, *Red Carolinians* 182 n. 23 (1940).

40. *Cherokee Phoenix,* Feb. 18, 1829, p. 2, col. 5.

41. See supra.

42. William Shedrick Willis, supra note 15, 243.

NOTES FOR CHAPTER FIFTEEN

1. R. S. Cotterill, *The Southern Indians: The Story of the Civilized Tribes Before Removal* 11 (1954).

2. Compare Knowles, "The Torture of Captives by the Indians of Eastern

North America," 82 *Proceedings Am. Philosophical Soc'y* 151, 152 (1940), to Verner W. Crane, *The Southern Frontier, 1670–1732* 182 (1928).

3. Swanton, "The Indians of the Southeastern United States," *Bulletin 137 Bureau Am. Ethnology* 111 & 117 (1946).

4. John Haywood, *The Natural and Aboriginal History of Tennessee* 225 (Mary U. Rothrock, ed. 1959); Corkran, "Cherokee Pre-History," 34 *N. C. Hist. Rev.* 455, 465 (1957). But see William Shedrick Willis, *Colonial Conflict and the Cherokee Indians, 1710–1760* 170 (unpublished doctoral dissertation, Columbia University, 1955).

5. Henry Thompson Malone, *A Social History of the Eastern Cherokee Indians From the Revolution to Removal* 8 (unpublished doctoral dissertation, Emory University, 1952). But see William Shedrick Willis, supra note 4, 32.

6. But see Frederick O. Gearing, *Cherokee Political Organizations, 1730–1775* 67 n. 1 (unpublished doctoral dissertation, University of Chicago, 1956).

7. *Adair's History of the American Indians* 5 (Samuel Cole Williams, ed., 1930).

8. Frederick O. Gearing, supra note 6, 67 n. 1.

9. *An Enquiry into the Origin of the Cherokees in a Letter to Parliament* 21 (1762).

10. Letter From the Little Carpenter to James Glen, Feb. 12, 1756, *Third S. C. Indian Book,* 93.

11. Letter From Raymond Demere to W. H. Lyttelton, March 27, 1757, ibid.

12. William Shedrick Willis, supra note 4, 32.

13. Letter From Raymond Demere to W. H. Lyttelton, March 27, 1757, *Third S. C. Indian Book.*

14. Letter From Raymond Demere to W. H. Lyttelton, July 30, 1757, ibid. 396.

15. "Tobias Fitch's Journal to the Creeks [1725]," *Travels in the American Colonies,* 176, 181 (Newton D. Mereness, ed., 1916). See also Report of Tobias Fitch, Aug. 4, 1725, *S. C. Council Journal* [3], 54.

16. Letter From James Glen to Edward Fenwick, June 1, 1756, *Lyttelton Papers.*

17. Fred Gearing, *Priests and Warriors: Social Structures for Cherokee Politics in the 18th Century* 85 (1962).

18. Minutes of April 17, 1946, *S. C. Council Journal* [photostat 3], 92.

19. Davis, "Early Life Among the Five Civilized Tribes," 15 *Chronicles of Oklahoma* 70, 89 (1937).

20. Fred Gearing, supra note 17, 4.

21. *Adair's History* . . . , supra note 7, 460. See Gilbert, "The Eastern Cherokees," *Bulletin 133 Bureau Am. Ethnology* 35 (1943).

22. See *e.g.,* Letter From White Outerbridge to W. H. Lyttelton, March 8, 1757, *Lyttelton Papers.*

23. See Timberlake's remarks, *Lieut. Henry Timberlake's Memoirs 1756–1765* 105–06 (Samuel Cole Williams, ed., 1948).

24. Talk of the Head Men of Ioree, April 17, 1752, *Second S. C. Indian Book*, 254. See also the revenge of Cusseta, a Creek town, upon the Cherokees. Minutes of Jan. 18, 1749/50 *S. C. Council Journal* [photostat 4].

25. Talk of the Red Coat King to James Glen, July 26, 1753, *Second S. C. Indian Book*, 380.

26. Proceedings of the Council Concerning Indian Affairs (June 13, 1753), ibid. 414.

27. Talk of the Red Coat King to James Glen, July 26, 1753, ibid. 380.

28. Letter From David Douglas to John McQueen, April 26, 1758, *Lyttelton Papers*.

29. Letter From John Stuart to Lord Amherst, July 30, 1763, *Amherst Papers*, Clements Library, University of Michigan, Ann Arbor.

30. John Richard Alden, *John Stuart and the Southern Colonial Frontier: A Study of Indian Relations, War, Trade, and Land Problems in the Southern Wilderness, 1754–1775* 30 (1944). See also Letter From James Glen to Thomas Lee, June 7, 1750, Minutes of Aug. 10, 1750, *S. C. Council Journal* [photostat 4].

31. Letter From James Glen to W. H. Lyttelton, Aug. 10, 1756, *Lyttelton Papers*.

32. Letter From Henry Ellis to W. H. Lyttelton, March 7, 1760, *Lyttelton Papers*.

33. Letter From Henry Ellis to W. H. Lyttelton, Feb. 9, 1760, ibid.

34. *Adair's History* . . . , supra note 7, 155–56.

35. Ibid.

36. William Shedrick Willis, supra note 4, 152.

37. Talk of Paul Demere to the Cherokees at Fort Loudoun, Aug. 25, 1757, *Lyttelton Papers;* Talk of the Little Carpenter to Paul Demere, Aug. 30, 1757, ibid.; William Shedrick Willis, supra note 4, 151.

38. Letter From Raymond Demere to W. H. Lyttelton, June 13, 1757, *Third S. C. Indian Book,* 384.

39. Ibid.

40. Letter From John Stuart to W. H. Lyttelton, June 12, 1757, *Lyttelton Papers.*

41. Letter From Paul Demere to W. H. Lyttelton, Dec. 30, 1757, *Third S. C. Indian Book,* 429.

42. Letter From Raymond Demere to W. H. Lyttelton, June 13, 1757, ibid. 384.

43. *Adair's History* . . . , supra note 5, 460.

44. Information of George Johnston, Oct. 2, 1754, *Third S. C. Indian Book,* 12; Letter From Lachlan McGillivray to James Glen, Sept. 8, 1754, ibid. 7.

45. Letter From James Beamor to W. H. Lyttelton, Sept. 10, 1759, *Lyttelton Papers*. See also John Richard Alden, supra note 30, 82.

46. David H. Corkran, *The Cherokee Frontier: Conflict and Survival, 1740–62* 225 (1962).

47. Ibid. 232.

NOTES FOR CHAPTER SIXTEEN

1. See, *e.g.*, Testimony of Ambrose Davis, Sept. 17, 1746, *The Journal of the [S.C.] Commons House of Assembly September 10, 1746–June 13, 1747* 26 (J. H. Easterby, ed., 1958).

2. 2 Frederick Webb Hodge, *Handbook of American Indians North of Mexico* 530-31 (House Doc. 926, 59th Cong., 1st Sess., 1906).

3. William Shedrick Willis, *Colonial Conflict and the Cherokee Indians, 1710–1760* 199 (unpublished doctoral dissertation, Columbia University, 1955).

4. John Richard Alden, *John Stuart and the Southern Colonial Frontier: A Study of Indian Relations, War, Trade, and Land Problems in the Southern Wilderness, 1754–1775* 24 (1944).

5. William Shedrick Willis, supra note 3, 199.

6. Letter From Ludovic Grant to James Glen, June 20, 1748, Minutes of July 13, 1748, *S. C. Council Journal* [15], 361-62.

7. Letter From Andrew Duche to James Glen, April 1, 1748, Minutes of April 9, 1748, ibid. 211.

8. Letter From the Cherokee Traders to James Glen, April 13, 1748, Minutes of April 21, 1748, ibid. 218-19.

9. See Message From Governor James Glen to the Commons House of Assembly, March 15, 1750, *The Journal of the [S. C.] Commons House of Assembly March 28, 1749–March 19, 1750* 467 (J. H. Easterby, ed., 1962).

10. Letter From Raymond Demere to W. H. Lyttelton, July 2, 1756, *Third S. C. Indian Book*.

11. Minutes of March 15, 1746, *The Journal of the [S. C.] Commons House of Assembly September 10, 1745–June 17, 1746* 141 (J. H. Easterby, ed., 1956).

12. Proceedings of the Council Concerning Indian Affairs (May 30, 1753), *Second S. C. Indian Book,* 390.

13. *Adair's History of the American Indians* 297-98 (Samuel Cole Williams, ed., 1930).

14. Proceedings of the Council Concerning Indian Affairs (May 30, 1753), *Second S. C. Indian Book,* 390.

15. Talk From the Squirrel King to the Head Men of Keowee, March 30, 1752, ibid. 252.

16. Chapman J. Milling, *Red Carolinians* 194-95 (1940).

17. Letter From Ludovic Grant to James Glen, March 5, 1752, *Second S. C. Indian Book*, 224.

18. Letter From Ludovic Grant to James Glen, July 22, 1754, *Third S. C. Indian Book*, 16.

19. *Adair's History* . . ., supra note 13, 372–73.

20. Letter From Ludovic Grant to James Glen, June 16, 1748, Minutes of July 13, 1748, *S. C. Council Journal* [15], 360.

21. Letter From Ludovic Grant to James Glen, Feb. 8, 1754, *Second S. C. Indian Book*, 474.

22. Proceedings of the Council Concerning Indian Affairs (May 31, 1753), ibid. 399.

23. "Colonel Chicken's Journal to the Cherokees, 1725," *Travels in the American Colonies* 97, 135 (Newton D. Mereness, ed., 1916).

24. James Mooney, *Myths of the Cherokee* 364 (1900).

25. Letter From Lachlen McGillivray to James Glen, April 5, 1750, Minutes of May 7, 1750, *S. C. Council Journal* [photostat 4].

26. Letter From John Stuart to the Great Chiefs of the Upper Creek Nation, Jan. 20, 1772, *Travels in the American Colonies* 520 n. 1 (Newton D. Mereness, ed., 1916).

27. Talk From the Little Carpenter to W. H. Lyttelton, June 3, 1758, *Third S. C. Indian Book*, 463.

28. John Richard Alden, supra note 4, 84.

29. W. W. Abbot, *The Royal Governors of Georgia 1754–1775* 80 (1959).

30. John Archdale, *A New Description of that Fertile and Pleasant Province of Carolina: With a Brief Account of Its Discovery and Settling and the Government Thereof to this Time* (1707), reprinted in 2 B. R. Carroll, *Historical Collections of South Carolina* 94–95 (1836).

31. See *e.g.*, Minutes of Oct. 5, 1744, *S. C. Council Journal* [11], 477–78; Chapman J. Milling, supra note 16, 241.

32. Minutes of July 3, 1739, *S. C. Council Journal* [photostat 2].

33. Letter From Malatchi to James Glen, May 7, 1754, *Second S. C. Indian Book*, 508.

34. Letter From Thomas Brown to William Bull, July 23, 1744, *S. C. Council Journal* [11], 428.

35. Chapman J. Milling, supra note 16, 239.

36. Wilbur R. Jacobs, *Diplomacy and Indian Gifts: Anglo-French Rivalry Along the Ohio and Northwest Frontiers, 1784–1763* 17 (1950).

37. See David H. Corkran, *The Cherokee Frontier: Conflict and Survival, 1740–62* 143 (1962).

38. Letter From Raymond Demere to W. H. Lyttelton, July 20, 1757, *Lyttelton Papers*.

39. Letter From John Stuart to John Blair, Oct. 17, 1768, "Virginia and the Cherokee, &c.—The Treaties of 1768 and 1770," 13 *Vir. Mag. Hist. & Bio.* 20, 22 (1905).

NOTES FOR CHAPTER SEVENTEEN

1. "Colonel Chicken's Journal to the Cherokees, 1725," *Travels in the American Colonies* 97, 122 (Newton D. Mereness, ed., 1916).

2. *The London Chronicle or, Universal Evening Post,* April 19 to April 22, 1760.

3. Gilbert, "The Eastern Cherokees," *Bulletin 133 Bureau Am. Ethnology* 312 (1943).

4. John P. Brown, *Old Frontiers: The Story of the Cherokee Indians From the Earliest Times to the Date of their Removal to the West, 1838* 528 (1938).

5. Letter From Raymond Demere to W. H. Lyttelton, Oct. 13, 1756, *Third S. C. Indian Book.*

6. Wilbur R. Jacobs, *Diplomacy and Indian Gifts: Anglo-French Rivalry Along the Ohio and Northwest Frontiers, 1748–1763* 13 (1950).

7. Message of the Principal Chief to the National Council, Oct. 31, 1859, *John Ross Papers* (folder #59-7), Gilcrease Institute, Tulsa.

8. Proposed Talk to the Cherokees, June 20, 1748, *The Journal of the [S.C.] Commons House of Assembly January 19, 1748—June 29, 1748* 334 (J. H. Easterby, ed., 1961).

9. Talk From King Haigler and the Other Catawba Headmen to W. H. Lyttelton, June 16, 1757, *Lyttelton Papers.*

10. Letter From Peter Henley to Arthur Dobbs, June 27, 1757, *Lyttelton Papers.* For a similar incident involving the same Cherokee headman and the Catawbas see Chapman J. Milling, *Red Carolinians* 248 (1940).

11. David Duncan Wallace, *South Carolina: A Short History, 1520–1948* 89 (1961).

12. Quoted in Verner W. Crane, *The Southern Frontier, 1670–1732* 182 (1928).

13. William Shedrick Willis, *Colonial Conflict and the Cherokee Indians, 1710–1760* 45 (unpublished doctoral dissertation, Columbia University, 1955).

14. David Duncan Wallace, supra note 11, 89.

15. Ibid. 89–90; Verner W. Crane, supra note 12, 184.

16. Bloom, 'The Acculturation of the Eastern Cherokees: Historical Aspects," 19 *N.C. Hist. Rev.* 323, 330 (1942).

17. *Lieut. Henry Timberlake's Memoirs 1756–1765* 94 n. 55 (Samuel Cole Williams, ed., 1948); 2 Frederick Webb Hodge, *Handbook of American Indians North of Mexico* 175 (House Doc. 926, 59th Cong., 1st Sess., 1906).

18. Gilbert, supra note 3, 346 n. 45 & 348.

19. Ibid. 348–49.

20. Ibid. 355.

21. Ibid. 318 & 348; Frederick O. Gearing, *Cherokee Political Organizations,*

1730–1775 61 & 66 (unpublished doctoral dissertation, University of Chicago, 1956).

22. Ibid. 47–48.

23. See William Shedrick Willis, supra note 13, 195 (citing *Adair's History*).

24. C. Hale Sipe, *The Indian Wars of Pennsylvania* 383 (1929).

25. James Mooney, *Myths of the Cherokee* 384–85 (1900); Swanton, "The Indians of the Southeastern United States," *Buletin 137 Bureau Am. Ethnology* 111–12 (1946); John P. Brown, supra note 4, 26; Frederick O. Gearing, supra note 21, 97.

26. Bloom, supra note 16, 343; Frederick O. Gearing, supra note 21, 48.

27. William Shedrick Willis, supra note 13, 194.

28. Letter From O Tassity [Judd's Friend] to Connecotte [Old Hop], May 22, 1757, *Lyttelton Papers*.

29. William Shedrick Willis, supra note 13, 190.

30. *Lieut. Henry Timberlake's Memoirs . . .*, supra note 17, 93.

31. Harriette Simpson Arnow, *Seedtime on the Cumberland* 176 (1960). For an account of Lewis's problems see *William Preston's Diary—Sandy Creek Expedition February 9-—March 13, 1756* (photostat of typescript), Georgia Historical Soc'y, Savannah.

32. 1 *Correspondence of William Pitt When Secretary of State With Colonial Governors and Military and Naval Commissioners in America* xlii (Gertrude Selwyn Kimball, ed., 1906).

33. Letter From Christopher Gist to Edmund Atkin, Aug. 8, 1758, *Lyttelton Papers*.

34. Quoted in Fred Gearing, *Priests and Warriors: Social Structures for Cherokee Politics in the 18th Century* 49 (1962); Frederick O. Gearing, supra note 21, 63.

35. Letter From Raymond Demere to W. H. Lyttelton, Oct. 26, 1756, *Third S. C. Indian Book*. For the Little Carpenter's refusing even to commence a promised expedition because conjurers warned of death see Affidavit of the Little Carpenter, *et al*, June 22, 1758, *Journal of the House of Burgesses of Virginia 1758–1761* 263 (H.R. McIlwaine, ed., 1908).

36. See also Letter From George Turner to W. H. Lyttelton, July 2, 1758, *Third S. C. Indian Book*.

37. *Lieut. Henry Timberlake's Memoirs . . .*, supra note 17, 93.

38. John Haywood, *The Natural and Aboriginal History of Tennessee* 231 & 233 (Mary U. Rothrock, ed., 1959); Frederick O. Gearing, supra note 21, 47.

39. David Duncan Wallace, supra note 11, 10.

40. But see Frederick O. Gearing, supra note 21, 61.

41. Letter From Raymond Demere to W. H. Lyttelton, June 26, 1757, *Lyttelton Papers*.

42. Letter From O Tassity [Judd's Friend] to Connecotte [Old Hop], May 26, 1757, *Lyttelton Papers.*

43. *Adair's History of the American Indians* xv (Samuel Cole Williams, ed., 1930).

44. Journal of John Buckles, Feb. 22, 1753, *Second S. C. Indian Book,* 384.

45. Letter From the Little Carpenter to Paul Demere, Jan. 4, 1758, *Third S. C. Indian Book,* 434–35.

46. Bloom, supra note 16, 343.

47. See *e.g.* Letter From Theodore Hastings to Arthur Middleton, July 17, 1725, *S. C. Council Journal* [3], 69; Letter From Tobias Fitch to Francis Nicholson, Aug. 23, 1725, ibid. 146.

48. Letter From George Chicken to Francis Nicholson, April 21, 1725, ibid. 136. See also Letter From Arthur Middleton to George Chicken, Aug. 29, 1725, "Colonel Chicken's Journal . . . ," supra note 1, 144 & 146–47.

49. Ibid. 150.

50. Letter From Eleazer Wiggin to George Chicken, Sept. 25, 1725, ibid. 155.

51. Ibid. 117.

52. Ibid. 153.

53. William Shedrick Willis, supra note 13, 149–50.

54. *Monypenny Journal* (mss.), Gilcrease Institute, Tulsa.

55. "Colonel Chicken's Journal . . . ," supra note 1, 153.

56. Ibid. 153–54.

57. Letters From Tobias Fitch to Francis Nicholson, Aug. 23, 1725 and Oct. 15, 1725, *S. C. Council Journal* [3], 147 & 152.

NOTES FOR CHAPTER EIGHTEEN

1. Letter From Ludovic Grant to James Glen, April 29, 1755, *Third S. C. Indian Book,* 53. See also post note 59.

2. Quoted in Henry Thompson Malone, *A Social History of the Eastern Cherokee Indians From the Revolution to Removal* 9 (unpublished doctoral dissertation, Emory University, 1952).

3. Gilbert, "The Eastern Cherokees," *Bulletin 133 Bureau Am. Ethnology* 181 & 187 (1943).

4. John Haywood, *The Natural and Aboriginal History of Tennessee* 222 (Mary U. Rothrock, ed., 1959).

5. Quoted in Grace Steele Woodward, *The Cherokees* 33 (1963).

6. Kilpatrick & Kilpatrick, "Chronicles of Wolftown: Social Documents of the North Carolina Cherokees, 1850–1862," *Bulletin 196 Bureau Am. Ethnology* 1, 67 n. 90 (1966).

7. See *e.g.*, Edmund Kirke, *The Rear-Guard of the Revolution* 87 (1886). See also Henry Thompson Malone, supra note 2, 56.

8. Emmet Starr, *History of the Cherokee Indians and Their Legends and Folk Lore* 468 (1921).

9. Fred Gearing, *Priests and Warriors: Social Structures for Cherokee Politics in the 18th Century* 26 (1962); James Mooney, *Myths of the Cherokee* 489 n. 93 (1900); Knowles, "The Torture of Captives by the Indians of Eastern North America," 82 *Proceedings Am. Philosophical Soc'y* 151, 177 (1940).

10. James Mooney, supra note 9, 48.

11. *Lieut. Henry Timberlake's Memoirs 1756–1765* 93 (Samuel Cole Williams, ed. 1948); Emmet Starr, supra note 8, 468.

12. James Mooney, supra note 9, 360 & 363.

13. Ibid. 489 n. 93.

14. *The Travels of William Bartram* 135 (Francis Harper, ed., 1958).

15. *Adair's History of the American Indians* 162 (Samuel Cole Williams, ed., 1930).

16. Knowles, supra note 9, 167.

17. R. S. Cotterill, *The Southern Indians: The Story of the Civilized Tribes Before Removal* 11 (1954).

18. Letter From James Grant to William Bull, June 4, 1760, 29 *The London Magazine or, Gentleman's Monthly Intelligencer* 425 (Aug., 1760); David H. Corkran, *The Cherokee Frontier: Conflict and Survival, 1740–62* 226, 234 & 236 (1962).

19. James Mooney, supra note 9, 48.

20. David H. Corkran, supra note 18, 202–03.

21. Letter From William Fyffe to John Fyffe, Feb. 1, 1761, Gilcrease Institute, Tulsa.

22. Knowles, supra note 9, 176 (quoting *Adair's History*).

23. William Shedrick Willis, *Colonial Conflict and the Cherokee Indians, 1710–1760* 167 (unpublished doctoral dissertation, Columbia University, 1955).

24. *Documents Connected With the History of South Carolina* 219 (Plowden C. J. Weston, ed., 1856).

25. Letter From Raymond Demere to W. H. Lyttelton, July 2, 1756, *Third S. C. Indian Book,* 130.

26. Letter From William Fyffe . . . , supra note 21.

27. "A True Relation of the Unheard-Of Sufferings of David Menzies, Surgeon, Among the Cherokees," The Royal Magazine 27–28 (July, 1761).

28. Minutes of Feb. 12, 1757, *S.C. Council Journal.*

29. "Journal of Antoine Bonnefoy (1741–1742)," *Early Travels in the Tennessee Country, 1750–1800* 149, 150 (Samuel Cole Williams, ed. 1928). Bonnefoy's Journal is also printed in *Travels in the American Colonies* 241–55

(Newton D. Mereness, ed., 1916). See also Harriette Simpson Arnow, *Seedtime on the Cumberland* 114 (1960).

30. "Journal of Antoine Bonnefoy . . . ," supra note 29, 151.

31. Ibid. 152.

32. Ibid. 155.

33. *Lieut. Henry Timberlake's Memoirs . . .*, supra note 11, 111.

34. Henry M. Owl, *The Eastern Band of Cherokee Indians Before and After the Removal* 23 (unpublished masters thesis, University of North Carolina, 1929); Almon Wheeler Lauber, *Indian Slavery in Colonial Times Within the Present Limits of the United States* 134 (1913); William Shedrick Willis, supra note 23, 156; Verner W. Crane, *The Southern Frontier, 1670–1732* 147 (1928).

35. Minutes of Nov. 17, 1747, *S. C. Council* [15], 9.

36. Letter From Raymond Demere to W. H. Lyttelton, July 11, 1757, *Lyttelton Papers.*

37. Letter From Raymond Demere to W. H. Lyttelton, Aug. 10, 1757, *Lyttelton Papers.*

38. "Journal of Antonine Bonnefoy, 1741–1742," *Travels in the American Colonies* 241, 246 (Newton D. Mereness, ed., 1916); "Journal of Antoine Bonnefoy . . . ," supra note 29, 153.

39. Rothrock, "Carolina Traders Among the Overhill Cherokees, 1690–1760," 1 *East Tenn. Hist. Soc'y Pub.* 3, 16 (1929).

40. Henry Thompson Malone, supra note 2, 20.

41. 1 Frederick Webb Hodge, *Handbook of American Indians North of Mexico* 15 (House Doc. 926, 59th Cong., 1st Sess., 1906).

42. But see James Mooney, supra note 9, 489 n. 93.

43. 1 Cadwallader Colden, *The History of the Five Indian Nations of Canada* xxix (1922 edition).

44. Davis, "Early Life Among the Five Civilized Tribes," 15 *Chronicles of Oklahoma* 70, 74–75 (1937); 2 Frederick Webb Hodge, supra note 41, 914.

45. *Indians of the Southern Colonial Frontier: The Edmond Atkin Report and Plan of 1755* 52 (Wilber R. Jacobs, ed., 1954).

46. James Mooney, supra note 9, 353.

47. *Lieut. Henry Timberlake's Memoirs . . .* , supra note 11, 82 footnote.

48. Swanton, "The Indians of the Southeastern United States," *Bulletin 137 Bureau Am. Ethnology* 692 (1946).

49. 1 Frederick Webb Hodge, supra note 41, 15–16.

50. 2 Frederick Webb Hodge, supra note 41, 484.

51. Chapman J. Milling, *Red Carolinians* 182 & 186 (1940).

52. 2 Frederick Webb Hodge, supra note 41, 846–47.

53. 1 Frederick Webb Hodge, supra note 41, 15–16.

54. Minutes of Dec. 14, 1737, *The Journal of the [S.C.] Commons House of Assembly November 10, 1736–June 7, 1739* 374 (J. H. Easterby, ed., 1951).

55. Journal of John Buckles, April 12, 1754, *Second S. C. Indian Book,* 512.

56. 2 Frederick Webb Hodge, supra note 41, 36; John Haywood, supra note 4, 98–99; James Mooney, supra note 9, 388; *Early Travels . . .* , supra note 28, 158 n. 15; Swanton, supra note 48, 160; *Travels . . .* , supra note 38, 251. It is possible but not certain that the Natchez were adopted by one Cherokee town, Estatoe.

57. 2 Frederick Webb Hodge, supra note 41, 695–96.

58. See *e.g., Charles Journeycake, Principal Chief of the Delaware Indians* v. *The Cherokee Nation and the United States,* 28 Ct. Claims 281 (1893); Act of Nov. 3, 1859, *John Ross Papers* (file # 59–9), Gilcrease Institute, Tulsa; "Instructions to the Delegation," Acts of Nov. 3, 4, & 11, 1859, *John Ross Papers (file # 59–8),* ibid.

59. Letter From Tobias Fitch to Francis Nicholson, Oct. 15, 1725, *S. C. Council Journal* [3], 152.

60. Talk of the Raven of Hywassee to James Glen, June 5, 1748, Minutes of July 13, 1748, *S. C. Council Journal* [15], 364.

61. See supra page 81.

NOTES FOR CHAPTER NINETEEN

1. R. S. Cotterill, *The Southern Indians: The Story of the Civilized Tribes Before Removal* 22 & 28 (1954).

2. See, *e.g.,* Instructions to Col. George Chicken, May 6, 1726, *S. C. Council Journal* [3], 306; Minutes of March 18, 1748/49, June 2, 1749, June 9, 1749, Sept. 5, 1749, *S. C. Council Journal.*

3. William Shedrick Willis, *Colonial Conflict and the Cherokee Indians, 1710–1760* 173 (unpublished doctoral dissertation, Columbia University, 1955).

4. "Tobias Fitch's Journal to the Creeks [1725]," *Travels in the American Colonies* 176, 198 (Newton D. Mereness, ed., 1916).

5. Proceedings of the Council Concerning Indian Affairs (July 7, 1753), *Second S. C. Indian Book,* 453.

6. Ibid. 444 (July 5, 1753); Journal of Thomas Bosomworth, Agent of South Carolina to Creek Nation, July—October 1752 (July 16, 1752), *Second S. C. Indian Book,* 270. See also Letter From James Francis to James Glen, April 14, 1752, *Second S. C. Indian Book,* 250.

7. See *e.g.,* Letter From William Gray to Enos Dexter, n.d., Minutes of April 27, 1748, *S. C. Council Journal* [15], 229.

8. James Mooney, *Myths of the Cherokee* 485 (1900).

9. Letter From William Sludders & Thomas Devall to James Glen, May 2,

1749, *The Journal of the [S.C.] Commons House of Assembly March 28, 1749—March 19, 1750* 193 (J. H. Easterby, ed. 1962).

10. "Colonel Chicken's Journal to the Cherokees, 1725," *Travels in the American Colonies* 97, 120 (Newton D. Mereness, ed., 1916); Report of Colonel George Chicken, Aug. 30, 1725, *S. C. Council Journal* [3], 118.

11. Letter From William Sludders to James Glen, July 11, 1750, Minutes of Sept. 5, 1750, *S. C. Council Journal* [photostat 4].

12. Proceedings . . . , supra note 5, 453 (July 7, 1753).

13. Letter From the Red Coat King to James Glen, July 26, 1753, *Second S. C. Indian Book,* 380.

14. Letter From James Germany to Lachlan McGillvery, July 15, 1753, ibid. 379.

15. Talk of the Upper Creeks to James Glen, July 11, 1750, Minutes of Sept. 5, 1750, *S. C. Council Journal* [photostat 4].

16. James Mooney, supra note 8, 355–56.

17. Ibid. 487–88.

18. See talk of Judd's Friend text to footnote 49 post.

19. Report of Tobias Fitch, Aug. 4, 1725, *S. C. Council Journal* [3], 55.

20. *Journal of Colonel John Herbert Commissioner of Indian Affairs for the Province of South Carolina October 17, 1727, to March 19, 1727/8* 11 (A. S. Salley, ed. 1936).

21. Chapman J. Milling, *Red Carolinians* 164 (1940).

22. Instructions to Major Butler, June 29, 1737, *S. C. Council Journal* [photostat 1].

23. Letter From Lachlen McGillivery to James Glen, April 5, 1750, Minutes of May 7, 1750, *S. C. Council Journal* [photostat 4].

24. Talk of the Upper Creeks to James Glen, July 11, 1750, Minutes of Sept. 5, 1750, ibid.

25. Letter From William Sludders to James Glen, July 11, 1750, Minutes of Sept. 5, 1750, ibid.

26. Ibid.

27. Reid, "Law and the Indians on the Arksansas Frontier," 18 *Ark. L. Rev.* 1, 24 (1964).

28. See supra 84 text to footnote 34.

29. Letter From William Sludders to James Glen, July 20, 1750, Minutes of Sept. 5, 1750, *S. C. Council Journal* [photostat 4].

30. Ibid.

31. Talk of Governor Glen to the Cherokees Concerning Their Treaty, Nov. 26, 1751, *Second S. C. Indian Book,* 190.

32. Proceedings of the Council Concerning Indian Affairs (July 7, 1753), *Second S. C. Indian Book,* 453.

33. Ibid. 444 (July 5, 1753).

34. Ibid. 403 (June 2, 1753).

35. Ibid. 395 (May 31, 1753).

36. Ibid. 399–400 (May 31, 1753).

37. "Tobias Fitch's Journal . . . ," supra note 4, 198.

38. "Colonel Chicken's Journal . . . ," supra note 10, 121.

39. "Tobias Fitch's Journal . . . ," supra note 4, 189. See also Letter From Tobias Fitch to Francis Nicholson, Aug. 23, 1725, *S. C. Council Journal* [3], 145.

40. *The Journal of the [S.C.] Commons House of Assembly March 28, 1749 —March 19, 1750* 194 (J. H. Easterby, ed., 1962); Letter From William Sludders & Thomas Devall to James Glen, May 2, 1749, Minutes of May 22, 1749, *S. C. Council Journal.*

41. James Mooney, supra note 8, 488.

42. "Colonel Chicken's Journal . . . ," supra note 10, 120. See also Report of Colonel George Chicken, Aug. 30, 1725, *S. C. Council Journal* [3], 119.

43. Letter From William Sludders & Thomas Devall to James Glen, May 2, 1749, supra note 9, 193–94.

44. John Haywood, *The Natural and Aboriginal History of Tennessee* 233 (Mary U. Rothrock, ed., 1959).

45. Verner W. Crane, *The Southern Frontier, 1670–1732* 260 (1928).

46. *Virginia Gazette,* Aug. 8, 1751, p. 3, col. 1.

47. *Virginia Gazette,* Aug. 16, 1751, p. 3, col. 1.

48. James Mooney, supra note 8, 488.

49. Talk of Judd's Friend, Report of Colonel Andrew Lewis & Dr. Thomas Walker to Lord Botetort, Feb. 2, 1769, "Virginia and the Cherokees, &c. —The Treaties of 1768 and 1770," 13 *Vir. Mag. Hist. & Bio.* 20, 33 (1905).

NOTES FOR CHAPTER TWENTY

1. Message From Governor James Glen to the Commons House of Assembly, March 15, 1750, *The Journal of the [S.C.] Commons House of Assembly March 28, 1794–March 19, 1750* 467 (J. H. Easterby, ed., 1962).

2. Talk of the Upper Creeks to James Glen, July 11, 1750, Minutes of Sept. 5, 1750, *S. C. Council Journal* [photostat 4].

3. Talk of the Lower Creeks to James Glen, July 25, 1750, ibid.

4. Journal of Thomas Bosomworth, Agent of South Carolina to the Creek Nation, July—October 1752 (July 16, 1752), *Second S. C. Indian Book,* 270.

5. Talk From Malatchi to James Glen, June 26, 1753, ibid. 381.

6. Second Journal of Thomas Bosomworth, October 1752–January 1753 (Nov. 17, 1752), *Second S. C. Indian Book,* 320.

7. Letter From Tasattee [Raven] of Hywassee to James Glen, Nov. 28,

1752, *Second S. C. Indian Book,* 363. For a similar situation reported by the Raven see Talk of the Raven of Hywassee to James Glen, June 5, 1748, Minutes of July 13, 1748, *S. C. Council Journal* [15], 365.

8. Second Journal . . . , supra note 6, 322 (Dec. 8, 1752).

9. Talk From Malatchi to James Glen, June 26, 1753, *Second S. C. Indian Book,* 381.

10. Second Journal . . . , supra note 6, 318 (Nov. 5, 1752).

11. Report of Tobias Fitch, Aug. 4, 1725, *S. C. Council Journal* [3], 54. See also ".Tobias Fitch's Journal to the Creeks [1725]," *Travels in the American Colonies* 176, 181 (Newton D. Mereness, ed., 1916).

12. Talk of the Cherokees to the Virginia Council, March 25, 1741, "Journals of the Council of Virginia in Executive Sessions, 1737–1763," 15 *Vir. Mag. Hist. & Bio.* 113, 119 (1907).

13. See supra pages 170–71.

14. "Colonel Chicken's Journal to the Cherokees, 1725," *Travels in the American Colonies* 97, 117 (Newton D. Mereness, ed., 1916).

15. See supra pages 209–10.

16. Proceedings of the Council Concerning Indian Affairs (July 5, 1753), *Second S. C. Indian Book,* 444.

17. Letter From the Red Coat King to James Glen, July 26, 1753, ibid. 380; Letter From Malatchi to James Glen, June 26, 1753, ibid. 381.

18. Letter From Ifa Tuskenia to James Glen, July 26, 1753, ibid. 381.

19. Letter From George Golphin to James Glen, Aug. 1, 1753, ibid. 378.

20. Letter From Lachlen McGillivray to James Glen, April 5, 1750, Minutes of May 7, 1750, *S. C. Council Journal* [photostat 4].

21. Letter From William Sludders to James Glen, July 11, 1750, Minutes of Sept. 5, 1750, ibid.

22. Ibid.

23. Information of George Johnston, Oct. 2, 1754, *Third S. C. Indian Book,* 12.

24. Bloom, "The Acculturation of the Eastern Cherokee: Historical Aspects," 19 *N. C. Hist. Rev.* 323, 324 (1942).

25. Letter From Charles R. Hicks to John Ross, May 4, 1826, 7 *Payne Papers* 9.

26. *Journals of the House of Burgesses of Virginia 1761–1765* ix (John Pendelton Kennedy, ed., 1907).

27. Letter From Lachlan McGillivray to James Glen, April 14, 1754, *Second S. C. Indian Book,* 502.

28. See, *e.g.,* Talk of the Lower Creeks to James Glen, July 25, 1750, Minutes of Sept. 5, 1750, *S. C. Council Journal* [photostat 4].

29. Letter From Ludovic Grant to James Glen, Feb. 8, 1753, *Second S. C. Indian Book,* 367.

30. Proceedings of the Council . . . , supra note 16, 444 (July 5, 1753).

31. Letter From the Red Coat King to James Glen, July 26, 1753, *Second S. C. Indian Book,* 380.

32. Letter From Malatchi to James Glen, May 7, 1754, ibid. 507-08.

33. Minutes of Oct. 2, 1754, *S. C. Council Journal* [photostat 5].

34. Information of George Johnston, Oct. 2, 1754, *Third S. C. Indian Book,* 10.

35. Journal of an Indian Trader, April 22, 1755, *Third S. C. Indian Book,* 62.

36. E.g., Skandawati, an Onondaga *The American Heritage Book of Indians* 189 (Alvin M. Josephy, Jr., ed., 1961).

37. 1 Cadwallader Colden, *The History of the Five Indian Nations of Canada* 26 (1922 edition).

38. William Shedrick Willis, *Colonial Conflict and the Cherokee Indians, 1710-1760* 165 (unpublished doctoral dissertation, Columbia University, 1955).

39. Talk of the Upper Creeks . . . , supra note 2.

NOTES FOR CHAPTER TWENTY-ONE

1. *Lieut. Henry Timberlake's Memoirs 1756-1765* 87 (Samuel Cole Williams, ed., 1948).

2. Frederic William Maitland, *Domesday Book and Beyond* 356 (Norton Library edition, 1966).

3. Landman, "Primitive Law, Evolution, and Sir Henry Sumner Maine," 28 *Mich. L. Rev.* 404, 408 (1930).

4. Schuyler, "The Historical Spirit Incarnate: Frederic William Maitland," 57 *Am. Hist. Rev.* 303, 315 (1952).

5. A. L. Smith, *Frederic William Maitland: Two Lectures and a Bibliography* 15 (1908).

6. Akers, "Toward a Comparative Definition of Law," 56 *J. Criminal L., Criminology & Police Science* 301, 302 (1965).

7. Max Gluckman, *Politics, Law and Ritual in Tribal Society* 201-02 (1965).

8. Letter From William Fyffe to John Fyffe, Feb. 1, 1761, Gilcrease Institute, Tulsa.

9. *Lieut. Henry Timberlake's Memoirs . . . ,* supra note 1, 168.

10. Ibid. 91.

11. Pound, "Benjamin Hawkins, Indian Agent," 13 *Georgia Hist. Q.* 392, 397 (1929).

12. See *Adair's History of the American Indians* 467 (Samuel Cole Williams, ed., 1930).

13. William Seagle, *The Quest for Law* 34 (1961); Seagle, "Primitive Law and Professor Malinowski," 39 *Am. Anthropologist* 280 (1937).

14. Letter From Johnson Pridget to John Howard Payne, Dec. 15, 1835, "Letters and Notes," 4 *Payne Papers* 21. See also ibid. 49 & 332.

15. Gilbert, "The Eastern Cherokees," *Bulletin 133 Bureau Am. Ethnology* 323 (1943).

16. *Adair's History* . . . , supra note 12, 51–52.

17. Hoebel, "Law and Anthropology," 32 *Vir. L. Rev.* 835, 842 (1946).

18. Robert H. Lowie, *Primitive Society* 397 (1920).

19. Hoebel, supra note 17, 845.

20. E. Adamson Hoebel, *The Law of Primitive Man: A Study in Comparative Legal Dynamics* 28 (1954); Hoebel, "Political Organizations and Law-Ways of the Comanche Indians," 54 *Memoirs Am. Anthropological Ass'n* 47 (1940).

21. See generally Gilbert, "Eastern Cherokee Social Organization," *Social Anthropology of North American Tribes* 285 ff (F. Eggan, ed., 1937).

22. See, *e.g.* discussion of Seminole clans. *The Travels of William Bartram* 72 (Francis Harper, ed., 1958).

23. See "Letters and Notes," 4 *Payne Papers* 332.

24. William Shedrick Willis, *Colonial Conflict and the Cherokee Indians, 1710–1760* 95 (unpublished doctoral dissertation, Columbia University, 1955); Henry Thompson Malone, *A Social History of the Eastern Cherokee Indians From the Revolution to Removal* 49 (unpublished doctoral dissertation, Emory University, 1952); Gilbert, supra note 15, 188.

25. Frederick O. Gearing, *Cherokee Political Organizations, 1730–1775* 42-43 (unpublished doctoral dissertation, University of Chicago, 1956). See K. N. Llewellyn & E. Adamson Hoebel, *The Cheyenne Way: Conflict and Case Law in Primitive Jurisprudence* 106–07 (1941).

26. Jean de Brebeuf, *Relation of the Hurons* (1636), reprinted in 10 *The Jesuit Relations and Allied Documents: Travels and Explorations of the Jesuit Missionaries in New France, 1610–1791* 223 (Reuben Gold Thwaites, ed., 1959 edition).

27. But see "Letters and Notes," 4 *Payne Papers* 331.

28. Anon., "Reflections on the Institutions of the Cherokee Indians," *The Analectic Magazine* 36, 42 (July, 1818); *Lieut Henry Timberlake's Memoirs . . .* , supra note 1, 91.

29. 2 Cadwallader Colden, *The History of the Five Indian Nations of Canada* 94–95, (1922 edition).

30. *An Enquiry into the Origin of the Cherokees, in a Letter to a Member of Parliament* 20–21 (1762).

31. See *e.g., South Carolina Gazette,* Jan. 27, 1732/33.

32. William Shedrick Willis, supra note 24, 127.

33. Cotterill, "Book Review," 21 *J. Southern Hist.* 102, 103 (1955).

34. Fred Gearing, *Priests and Warriors: Social Structures for Cherokee Politics in the 18th Century* 45 (1962).

35. But see unsubstantiated assertions that a Cherokee was dishonored if he failed to avenge an insult. Letter From William Fyffe . . . , supra note 8; Grace Steele Woodward, *The Cherokees* 33 (1963).

36. Talk of the Cherokees to James Glen, Nov. 15, 1751, *Second S. C. Indian Book,* 179.

37. David H. Corkran, *The Cherokee Frontier: Conflict and Survival, 1740– 62* 270–71 (1962).

38. James Mooney, *Myths of the Cherokee* 351 (1900).

39. Fred Gearing, supra note 34, 35.

40. Ibid. 36.

41. Ibid. 31–32.

42. *Adair's History* . . . , supra note 12, 461.

43. Fred Gearing, supra note 34, 32.

44. Letter From William Fyffe . . . , supra note 8.

45. Fred Gearing, supra note 34, 34.

46. See supra pages 97–98 and 104.

47. Frederick O. Gearing, supra note 25, 31.

48. "Colonel Chicken's Journal to the Cherokees, 1725," *Travels in the American Colonies* 97, 154 (Newton D. Mereness, ed., 1916).

49. William Shedrick Willis, supra note 24, 109.

50. Letter From Paul Demere to W. H. Lyttelton, Aug. 18, 1757, *Third S. C. Indian Book,* 402.

51. See *e.g.,* Letter From James Glen to Tacite of Hywassee, n.d. [c. June, 1751], *Second S. C. Indian Book,* 68. See also Samuel Cole Williams, *Tennessee During the Revolutionary War* 263–64 (1944).

52. Proceedings of the Council Concerning Indian Affairs (July 4, 1753), *Second S. C. Indian Book,* 434.

53. Ibid. 443–44 (July 5, 1753).

54. Ibid. 445–46 (July 5, 1753).

55. Ibid. 448 (July 6, 1753).

56. Ibid. 450 (July 7, 1753).

57. Letter From Ludovic Grant to James Glen, July 27, 1754, *Third S. C. Indian Book,* 19.

58. Talk of Cherokee Head Men of Seven Towns to James Glen, Sept. 21, 1754, ibid. 8.

59. David H. Corkran, supra note 37, 135.

60. Fred Gearing, supra note 34, 38.

61. Ibid. 39.

62. Ibid. 32.

63. Akers, supra note 6, 306.

64. Hoebel, supra note 17, 843.

65. John H. Provinse, "The Underlying Sanctions of Plains Indian Culture," *Social Anthropology of North American Tribes*—, 369 (Fred Eggan, ed. 1937).

See also A. R. Radcliffe-Brown, *Structure and Function in Primitive Society* 212 (1952).

66. But see broader definition of religion and law among the American Indians, K. N. Llewellyn & E. Adamson Hoebel, supra note 25, 58.

67. A. R. Radcliffe-Brown, supra note 65, 205.

68. 2 Paul Vinogradoff, *Outlines of Historical Jurisprudence* 265 (1922).

69. "Letters and Notes," 4 *Payne Papers* 177 & 332.

70. Williams, "An Account of the Presbyterian Mission to the Cherokees, 1757–1759," 1 (2d series) *Tenn. Hist. Mag.* 125, 136 (1931).

71. Letter From Paul Demere to W. H. Lyttelton, Feb. 26, 1759, *Lyttelton Papers.*

72. John Haywood, *The Natural and Aboriginal History of Tennessee* 254 (Mary U. Rothrock, ed. 1959); Harriette Simpson Arnow, *Seedtime on the Cumberland* 176 n. 13 (1960) (quoting *Adair's History*).

73. Letter From William Fyffe . . . , supra note 8. See also Grace Steele Woodward, supra note 35, 33.

74. *Adair's History* . . . , supra note 16, 461.

75. 1 Cadwallader Colden, supra note 29, xvi.

76. *Adair's History* . . . , supra note 16, 469.

77. Robert H. Lowie, supra note 18, 385.

78. Fred Gearing, supra note 34. 109.

79. Frederick O. Gearing, supra note 25, 26.

80. See *e.g.,* Ratcliff, "What Life was Like 20,000 Years Ago," 1 (#3) *Mankind: The Magazine of Popular History* 67, 68 (1967).

81. James Mooney, supra note 38, 304.

82. Robert H. Lowie, supra note 18, 398.

83. Frederick O. Gearing, supra note 25, 27.

84. R. S. Cotterill, *The Southern Indians: The Story of the Civilized Tribes Before Removal* 13 (1954).

85. *Cherokee Phoenix,* Feb. 18, 1829, p. 2, col. 5.

86. *The Travels of William Bartram,* supra note 22, 313.

87. Letter From William Fyffe . . . , supra note 8.

NOTES FOR CHAPTER TWENTY-TWO

1. John Richard Alden, *John Stuart and the Southern Colonial Frontier: A Study of Indian Relations, War, Trade, and Land Problems in the Southern Wilderness, 1754–1775* 218 (1944).

2. Talk of James Glen to the Cherokees, Nov. 28, 1751, *Second S. C. Indian Book,* 196–97.

3. Using James Adair's phraseology. See *Adair's History of the American Indians* 92 (Samuel Cole Williams, ed., 1930).

4. Fred Gearing, *Priests and Warriors: Social Structures for Cherokee Politics in the 18th Century* 52 (1962).

5. *Adair's History* . . . , supra note 3, 466–67.

6. Letter From James Adair to William Pinckney, April 27, 1750, Minutes of April 11, 1750, *S. C. Council Journal.*

7. Williams, "An Account of the Presbyterian Mission to the Cherokees, 1757–1759," 1 (2d series) *Tenn. Hist. Mag.* 125, 126 (1931).

8. Wigmore, "Responsibility for Tortious Acts: Its History," 7 *Harv. L. Rev.* 315, 328–29 (1894).

9. Kilpatrick & Kilpatrick, "Chronicles of Wolftown: Social Documents of the North Carolina Cherokees, 1850–1862," *Bulletin 916 Bureau Am. Ethnology* 58 (1966).

10. Williams, supra note 7, 133.

11. Samuel Cole Williams, *Tennessee During the Revolutionary War* 265 (1944).

12. Letter From John Stuart to Lord Amherst, July 30, 1763, *Amherst Papers,* Clements Library, University of Michigan, Ann Arbor.

13. Talk of the Little Carpenter to John Stuart, Aug. 5, 1763, ibid.

14. Proceedings of the Council Concerning Indian Affairs (July 4, 1753), *Second S. C. Indian Book,* 433.

15. Ibid. 433–34 (July 4, 1753).

16. Ibid. 439 (July 5, 1753).

17. Compare ibid. 434 (July 4, 1753) to 1 John H. Logan, *A History of the Upper Country of South Carolina From the Earliest Periods to the Close of the War of Independence* 461 (1859).

18. Proceedings . . . , supra note 14, 434 (July 4, 1753).

19. Ibid.

20. Ibid.

21. Ibid.

22. Ibid. 441 (July 5, 1753).

23. Ibid. 434 (July 4, 1753).

24. Ibid.

25. Ibid.

26. See supra pages 238-39.

27. Kilpatrick & Kilpatrick, supra note 9, 10. For a not dissimilar comment regarding contemporary Cherokees, see Muriel H. Wright, *A Guide to the Indian Tribes of Oklahoma* 57 (1951).

28. David H. Corkran, *The Cherokee Frontier: Conflict and Survival, 1740–62* 11 (1962).

29. John P. Brown, *Old Frontiers: The Story of the Cherokee Indians From the Earliest Times to the Date of Their Removal to the West, 1838* 68–69 (1938). See also Letter From Raymond Demere to W. H. Lyttelton, April 2, 1757, *Third S. C. Indian Book,* 359.

30. William Shedrick Willis, *Colonial Conflict and the Cherokee Indians,*

1710–1760 56–57 (unpublished doctoral dissertation, Columbia University, 1955).

31. Letter From George Turner to W. H. Lyttelton, May 20, 1758, *Lyttelton Papers.*

32. Letter From Raymond Demere to W. H. Lyttelton, July 30, 1757, *Third S. C. Indian Book,* 395.

33. "Colonel Chicken's Journal to the Cherokees, 1725," *Travels in the American Colonies* 97, 128 (Newton D. Mereness, ed., 1916).

34. Letter From George Turner to W. H. Lyttelton, July 2, 1758, *Third S. C. Indian Book,* 471.

35. Letter from Lach. Mackintosh to W. H. Lyttelton, Feb. 17, 1758, ibid. 448.

36. Letter From Ludovic Grant to James Glen, April 29, 1755, ibid. 55.

37. *Adair's History* . . . , supra note 3, 5.

38. For the British theory of retribution regarding Cherokee "crimes" see: Letter From James Glen to James Maxwell, March 24, 1747/48, Minutes of March 29, 1748, *S. C. Council Journal* [15], 192; Minutes of April [sic May] 7, 1748, ibid., 254; Talk From James Glen to the Cherokee Emperor, June 8, 1751, *Second S. C. Indian Book,* 174; Talk From James Glen to Tacite of Hywassee, n.d. [1751], ibid. 67–68; Talk From James Glen to Tucosigia, n.d. [1751], ibid. 79; Talk From James Glen to the Head Men of Tomasey, June 8, 1751, ibid. 79–80; Talk From James Glen to Head Men of Oustenalley, n.d. [1751], ibid. 81–82; Talk From James Glen to the Cherokees, Nov. 13, 1751, ibid. 158; Letter From Lord Amherst to W. H. Lyttelton, Dec. 21, 1759, *Lyttelton Papers;* Letter From William Knox to Robert Knox, June 28, 1761, *William Knox Papers,* Clements Library, University of Michigan, Ann Arbor; *Adair's* History . . . , supra note 3, 163; 1 *Correspondence of William Pitt When Secretary of State With Colonial Governors and Military and Naval Commissioners in America* xliii (Gertrude Selwyn Kimball, ed., 1906).

39. James Mooney, *Myths of the Cherokee* 453 n. 35 (1900).

40. Fred Gearing, supra note 4, 91; Frederick O. Gearing, *Cherokee Political Organizations, 1730–1775* 15 (unpublished doctoral dissertation, University of Chicago, 1956).

41. Talk of the Over Hill Cherokees, given out in their Town House of Great Telliquo, April 9, 1751. Directed to his Excellency James Glen Esq., and the Honorable Gentleman of the Assembly and Council, *Second S. C. Indian Book,* 64.

42. For more regarding the plea of mistake see Affidavit of James Maxwell, June 12, 1751, ibid. 69.

43. Talk From the Head Men and Warriors of the Lower Cherokees to James Glen, May 10, 1751, ibid. 62.

44. Talk of the Cherokee Indians to James Glen, Nov. 14, 1751, ibid. 175.

45. James Glen's Talk to the Cherokees, Nov. 13, 1751, ibid. 157.

46. Letter From Paul Demere to W. H. Lyttelton, Oct. 11, 1757, *Lyttelton Papers*.

47. Speech of the Little Carpenter to Raymond Demere, July 13, 1756, *Third S. C. Indian Book,* 137.

48. David H. Corkran, supra note 28, 134.

49. Ibid.; Talk of the Little Carpenter to W. H. Lyttelton, May 2, 1758, *Third S. C. Indian Book,* 478.

50. Letter From James May to James Glen, Sept. 27, 1755, ibid., 81.

51. Letter From Paul Demere to W. H. Lyttelton, March 7, 1758 (postscript), ibid., 440.

52. David H. Corkran, supra note 28, 66.

53. Letter From Old Hop to Raymond Demere, April 5, 1757, *Third S. C. Indian Book,* 409.

54. Frederick O. Gearing, supra note 40, 64; Talk From the Great Warrior of Chota to Raymond Demere, April 5, 1757, *Third S. C. Indian Book,* 410.

55. Letter From Robert Wall to John Hatton, June 1, 1757, ibid. 409.

56. Talk of Old Hop to Paul Demere, Aug. 30, 1757, *Lyttelton Papers*.

57. Minutes of June 20, 1757, *S. C. Council Journal; South-Carolina Gazette,* June 23, 1757.

58. Minutes of Nov. 17, 1747, *S. C. Council Journal;* Minutes of June 10, 1747, *Upper House Journal*.

NOTES FOR CHAPTER TWENTY-THREE

1. See, *e.g.,* Act of Oct. 27, 1825, *Cherokee Laws*.

2. Petitions for clemency are preserved in the executive papers of the nation at the University of Oklahoma. For the period of 1830 to 1860 petitions may be seen in the *John Ross Papers,* Gilcrease Institute, Tulsa.

3. Josiah Gregg, *Commerce of the Prairies, or The Journal of a Santa Fé Trader,* reprinted as 20 *Early Western Travels 1748-1846* 309-10 (Rueben Gold Thwaites, ed., 1905).

4. *Lieut. Henry Timberlake's Memoirs 1756-1765* 79 (Samuel Cole Williams, ed., 1948).

5. Alexander Spoehr, *Changing Kinship Systems: A Study of the Acculturation of the Creeks, Cherokee, and Choctaw* 199-200 (Pub. 583, Anthropological Series Field Museum of Natural Hist., vol. 33, number 4, Jan. 17, 1947); William Shedrick Willis, *Colonial Conflict and the Cherokee Indians, 1710-1760* 278-79 (unpublished doctoral dissertation, Columbia University, 1955).

6. Donald Davidson, *The Tennessee—The Old River: Frontier to Seccession* 43 (1946). See also *Adair's History of the American Indians* 187 (Samuel Cole Williams, ed., 1930).

7. *Virginia Gazette,* Sept. 19, 1755, p. 1, col. 2.

8. *Cherokee Phoenix,* July 30, 1828, p. 3, col. 1; April 1, 1829, p. 1, col. 5; July 15, 1829, p. 2, col. 1–2; Jan. 1, 1830, p. 1, col. 3 (extra).

9. *Early Travels in the Tennessee Country, 1540–1800* 436 (Samuel Cole Williams, ed. 1928).

10. James Mooney, *Myths of the Cherokee* 229-32 (1900); Thomas Nuttall, *Journal of Travels into the Arkansa Territory, During the Year 1819,* reprinted as 13 *Early Western Travels 1748–1846* 184 (Rueben Gold Thwaites, ed., 1905). But see Letter From William Chamberlin to Calvin Jones, Oct. 10, 1818, Miscellaneous File, Tennessee Historical Society, Nashville.

11. James Mooney, supra note 10, 332.

12. *Virginia Gazette,* Sept. 19, 1755, p. 2, col. 1; 2 Alexander Hewatt, *An Historical Account of the Rise and Progress of the Colonies of South Carolina and Georgia* 203 (1779); David H. Corkran, *The Cherokee Frontier: Conflict and Survival, 1740–62* 60–61 (1962). See also Talk of the Little Carpenter "for all the Warriors" to John Stuart, Aug. 1, 1763, *Amherst Papers,* Clements Library, University of Michigan, Ann Arbor; *Early Travels* . . . , supra note 9, 142.

13. Alden, "The Eighteneeth Century Cherokee Archives," 5 *Am. Archivist* 240 (1942); Letter From William Fyffe to John Fyffe, Feb. 1, 1761, Gilcrease Institute, Tulsa.

ACKNOWLEDGMENTS

To write of the primitive customs of the Cherokees from the perspective of law and history has been an unusual challenge, not merely for the obvious reason that the study of primitive laws has long been preempted by a different discipline which has different values, seeks different answers, and uses different methods of proof. It has also been challenging because the available evidence, arguments, and primary sources are not to be found in the conventional literature of the law or in the familiar materials from which most legal history is fashioned. All too often the evidence is unavailable, or at best, well hidden in obscure documents. It follows, therefore, that the writer of a book such as this owes a more than ordinary debt to the many people who helped him uncover clues or who pointed the way to obscure manuscripts and specialized monographs. Surely this book could not have been written without the assistance of more than can be mentioned. In Oklahoma there was Daniel M. McPike of Tulsa's Gilcrease Institute, A. M. Gibson of the Division of Manuscripts at the University of Oklahoma Library, and Earl Boyd Pierce, Esq.,

331

Counsel of the Cherokee Nation. In Washington there was Mrs. Margaret C. Blaker of the Smithsonian Institute and in Michigan, William F. Ewing of the Clements Library at the University in Ann Arbor. In Tennessee there was Mrs. Penelope J. Allen of Chattanooga, and Mrs. Harriet Chappel Owsley and Mrs. Gracia M. Hardacre of the Tennessee State Library and Archives. At New York University there was Robert B. McKay, Esq., Maribeth Kirk, Arlene Spieler, Dusan J. Djonovich, Esq., G. O. W. Mueller, Peter Anthony Irwin, and Christopher P. Thomas, Esq., of the Oregon bar. Finally, particular mention must be made of the two erudite, adjuvant, and argute guardians of what surely is the outstanding institution of its kind in the United States, Charles E. Lee and William L. McDowell, Jr., of the South Carolina Archives Department. Without their guidance through the wealth of Carolina manuscripts, this first volume of a projected legal history of the Cherokee Nation, would have commenced with a later epoch and laid a less firm foundation.

Hayden Hall   John Phillip Reid
Washington Square
September 15, 1969

INDEX

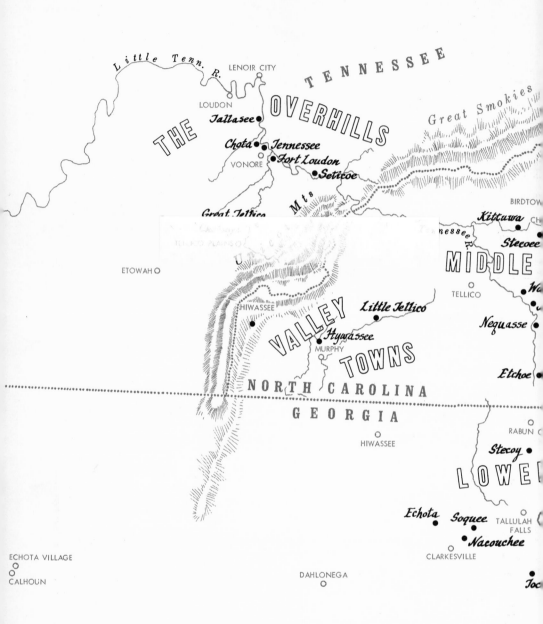